Dr Famahan SAMAKÉ

ZOLA'S NATURALISM IN THE ROUGON-MACQUART: THE FATALITY OF SEXUALITY

A submission presented in partial fulfilment of the
Requirements of the University of Glamorgan/Pryfisgol Morgannwg
For the degree of Doctor of Philosophy

May 2003

Dr Famahan SAMAKÉ

ZOLA'S NATURALISM IN THE ROUGON-MACQUART: THE FATALITY OF SEXUALITY

A submission presented in partial fulfilment of the
Requirements of the University of Glamorgan/Pryfisgol Morgannwg
For the degree of Doctor of Philosophy

May 20

ABSTRACT

My proposed PhD, titled *Zola's Naturalism in The Rougon-Macquart: The Fatality of Sexuality*, aims to study the foundation of the naturalistic novel in the second half of the nineteenth-century France.

Firstly, I have looked back at previous critical studies that were dedicated to the themes of sexuality and/or fatality in Zola's writing. This introductory chapter helped me assess how far critics have investigated this matter and what a long way we still have to go before we can fully appreciate the importance of these themes in the context of Zola's naturalism.

Throughout the twenty novels that make up **The Rougon-Macquart** series, I studied the characters in their being, their appearance and their evolution in space and time. To that effect, I investigated whether or not those characters were masters or slaves of their space and time, and beyond that, I questioned what influences they had on each other. Afterwards, I questioned the fecundity of the theme of sexuality in Zola's work to find out both the aspects of originality in his writing and his contribution to the modern novel as a whole. Nevertheless, I have criticized Zola on a wider angle as an emeritus writer despite the scientific "weaknesses" in his theory of naturalism.

Methodologically, I have largely used the semiotics approach along with psychoanalysis due to the specificity of the theme of sexuality. Despite the wide range of critical studies on Zola's novels, in my sense, most of them have so far failed to tackle naturalism at its foundation, i.e. sexuality. In fact, if one attempts to free **The Rougon-Macquart** series from the theme of sexuality, neither the Rougon-Macquart family would ever exist nor would be written the twenty novels they generated. Studying sexuality, therefore, appeared to be essential to the understanding of the naturalistic theory. However, and surprisingly so, most of Zola's critics have avoided that rather inescapable theme, perhaps more likely for reasons of decency, rather than for scientific ones. It was in such a context that I decided to bring it to light for the sake of truth about the knowledge of Zola and the understanding of his works.

STATEMENT OF THE CANDIDATE

Ever since I started studying Émile Zola back in 1992, I was struck by his tendency to constantly mention sexuality in all of his novels. In Zola's works, dramas and tragedies were the direct consequences of adultery, infidelity, incest, paedophilia, and so on. I then questioned his motives in doing so: was it as if he were a sex maniac, or did he have a morally higher - and a better - reason to mention sexuality so ceaselessly in his works?

Meanwhile, I noticed that Zola's specialists almost neglected that iterative and essential theme, seemingly avoiding it as much as they could, maybe because they would not afford to sound low or immoral. That is when I decided to investigate the matter more deeply, avoiding going about it with any preconceived ideas, but with the sole aim of discovering the naked truth.

I found out, as this study shows, that although Zola had reasons to be sexually frustrated - as he failed to father a single child for nearly thirty years, despite living with his partner, Gabrielle-Alexandrine Meley -, he genuinely focused on the theme of sexuality as the foundation of his naturalistic theory. I then investigated the reasons why it had to be sexuality rather than any other theme, and what substantial benefit sexuality actually brought to his aesthetic theory. I also questioned Zola's contribution to the modern novel in general, and why this writer has been subjected to so many outrageous pamphlets, as well as so many laudatory applauses.

Famahan SAMAKÉ

DEDICATION

I dedicate this book to my uncle, Yaya Samaké, and to all my teachers of French. I also dedicate it to all my students in Ouragahio, in Gagnoa and in Bouaké - in Côte d'Ivoire - as well as to my wife and children.

ACKNOWLEDGEMENTS

I cannot be thankful enough towards Professor Gérard LÉZOU DAGO and towards the late Dr Mermoz KOUASSI KOUADIO of the University of Cocody, Abidjan, as well as to Professor Margaret Majumdar and to Professor Sharif Gemie of the University of Glamorgan, now known as the University of South Wales in the United Kingdom, for their great work as supervisors of my PhD research which allowed me to write the present book.

> «Quoiqu'on inventât, le roman ne pouvait se résumer à ces quelques lignes : savoir pourquoi Monsieur Untel commettait ou ne commettait pas l'adultère avec Madame Une telle»[1].

ZOLA'S NATURALISM IN THE ROUGON-MACQUART: THE FATALITY OF SEXUALITY

---

[1] Joris-Karl Huysmans: *Préface* to the second edition of **À Rebours,** Paris, Édition Gallimard, 1977, p. 57.

PREAMBLE

This book derives from my doctoral thesis defended at the University of Glamorgan – now known as the University of South Wales, Wales, United Kingdom, on the 23rd August 2003. It is an edited version of that thesis to take into account the needs of the book publishing industry and the larger public to which it is addressed from now on. However, I decided to minimise the changes as much as possible, in order to stay as close as possible to the original version of my research work.

Moreover, in the following study, a need for conciseness has commanded me to analyse only the most recurrent, and the most relevant aspects of the theme of sexuality in the corpus despite the abundance of the information collected. The concision of my analyses is therefore the result of a deliberate choice.

SUMMARY

	Pages
ABSTRACT	3
STATEMENT OF THE CANDIDATE	5
DEDICATION	6
THANKS	7
PREAMBLE	8
SUMMARY	9
INTRODUCTION	10
INTRODUCTORY CHAPTER: STATUS OF ZOLA'S CRITICISM IN RELATION TO SEXUALITY AND FATALITY	18
PART I: FOUNDATIONS AND CHARACTERISTCS OF SEXUALITY IN THE ROUGON-MACQUART	29
CHAPTER 1 : FOUNDATIONS OF SEXUALITY IN THE ROUGON-MACQUART	30
CHAPTER 2 : CHARACTERISTICS OF SEXUALITY IN THE CORPUS	40
PART II : SEXUAL AGENTS AND THE QUESTION OF SEXUALITY	71
Genealogical tree of the ROUGON-MACQUART	72
CHAPTER 1 : THE BEING OF THE CHARACTERS OR THE PROLIFERATION OF PUPPETS	73
CHAPTER 2 : THE DEEDS AND THE BECOMING OF THE CHARACTERS OR THEIR PERFORMANCE AND SANCTION	105
CHAPTER 3 : THE METALINGUISTIC FUNCTION AND THE POETIC FUNCTION IN THE ROUGON-MACQUART OR THE PREDICTABILITY OF THE SEXUALITY-RELATED FATALITY	141
PART III : THE RELEVANCE OF THE SPATIO-TEMPORAL COMBINATORICS IN THE FATALITY OF SEXUALITY	177
CHAPTER 1 : THE TIME IN THE ROUGON-MACQUART : THE PROGRAMMED AND THE TIMED OUT SEXUALITY	178
CHAPTER 2 : THE SPACE IN THE ROUGON-MACQUART : THE FRAGMENTED BUT DELIMITED SEXUALITY	209
PART IV : THE FECUNDITY OF THE THEMATICS OF SEXUALITY IN THE ROUGON-MACQUART	234
CHAPTER 1 : SEXUALITY AND THE RENEWAL OF THE ROMANESQUE WRITING	235
CHAPTER 2 : ZOLA AND NATURALISM	244
CONCLUSION	283
BIBLIOGRAPHY	290
TABLE OF CONTENTS	312

INTRODUCTION

INTRODUCTION

It is fair to argue that the seventeenth Century French literature was overwhelmingly dominated by the playwriters in their diversity - tragedy, comedy, tragi-comedy, melodrama, etc. - and the eighteenth Century by the philosophy of enlightenment. The nineteenth Century, however, was notorious for its poetry - romanticism, symbolism, parnassus, etc. - and for fiction writing - realism and naturalism in particular. Still, while the first half of that latter Century was dominated by romantic poets such as Victor Hugo and Lamartine, the second half owes its notoriety especially to the naturalistic fiction writers.

Indeed, from the end of the 1860s, Émile Zola led a new literary school called *naturalism* which gathered around him some young novelists subjugated by the scientific progress registered in the field of biology. They were especially interested in the *experimental method* championed by Claude Bernard and his peers[2]. From then on, literature and science would combine their efforts to provide an explanation of the world, the former borrowing from the latter its tools and its method of investigation.

Like a geneticist studying a given species, Zola endeavoured to study in the twenty novels that make up **Les Rougon-Macquart** series, *the natural and social history of a family under the Second Empire*[3]. As a result, the human reproduction process and the genetic transmissions within this ''human group'' had to be the core subject of a particular investigation by the novelist considering himself more as a researcher, and to be more specific, as a scientist. On the one hand, there is therefore no surprise as to the recurrence of the theme of sexuality in the novels of the series.

On the other hand, what is subject to investigation here is that in Zola's works, sexuality is characterised by a certain inevitability[4] for his characters cannot be, do, or become anything other than what their hereditary programme has inscribed in their destiny. From this point of view, Zola's characters are very much like puppets that passively perform narrative programmes designed by their ancestry. Those programmes are transmitted to them through the genes they received from their parents.

It can also be noted that Zola's biggest obsession throughout his entire production, novels and short stories combined, consciously or unconsciously, is sexuality. Sometimes it refers to nature – trees and grass -, sometimes to animals

---

[2] I'll get back to that in the 1st Part, chapter I. 4. The epistemological foundations of this choice.
[3] I'll investigate this area further in light of the studies by Jean Kaempfer, also in the 1st Part, chapter I. 4.
[4] Brian Nelson asserts that the central theme in Zola's fiction is indeed << *the disruptive nature of a sexuality seen as an irresistible fatality* >>, in **Zola and the Bourgeoisie**, London, MacMillan, 1983, pp-96-97.

or to humans, but overall sexuality appears in **Les Rougon-Macquart** in several aspects - chaste and reproductive, morbid and depraved, even incestuous, etc. The consequences are then either invigorating or fatal, with the complicity of the elements of temporality and the various spaces, and even with the different narrative structures, all things that led me to choose as the subject of this book - PhD thesis originally – **Zola's naturalism in the Rougon-Macquart: the fatality of sexuality.**

I would thus like to participate in the various debates raised by naturalism nowadays. And I do so by focusing first on the question of sexuality, the unifying theme of the famous novelistic cycle – which remains by far the major work of the entire naturalism literary movement. Nevertheless, I will have to start with a series of definitions of certain lexemes of the title of my research subject in order to remove any ambiguity.

The key word of this title, the one around which everything gravitates, is the substantive *sexuality*. The first meaning of this term refers to the sexual instinct and its satisfaction[5]. However, this definition from the **Petit Robert** remains incomplete when compared to what I envision: that is to say sexuality from a more dynamic angle. I will therefore extend it to the many consequences of sexual practices. In psychoanalysis, the term refers to the drives and behaviours related to the libido[6]. It was in this psychoanalytic context that Freud distinguished *genitality* from *sexuality*, the former manifesting itself from puberty, the latter from the very first years of childhood[7]. This second definition is better suited to my ambition and to the context in which I intend to study sexuality in the corpus as any attitude, any behaviour in the face of the sexual impulse and any consequences of sexual practices such as seduction, interpersonal conflicts as well as individual conflicts due to jealousy, sexual intercourse, child production, genetic transmissions and the immanent punishments of sexually-labelled characters and their offspring in the corpus.

The second lexeme to be defined is the *fatality* perceived as a supernatural force by which all that happens is *predetermined*[8]. We know that Zola refuted this classic fate with vehemence and preferred the term of *determinism*[9]. The word

---

[5] **Le Petit Robert 1,** Paris, Le Robert, 1979, p. 1810.
[6] **Le Grand Robert de la Langue Française, VIII**, Paris, Dictionnaires Robert, 1992, p. 749.
[7] **Ibidem**, p. 749.
[8] **Le Petit Robert 1**, op. cit. p. 761.
[9] Émile Zola denounced in his article Le Roman Expérimental, published for the first time in **Le Messager de l'Europe** in August 1879, and then in **Le Voltaire** of the 16th to the 20th October of the same year, before being published the following year as an essay in its own right, the adversaries of the naturalist writers, who branded them *fatalists* as long as in their works, man remained like a mere machine-like animal, acting only under the influence of heredity. He then defined the naturalist writers not so much as *fatalists,* but rather as *determinists,* for they sought to determine the conditions of the phenomena without ever going beyond the laws of nature. However, as he stressed, one cannot do anything against *fatalism*, which determines things necessarily according to its own agenda, and regardless of the natural conditions. For further

admits, in fact, for synonyms "destin", "destinée", "fatum". That is to say, according to Littré, the « *enchaînement de choses fatales, de ce qui est réglé d'avance, qui porte en soi une destinée irrévocable* »[10]. But fatality is also a « *suite de coïncidences fâcheuses, inexpliquées, qui semblent manifester une finalité supérieure et inconnue ; un hasard malencontreux, malheureux, une malédiction* »[11]. This definition is opposed to that of Zola, who intends to explain scientifically what the ancients had divinely explained. In short, the fatality linked to sexuality is the sort of curse that crowns sexuality; the unfortunate chance that sanctions the culmination of the sexual act; the bad fatum that determines the being; the doing and even the becoming of the begotten character.

The other key word in this title, *naturalism*, appeared in 1582, deriving from the Latin word *naturalis*, which originally referred to the philosophical doctrine which accepted that nothing does exist outside of nature. De facto, naturalism excluded any supernatural or metaphysical explanation. Gérard Gengembre reminds us that in the **Encyclopédie**, Diderot gave it the following definition: « *Les naturalistes sont ceux qui n'admettent point de Dieu, mais qui croient qu'il n'y a qu'une substance matérielle... Naturaliste en ce sens est synonyme d'athée, spinoziste, matérialiste, etc.* »[12]. This acceptation of the word is close to that of Littré, who considers that naturalism is the « *système de ceux qui attribuent tout à la nature, comme premier principe,* [la] *religion de la nature* »[13].

While in the sixteenth Century the word *naturalist* meant more specifically a scholar who dealt with natural sciences in general and with biology in particular, it's worth noting that the concept experienced a semantic shift towards the end of the century to also mean a philosopher taking interest in naturalism. Thus. Furetière defined the naturalist in his **Dictionnaire** in 1727, as the one who explains « *les phénomènes par les lois du mécanisme et sans recourir à des causes surnaturelles* »[14].

However, the lexeme *naturalism* took its aesthetic sense from 1839 with a new school in painting that claimed to represent nature with realism, better still, to achieve an exact imitation of nature. The literary concept was born from there with Émile Zola who, in 1865, owned the word by granting it all the three meanings above. In literature, therefore, *naturalism* is the « *doctrine et* [l'] *école*

---

study on this point, please refer to Émile Zola: **Le Roman Expérimental**, in **Œuvres Complètes**, under the direction of Henri Mitterand, Volume 9: **Nana 1880**, presentation, notices, chronology and bibliography by Chantal Pierre-Gnassounou, Paris, Nouveau Monde Éditions, 2004, p. 336.

[10] Maximilien Paul Émile Littré: **Dictionnaire de la Langue Française, Q-Z**, Paris, Librairie Hachette et Cie, 1883, p. 1623.

[11] **Le Petit Robert 1**, op. cit. p. 761.

[12] Gérard Gengembre : "*Au Fil du Texte*' in **La Faute de l'Abbé Mouret** by Zola, Paris, Édition Pocket Classiques, 1993, p. XXXVII.

[13] Maximilien Paul Émile Littré: **Dictionnaire de la Langue Française, I-P**, Paris, Librairie Hachette et Cie, 1883, p. 693.

[14] Gérard Gengembre, p. XXXVII, see note 12.

qui proscrit toute idéalisation de la nature et insiste principalement sur les aspects qui, dans l'homme, relèvent de la nature et de ses lois »[15]. For a few years, naturalism and realism were often confused - and wrongly so. The main distinction between the two literary movements lies in the scientific intent clearly displayed by the naturalist writers. Let us add that the Zolian adjective specifies the framework in which I will work, namely naturalism in Zola's own perspective, because, as the late David Baguley noted so well, there is no single, unified naturalistic theory[16]. Roughly, one can admit with him that naturalism is less a rhetoric than a method[17] - that of scientific objectivity - aimed at reconciling humanity with nature[18].

In total, my task will consist in identifying and in analysing all that is related to sexuality in the corpus, from its origins, its motivations to its various implications, and its unfortunate consequences on the fictional character. One will wonder why and how the characters are victims of such a harsh determinism; why does a bad fatum seem to be beating down on them from generation to generation, and how does that manifest itself? In the same way, one wonders why and how Zola depicted all this as tirelessly and as redundantly in his novels? What were the psychological, the psychoanalytic, and especially the literary motivations that prompted Zola to attach so much importance to that theme, which had remained taboo in literature for several centuries? What is the meaning of that omnipresence of sexuality in **Les Rougon-Macquart** series and what makes its particularity in the corpus? What is the place of time and space in the process of fulfilling the sexual act? Are the characters masters or slaves of the spatio-temporal component? In other words, I am trying to grasp the theme of sexuality in all its latitudes in order to explain the inevitability that is linked to it.

To achieve this, I will use two reading methods: the semiotics and the psychoanalysis methods. The first is nothing less than a structural approach to the narration process, an investigation through the immanent elements of the literary text. The Entrevernes Group, describing semiotics, simply compared it to a game of deconstruction: *« En se donnant pour but l'examen des racines du sens, en mettant les textes « **sens dessus dessous** », afin d'élucider « **les dessous du sens** », la sémiotique ne ressemble-t-elle pas à un jeu de la déconstruction ? »*[19].

---

[15] **Le Grand Robert de la Langue Française, VI**, Paris, Dictionnaires Robert, 1992, p. 695.
[16] David Baguley writes: << *The problem is due in part to the fact that there was no coherent, unified body of theory among the naturalists. Not only did the French naturalists, to take them again as our primary object of study, tend, surprisingly so, to be largely indifferent to theoretical questions, but also many of their programmatic statements were in fact directed against the views of Zola, who was supposedly their chief theoretician* >>, in **Naturalist Fiction. The Entropic Vision**, Cambridge, Cambridge University Press, 1990, p. 40.
[17] **Ibidem,** p. 45.
[18] **Ibidem,** p. 44.
[19] Le Groupe d'Entrevernes : **Analyse Sémiotique des Textes**, Lyon, Presses Universitaires de Lyon, 1984, p. 7.

For the semiotician, therefore, the fundamental question to ask is: « *non pas « que dit ce texte ? » - non pas « qui dit ce texte ? », mais « comment ce texte dit ce qu'il dit ? »»*[20]. Consequently, semiotics considers the text as a sufficient object of study, and that it suffices to question it in order to grasp its meaning. It investigates the *signifiance* in the production, that is to say, in the structure of the narrative texts, in the writing processes by a given author. And I use *signifiance* here rather than significance, the former meaning all the literary process that might help to produce meaning and understanding and the latter refers to the mere meaning of the literary text. I will study the characters in their being and in their deeds, through their evolution in space and time, and also through their interpersonal relationships. This will include the ability to grasp the surface level with its two components - the discursive and the narrative aspects - and then the deep level that includes the network of relationships and the system of operations. To carry this out efficiently, I will use the work of the Entrevernes Group to a large extent without leaving aside those of Philippe Hamon, Gérard Genette, Michel Raimond, Roland Barthes and Claude Bremond, to name only a few literary critics.

The second reading method is psychoanalysis and its use is justified by the nature of sexuality also referred to as the libido. The libido is essentially made of impulses, sublimations, repressions, transfers and neuroses. Therefore, it is central to the field of psychoanalysis. Starting with the works of Sigmund Freud and Charles Mauron[21], I will approach the four moments of the psychoanalysis that are:

The fundamental operation which consists in the superposition of the texts of the same author, Zola in this case, in order to discover « *Les réseaux d'associations ou des groupements d'images, obsédants et probablement involontaires* »[22], which are the metaphorical networks and repetitive mythical figures, including the haunting ones.

Then, from the foregoing, it will be necessary to identify the personal myth of the author[23] as the overall structure of his work. At this level, it will be necessary to investigate « *comment se répètent et se modifient les réseaux, les groupements, ou d'un mot plus général, les structures révélées par la première opération.*

---

[20] Le Groupe d'Entrevernes : **Analyse Sémiotique des Textes**, Lyon, Presses Universitaires de Lyon, 1984, p. 7
[21] Charles Mauron: **Des Métaphores Obsédantes au Mythe Personnel**, Paris, José Corti, 1952.
[22] **Ibidem**, p. 8.
[23] **Ibidem**, p. 8. On the same topic, refer to Maarten Van Buuren, in **Les Rougon-Macquart d'Émile Zola. De la Métaphore au Mythe**, Paris, José Corti, 1986, who says that the personal myth, in such context, has got a narrow meaning since it refers to the unconscious of the author, which has been uncovered by the haunting of a small group of characters and the drama that unfolds between them p. 46.

Car, en pratique, ces structures dessinent rapidement des figures et des situations dramatiques [...] la seconde opération combine ainsi l'analyse des thèmes variés avec celle des rêves et de leurs métamorphoses. Elle aboutit normalement à l'image d'un mythe personnel »[24].

The third operation is an interpretation of the results obtained on the basis that the myth is a staging of the unconscious fantasy of the author, which was betrayed by his work[25].

Finally, the ultimate operation aims to check the results of the previous operations by confronting them with the biography of the author for a simple verification process.

My vocabulary, needless to say, will be plural, depending on the method used at any given time, or whether the critical or theoretical authors I rely on will be different within any given method. The reader, I wish, would to be indulgent for the plurality of the methods used, which is justified by my desire to grasp with as much clarity as possible the signifiance of the **Rougon-Macquart** series in the particular context of sexuality.

I will begin by making a quick tour of the previous critical studies that have been published on Zola in the precise frameworks of sexuality and fatality. This reminder will allow me to assess where critical studies are standing right now on this subject matter and also to explain the opportunity of the present work. It is only from there that I can establish the originality of this contribution in the concert of the Zolian studies.

Then, the first part of this book will focus on the foundations and the characteristics of sexuality in the corpus. We will therefore focus on the religious, the biological, the epistemological, the ideological and the literary motivations that led Zola to pose sexuality as the cornerstone of his literary theory which is naturalism. In the same vein, I will study the various forms of sexuality such as the animalistic, the diabolical, the mythical, the apocalyptic and the infernal approaches that the author has to the theme of sexuality.

The second part of the book will be devoted to the sexual *agents* - as opposed to the lexeme *characters* - facing the central question of fatality. I will use this word of *agent* in its greimasian sense, that is to say, not as a character, but rather as any entity likely to play a role in a given actantial diagram, either as a sexual subject or as a sexual object, or as an adjuvant or an opponent, or as a sender or a beneficiary. I will distinguish the being - *l'être* - of the sexual agents from their appearance before evaluating their various deeds - *le faire* - and lastly, their various sanctions. It is obvious that I will not neglect the actantial

---

[24] Charles Mauron: **Des Métaphores Obsédantes au Mythe Personnel**, op. cit. p. 8.
[25] **Ibidem**, p. 8.

diagram at this stage since it makes it possible to visualise the networks of interpersonal relationships between the sexual agents in a synthetic way. I will end this part with a brief study of the poetic and the metalinguistic functions as long as they accentuate the predictability of the inevitability of sexuality.

The third part of the book will deal with the relevance of the spatio-temporal combinatory in the field of fatality. I will then investigate how the external and the internal times can constitute relevant elements in the programming and the timing of sexuality in the corpus. Furthermore, I will address the question of the spatial component which seems to be involved in an open conflict with the sexual agents that it transforms to the point that, sometimes, they feel obliged to take revenge on the space in a burst of nihilism by arson.

Finally, the fourth and the last part of this book will show the fertility of the theme of sexuality in Zola's fiction works, especially with the new form of art that he introduced in the novel writing known as *naturalist fiction*. I will end this work with a final act that will cast a glance at the man Zola facing the question of naturalism. This will allow me to grasp other dimensions of the novelist and to question his relationships with his contemporary peers without forgetting the reception his works received from literary critics of his time and beyond.

INTRODUCTORY CHAPTER: STATUS OF ZOLA'S CRITICISM IN RELATION TO SEXUALITY AND FATALITY

Since the publication of **Thérèse Raquin** in 1867 to the present day, literary criticism has not ceased to be interested in Émile Zola. The most striking thing about this is that, at the beginning of Zola's naturalistic adventure, his critics - his fellow journalists and writers - were bent on denouncing his penchant for the monstrosities of the flesh, whereas the critics of our time – the exegetes and the specialists of literature - have taken a positive approach. In fact, instead of focusing on the moral aspects of Zola's fictional universe - as Chapter 2 in Part IV will show – for example with Anatole France and Louis Ulbach - they are far more interested in its *littéralité*.

This change of angle of study allowed me to analyse Zola's work in the light of the sociocritical, the thematic, the psychoanalytic, the narratological and the semiotic methods. In short, this new criticism - if we consider the previous one as the traditional criticism - is not so much interested in denouncing Zola's propensity to stack up *"piles of filth"*, even less so in studying the fidelity of his texts in relation to the reality of the Second Empire era, but rather in establishing the formal principles of Zola's aesthetics - because there is one. Then, I sought to discover the deep meaning of the texts in the chosen corpus by passing them through the semiotic comb.

However, that is not to say that the great question of the flesh in Zola's novels has now fallen into oblivion. If anything, many insightful studies have been published over the past five decades, which have addressed the theme of sexuality and/or that of fatality in Zola's works. Among the best known and the most decisive works to date, I can mention **Zola et les Mythes, ou de la Nausée au Salut** by Jean Borie in 1971 and **L'Éros et la Femme chez Zola** by Chantal Bertrand-Jennings in 1977. Also, there was **La Logique du Sens** by Gilles Deleuze in 1969 on the crack – *la fêlure* - in Zola's novels. In the same psychoanalytical vein, I can recall Michel Serres, who attempted to explain **Les Rougon-Macquart** in 1975 in his **Feux et Signaux de Brume: Zola** from the theories of heredity and thermodynamics of the 19th Century. We can also mention **Le Romancier et la Machine, I. L'Univers de Zola** by Jacques Noiray in 1981 on the relationship between the machine and the human body in Zola's works. Later on, Maarten Van Buuren, in 1986, was more interested in the relationship between the networks of metaphors and the myths in his book **Les Rougon-Macquart d'Émile Zola. De La Métaphore au Mythe.** As for Sylvie Collot, she published in 1992 a study on the relationship between the space and the theme of love in Zola's works, in her book **Les Lieux du Désir: Topologie Amoureuse de Zola.** Without rehashing all those previous works, I will be interested in the two main works by Bertrand-Jennings and Jean Borie of which

I will give an analytical summary to see how those previous studies - while remaining precious - do not satisfy me entirely since they are all characterised by both their singularity and their generalities. I will then briefly refer to the other critical studies that have dealt with this theme before I finally insist on the novelty of my approach, which is essentially down to semiotics.

Thematically and psychoanalytically inspired, **L'Éros et la Femme chez Zola** by Bertrand-Jennings poses the woman as the Other opposed to an ego - the man - who would be wary of her. The justification for this mistrust is to be looked at from within the woman, who haunts the male unconscious because she is protean, that is to say both a goddess and a demon[26]. This project undoubtedly allows her readers to deepen the knowledge of the woman with regard to the question of sexuality but it does also present the danger of offering only a sexist reading of the corpus.

At first sight, speaking of a **Descent into Hell**, the author insists on the catastrophic and the infernal vision of sexuality in the books of Zola where sex seems linked to sin and ransom because << *on ne jouit jamais impunément dans les romans de Zola* >>[27]. This point of view seems indisputable and this study will show it too. Bertrand-Jennings deduces from such sanction of sexuality the moralising counterpart of the Zolian text, even though the idea of sin is not be a tendency to magnify religion, which remains the enemy of the people in the eyes of Zola. This point of view also seems indisputable as it will be seen in the very last part of this study. The author further notes that the catastrophe and the fall will be conjured only in the last two cycles of Zola: << *Le discours de Zola sur la sexualité part de la catastrophe de la chute abordée dès les premiers romans et ressassée à travers la totalité de l'œuvre pour s'ouvrir sur la rédemption et la vision d'un paradis retrouvé, loin des anciennes valeurs corruptrices et décadentes* >>[28]. This is a judicious conclusion that cannot be disputed either.

Furthermore, Bertrand-Jennings says that in Zola's fiction works, the woman is an essentially malefic character. She then releases a class of women she calls << *indomptées* >>[29] such as virgins, lesbians and other women who are indifferent to men, and are therefore so capable of aggressiveness, of revolt and of resistance - I will discuss that in the section on the discursive modalities. The author further asserts that the hysterical and the superstitious woman leads her man into sinning. If this is true in some cases, for example with Marthe Mouret and Nana, it must be highlighted, however, that its frequency is far too low - if not marginal - in the corpus to the point that it would be dangerous to generalise it to such an extent.

---

[26] Chantal Bertrand-Jennings: **L'Éros et la Femme chez Zola**, Paris, Klincksieck, 1977, pp.7-9.
[27] **Ibidem**, p. 13.
[28] **Ibidem**, p. 36
[29] **Ibidem**, p. 37.

However, all credit goes to Chantal Bertrand-Jennings when she mentions the << *péril érotique* >>[30] related to the femme fatale, the nymphomaniac and the man-eater.

However, the femme fatale finds her opposite in the ideal woman, who is present too - although rare - in Zola's fiction. She is a motherly woman that is sometimes a foster and a sterile mother, who would have the face of Mme Caroline in **L'Argent** or Pauline in **La Joie de Vivre**. In short << *le mal féminin* >>[31] derives from the fact that the woman is the fault through which the evil spell penetrates, and that is why Nana was the allegory of the Empire by design. That is why the decomposition of the former finds its echo in the fate of the latter. It is imperative to note at this point that there is also a male evil - that unfortunately the author does not mention, probably because her subject of study is limited to the woman and that was a major handicap.

That evident male evil possesses the likes of Jacques Lantier, Buteau Fouan and Victor Saccard. However, in the face of the femme fatale, there are, according to Bertrand-Jennings, some << *ripostes masculines* >>[32] through misogynistic characters - Archangias from **La Faute de l'Abbé Mouret** and the abbot Faujas from La **Conquête de Plassans**. Those ones include protagonists such as Eugène Rougon and Gundermann and they are supposedly driven by non-libidinal interests. That particular category of evil men, in resisting the woman, become << *conquérants* >>[33]. I will study them simply in the class of chaste characters.

Taking her argument further still, Chantal Bertrand-Jennings finds that church women are hysterical and negative characters whereas atheist women are positive. Such dichotomy imposes a << *rejet de l'église* >>[34] in her view. Critics of Zola seem to unanimously agree on that assertion. Bertrand-Jennings goes on to call for the << *maternité panacée* >>[35] because of the fact that a lot of bad women in Zola's fiction are deprived of children[36]. Apart from the rejection of the church and the evident maternity panacea, it would seem that the ultimate means of redemption for women is belonging to the privileged class of the so-called << *vierges martyres, saintes femmes, Immaculée Conception* >>[37] women. Starting with examples of young girls who died on the threshold of their puberty, the author summarises her thoughts this way: << *Toutes ces enfants sacrifiées*

---

[30] Chantal Bertrand-Jennings: **L'Éros et la Femme chez Zola**, op. cit. p. 54.
[31] **Ibidem**, p. 72.
[32] **Ibidem**, p. 77.
[33] **Ibidem**, p. 81.
[34] **Ibidem,** p. 88.
[35] **Ibidem**, p. 92.
[36] **Ibidem,** Chantal Bertrand-Jennings writes: << *Il est vrai que la maternité devient le rachat de la faute sexuelle, que seule la femme considérée comme une bonne mère peut être acceptée, alors que les autres sont présentées soit comme des personnages négatifs soit comme des femmes fatales* >>, op. cit. p. 97.
[37] **Ibidem**, op. cit. p. 102.

avant la faute à une conception puritaine de la sexualité n'accèdent à la sainteté que par leur état de virginité symbolique ou réelle >>[38].

Lastly, the author denonces in Zola's works a blatant << *patriarcat* >>[39] marked by the couple made up of a much younger woman, who is subjected to a much older man that would be her master. Therefore, the << *Pygmalion* >>[40] crowns the patriarchy since the man, by impregnating the woman, marks her forever and creates her so to speak, or recreates her in order to save her by impregnating her. In the end, the author recalls that only << *la femme castrée* >>[41] would be valued as a holy woman, a virgin martyr in Zola's works. Any other woman would be at once a << *bouc émissaire* >>, a << *monster* >>, and a << *diable* >>[42].

In total, Bertrand-Jennings emphasises the woman alone as the force that regulates the dynamics of sexuality. I believe that monstrosity and devilery are not defects that can only be seen in women in Zola's novels because they are also found in many male characters in the corpus, which the critical author does not study, nor emphasise. Therefore, I propose another approach that will pose the problem of the role of each gender and the interaction of the two sexes in the dialectic of sexuality in Zola's novels.

If Bertrand-Jennings is interested in the Eros only in relation to the woman - leaving the man aside - she does not grant any place to the situation of the sexually marked character either. She does not grant any careful consideration to his situation in relation to his space and time. To the contrary, I consider that not only is there a space of sexuality in the corpus, but also a time of well-defined sexuality with great importance in the process of accomplishing and sanctioning the sexual act. Furthermore, contrary to the common position taken by both Bertrand-Jennings and Philippe Hamon, there are many male characters in the novels of Zola that can hardly be ignored and who have nothing to envy Dom Juan. Octave Mouret is a living proof of it, he who is a patent womaniser who seduces both girls, housewives and middle-class women not only in **La Conquête de Plassans** but also in **Pot-Bouille** and **Au Bonheur des Dames**. According to Baguley, he remains << *un fieffé coureur de jupons* >>[43] who << *passe de ménage en ménage pour séduire les dames* >>[44].

Moreover, how can anyone apprehend the character of Renée Saccard without considering Maxime at the same time? How can we study Nana without Count

---

[38] Chantal Bertrand-Jennings: **L'Éros et la Femme chez Zola**, op. cit. p. 103.
[39] **Ibidem**, p. 115.
[40] **Ibidem**, p. 121.
[41] **Ibidem**, p. 128.
[42] **Ibidem**, p. 129.
[43] David Baguley : **Le Naturalisme et ses Genres**, Paris, Nathan, 1995, p. 122. This book is the French revised and corrected version of an English original version, which was titled **Naturalist Fiction. The Entropic Vision**, op. cit.
[44] **Ibidem**, p. 122.

Muffat, or Albine without Abbé Mouret? These are indissociable couples that must be studied together and not separately because, finally, Zola's sexuality functions as a dialectic.

Jean Borie tackles the issue from a more theoretical and a general point of view in **Zola et les Mythes, ou de la Nausée au Salut,** in the sense that he does not focus on sexuality as such, and much less so on the female character in particular. In a psychoanalytic approach largely inspired by Freud, Jean Borie attempts to establish the generating myth of Zola's fictional universe. When that method illuminates the Zolian text in the sense of an introduction to the critical study of his work, it lacks, however, close enough rapport to the theme of sexuality in Zola's fiction works. Indeed, neither the characters nor the narrative structures are taken into account in his book. In fact, his study merely analyses a series of recurring figures relating to nausea. From the beginning, the author opposes the myths of Nausea and Resignation on the one hand to the Messianic and the imperialist myths on the other hand; these corresponding to the **Trois Villes** and to the **Quatre Évangiles,** those corresponding to the first novels of the **Rougon-Macquart** series.

Tackling what he calls *Les fatalités du corps dans les Rougon-Macquart*, Borie took interest first and foremost in the << *fêlure* >>[45] like an inheritance, a fatality and even death. However, the author does not go into much details to show how such fatality manifests itself as I intend to do here.

Focusing on the body as a whole, Borie writes that :<< *Zola est vraiment obsédé par le corps et la malédiction de l'ordure* >>[46]. In trying to prove that point, Borie refers to the recurrence in the Zolian texts of the notion of the belly, which does not go without food, digestion, excrement and fertility with the liquids of childbirth. If fertility sanctifies the sexual act - in agreement here with Bertrand-Jennings and other critics[47] such as Philippe Hamon -, it is nonetheless true that the body and the instincts harbour an infernal and a catastrophic vision. But what is << *descente aux enfers* >>[48] in Bertrand-Jennings' essay announces rather an exit from the underworld in Borie's words : << *Or, sortir des enfers, c'est précisément le sens de l'entreprise de Zola, de son difficile nettoyage du corps et du monde* >>[49]. Borie justifies this optimism by comparing Zola's works to that of Freud in these terms : << *Comme celle de Freud, elle libère des secrets honteux, part de la révélation d'un scandale et tâtonne vers sa guérison* >>[50]. It will be noticed that according to those critics, Zola is portrayed as a moralizing and a healing author. Those positive qualifiers already come about as

---

[45] Jean Borie: **Zola et les Mythes, ou de la Nausée au Salut,** Paris, Seuil, 1971, p.p.20-21.
[46] **Ibidem**, p. 36.
[47] **Ibidem**, p. 31. Let us say that Bertrand-Jennings goes back to the same idea in **L'Éros et la Femme chez Zola**, op. cit. p. 94.
[48] **Ibidem**, pp. 11-36.
[49] **Ibidem**, p. 38.
[50] **Ibidem**, p. 39.

revolutionary in the context of the Zolian criticism that has long focused on the garbage and the filth in Zola's novels as already mentioned.

Jean Borie goes on to posit the hypothesis of an << *anthropologie mythique de Zola* >>[51] whose foundation is the primitive man, the brutal man and ready to disembowel his wife who has betrayed him. This original betrayal brought about his resentment for their descendants. Borie puts this conception in line with Freud's, where, on the contrary, it is rather the Oedipus myth that prevails with a son who hopes to marry a mother-woman after killing his father-love rival. If sex and death are linked, Borie finds that it is because the murder is virilising since it makes it possible to find the ancestor in man.

However, a careful study of the characters in the corpus does not confirm such dramatic statement. To the contrary, two main facts can destroy that argument by Jean Borie: it is enough to look closely at the case of Roubaud who kills his love rival in **La Bête Humaine** and then goes on to lose any interest in sex from that moment on. It is the same for Laurent who kills the husband - Camille - in **Thérèse Raquin**, without being capable, from that point on, of reclaiming his virility when he finds himself with Thérèse, the loving widow. Murder in both cases is everything but virilising; it rather signals the death of manhood in those two jealous characters' cases. In Zola's fiction works, murder makes man impotent in my view and I am sharply in disagreement with Jean Borie here.

Basically, sexuality, for Borie, only leads to three possible outcomes: asphyxiation, murder and exhaustion, hence nausea : << *la nausée, le dégoût de la vie organique, pullulante et pourrissante, sale et malodorante, n'ont pas fini de reparaître dans l'œuvre de Zola* >>[52]. Generally speaking, the great Zolian myth is that of heredity, which is only the inevitability of a return, a repetition within the same family, as this study will show.

Finally, taking interest in the *Maison*[53], the author points out that the wall is a strategic place because it expresses both rêverie and intimacy in Zola's works. The opening of a house would therefore be seen as diabolical as it is in the eyes of Nana, or in those of Clorinde in **Son Excellence Eugène Rougon**. The same goes for hermetically closed houses - as with those he calls << *les tartufes des* **Rougon-Macquart** >>[54] - in **Pot-Bouille** and in **Le Ventre de Paris**. I will expand on all these aspects in the chapter studying the space in the corpus - part three. Borie ends his study by << *les sanctuaires* >> which are << *la chamber* >> and << *l'église* >>. He assumes that the room is a soft and a good shelter when it is open while it becomes cursed if closed[55]. The room of a woman has the peculiarity of reflecting the adornment of her body, a place where metaphors of

---

[51] Jean Borie : **Zola et les Mythes, ou de la Nausée au Salut**, op. cit. pp. 43-45.
[52] **Ibidem,** p. 62.
[53] **Ibidem.** pp. 125-229.
[54] **Ibidem,** p. 142.
[55] **Ibidem,** p. 191 et p. 201.

satin refer to the throat of the woman; those of silk to her thighs[56] while the bed is all the greater as the occupant is marked by lust. This is a solid argument which is unchallengeable in my view. In contrast, the church is promised to destruction because it is first and foremost an arrow – which rises to the sky – and a cave – like a tomb, a burial place, an abyss or a vagina. Inhabited by a man-woman wearing a dress, a virtual homosexual[57] so to speak, the church is seen both as an external threat as much as an internal one. On the outside, it indeed steals the bride from the husband, like Marthe Mouret who was stolen from François in **La Conquête de Plassans.** On the inside, it steals the woman's sound mind, making her hysterical, with erotic dreams, as it happened to Marthe once more. Such conception of the church seems to be unanimously agreed by critics. Still, I will show it from an immanent study of the Zolian novels. I will refer in particular to the church of Artaud, the parish of the abbot Mouret. Jean Borie concludes his book with a denial of Jesus in Zola's works: << *Zola ne montre guère, à quelque moment de son œuvre que ce soit, une grande admiration pour le Christ qui demeure toujours une figure de renoncement, de démission, de masochisme et de mort* >>[58].

In short, Jean Borie studies the relationship between the imaginary and the myth in Zola's works from a rather theoretical and a masterly angle. His study of the mythological anthropology in Zola's novels unfortunately does not take into account the myths clearly expressed in the corpus although such myths are many and widely varied. The fatality that interests him seems to be limited to the threshold of nausea and salvation. Yet, as this study will show, these myths constitute a fatality in their own right in addition to being otherwise more revealing of the sexual tendencies of the characters identified with mythical heroes. In Borie's book, there is also a lack of connection between the character and his spatio-temporal universe despite the long chapter devoted to the house which is treated as an independent and a meaningful instance in its own right; a meaningful place even if not inhabited by an anthropomorphic character.

To return briefly to the other studies mentioned above, I could start with Jacques Noiray for whom perversion and death are fatalities deriving from the machine[59]. It seems to me that the reading of **La Bête Humaine** confirms that statement by Noiray if one refers to the ambiguous rapport that Jacques Lantier has with the Lison the one hand and, on the other hand, to all the assassinations that took place in the book. It must be pointed out that all the tragedies in that novel

---

[56] Jean Borie : **Zola et les Mythes, ou de la Nausée au Salut**, op. cit. p. 195.
[57] **Ibidem**, p. 218.
[58] **Ibidem**, p. 226.
[59] Jacques Noiray : << *C'est comme corps mécanique érotisé que la machine développe avec l'homme ou la femme des rapports pervertis et finalement meurtriers ; c'est comme incarnation des instincts de mort qu'elle trouve à la fois sa suprême puissance et sa fin cataclysmique. Ainsi l'univers de la technique est-il saturé de forces meurtrières, dont la machine est à la fois l'instrument et la victime* >> in **Le Romancier et la Machine I. L'Univers de Zola**, Paris, José Corti, 1981, p. 448.

took place in a large theatre: the machine branded as La Lison. I will not lose sight of the cataclysms of which La Lison was both the agent, the victim and the set of the action. If, therefore, scientific and technological progress must inevitably be pursued, in Zola's eyes, it is advisable to bear in mind its catastrophic consequences in order to better ward them off.

However, Gilles Deleuze does not go so far; for, in his eyes, fatality is called by a name: the crack that transcends the individual: << [...] *il n'y a de commun et de transindividuel que la fêlure elle-même, passant d'une histoire ou d'un corps à l'autre, formant le fil rouge des* **Rougon-Macquart** *et la transcendance d'un destin épique. À cet égard,* **La Bête Humaine** *est exemplaire* >>[60]. Philippe Hamon fully shares this idea of the hereditary fatality when he notes that surnames such as Rougon and Macquart mark the persistence of a heredity, a destiny and, consequently, the persistence of a threatening catastrophe[61]. << *Le fil rouge* >> in Deleuze's terminology is nothing but the symbol of blood, disaster and death, all things that Michel Serres brings together under the concept of << *entropie* >> : << *Rien ne dit mieux que* **Les Rougon-Macquart** *l'écrasement, le gaspillage, la dissémination, la perte, l'irréversible jusant vers la mort-désordre ; la déchéance, l'épuisement, la dégénérescence. Ils le disent : ça brûle trop vite. Épopée d'entropie* >>. The concept of entropy is also manifested by the irreversible fall of Zola's characters as David Baguley rightly notes : << *les personnages ''régressent'' pour sombrer dans la poursuite de la satisfaction de leurs appétits, de leurs instincts, de leur animalité* >>[62]. In a global way, Baguley, like Bertrand-Jennings, denounces << *la misogynie habituelle du discours naturaliste* >>[63]. In the first part of this study, I will address this idea of entropy in the section focussing on the catastrophic vision of sexuality in **Les Rougon-Macquart**. In the section devoted to the animalistic vision of sexuality, I will study the phenomenon of the regression of sexual agents in human form as they undergo a fatal striking metamorphosis through myths, the animalistic metaphors and through processes of reification.

As for Philippe Hamon, he believes that in Zola's works, characters are first and foremost victims of a first fatality inflicted to them by the author as early as from the very first draft of his novels : << *Avant d'être déterminé par une hérédité, des influences, des milieux etc., le personnage zolien est donc prédéterminé, ce qui n'était pas évident a priori pour un personnage relevant de l'esthétique réaliste-naturaliste* >>[64]. Addressing the important section of

---

[60] Gilles Deleuze : **La Logique du Sens**, chapter *Zola et la fêlure*, Paris, Édition de Minuit, 1969, p. 91.
[61] Philippe Hamon : **Le Personnel du Roman. Le Système des Personnages dans les Rougon-Macquart d'Émile Zola**, Genève, Droz, seconde édition, 1998, p. 108.
[62] David Baguley : **Zola et les Genres**, chapter III: *La Curée : La Bête et la Belle*, Glasgow, University of Glasgow French and German Publications, 1993, p. 39.
[63] **Ibidem**, chapter VII : *L'Œuvre, künstlerroman à thèse*, p. 87.
[64] Philippe Hamon : **Le Personnel du Roman. Le Système des Personnages dans Les Rougon-Macquart d'Émile Zola**, op. cit. p. 55.

the << *sexe du personage* >>[65], Hamon, draws on Bertrand-Jennings' assertion that female characters are depositories of sexuality because they are the seat of impulses, repulsions, then the instigators and the regulators of eroticism, in short: << *la sexualité est, d'abord, celle de la femme* >>[66]. There is no need to repeat that I do not share that opinion at all.

Philippe Hamon, in justifying his assertion, argues that male sexuality is at the same time less represented, less differentiated and less rich than its female counterpart in the corpus[67]. I will have the opportunity to demonstrate that this is not sustainable since male characters in the corpus actually offer a more varied sexuality than their female counterparts. Nevertheless, Hamon's assertion seems to be based on the lack of a Don Juan in **Les Rougon-Macquart**[68] and that seems particularly questionable too, if not downright unfounded since we have Octave Mouret to contradict it.

Let us note that the studies above are sometimes too general in the sense that they do not really rely on a rigorous analysis of the textual signs in order to release their significance, which only a semiotics reading would be able to do in my opinion. Hamon and Seassau tried this semiotic exercise, but on the onomastic level[69] only and not in relation to the themes of sexuality and fate at large.

My contribution, let us stress this again, does not have a revolutionary ambition in the concert of the Zolian studies, but rather a complementary one. Indeed, far from rejecting the works of Bertrand-Jennings, Jean Borie, Philippe Hamon or those of Claude Seassau, Roger Ripoll and Van Buuren, I will complete them by recalling the common thread that connects them all: sexuality. For these works have very often touched on essential elements of Zola's naturalism, but each time, they did it from a fragmentary and a narrow angle, thus offering an incomplete assessment of the theme of sexuality.

For example, I intend to abandon the sexist approach by Chantal Bertrand-Jennings to take into account the male gender put on the same footing as the female gender. In addition to that, I will complete the study of Jean Borie with an analysis of the Christian and the Greco-Roman myths clearly indicated in the corpus. In the same way, I will take into account the study of the characters that interests Philippe Hamon so much, putting it in close connection with the study by Roger Ripoll on the myths in Zola's novels. I will also take into account the stylistic aspects of the metaphors and the symbols that Maarten Van Buuren

---

[65] Philippe Hamon : **Le Personnel du Roman. Le Système des Personnages dans Les Rougon-Macquart d'Émile Zola**, op. cit. p. 188-204.
[66] **Ibidem**, p. 190.
[66] **Ibidem**, p. 191.
[67] **Ibidem**, p. 191.
[68] **Ibidem**, p. 191.
[69] I'll get back to that in the second part of this book, which talks about the sexual agents.

and Claude Seassau have already studied separately. I will present, for the first time ever, a unique study that includes both the system of characters and their location in time and space, the metaphors, the symbols and the myths and the narrative structures in the framework of sexuality. This will show how sexuality is a fruitful and a unifying theme in Zola's works. Although I do not completely abandon the psychoanalysis method as applied by Maarten Van Buuren, Jean Borie and Chantal Bertrand-Jennings, I will keep it only in the background, insisting more on a semiotic reading of the corpus. That is to say that I will give primacy to the text, or to be more precise, to the analysis of the textual signs.

In short, unlike Bertrand-Jennings and Borie, I will consider a study of the theme of sexuality as comprehensively as possible and as punctiliously as possible. My hypothesis is that sexuality is fundamental in the **Rougon-Macquart** series and that only a semiotic study can bring about a wider manifestation of the truth about it. Sexual agents will be studied on an equal footing - women being equal to men - and all variants of sexuality in Zola's works will be treated - such as heterosexuality, lesbianism, pederasty, paedophilia, sexual immaturity, sadism and masochism, stopping on intermediate relations, disguise and hermaphroditism - as well as their consequences, that is to say the various hereditary diseases, degeneration, animalisation, reification and evanescence and death suffered by the anthropomorphic characters. To this study, I will add that of the myths clearly indentified in the corpus: their classification, their representations and their impact on the character and on the naturalistic text - which is sorely lacking in Jean Borie's book. In addition, it seems important to note that in Zola's works there are three forms of fatalities: one is linked to heredity, another to the assimilation of the fictional characters to mythical figures, thus limiting their freedom and finally, a kind of fatality linked to the influence of the natural and the social environments on the character. This means that the notion of fatality is rather more dynamic in Zola's view than static, more polymorphic than monolithic as I will show in the second part of this study.

I will then put the sexually marked characters in their temporal and their spatial environments to observe their interaction and effects, all things that Philippe Hamon superficially studies before moving on very quickly. Lastly, this picture cannot be complete unless one conducts an investigation of a poetic element to try to understand the constraints that the theme of sexuality imposes on the novelist as well as the repercussions of that theme at the literary level. Roger Ripoll, Maarten Van Buuren and Claude Seassau both did a remarkable job on that sense. However, once again, they somehow put the spatio-temporal component into oblivion.

Nonetheless, before proceeding with such study of the deep structures of the corpus, I will investigate the main characteristics of sexuality in the Zolian novels.

FIRST PART:
FOUNDATIONS AND CHARACTERISTICS OF SEXUALITY IN THE ROUGON-MACQUART SERIES

This part will consist in two separate chapters. The first one will study the foundations of sexuality in the naturalistic novel in general and, as far as I am concerned, in the specific series of the **Rougon-Macquart**. It is a question of trying to answer the following questions: for what reasons or for what literary, psychological, sociological, psychoanalytic and religious reasons is sexuality the generative grammar of Zola's naturalism? What justifies this preponderant place of sexuality in the corpus? And why sexuality rather than another theme?

Secondly, I will devote myself to the immanent study of the theme of sexuality in order to discover how it is approached and treated by Zola, what characterises it, in short, all the elements allowing us to apprehend it, to specify it and to produce its meaning.

CHAPTER I: THE FOUNDATIONS OF SEXUALITY IN THE ROUGON-MACQUART SERIES

Basically, I mean here the deep motivations that led Zola to put sexuality at the centre of his naturalism. These foundations seem to me to be of several orders. So, I will try to grasp them individually for clarity reasons. I will begin with the religious foundations of his literary aesthetical choice.

1. THE RELIGIOUS FOUNDATIONS

According to the **Bible**, first Adam and Eve were ordered to multiply and fill the earth. Much later on, after the flood, God again ordered Noah to go out into the world with his family and to populate the earth. Therefore, from a theological point of view, sexuality is first and foremost of a sacred nature; it answers a divine prescription so to speak. Therefore, to satisfy one's libido is above all to obey a divine prescription; to show one's allegiance to God by fulfilling the order he gave our biblical ancestors.

Sexuality sows indeed the invigorating and reproductive seed that perpetuate the human species. However, we must not lose sight of the ethical value of sexuality because God, although preoccupied with the continuity of the human race on earth, did not allow concupiscence and defilement. For that reason, the **Bible** insists on the prescription that makes marriage a sacred institution which is recommended by the first creator, starting with the wedding of Eve to Adam in the Garden of Eden.

Since the introduction of this study, I have insisted that the whole **Rougon-Macquart** series is that of a family; Adélaïde Fouque also called Aunt Dide being at the core of its first social fabric. In **La Fortune des Rougon**, the narrator shows six weddings: that of Adélaïde Fouque and Rougon first of all, then that of her eldest son, Pierre Rougon, with Félicité Puech; that of their son, Aristide Rougon, with Angèle Sicardot; that of their daughter, Marthe Rougon, with

François Mouret; then the one that unites "the bastard", Antoine Macquart, with Josephine Gavaudan and finally, that of their daughter, Ursule Macquart, with the hatter Mouret.

Paradoxically, this first avalanche of weddings will be followed by a great wind of debauchery that will blow on the characters of the **Rougon-Macquart** series and which will tolerate only a handful of almost unfruitful marriages (Aristide and Renée; then Maxime and Louise in **La Curée**; Jean Macquart and Françoise Mouche in **La Terre**; Angélique and Félicien de Hautecour in **Le Rêve**, to name only these typical cases). Those unsuccessful marriages are a harbinger of both the planned extinction of the **Rougon-Macquart** race and of a world that is irremediably doomed and which is heading towards disappearance. Indeed, the Second Empire is condemned to sterility and barenness. That is why its disappearance in Zola's point of view in inevitable because it is a world that has committed an unforgivable sin by abandoning the path of reproduction to follow that of extreme debauchery and endless lust. What is questioned in Zola's novels is not the legitimacy of sexual practices as long as they remain attached to morality but rather the licence that characterises them. In fact, sexuality here is marked by debauchery and by all the depravations and perversions that I will study in the next chapter. In this sense, sexuality seems to have deviated from the divine way to follow the path of destruction and self-destruction.

Finally, one must remember that there is a sort of divine voice in Zola's novels that desperately tries to restrict the field of sexuality to the only religious and ethical foundations. This voice is that of the clerics such and priests and assimilated - the abbots Madeline and Godard in **La Terre**; Brother Archangias in **La Faute de l'Abbé Mouret** - and religious figures like Venot in **Nana**.

Still, sexuality in the corpus is not only motivated by religious considerations. On the contrary, as a naturalist writer, physiology could not renounce its rights in Zola's novelistic creation.

2. THE BIOLOGICAL AND SOCIOLOGICAL FOUNDATIONS

Human physiology has clearly distinguished two fundamental genres, namely the male and the female. This biological diversity is however not inconsequential since the laws of nature attract one towards the other. This reciprocal attraction is of a natural and animalistic nature in the sense that the opposites ostensibly attract each other as if to complete each other. They work together like opposite signs would do in electricity or in chemistry. Moreover, biologically speaking, man is nothing less than an animal made up of organs with specific functions. But these organs - especially the genital devices - have needs whose satisfaction passes through copulation or sexual intercourse.

For Zola, it's important to deal with what he calls << *la bête humaine* >>. Is it necessary to specify that this nominal group can be broken down in the following way: the essential nominal constituent / the beast / has the traits [+ animal], [+ wild], [+ instinctive], [+ brutal], [+ aggressive], [-reflective], [- civilised] and [- intelligent] while the optional adjectival constituent / human / has the traits [+ human], [-wild], [+ reflective], [+ intelligent] and [+ civilised]. One must admit that the combination of all those features gives a complex narrative programme, even an ambivalent and an ambiguous one at that.

Moreover, the animalistic and the deeply instinctive nature of the coitus is an inescapable reality. It suffices to refer to the assaults of Buteau on his sister-in-law, Françoise, in **La Terre** to prove that. Those assaults are designated by the word << *rut* >>, which normally applies to animals in heat. The biological need for copulation also responds to a sociological necessity, that of maintaining the human race alive by multiplying it. Therefore, sexuality also has a utility value closely related to the divine prescription that was mentioned above. With this sociological value, we have something that allows the novelist to build the story of his twenty volumes on a range of protagonists spread over several generations, the oldest being the most numerous unlike the younger dwindling generations[70].

On an arithmetic point of view, there are only three agents for the first generation: Adélaïde, Rougon and Macquart. The second generation, which comes from that primary nucleus, includes three other agents: Pierre Rougon, Ursule Macquart and Antoine Macquart. The third generation consists of the five children for the couple formed by Pierre and Félicité; the three children for the Ursule-Mouret couple and three other children for the Antoine-Joséphine couple. In total, therefore, that generation amounts to eleven characters generated by these three children of the grandmother Aunt Dide. The fourth generation goes up to seventeen children while the fifth, paradoxically, falls sharply to only five individuals. In all, we count thirty individuals deriving from Adélaïde Fouque but to understand the sudden and drastic fall in the birthrate within the family of the Rougon-Macquart, in particular from the fifth generation[71], we will have to refer to our third part - **2. Recognition and sanction of the character.** For now, let us draw a graph of the number of individuals born in the Rougon-Macquart family to evaluate the fertility curve within. I will assume that Father Fouque makes up generation zero because he has virtually no narrative interest in the corpus. The story really begins with his only daughter, Adélaïde, who is our first

---

[70] Please refer to the previous point where I announced the supreme sanction which strikes the world of the Second Empire beyond the family of the Rougon-Macquart.

[71] Roger Ripoll recalls in his PhD thesis, **Réalité et Mythe chez Zola**, volume I, Paris, Honoré Champion, 1977, p. 168, this passage of Dr Prosper Lucas, written in his **Traité Philosophique et Physiologique de l'Hérédité Naturelle**, page 590, that the ineluctable fate of any family was degeneration: << *Il est digne de remarque que le mouvement ascendant des hautes facultés d'un assez grand nombre de fondateurs de races, s'arrête presque toujours à la troisième, se continue rarement jusqu'à la quatrième, et presque jamais ne dépasse la cinquième génération* >>. This decline is manifested by helplessness, a lack of virility and, ultimately, by death. We will return to the influence of this scientific study of Dr. Lucas on Zola at the time of the development of the **Rougon-Macquart** series, in point 4. The epistemological foundations.

generation. The second will be composed of her offspring. Starting from this principle, we can draw the following diagram:

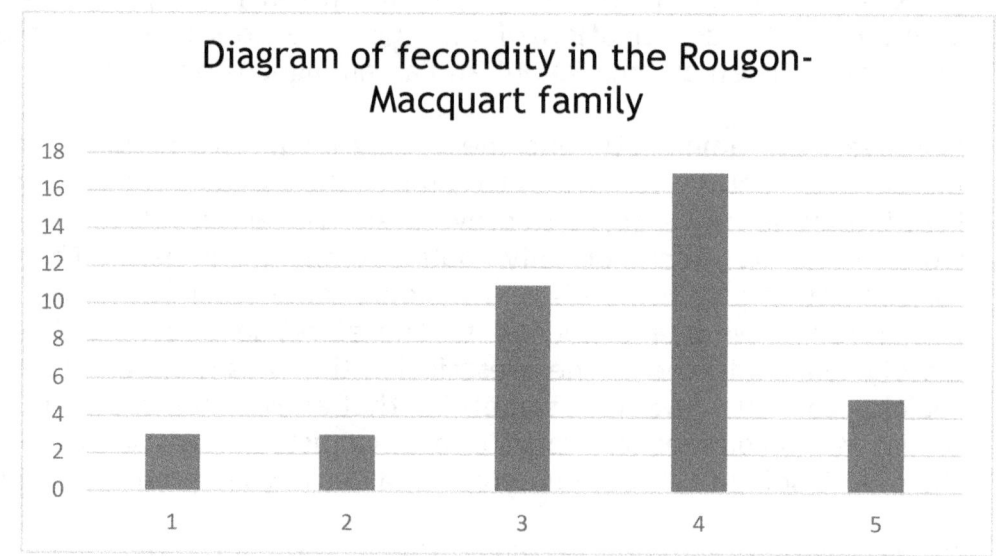

the generations

This diagram shows that the generation zero - the father Fouque - has generated only one individual - Adélaïde - who, in turn, founded the first generation with her successive unions with Rougon then Macquart. The three of them gave birth to three children who multiplied to give birth to eleven new individuals, then to seventeen. If the fourth generation was the most fertile with its seventeen daughters and sons, the fifth began a vertiginous fall with only five children born and, worse still, none of them procreated in turn, leaving the Rougon- Macquart race to die down around the year 1874.

Beyond this demographic data, it will be necessary to question the purely literary and ideological foundations of sexuality in the corpus since the writer also clearly carries an ideology.

3. THE LITERARY AND THE IDEOLOGICAL FOUNDATIONS.

In the following point 4, I will approach the fiduciary contract which bound the author to his characters from the preface of July 1st, 1871. That preface which was valid for the whole series of the Rougon-Macquart, alluded to << *this race*

>>, a deliberately genetic vocabulary. It went on to mention its << *instincts* >>[72] and to << *l'hérédité* >>[73]. The author wanted to position himself in the absolutely new aesthetic context of naturalism.

In terms of literary creation, naturalism was a scientific approach to literature with the introduction of the experimental method inspired by Claude Bernard. Indeed, Zola intended to end the compartmentalisation that seemed to keep scientists away from men of literature: << *[...] si nous mettons la forme, le style à part, le romancier expérimentateur n'est plus qu'un savant spécial, qui emploie l'outil des autres savants, l'observation et l'analyse* >>[74]. Genetics being its creed, the new school led by Zola made a wide opening on all factors related to the reproduction of the characters - the phenomena of copulation, fertilisation, gestation and parturition - at a primary level.

At a secondary level, the novelist had to follow the biological, the physiological and the psychological evolution of his characters without dissociating these aspects form their links with the social, the historical and the family environment to which they belong. The naturalistic approach was therefore as effective as possible because of its globalising and multidisciplinary nature; science and history coming together to meet with literature in order to avoid any partitioning between them. This decompartmentalisation, or the fact of grasping them together as they exist in nature, constituted a literary and an ideological motive at the same time. Indeed, Zola and his followers, by initiating naturalism, thus operated an ideological revolution in the history of literature in general and in the fiction writing in particular. For Zola, naturalism had to differentiate from classical literature by rejecting its metaphysical tendencies and by substituting them with a scientific explanation of social facts. That is why he wrote in October 1879: << *Justement, nous voulons recommencer* **Phèdre**. *[...] Nous trouvons que le terrain métaphysique cédant la place au terrain scientifique, la littérature théologique et classique doit céder la place à la littérature naturaliste [...]. Phèdre est malade, eh bien ! voyons sa maladie, démontons-la, rendons-nous-en les maîtres, s'il est possible [...]* >>[75].

On the other hand, Zola was ideologically opposed to Malthus and his advocacy for birth control or, at worst, his encouragement to promote war as an effective means to curb galloping demography. Basically, this novelist was a writer of the people; he was in essence a natalist whose drama was all the harder to bear because he founded a sterile famil with his wife, Alexandrine Meley. His

---

[72] Roger Ripoll: **Réalité et Mythe chez Zola**, op.cit. p. 3.
[73] **Ibidem**, p. 3.
[74] Émile Zola : **Le Roman Expérimental**, in **Œuvres Complètes**, under the direction of Henri Mitterand, volume 9 : **Nana 1880**, presentation, notices, chronology and bibliography by Chantal Pierre-Gnassounou, op. cit. p. 346.
[75] Response to Charles Bigot, in **Le Salut Public** in Octobre 1879, article published later on in the above book, op.cit. p. 454.

novelistic production, from the **Rougon-Macquart** to the **Trois Villes**, can be seen as a way out of his personal heartbreak, just like a catharsis.

Indeed, because literary creation gave him the power to create characters and to make them go through different experiences, and especially to have them procreate as he pleased, it seemed to have helped Zola fill his initial lack of children. Naturalism therefore came about as the perfect answer to his personal issues of infertility. Do not novelists claim to be the emulators of God? Certainly, they are gods who proceed by substitution, replacing their essential lacks by a literary omnipotence, thus factitious. In Zola's works, this translates into his omnipotence to allow child biths in his novels when, in real life, he remained deprived of them for many years.

Perhaps it is necessary to ask oneself why precisely the theme of sexuality has obsessed Zola in the corpus rather than any other? In fact, this question has been partially resolved in the previous section. It should only be added that sex is the reproductive element of animal species and therefore the instance that transmits all genetic and hereditary data at the same time as it produces babies. Now this sums up all the naturalistic aesthetics.

Whether it be religious, biological, sociological or even literary and ideological, everything obviously contributes to justify the preponderance of the theme of sexuality in **Les Rougon-Macquart**. It is nothing more nor less than what must be perceived as the cornerstone of this monumental literary edifice. This is the time now to analyse the epistemological foundations that might have justified this prominence of sexuality in the corpus.

4. THE EPISTEMOLOGICAL FOUNDATIONS

I propose here to return to the general preface to the **Rougon-Macquart** series written by Zola in July 1871. The text of this preface indeed had a very strong accent of predictability and readability of the twenty novels that were to follow, at least in regard to the epistemological foundations. For example, Zola wrote, somewhat peremptorily : << *L'hérédité a ses lois, comme la pesanteur* >>[76].

The tone was thus given which consecrated heredity, thus genetics, as the basis for his romantic enterprise on the one hand. The author's mission was therefore, on the one hand, to formulate hypotheses that would be subjected to a rigorous experimentation on a *"human"* material and, on the other hand, to identify any laws in order to draw conclusions that would have been *"scientifically"* proven.

Posing as an experimental biologist, Zola proposed to proceed from a hypothesis : << *la famille que je me propose d'étudier, a pour caractéristique le débordement des appétits, le large soulèvement de notre âge qui se rue aux*

---

[76] Émile Zola : **R. M, I**, op. cit. p. 3.

jouissances >>[77]. Clearly, this basic predicate was not an analysis but simply a mere statement that asked the questions of why and how. To answer these fundamental questions, the author envisaged finding and following << [..] *le fil qui conduit mathématiquement d'un homme à un autre homme* >>[78]. The epistemological ambitions thus revealed are reinforced by the presence of the terms << *étude* >>, << *analyse* >> and << *scientifique* >> in the same preface. It can be deduced that the novelist, essentially a man of letters, was somewhat subjugated by scientific advances and, more precisely, by the experimental method whose rigour he appreciated so much that he undertook to bend the subjective - the romantic literary creation - to the rigidity[79] of experimental science.

Later on, in 1880, Zola published **Le Roman Expérimental** which was nothing else but a redacted synthesis of the **Introduction à l'Étude de la Médecine Expérimentale** by Claude Bernard that was published in 1865. It is not without naivety that Zola wrote as early as in the introductory chapter of this essay : << *Je n'aurai à faire ici qu'un travail d'adaptation car la méthode expérimentale a été établie avec une force et une clarté merveilleuses par Claude Bernard, dans son* **Introduction à l'étude de la médecine expérimentale**. *Ce livre, d'un savant dont l'autorité est décisive, va me servir de terrain solide. Je trouverai là toute la question traitée, et je me bornerai, comme arguments irréfutables, à donner les citations qui me seront nécessaires. Ce ne sera donc qu'une compilation de textes ; car je compte, sur tous les points, me retrancher derrière Claude Bernard. Le plus souvent, il me suffira de remplacer le mot << médecin >> par le mot << romancier >> pour rendre ma pensée claire et lui apporter la rigueur d'une vérité scientifique* >>[80].

If it is legitimate to reproach Zola for his unfortunate tendency to equate the novelist with the doctor with no restrictions, it must be conceded to him that the experimental novelist is the product of a Century dominated by scientists such as Charles Darwin and Claude Bernard. Zola wrote exactly about that in the following words : << *J'en suis donc arrivé à ce point : le roman expérimental est une conséquence de l'évolution scientifique du siècle ; il continue et complète la physiologie, qui elle-même s'appuie sur la chimie et la physique ; il substitue à l'étude de l'homme abstrait, de l'homme métaphysique, l'étude de l'homme naturel, soumis aux lois physico-chimiques et déterminé par les influences du milieu ; il est en un mot la littérature de notre âge scientifique,*

---

[77] Émile Zola : **R. M, I**, op. cit. p. 3.
[78] **Ibidem,** p. 3.
[79] We are not going to waste time on the skepticism inherent to such a programmatic vision. Suffices it to return the reader to the book by David Baguley: **Naturalist Fiction. The Entropic Vison**, op. cit. p. 59.
[80] Émile Zola : **Le Roman Expérimental**, in **Œuvres Complètes**, sous la direction de Henri Mitterand, Tome 9 : **Nana 1880**, op. cit. p. 324.

comme la littérature classique et romantique a correspondu à un âge de scolastique et de théologie >>[81].

In the second half of the nineteenth Century, in fact, Auguste Comte's doctrine was very popular amongst intellectuals. His doctrine described a humanity guided by reasoning and the progressive discovery of the intellectual laws which alone would be capable of explaining natural phenomena. Maarten Van Buuren has already shown that Broussais, who defined it in 1828 as a serious disturbance, owns the notion of lesion, and that Comte has taken up the word after him. Zola had probably discovered it by reading Auguste Comte[82] whose ideas were broadly spread across Europe. However, since the lesion is an injury, a slit through which the ego escapes from the individual who then goes on to be dominated by their instincts alone, Van Buuren notes that the very notion of lesion is obsolete today and that it no longer has any scientific value. The bookshop Hachette – let us remember that Zola worked there - published works of all kinds including the famous **Dictionnaire** by Littré from 1863 to 1877. The influence of Littré, a doctor, an historian and a positivist philologist on Zola is undeniable[83].

Elsewhere, **The Origin of Species** by Charles Darwin was translated into French in 1862 and was seen as a scientific revolution at that time. In Darwin's view, living species are transformed because of the action of the environment in which they live, and as a result of what he calls the mechanism of natural selection and the hereditary transmission of acquired characters. Nonetheless, Zola was not really inspired directly by Darwin as it was the case with Lucas and Claude Bernard. According to Ripoll, the reference to Darwin remains brief and almost anecdotal : << *Par exemple Zola cite le nom de Darwin sans qu'on puisse savoir s'il s'est réellement attaché à le lire ou s'il s'est contenté de reprendre l'image que l'on se faisait couramment de sa pensée. Dans* **Le Roman Expérimental** *il parle des théories de Darwin comme d'hypothèses qui seraient susceptibles d'aider le romancier dans son travail, mais il ne s'y attarde pas* >>[84].

Generally speaking, the nineteenth Century saw science leaving the closed circle of scientists only to reach the general public and Taine - whom Zola knew personally - was the first to apply Darwinian theories to the human sciences by considering that the race, the milieu – which is about the environment - and the era were the essential factors of human determinism. Zola especially admired

---

[81] Émile Zola : **Le Roman Expérimental**, in Œuvres Complètes, sous la direction de Henri Mitterand, Tome 9 : **Nana 1880**, op. cit. p.333.
[82] Maarten Van Buuren : **Les Rougon-Macquart d'Émile Zola. De la Métaphore au Mythe**, op. cit. p. 190.
[83] Roger Ripoll has sufficiently showed in **Réalité et Mythe chez Zola**, volume I, the direct influence of Littré on Zola; the latter admiring the modesty and the abnegation of the scholar that was the former, op. cit, p. 160.
[84] **Ibidem**, op. cit. pp. 159-160.

the literary critic Hippolyte Taine, whom he highly regarded[85] because of his scientific method.

When he put himself in the shoes of the literary critic, Zola blithely equated the fiction work with a baby that the critic – just like a scientist - must dissect[86]. Amazingly enough, this metaphorical dissection of a baby is a sadism that remains a fundamental aspect of naturalism according to Jean Kaempfer[87]. After having revealed the referential absurdity of this Zolian statement which is an insane but a harmless madness[88], Kaempfer believes this is a perverse statement : << *Telle est l'efficacité de la formule qui nous arrêtait tout à l'heure : faire l'autopsie d'un nouveau-né, littéralement, ça ne veut rien dire ; aussi le lecteur est-il seul responsable de l'esprit qu'il voudra bien prêter à cet énoncé absurde. Quant à l'auteur, il l'a bien dite, la formule, mais il ne s'y trouve pas ... Contrairement à son perplexe lecteur, qui s'y perd, et finit par porter le chapeau d'une folie qui n'est pas la sienne ! C'est un comble, - le comble machiné par un pervers* >>[89].

Nevertheless, Zola firmly claimed the use of the experimental method that would make the difference between the naturalistic novelists and poets - especially the romantics - and the philosophers : << *En un mot, nous travaillons avec tout le siècle à la grande œuvre qui est la conquête de la nature, la puissance de l'homme décuplée. Et voyez à côté de la nôtre, la besogne des écrivains idéalistes, qui s'appuient sur l'irrationnel et le surnaturel, et dont chaque élan est suivi d'une chute profonde dans le chaos métaphysique. C'est nous qui avons la force, c'est nous qui avons la morale* >>[90].

Still, how should naturalist novelists go about reaching such a high summit? Well, for Zola, the way seems all carved out: << *Et c'est là ce qui constitue le roman expérimental : posséder le mécanisme des phénomènes chez l'homme, montrer les rouages des manifestations intellectuelles et sensuelles telles que la physiologie nous les expliquera, sous les influences de l'hérédité et des circonstances ambiantes, puis montrer l'homme vivant dans le milieu social qu'il a produit lui-même, qu'il modifie tous les jours, et au sein duquel il éprouve à son tour une transformation continue. Ainsi donc, nous nous appuyons sur la physiologie, nous prenons l'homme isolé des mains du physiologiste, pour*

---

[85] Émile Zola : **Le Roman Expérimental**, in **Œuvres Complètes**, volume 9 : **Nana 1880**, op. cit, p. 422.
[86] **Ibidem**, p.376, Zola takes the comparison between the experimental novelist and the forensic doctor further by writing, with regard to the naturalistic novelists, including Balzac and Stendhal, that << *Leur besogne consistait à prendre l'homme, à le disséquer, à l'analyser dans sa chair et dans son cerveau* >>, p. 376.
[87] Jean Kaempfer : **D'Un Naturalisme Pervers**, Paris, José Corti, 1989, p. 202.
[88] **Ibidem**, p. 191.
[89] **Ibidem**, op. cit. p. 193.
[90] Émile Zola : **Le Roman Expérimental**, in **Œuvres Complètes**, volume 9 : **Nana 1880**, op. cit. p. 337.

continuer la solution du problème et résoudre scientifiquement la question de savoir comment se comportent les hommes dès qu'ils sont en société >>[91].

This study of the interaction between man and society is what Zola called << *la sociologie pratique* >>, of which he expected utopian results, to say the least: << *C'est ainsi que nous faisons de la sociologie pratique et que notre besogne aide aux sciences politiques et économiques. Je ne sais pas, je le répète, de travail plus noble ni d'une application plus large. Être maître du bien et du mal, régler la vie, régler la société, résoudre à la longue tous les problèmes du socialisme, apporter surtout des bases solides à la justice en résolvant par l'expérience les questions de criminalité, n'est-ce pas là être les ouvriers les plus utiles et les plus moraux du travail humain ? >>*[92]

Those were utopian aspirations indeed, and never before him, nor after him, such a challenge had been undertaken by any of his peers. The audacity was great and the merit of Zola was above all to have dared to take up that challenge in the first place. Never mind that some critics continue to claim that it was a losing bet[93], To say the least, the courageous initiative in itself must be unreservedly welcomed. At the end of the Century marked by the triumphs of scientists such as Claude Bernard and Lucas, it was up to men of letters to follow the general momentum and innovate literature if necessary. It was up to them to show that the watertight partitions erected between those different fields of human knowledge were unfounded. Roger Ripoll insisted on the fact that Claude Bernard's contribution was decisive in the formation of Zola's scientific ideas[94]. He went on to aptly argue there was a similarity of method between science and naturalistic literature (not to be confused with an integral application of the experimental method to naturalistic novels)[95]. Above all, he has shown how faithful Zola's theories of heredity were to those of Dr. Prosper Lucas, for

---

[91] Émile Zola : **Le Roman Expérimental**, in **Œuvres Complètes**, volume 9 : **Nana 1880**, op. cit. p. 332.

[92] **Ibidem**, Chapter III, op. cit. p. 183

[93] David Baguley recognises, following Céard and Brunetière, the impossibility of literary experimentation: << *Obviously, as Céard and Brunetière pointed out, a novelist cannot strictly speaking perform an experiment whose outcome is unknown, since the novelist is constantly in control of the conditions and the result*>>, in **Naturalist Fiction. The Entropic Vison**, op. cit. p. 59.

Claude Seassau analysed the difference between **Le Roman Expérimental** and Zola's works and denounced the hiatus between the naturalist practice and theory in **Émile Zola, Le Réalisme Symbolique**, op. cit. p. 275.

As for Maarten Van Buuren, he believes that Zola's scientific claims are not taken seriously, and that his scientism is undercut by myth, in **Les Rougon-Macquart d'Émile Zola. De la Métaphore au Mythe**, op. cit. p. 15.

Lastly, let us mention **D'Un Naturalisme Pervers** by Jean Kaempfer for whom the naturalistic theory is nothing more than a usurpation (p. 163), especially since naturalism does not exist, or rather the so-called naturalist novels should be written otherwise (p. 162)..

[94] Roger Ripoll : **Réalité et Mythe chez Zola**, op. cit. p. 161.

[95] **Ibidem**, p. 162.

example, with regard to the link between animality and hereditary defect[96]. The inevitable degeneration of families on the threshold of the fifth generation[97], or the perception of heredity as a fatality weighing on the whole family, and finally, the thought that drunken parents beget crazy children[98]. It is for all those reasons that for Ripoll, there is no need to oppose **Le Roman Expérimental** to **Nana** for they complete each other[99].

With Zola, the novel, genetics, psychoanalysis, sociology and history would henceforth merge into a single crucible to analyze the world (that of the Second Empire) and explain it globally. Claude Bernard himself did not escape this temptation when the geneticist that he was turned into a philosopher and a rather prolific writer. This can be seen as a fair return to the things of the old days, because in ancient Greece, the great philosophers such as Thales, Plato, Aristotle or Pythagoras, were also geometers, mathematicians, physicists, astronomers, even theorists of literature.

All in all, the foundations studied here are hardly contradictory. On the contrary, they remain complementary to show that Zola had many reasons to place sexuality at the core of his literary conception, not because he was the voyeur or the pornographer that some Puritan minds saw in him, i.e. his irreducible detractors, but for nobler reasons as I have just shown.

Let us not forget, moreover, to question **Les Rougon-Macquart** about the effective characteristics of sexuality, the thematics that is dear to me.

---

[96] Roger Ripoll : **Réalité et Mythe chez Zola**, op. cit. p. 167.
[97] **Ibidem**, p. 168.
[98] **Ibidem**, p. 169.
[99] **Ibidem**, p. 479.

CHAPTER 2 : THE CHARACTERISTICS OF SEXUALITY IN THE CORPUS

The substantive "characteristics" designates that which serves to characterise, to particularise something or someone. By character, I mean any textual sign allowing the reader to recognise and to specify the sexuality of the anthropomorphic agent or that of the non-anthropomorphic agent. It is any element of appreciation that distinguishes sexuality in the naturalistic text from what may be found elsewhere. In summary, therefore, I intend to study in this chapter everything that makes it possible to recognise, to particularise and to constitute the originality of sexuality in the corpus.

How is the treatment of the theme of sexuality in **Les Rougon-Macquart** specific and, therefore, different from what can be seen elsewhere? The answer to that question will be revealed throughout the following six points. The first of which is undoubtedly the recurrence of hereditary diseases that strike most of the main characters in the series that is the focus of this study.

1. THE HEREDITARY DISEASES AND THE NARRATIVE GRAMMAR

From **La Fortune des Rougon** to **Le Docteur Pascal**, the lexematic figure that is the crack is at the heart of the **Rougon-Macquart** series. It goes through many declensions throughout the twenty novels that make up the **Rougon-Macquart**. The crack also travels several semanmic paths, that is to say different possibilities of actualisation, or different uses and meanings. Among those sememic journeys, one will find lucid madness, murderous madness, derailment, nervousness, animality, ferocious appetite, brutality and aggressiveness, to name but a few major examples of the crack's declensions.

Finally, the crack positions itself as an isotopy because it guarantees the homogeneity of the Zolian naturalistic discourse. I can say with Jean Borie that the crack is both a fatality and a heredity[100], whereas for Gilles Deleuze: << *L'hérédité n'est pas ce qui passe par la fêlure, elle est la fêlure elle-même : la cassure ou le trou, imperceptibles* >>[101].

Indeed, the crack of the grandmother Aunt Dide explains the behaviour of each member of her numerous descendants by the fatal and the inexorable game of heredity that weighs on them[102]. It is also undeniable that it is the condensation of the whole theory of heredity - or rather the whole theory of naturalism - according to Émile Zola ; the principle that presided over the genesis of the

---

[100] Jean Borie : **Zola et les Mythes, ou de la Nausée au Salut**, op. cit. p. 20-21.
[101] Gilles Deleuze : **La Logique du Sens**, *chapitre : Zola et la fêlure*, op. cit. p. 91.
[102] Roger Ripoll writes that Tante Dide is the << *Figure de la fatalité* >> and that << *En Tante Dide, il faut reconnaître, malgré la différence d'âge, cette figure de femme fatale dominée par les puissances de destruction* >>, in **Réalité et Mythe chez Zola**, op. cit. p. 478.

Rougon-Macquart. The crack that Aunt Dide thus transmits to her descendants (as a hereditary disease) is undoubtedly the generative grammar of the Romanesque cycle of **Les Rougon-Macquart**, because without it, no logical organisation of the different discursive and narrative elements would be possible.

In what Zola called the novel of the origins, **La Fortune des Rougon**, Adélaïde Fouque is labelled as having << *le cerveau fêlé comme son père* >>, while her great-grandson, Claude Lantier, is the victim of a << *détraquement héréditaire* >> who would go on to become << *un fou* >> because of the << *déséquilibrement des nerfs dont il souffrait* >>[103]. Meanwhle, his junior broher, Jacques Lantier, is << *emporté par l'hérédité de violence, par ce besoin de meurtre* >>[104], which makes him another type of madman and a ripper. Nana, the half-sister of the two previous ones, is called << *folle* >>[105] by her lover, Earl Muffat[106].

Yet, to each character their particular form of madness. Thus, Renée is the victim of a nervous breakdown that pushes her to demand a trip to America with her incestuous lover, Maxime Rougon dit Saccard, the son to her lawful husband in **La Curée**. In a realistic novel, such an unrealistic venture fails naturally and miserably, and the heroine becomes somewhat amnesic and gradually fades away until her complete extinction[107]. It is fair to argue that the Renée who dies in the prime of her life is only an allegory of the decadent Second Empire that will also collapse at the age of eighteen.

As for Georges Hugon for example, his folly is rather transient in **Nana** and it stems directly from jealousy from the moment he discovers the incestuous affair of his older brother, Philippe, with his mistress, Nana. It is only then that he loses his mind to the point of killing himself before the culprit. He summarises the loss of innocence of the imperial youth; a youth raised in a ring of vice and running to its own loss.

---

[103] Émile Zola : **R. M. IV**, Paris, Gallimard, 1966, p. 245.
[104] **Ibidem**, p. 1299.
[105] Émile Zola : **R. M. II**, Paris, Gallimard, 1961, p. 1411.
[106] In **Les Rougon-Macquart d'Émile Zola. De la Métaphore au Mythe**, op. cit. pp. 193-195, Maarten Van Buuren has shown how meaningful is the notion of the *fêlure* – the crack - in Zola's works, which admits the following meanings: hereditary blemish, social decay, mental imbalance and fever. He then counted the metaphors of illness dominated by << *la fièvre* >>, 355 occurrences, << *maladie* >>, 31 times ; << *mal* >>, 24 occurrences; << *peste* >>, 20 times; << *épidémie* >>, 8 times; << *choléra* >>, 8 times ; << *contagion n*>>, 9 times ; << *virus* >>, 1 time; << *pourrir* >>, 56 occurrences; << *gâter* >>, 79 times. Apart from those metaphors, he underlined the synonyms of imbalance such as << *bouleverser* >>, 130 occurrences ; << *ébranler* >>, 82 times; << *chanceler* >>, 10 times and << *chavirer* >>, 3 occurrences.
[107] In David Baguley's book, this phenomenon bears the following names: << [the] *poetics of dissolution* >> and << *the dynamics of disintegration* >>, refer to his **Naturalist Fiction. The Entropic Vision**, op. cit. p. 200 et p. 202.

In **La Bête Humaine**, Roubaud's situation is quite specific: having murdered President Grandmorin out of jealousy, he remains paradoxically amnesiac and amorphous about the subsequent infidelity of his wife, Séverine. His sex drive seems to have died down with the murder committed by passion, giving the impression that violent madness is followed by lucid and passive madness. In the same novel, Flore manifests a madness that is downright violent as it provokes carnage - the derailment of a train - to avenge her unsatisfied love and to punish what she sees as traitors, namely Jacques Lantier and Séverine. In Zola's world, sexual subjects are wild animals that evolve in a ruthless jungle[108] and who eat up their prey to the very last bone.

To tell the truth, madness is found at each end of the **Rougon-Macquart** not as a cosmetic feature, but rather as the very essence of the naturalistic doctrine. The crack of the grandmother Dide is the starting point of the narrative grammar of Zola's novelistic series, thus the generating element of the story. The generative and transformational grammar gives the kernel-phrase (P) the following structure:

$$P \longrightarrow NP + VP + (PS)\ n^{109}.$$

This means that the core of the noted sentence (P) is reduced to the concatenation of a noun phrase (NP) and a verbal phrase (VP) at the primary and mandatory level. At the secondary or optional level, one or more prepositional syntagmas (PS), complements of the sentence must be added on to the core structure to expand it. In a very theoretical way, we can project the image of that canonical structure of the sentence on Zola's naturalistic doctrine in these terms:

P ⇔ naturalism.
NP ⇔ the cracked or deranged parents.
VP ⇔ sexuality (V) + heredity (Compl.).
PS ⇔ typical or stereotyped children that are all infected.

It must be understood that if naturalism were to be read as a great sentence, the cracked parents would be its subjects, that is to say, the first agents who carry out the action. These subjects would conjugate sexuality as a direct transitive verb admitting therefore a complement of direct object (CDO) which would be nothing other than heredity. The complements of the sentence are known for their optional character. That is why they would be made up – or not – of children. Yet, if these children were to be born at all, they would all be typified or stereotyped depending on the case, but they would always be contaminated by the genes received from their parents.

---

[108] Paris remains the most iconic symbol of that jungle.
[109] Louis Lalaire : **Le Verbe et le Classement Syntaxique du Verbe**, collection Les Cahiers de Grammaire, n°. 4, Abidjan, ENS, 1990, p. 4.

What also strikes the reader of the **Rougon-Macquart** series is this panoply of aberrations and other sexual perversions in practically each of the twenty novels of the cycle. One of Zola's originalities is precisely this perception that he shows a sexuality made up of aberrations and perversions[110].

2. THE SEXUAL ABERRATIONS

Let us remind ourselves that Sigmund Freud thus named the set of perversions and sexual deviations in his **Trois Essais sur la Théorie de la Sexualité** published in 1905. I will refer to Freud not only because he was a contemporary of the author, but especially because on the one hand, his theories are sometimes a direct confirmation of Zola's views on the issue of sexuality, and, on the other hand, because in his time, he was the most authoritative scholar on the subject. Freud classified sexual aberrations into two categories: deviations from the sexual object first, then deviations from the sexual goal.

2.1. The deviations from the sexual object

These deviations are about inversions, which are broken down into three classes in the Freudian theory: *les inversions absolues, les inversions amphigènes* and *les inversions occasionnelles*.

2.1.1 The absolute inversions

Any sexual subject having an aversion for the opposite sex and de facto, the one whose sexual object is always homosexual, is said *inverti absolu* for the inversion he manifests is innate. In this category, we find the hermaphrodites, the homosexuals and the sexual immature subjects.

In the corpus, there are no true hermaphrodites, strictly speaking. Though, there is an absolute homosexual character in **La Curée**, Baptiste, the butler of Aristide Rougon dit Saccard and two absolute lesbians in **Nana**, Satin and Mme Robert. The epithet *absolute* characterises them for the simple reason that these three protagonists have sex only with their peers of the same sex. Freud quotes Ferenczi who proposed the term homoerotic to describe such people instead of homosexual. For the latter, a homoerotic subject is the one << *qui est pleinement viril et ne fait qu'échanger l'objet féminin contre un objet du même sexe que lui* >>[111]. It is right, therefore, for Freud to classify such sexual subjects as obsessional neurotics since they can enjoy the opposite sex although they stubbornly turn away from it.

---

[110] I shall follow in Sigmund Freud's footsteps by using those terms as he defined them in his **Trois Essais sur la Théorie de la Sexualité**, Vienne, 1905, Paris, Gallimard, 1981, for the second French translation.
[111] Sigmund Freud citing Ferenczi in **Trois Essais sur la Théorie de la Sexualité**, op. cit. p.32.

In that category, we can also find a place for sexual immature characters, that is to say the sexual subjects who exercise their virility on children - paedophiles for whom President Grandmorin is the torchbearer in **La Bête Humaine.** They can also direct their sexual interests towards animals, or even towards physical objects that belonged to the beloved character. Those objects they treasure are also known as fetishes. There are two sexual immature characters in the corpus: Saturnin Josserand of **Pot-Bouille** and Cabuche in **La Bête Humaine.** The latter is content to cherish and adore the handkerchiefs of his beloved woman, Séverine Roubaud, thus limiting his sexual inclinations to a mere preliminary pleasure consisting in caressing and sniffing the scent of the fetish item. The former delights in extramarital love affairs of his sister. Here, only Grandmorin is punished severely because Zola abhors paedophilia which he saw as the most abject form of corruption in morals. The throat-sliting he suffers is indeed the harsh punishment that sanctions his deranged lust. On a larger scale, his murder is a sign of the upcoming cleansing of the upper middle class – the bourgeoisie - under Napoléon III. It also suggests the need to get rid of a rotten political system in order to hatch out a better world.

The corpus thus offers only those five protagonists called absolute *invertis*: Cabuche, Baptiste, Satin, Saturnin and Mme Robert. Nevertheless, if we were to provide a scientific explanation for this sexual aberration, we would only have to refer once again to Sigmund Freud who wrote: << *Nous avons établi de tous les cas examinés que les futurs invertis traversent, au cours des premières années de leur enfance, une phase de fixation très intense et cependant éphémère à la femme (le plus souvent la mère) et qu'après avoir surmonté cette phase, ils s'identifient à la femme et se prennent eux-mêmes comme objets sexuels, autrement dit que, partant du narcissisme, ils recherchent de jeunes hommes semblables à leur propre personne, qu'ils veulent aimer comme leur mère les a aimés eux-mêmes* >>[112]. Further down the line, Freud pointed out that << *Il n'est pas rare que l'absence d'un père fort dans l'enfance favorise l'inversion* >>.

Unfortunately, the narrator in Zola's works gives away almost no textual signs allowing us to grasp the childhood of the five absolutely inverted characters which would have allowed us to confirm or to refute the theories that Freud develops in these two quotations on a larger scale. The only background information in such cases appears in **Pot-Bouille** where Josserand, the father, is too weak and fades away before the coarse domination and disdainful presence of Madame Éleonore Josserand.

To use Roland Barthes' vocabulary, no *informant*[113] or immediately signifying pure data comes along directly to instruct the reader of their inversion. Only a

---

[112] Sigmund Freud : **Trois Essais sur la Théorie de la Sexualité**, op. cit., p. 50.
[113] Roland Barthes : *Introduction à l'Analyse Structurale des Récits* in **Communications, 8**, Paris, Seuil, 1982, p. 15.

few *indices*[114] are scattered here and there. Once they are cut out and analysed, they provide only a hint at their pederasty, their lesbianism and their sexual immaturity. It can be deduced that the criticisms directed at Zola about immorality and defilement in his novels must be put into perspective since the narrator in his works never bluntly exposes the sexual aberrations of the characters. Only by overlapping the innocuous and disparate indices scattered throughout his works, one can shed a light on those aberrations. This probably explains the narration of sexual aberrations in the **Rougon-Macquart** series under the regime of the *focalisation externe*[115] - and never under that of the *focalisation zéro*[116] -, to use Genette's terminology, that is, when the narrator knows as much as any of the characters. For example, in the case of Baptiste, the narrator knows even less than his characters. In such a case, he is limited to only ocnveying what we hear and see.

Finally, exceptionally, the focus is *interne*[117] in the case of Jacques Lantier and Cabuche when the narrator then knows more than any of his characters, penetrating into their consciousness as well as into their unconscious to narrate everything that happens there.

In the first case scenario - the external focus - the narrator seems to know less than Céleste, Renée's maid, who first discloses the secret of the pederast to her boss before the narrator lets his readers know of it. The narrator here merely operates as an additional listener, indiscreet by nature, who does not deliver it to their fictional and/or real audience. The novelist seems to clear his name thus by distancing himself from the conduct of his paper-beings. He pretends not to be informed of their secret dealings. In the case of the internal focus, he knows just as much as the characters who see and interpret the suspicious conduct of Satin in the arms of Nana and Cabuche hoarding the handkerchiefs of Séverine in his *"cave"*.

For the rest, the richness of the Freudian remarks I have mentioned above will be revealed far more boldly through the study of the acquired inversions, whether they be amphigenic or occasional.

2.1.2. The amphigenic inversions.

In the Freudian conception, the amphigenic inverted characters are psychosexual hermaphrodites, meaning those whose sexual object can be both homosexual and heterosexual. In today's language, we would speak of bisexuals. Maxime Rougon dit Saccard, the inseparable Adeline d'Espanet and Suzanne Haffner in **La Curée** and Nana in **Nana**, make up this class of inverted characters. These

---

[114] Roland Barthes : *Introduction à l'Analyse Structurale des Récits* in **Communications, 8**, op. cit. p. 15.
[115] Gérard Genette : **Figures III**, Paris, Seuil, 1973, p. 74.
[116] **Ibidem**, p. 74.
[117] **Ibidem**, p. 74.

are not victims of an innate inversion but rather of an acquired and a desired inversion. In contrast to their *absolute* counterparts, which the reader must apprehend by cross-checking the clues scattered around in the corpus, the amphigenic characters can be directly grasped thanks to the informants since the narrator appears to feel no discomfort in exposing their conscious and voluntary perversions on the spot because they refuse to disguise them in the first place. The denunciation on the part of the novelist is all the more clearer because he strongly condemns this shameless libertinage, this deliberate practice of debauchery that will cost the Second Empire so dearly. For debauchery is indeed the disease of the idle and carefree imperial bourgeoisie. When money and luxury are overflowing, nothing else is sought more fiercely than a rare enjoyment - like Renée puts it when looking for the *''jouissance rare''*. That indefined type of climax is supposed to cure her *''mal de vivre''*.

This is also how one must read the travesty of Maxime[118], a cross-dresser. Much later on, the young man becomes like a woman in the hands of his phallic mistress, Renée, especially when they indulge in incest in the greenhouse. This inversion of roles during their sexual intercourse encounters constitutes an acquired and a voluntary inversion whose foreseeable consequence is the degeneration of the individuals and, by extension, of the imperial society[119] of which they are, after all, a solid representation. It should also be remembered that these two characters all flirted with homosexuality in their childhood: Maxime with his classmates of the boarding school in Plassans and Renée at the ladies of the Visitation convent. The boarding school and the convent, by bringing together young people of the same sex, both push them to harbour homoerotic tendencies in the Zolian novel. These two spaces then become what Greimas calls *espaces paratopiques*[120], spaces where a given skill is acquired. This remains true for Adeline d'Espanet and Suzanne Haffner who, despite their

---

[118] Maxime indeed wears Renée's dresses and struts in front of the clients of the fashion designer, Worms, who were supposed to admire his elegant feminism!

[119] Maarten Van Buuren, in **Les Rougon-Macquart d'Émile Zola. De la Métaphore au Mythe**, op. cit. writes : << *Les métaphores qui représentent l'homme comme une femme et la femme comme un homme, servent des buts divers. Leur fonction principale est d'exprimer la corruption sous le Second Empire, mais ce n'est pas leur seule fonction* >> p. 185 and later on, he adds: << *Mais, le changement de sexe symbolise en premier lieu la dégénérescence que Zola considère comme caractéristique de l'époque du Second Empire* >>, p. 187.

[120] A. J. Greimas and J. Courtès write : << *Eu égard à un programme narratif donné, défini comme une transformation située entre deux éléments narratifs stables, on peut considérer comme* espace topique *le lieu où se manifeste syntaxiquement cette transformation, et comme* espace hétérotopique *les lieux qu'il englobe, en le précédant et/ou en le suivant* >>, p. 397, and << *Sous composante de l'espace topique, et opposé à l'espace paratopique (où s'acquièrent les compétences); l'espace utopique est celui où le héros accède à la victoire; c'est le lieu où se réalisent les performances* >>, refer to **Sémiotique. Dictionnaire Raisonné de la Théorie du Langage**, Paris, Hachette, 1979, p. 413.

respective marriages, continue their lesbian practices acquired at the convent where they met[121].

Tired of men, Nana ended up being initiated to lesbianism by her good friend Satin whom she accommodated temporarily in her mansion. Here again, this space is invested exclusively by three women: Nana, Zoe - her maid - and her friend Satin[122], just like a convent serving as a hotbed for vice.

Nevertheless, the spatial configuration alone is not enough to justify the acquired or the amphigenic inversion, since, as Freud argued above, it may be due to the absence of a strong father or to the intense attraction of a mother on her child.

On this subject, Aristide Rougon dit Saccard was totally absent during the childhood of his son, Maxime, who was deeply influenced by his mother, Angèle Sicardot, the soft and passive woman. There followed the sluggishness, the passivity and the effeminacy of the son who had become deeply narcissistic. To this hereditary baggage, we must add the harmful influence of the environments where he lived, including the boarding school of Plassans where he was initiated to homosexuality and the rotten environment of Paris[123], embalmed by the smell of women, and especially the almost nonexistent family environment at the Saccard house. All those elements exacerbate Maxime's innate appetites. If we consider the luxury[124] in which he lived, and the money he had at his disposal, enabling him to pay off all the demi-mondaines and for any other type of debauchery, we can easily picture a Maxime who was predestined to perversion and degeneration in later life.

On the other hand, although Father Béraud du Châtel was an authoritarian dad, he did not have the time to bring his daughter up, Renée, who was raised mainly in the convent after her mother's death. It is among the ladies of the Visitation that she became overly narcissistic and was initiated to lesbianism before receiving the jewel in the crown of her bad education with the rape she suffered

---

[121] Naomi Schor writes in this context: << *According to Zola (here, too, following in Balzac's footsteps), boarding schools are hotbeds of vice, breeding grounds for homosexuality* >>, in **Zola's Crowds**, Baltimore and London, The Johns Hopkins University Press, 1978, p. 94.

[122] This can be seen as a sort of boarding school since there is no authority - or rule - in this house, so much so that its inhabitants cohabit like ordinary schoolmates or student roommates, with all the licence and libertinism this implies.

[123] Maarten Van Buuren has well noticed this dimension of Paris - *coquette*, *dangereuse* and *frivole*, to borrow his words - in **Les Rougon-Macquart d'Émile Zola. De la Métaphore au Mythe**, op. cit. p. 73.

Roger Ripoll also returns to the metaphorical assimilation of Paris to the biblical cursed cities, Sodom and Gomorrah, to prophesy the fall of the Empire, see **Réalité et Mythe chez Zola**, op. cit. pp 100-101.

[124] **Les Rougon-Macquart d'Émile Zola. De la Métaphore au Mythe**, op. cit., p. 259, Maarten Van Buuren notes that << *les vices sont le produit du luxe qui est à son tour le produit des changements sociaux* >>.

as a young adult. This rape represented her true baptism, a baptism of fire under the sign of lust and decadence. It also prepared her to enter the imperial society where she would be celebrated and crowned as a sex symbol. Her marriage to Aristide brought her only a name and a roof instead of a matrimonial home[125]. That is why, luxury and money helping, she devoted her whole life to seeking entertainment, pleasure and happiness until she found the ultimate rare enjoyment, the *"jouissance rare"*.

The same paternal absence disoriented Nana, another mirror enthusiast whose father Coupeau, the disabled and the drunken former carpenter had absolutely no authority[126]. Coupeau died far too early to take care of the upbringing of his daughter. The poor environment she grew up in was a reason for Nana's resentment towards society, hence the concept of revenge. One must add to all that precedes the drunkenness of her parents which encompasses to make up her temperament as a future prostitute for it is known that in Zola's views on the theory of heredity, drunken parents are most likely to procreate prostitutes and murderers.

All in all, we do accept the degree of accuracy of the Freudian conception in the case of these *anaphoric characters*[127] that make up the core family of the Rougon-Macquart and their allies by bonds of marriage, the Mouret and the Lantier families. I will detail further this character classification in the second part of this book. With regards to the *personnages embrayeurs*[128] or *clutch characters*, Adeline and Suzanne - who are only allies of the *anaphoric characters* - we lack enough explicit informants about their respective parents. It's hard therefore to assess the influence of their family background on the development of their temperament. It must be pointed out, however, that the convent was the place where they were initiated to debauchery. Returning to live in Paris, although they were married to rich men[129] and they were enjoying all the liberties, they stopped at nothing on the path to debauchery.

It is still understood that the inversion can take many other forms that are less rigid and less permanent.

---

[125] In **Les Rougon-Macquart d'Émile Zola. De la Métaphore au Mythe**, op. cit. p. 175, Maarten Van Buuren believes that Renée is a mere goods for Saccard, and that erotic desire in him is often brought about in the corpus by the greed for money acting as a matchmaker. It was the same greed indeed that led to the marriage of Lisa Macquart with Quenu in **Le Ventre de Paris**, or the wedding of Renée with Saccard, not to mention that of Louise de Mareuil with Maxime in **La Curée**.
[126] For Claude Seassau, in **Émile Zola, Le Réalisme Symbolique**, Coupeau is a latent homosexual, op. cit. p. 53.
[127] Philippe Hamon : *Pour un Statut Sémiologique du Personnage* in **Poétique du Récit**, Paris, Seuil, 1977, p. 125.
[128] **Ibidem**, p. 125.
[129] Maarten Van Buuren highlighted the close link between the erotic desire and money in **Les Rougon-Macquart d'Émile Zola. De la Métaphore au Mythe**, op. cit. p. 175.

2.1.3. The occasional inversions

For Freud, sexual subjects who, under certain external conditions, can take a person of the same sex as themselves and enjoy them, are occasional inverts. In the corpus, there is unfortunately no occasional invert of this type but it must be remembered that this is a sporadic aberration that occurs only when the sexual urge of the subject is so compelling that it cannot be postponed[130].

Overall, if we accept that in Zola's works the deviations from the sexual object do exist, we must understand their meaning. Indeed, all the sexual aberrations already mentioned constitute as many grievances Zola levies against the imperial society which he accused of harbouring all evils. For him, the Empire emptied the sons of France of all their vital and life-giving substance. To achieve this, it championed a disgraceful degeneration process to the point where the grandsons - parody of the French people under Napoléon III - failed where the grandfathers were victorious - tribute to the French under Napoléon 1st. Isn't it true that the whole **Rougon-Macquart** series aim to parody in all its compartments the model of society that the Second Empire established? In this regard, sexual depravities described by Zola appeared to be related to his literary commitment and/or to his own fantasies[131].

Now is the time to study another sexual deviation which consists in remaining heterosexual while carrying one's desire for an unusual sexual purpose such as the anal part or the clothes of the desired sexual object.

2.2. The deviations from the sexual purpose

The normal sexual purpose, according to the Freudian classification, is the genital apparatus itself. Thus, the man will seek to reach the woman's vagina. The woman will also rely on the genitals of her male partner. The aim is to enjoy the sex of the other party during sexual intercourse and to soothe one's sexual desire. There is a deviation from the sexual purpose when a sexual subject chooses to value any other part of the body of their sexual object - or an inanimate object belonging to them - to the detriment of their genitals. Freud believes that there are basically two perversions of this type: *the anatomic transgressions* and *the limitation* of the coitus to the *intermediary relations*.

2.2.1. The anatomic transgressions

---

[130] Maarten Van Buuren shows that Zola accounts for the compelling sexual urge in the whiplash metaphor that directs the obedient human beast, refer to **Les Rougon-Macquart d'Émile Zola. De la Métaphore au Mythe**, op. cit. p. 57.
[131] Claude Seassau asserts in **Émile Zola, le Réalisme Symbolique,** that the structures of sexuality in the corpus do not reflect the reality of the time of the Second Empire, but they rather reflect the own fantasies of the author, Zola himself, op. cit. p. 203.

They include all attitudes overestimating the sexual object. A male subject capable of all transgressions easily replaces his female partner's vulva by her anus or by her oral cavity. If the sexual subject is a woman, the gonads and the penis of the sexual object will be sucked. This last manoeuvre is called fellatio while the previous one is sodomy. There is *fetishism* when inanimate objects - clothing, jewellery, etc. - or certain parts of the body - feet, hair, among others - of the sexual object become exclusively the aimed goals by the sexual subject who does not seek further sexual contacts such as sexual intercourse.

It shall be noted however that the Zolian narrator is not particularly fond of details when it comes to the conduct of the sexual act itself as if he were to show chastity and moral propriety. It is in this regard that Zola differs from the Marquis de Sade for whom morality is unnatural. Sade advocated for total sexual freedom by calling for criminal instincts[132]. For Zola, the Marquis de Sade was the triumphant Satan : << *Pour moi, il sort logiquement du catholicisme, il arrive à l'agonie du dix-huitième siècle, après les négations des philosophes, et il joue le rôle de Satan triomphant, le vieux Satan du Moyen Âge, monstrueux et lubrique, éventrant les femmes à coups de fourche, broyant les petits enfants d'une caresse, prêchant l'inceste et le meurtre, rêvant la désorganisation et l'écroulement final. [...] C'est, je le répète, le catholicisme retourné, Satan à la place de Dieu, l'enfer à la place du ciel, la flamme, les crocs, les tortures, les plaies, le sang, à la place de la musique des séraphins et de l'éternité sereine des bienheureux* >>[133]. Contrary to what can be seen in the Marquis de Sade's works, only the atmosphere around the lovers and the conscious or the unconscious sensations they experience are described in great details in Zola's fiction. We cannot objectively argue that sodomies - except in Baptiste's case in **La Curée** - or blowjobs are performed in the corpus[134].

On the other hand, a notorious case of fetishism in the corpus relates to Cabuche who adored Séverine's handkerchiefs in **La Bête Humaine**. One could add to that the voyeurism of the shepherd Soulas who always keeps an eye open to watch Jacqueline known as La Cognette in her innumerable sexual relations in **La Terre**. We must note that those two protagonists satisfy their sexual impulses by the scopic pleasure only - for the latter - and by the tactile and olfactory pleasures only - for the former. None of them seeks to profit more from their sexual objects and it is at that level that they are considered as pathological

---

[132] **Les 120 Journées de Sodome ou l'École du Libertinage** by the Marquis de Sade remains the prototype of the school of sexual libertinage in terms that cannot be more sordid, with everything that it implies in terms of incest, sodomy, paedophilia, criminal sadism, monsters born of senseless sexual unions and an evident denial of God.

[133] Émile Zola : **Documents Littéraires** (1882) and then in **Œuvres Complètes**, Paris, Tchou, Cercle du Livre Précieux, under the direction of Henri Mitterand and Armand Lanoux, 15 volumes, 1966-1970. Here, volume XI, p. 453.

[134] In **Émile Zola, Le Réalisme Symbolique**, Claude Seassau shows that **L'Assommoir** is dominated by the sexual theme of anality and that of the mugger, who often comes back in the Zolian text, originally means, heretic and sodomite, op. cit. pp. 216-218.

cases. Those neurotics are resigned in their repression of any desire to mate with the beloved woman. The case of Cabuche is all the more impressive that he fears to spill dirt on Séverine by sleeping with her, finding her too perfect for a man like him. Fetishism and voyeurism therefore remain nonviolent deviations from the sexual goal. This probably explains the indulgence, even the pity of Zola towards the subjects who suffer from them.

Fetishism and voyeurism have got their violent symmetries however: sadism and masochism, which are stops at intermediate relations.

2.2.2. The stops at intermediate relations

Two forms dominate the so-called intermediate relations : << *La plus fréquente et la plus significative de toutes les perversions, le penchant à infliger de la douleur à l'objet sexuel et sa contrepartie, a été nommée par Von Krafft-Ebing, sadisme et masochisme, en fonction de ses deux formes active et passive* >>[135]. Sadism, though not pathological in essence, is an aggressive component of the sexual desire inasmuch as the sadistic sexual subject climaxes by enslaving, by humiliating and by mortifying their sexual object[136]. A masochistic subject, on the contrary, enjoys sex in the pain felt, a pain inflicted by their sadistic sexual object[137].

The character of Nana best represents these two forms of perversions. With the actor Fontan, she becomes a masochist, adoring him through excruciating pain and in tears. As for her lover, he logically sits in the category of sadists. It is at the regular rate of slappings that he loves her for several months. Later on, Nana becomes sadistic by inflicting similar treatments to Muffat, her new lover who then occupies the position of the masochist. For example, when his beautiful lover kicks him around, Muffat launches: << *Tape plus fort [...]. Hou ! Hou ! Je suis enragé, tape donc !* >>[138]. It can be concluded that the same sexual subject can be both sadistic and masochistic since the two tendencies go hand in hand like in the case of Nana where these two perversions are the two faces of the same coin. Through count Muffat, Zola tries the old French aristocracy that did nothing to escape from the wind of debauchery that blew on the Empire. The aristocracy undergoes the same decadence as the bourgeoisie and the *demi-monde* in this universe devoid of moral ideals.

How can one ignore the particular form of Jacques Lantier's sadism in **La Bête Humaine**? This sexual subject combines indeed sexual impulse and the drive for

---

[135] Sigmund Freud : **Trois Essais sur la Théorie de la Sexualité**, op. cit. p. 68.
[136] Claude Seassau believes that violence is at the heart of the Zolian novel as an essential factor and a vision of the world, In **Émile Zola, Le Réalisme Symbolique**, op. cit. p. 188.
[137] Chantal Bertrand-Jennings shows in **L'Éros et la Femme chez Zola**, op. cit. p. 12, that *les violences sado-masochistes*, such as rapes, assassinations and murder are no less than *délices sexuels* in the corpus.
[138] Émile Zola: **R. M. II**, op. cit. p. 1461.

murder[139]. The more compelling the sexual urge is, the greater is the temptation to commit murder on his sexual object[140]. If he avoids sleeping with his cousin, Flore, it is simply to avoid slaughtering her because the exposure of her naked and white throat awakes in him the evil desire to seize his dagger and strike her neck. It is this combination of two impulses – the sexual and the murderous – that will bring about the death of his beloved mistress, Séverine. It is also that evil in him that explains his hostility towards the light during the intimate moments and his de facto preference for darkness. Indeed, darkness has the advantage of concealing the white female throats and necks, the sight of which sharpens his instinct for murder. The form of sadism that is his is totally pathological[141] and it is the result of a severe paranoid neurosis. The subject becomes totally helpless before the imperious awakening of his unconscious, and, unable to perform the least suppression on this deep evil in him, Jacques Lantier aspires to fulfil his sexual desire by cutting open his lover's throat. The flow of hot blood coming from his sexual object's body is the ultime climax for him. Jacques himself does not know where this mysterious evil comes from: the will to kill his mistresses[142]. In addition, he is unable to escape from it as this mysterious evil imposes itself on him[143]. At least five times, he initially succeeds in defeating the evil for murder, but ultimately, he fails to prevent the final straw which consists in slaughtering Séverine, the one lover he so badly wanted to spare the life of. It is only from this moment on that he experiences a temporary reprieval marked by a sense of complete fullness and total happiness. Nevertheless, the trigger goes off again when he is in Philomène's arms. Like the sexual impulse, the drive for murder is renewed in the psychopathic type of

---

[139] Geoff Woollen reckons that: << *he approached the correlation between sexuality and psychopathic killing* >>, in *Jacques The Ripper*, **Émile Zola Centenary Colloquium: 1893-1993**, edited by Patrick Pollard, London, The Émile Zola Society, 1995, p. 73.

[140] For Roger Ripoll, the animal ferocity derives from the ancestor, Tante Dide, in **Réalité et Mythe chez Zola**, op. cit. p. 479.

As for Claude Seassau, he admits, after studying Chaval, Étienne, Roubaud, Pecqueux and Jacques Lantier, that jealousy is at the origin of the urge to kill, see **Émile Zola, Le Réalisme Symbolique**, op. cit. pp. 198-199.

[141] Claude Seassau reaffirms that for the hero in **La Bête Humaine**, jealousy has a pathological essence, refer to **Émile Zola, Le Réalisme Symbolique**, op. cit. p. 199.

[142] This hereditary disease is what Jacques Noiray calls *la dégénérescence criminelle*, in **Le Romancier et la Machine, tome I : L'Univers de Zola**, op. cit. p. 179, and in David Baguley's critical works, it bears the name of *atavistic regression* or even better, according to a word he borrows from the American naturalist novelist Frank Norris, Jacques is a *hereditary evil*, in **Naturalist Fiction. The Entropic Vision**, op. cit. p. 213 et p. 214.

[143] Claude Seassau, in the above book, p. 257, opposes two distinct entities, le *moi* and *la bête* locked in a deadly fight within Jacques Lantier.

Maarten Van Buuren concurs with Noiray on that in **Les Rougon-Macquart d'Émile Zola. De la Métaphore au Mythe**, op. cit., to say that the ça (which is nothing else but the *bête* in Seassau's vocabulary) is what is innate and non-personal in man; the ça being the horse or the superior force (p. 54) and the *moi*, the horse rider who regulates the ça (p. 55). Jacques, who experienced *la fuite de son moi*, (p. 193), is not supposed to be accountable for his actions since he bears no *responsabilité de son acte*, just like Sylvine in **La Débâcle** (p. 57) because those characters are dominated by their irresistible ça – or the beast within themselves.

neurotic character he is. Such a sexual subject is the battleground where a fierce fight takes place between Eros and Thanatos. With Jacques Lantier, the industrial society is hung up to dry in the sense that it disrupts the machine and the machinist. It also makes man become a killing machine under the intoxication of smoke and grease.

In general, sexual aberrations are not very frequent in Zola's novels. Yet, they are very characteristic to the point where psychoanalysts[144] had to study them well after the completion of the **Rougon-Macquart** series. Zola's merit was, therefore, to have been a forerunner in the field of psychoanalysis, which did not fall specifically within his primary field. It was for that reason that Sigmund Freud paid the ultimate tribute to Zola by calling him a << *parfait connaisseur de l'âme humaine* >>[145], when referring especially to Pauline Quenu who continually strips herself of everything she owns only to try and make the happiness of her beloved Lazare Chanteau in **La Joie de Vivre**, without expecting anything in return.

From another point of view, the presence of sexual aberrations in the **Rougon-Macquart** series must be seen as a disqualification of the imperial society seen as an immoral and an amoral society, a neurotic, a pathological and a paranoid society that is doomed from the outset. It is no wonder why such a society may suffer the same fate as the biblical cities of Gomorrah and Sodome[146] or the prostitute of Babylon. **The Bible** reveals about the latter : << *Autant elle s'est glorifiée dans le luxe, autant donnez-lui de tourment et de deuil. Parce qu'elle dit en son cœur : Je suis assise en reine, je ne suis point veuve, et je ne verrai point de deuil ! À cause de cela, en un même jour, ces fléaux arriveront, la mort, le deuil et la famine, et elle sera consumée par le feu. Car il est puissant, le Seigneur Dieu qui l'a jugée* >>[147]. The god that passes judgment on the Second Empire here is called Zola !

In addition to this biblical sanction, there are other striking features of sexuality in the corpus, beginning with the animalistic approach.

3. THE ANIMALISTIC APPROACH TO SEXUALITY

---

[144] Maarten Van Buuren shows with great details in **Les Rougon-Macquart d'Émile Zola. De la Métaphore au Mythe**, op. cit, pp. 54-55, that psychoanalysts such as Groddeck, Freud, Laplanche and Pontalis have all confirmed Zola's concept of the "ça" and the "moi".
[145] Sigmund Freud : **Trois Essais sur la Théorie de la Sexualité**, op. cit. p. 169.
[146] Roger Ripoll writes in **Réalité et Mythe chez Zola**, op. cit. : << *Ce mythe des cités maudites, appelé dans Germinal par l'annonce de la ruine à la fin de la série des Rougon-Macquart, prophétisent ou racontent l'effondrement du Second Empire. Reprenant un motif abondamment exploité par les romantiques, Zola assimile Paris aux cités frappées par la colère divine dont la Bible a transmis le souvenir* >>, pp. 100-101.
[147] **La Sainte Bible** : "Apocalypse", chapter 18, verses 7-8, op. cit. p. 1248.

In **Les Rougon-Macquart** series, sexuality is indeed characterised by its fundamentally animalistic approach. The *anthropomorphic*[148] characters, to borrow that word from Philippe Hamon, are subjects or sexual objects that undergo a process of metaphorisation[149] that can be designated by the explicit term of animalisation. Philippe Bonnefis counted several thousands of metaphors in the animalistic sphere in the works of Zola, including 83 occurrences in **La Fortune des Rougon**; 86 in **La Curée**; 102 in **Le Ventre de Paris**; 122 in **Son Excellence Eugène Rougon**; 340 in **L'Assommoir**; 245 in **Germinal**; 251 in **Nana**; 140 in **Pot-Bouille**; 120 in **La Débâcle**; 35 in **Le Docteur Pascal**; 25 in **Le Rêve**; 22 in **L'Œuvre**; 293 in **Les Trois Villes** and 150 in **Vérité**[150]. Without studying each of these thousands of metaphors of animalisation - it would be a loss of time - I will try, from the seme *"animality"*, to find the corresponding paradigms according to the gender of the agents. We can begin with the female characters that are identifiable under the seme animality. We will look at the paradigms that correspond to each of them from one novel to another.

Then, we will proceed in the same way with regards to the equivalent male characters. It goes without saying that this census will not be exhaustive since the aim is to highlight the relevant and the redundant aspects that give sexuality an animalistic tone, therefore a strongly instinctive way to behave in Zola's novels. Of course, by paradigms, I simply mean all the variants that lead to the constitution of the seme of animality. This work of classification and detailed interpretation of the bestiary that I intend to do lacks in Bonnefis' study - who prefers to give an overall explanation to the phenomenon of the bestiary. It also lacks so badly in Maarten Van Buuren's study.

The latter saw, through animalisation, merely a tendentious representation of the reality and a position taken by the author in the social conflict, which would contradict the so-called Zolian correctness[151].

3.1. The female characters and animalisation

---

[148] Philippe Hamon : *Pour un Statut Sémiologique du Personnage* dans **Poétique du Récit**, op. cit. p. 126.
[149] Claude Seassau acknowledges that the animal imagery or *bestiaire* – as he calls it – has got the merit to split the characters into distinct categories (pp. 38-39) even if it still has the downside of having to transfigure the real into something else (p. 39), refer to **Émile Zola, Le Réalisme Symbolique**, op. cit.
[150] Philippe Bonnefis : *Le bestiaire d'Émile Zola: valeur et signification des images animales dans son œuvre romanesque* in **Europe : Zola**, avril-mai 1968, no. 468-469, op. cit. p. 98.
[151] This expression is borrowed from Maarten Van Buuren, in **Les Rougon-Macquart d'Émile Zola. De la Métaphore au Mythe**, op. cit. p. 35. He was referring to Zola's own affirmations, when he was claiming to be working in a literary field which was painting life with exactitude, clarity and truth, or in other words, a literature that was not tainted or biased by imagination, invention nor by fallacious exposition of social facts. For the literary critic, metaphors are simply the privileged place for Zola's creative mind.

Semes	Paradigms
Animality:	* Beast, snake, live snake, pretty domestic animal, little mouse, goat, sphinx, (**La Bête Humaine**).
	• Cat, the eyes of young cats, vermin, cicada, sheep, stubborn beast, poor beast, lamb, goat, wolf, (**La Fortune des Rougon**).
	• A cat in heat, rat, pussy, turkey, gold fly, vengeful gold fly, snake, (**Nana**).
	• Goat, pussy, (**La Terre**)
	• Beast in love, cat, snake, bear, sphinx, monster, (**La Curée**).

The study of the paradigmatic axis above gives to the following results: the agents designated by the metaphor of << *la chatte* >> will always be in search of affection and cuddles like Miette in **La Fortune des Rougon** or Renée in **La Curée**. << *La chatte en chaleur* >> will be associated with insatiable sexual desires and will feel broody. From a mythological point of view, it is an animal characterised by debauchery and lust, worse yet, the cat is suspected of being a servant of the Underworld, the Hades. To summarise this, we can argue that in the figure << *la chatte* >> corresponds to the following semic nucleus: / + affective /, / + insatiable /[152], / + demanding /, / + debauched / and / + infernal /. This is why, in the Zolian novel, the female characters aligned with the seme /cat/ are nymphomaniacs deeply involved in fierce debauchery that corrupts a rotten Parisian society symbolised by Nana and Renée. They are infernal figures like their biblical counterpart of the prostitute of Babylon.

The figures << *couleuvres* >> and << *serpents* >> refer to the following seminal nucleus: /+ suppleness/, /+ felony/, /+ venomous/, /+ mortal/, /+ corrupt/. Séverine, Nana and Renée are the components of this particular category. They seem harmless like the snake, but they are still venomous and deadly[153]. Séverine first contributed to the execution of her first lover, President Grandmorin, and planned the murder of her husband, Roubaud, while Nana engaged in two abortions. Nana, in particular, has been responsible for several manslaughters because if it was not her hand that stroke the victims, at least

---

[152] Claude Seassau insists on the metaphors of the female cat and that of the female dog which apply to Gervaise Macquart in **L'Assommoir** and which both imply the sexual appetite that caracterises her (needless to stress that the same figure of speech applies to Nana), for further reading on this, please refer to **Émile Zola, Le Réalisme Symbolique**, op. cit. p. 56.

[153] Chantal Bertrand-Jennings talks about a small number of women, "*femmes fatales*" as she calls them in **L'Éros et la Femme chez Zola**, who are maneaters and who gather around Nana and Renée in **Nana** and in **La Curée**. That category also inculdes Clarisse in **Pot-Bouille**, Irma Bécot and Christine in **L'Œuvre**, op. cit. pp. 66-67.

her dejected lovers were driven to commit suicide. They could not bear the thought of losing this beautiful woman's love and contemplate life without her.

At << *la chienne* >> corresponds the following traits: /+ without embarrassment/, /+ debauched/, /+ enraged/, /+ contagious/ and /+ domestic/. That is why Nana remains insatiable, frivolous, downright impudent and shameless despite the devastation she causes in families and especially in the high society of Paris and Europe. As a << *mouche d'or Vengeresse* >>, she has the followins traits: / + foul-smelling/, /+ fetish/, /+ golden/, /+ joking/, /+ frustrated/, /+ vengeful/, /+ poisonous/[154].

As for Renée, she is a << *sphinx* >> and a << *monster* >>. These two figures are of a complex nature since they are both stupid and mythical. Their mythical aspect will be the subject of a further study later on but for the time being, it is enough to grasp their purely animalistic dimension. Their semic nucleus can be split in the following way: /+ composite nature/, /+ fabulous/, /+ dangerous/, /+ tenacious/, /+ murderous /, /+ enigmatic/. Fighting Renée or Séverine therefore requires an Oedipal strength and intelligence because of their composite and mythical nature.

Without aiming to study each of the components of the paradigmatic axis above, I will have to look at these two figures that are << *l'agneau* >> and << *la louve* >>. These two animals recall the protagonists of the fable of La Fontaine and Zola seems to have updated them on purpose. Joséphine Gavaudan, wife of Macquart, is an << *agneau* >> whereas Tante Dide is a << *louve* >>. Meanwhile, Miette is a << *chèvre* >> in **La Fortune des Rougon**. << *La chèvre* >> and << *l'agneau* >> have got the following traits: /+ harmless/, /+ naive/, /+ innocent/, /+ victims/, /+ resigned/ while << *la louve* >> is: /+ warlike/, /+ unjust/, /+ cruel/, /+ guilty/, / + deadly/. Josephine perfectly honours these semic traits by becoming the resigned victim of her husband, Antoine Macquart, who is capable of all crimes under the influence of alcohol[155]. For her part, Miette remains naive and harmless until her brutal death caused by the army[156]. The overall point is that with regard to the female figures and their metaphorical

---

[154] For Patrick Wald Losowski, the fly represents << *[...] le défi à la structure: "remontant" du peuple à l'aristocratie en une fermentation puissante digne de tout germinal, la mouche dénonce la division des classes, et passe allègrement toutes les barrières, faisant communiquer en son vol innocent les charognes abjectes aux palais protégés, se revêtant de soleil à partir de l'ordure, disséminant le poison dans l'éclat des pierreries et des cuisses de neige* >>, refer to **Syphilis. Essais sur la Littérature Française du XIXème Siècle**, Paris, Gallimard, 1982, p. 52.

[155] For Claude Seassau, in **Émile Zola, Le Réalisme Symbolique**, op. cit. p. 39, it is evident that the images are far richer in connotations than the discourse to the extend that the word *loup* says far more how violent and cruel is a given character than any descriptive discourse about their behaviour.

[156] Maarten Van Buuren highlights that : << *Il suffit pour le moment de remarquer que l'ensemble des métaphores s'organise selon trois grandes articulations : la chasse, la domestication et la bête humaine qui ont toutes en commun l'opposition entre une partie soumise et une partie dominante* >>, in **Les Rougon-Macquart d'Émile Zola. De la Métaphore au Mythe**, op. cit. p. 40.

paradigms, there is some form of referential overload that shows how complex and ambiguous female nature can be. Beautiful and kind, Zola's woman is no less despicable, and sometimes cruel. Real and innocent, she remains mythical, fabulous and capable of the worst monstrosities. There is in Zola's works an enigma of the woman, an enigma not always obvious to elucidate. However, in the axiology of sexuality, women cannot go without their male counterpart.

3.2. The male characters and animalisation.

Semes: Paradigms:

Animality:
* Small snake, brute, good beast, howling beast, other species, the animal, a real wolf, wild boar, lion, human cattle, human beast, rabid beast, hunted beast, attacked beast, pig, horse, dog, werewolf, rat, furious dog, faithful dog, big beast, (**La Bête Humaine**).
- Monster, cat, toad, calf, sheep, viper, vermin, poor cat, (**La Fortune des Rougon**).
- Vulture, bird of prey, bull, rabbit, rooster, murderous brutes, old beast, devouring beasts, vampires, (**La Terre**).

On this paradigmatic axis, the figures of << *cochon* >>, and << *coq* >>, of << *chien* >>, << *lapin* >> and of << *cheval* >> are the most significant at a purely sexual level. However, from a behavioural point of view, it would be good to question << *le petit serpent* >>, << *la brute* >>, << *le lion* >>, << *la vipère* >>, << *le sanglier* >>, << *les bêtes meurtrières* >> and << *les vampires* >>.

<< *Le cochon* >> obeys this revealing semic nucleus: /+ dirty/, /+ depraved/, /+ immoral/, /+ repugnant/. Calling President Grandmorin a *pig* is a perfect fit for his lust for little girls[157] and the true rapist he is in **La Bête Humaine**.

<< *Le coq* >> is characterised by the semic features: / + heat /, / + constant /, / + harassment /, / + aggressiveness /. Buteau Fouan, in **La terre**, combines all these traits that he develops with hypertrophy. Like a rooster in heat, he never stops harassing his sister-in-law, Françoise, even after she has married Jean Macquart and she becomes pregnant by him.

---

[157] Claude Seassau states in **Émile Zola, Le Réalisme Symbolique**, that Zola has got a bourgeois vision of the people that he had been defending all along; the very same people he sometimes animalises while stopping short of animalising the bourgeois, op. cit. p. 55. However, I do not believe that statement is acurrate since the powerful President Grandmorin is truly assimilated to a *"pig"* in **La Bête Humaine**. Moreover, the bourgeois of Plassans that are gathered around Pierre are all assimilated to animals by Dr. Pascal in **La Fortune des Rougon**.

<< *Le sanglier* >> has the traits / + aggressive /, / + dark /, / + devious /, / + instinctive / and / + demonic /. Jacques Lantier and his locomotive receive the metaphor of the boar because of their enigmatic, dangerous and demonic nature[158].

One must associate << *le chien* >> to << *la chienne* >> already studied to avoid any annoying redundancy. On the other hand, << *le lapin* >> is a rather interesting figure because it can be read in the following way: / + heat /, / + virile /, / + constance / / + nymphomaniac / and / + insatiable /. Once again, Buteau Fouan is an insatiable rabbit whose sexual urge is as imperious as it is constant. As a result, he crossed the boundaries of morality by to engage into incest when he rapes the heavily pregnant younger sister of his wife. To add salt to injury, he rubs that right in his wife's face. Not even the victim's eight-month baby bump can turn him away him from his neurotic enterprise. << *The horse* >> joins << *the rabbit* >> because their standards are / + virile /, / + resistant, / + robust /. Count Muffat, by playing the horse with his mistress, Nana, exteriorises his character as an extremely virile and robust man who cannot abstain before his young and beautiful mistress. But because he is *horse*, he lets her ride him - just like a horse rider would do - in their sado-masochistic scenes. She is in total control of him just like the horse obeys its rider[159].

The figure of the << *petit serpent* >> is closely linked to that of the << *serpent* >> already mentioned. When it comes to the male charaters, Roubaud is the << *petit serpent* >> that kills its love-rival, Grandmorin, in a cold-blooded calculated and senseless murder in **La Bête Humaine**. He is also the << *brute* >> with the following traits /+ unreasoned /, /+ violent /, / + grotesque /, /+ gross /, /+ spontaneous/, and, according to the words of Geoff Woollen, /+ savage /, /+ rude /, /+ incomplete /, /+ unfinished /, /+ primitive /, /+ agressive/[160].

Those traits are also that of the << *brutes meurtrières* >> such as Buteau and his spouse, Lise, in **La Terre**, except that they should be given a new trait as /+ recidivists/ because they first murder the father figure, Fouan, then their sister-

---

[158] Claude Seassau writes to that end: << *Ce qui est particulièrement intéressant dans ce roman est que l'image du sanglier n'est pas seulement attribuée à Jacques, elle intervient à propos de la locomotive folle à la fin du roman, elle aussi, comparée à un << sanglier >>. Cela prouve la similitude entre Jacques et la machine folle, cette dernière est aussi une << bête humaine >>, le double de Jacques; ce sont deux éléments des plus tératologiques du roman. Par ce rapprochement entre Jacques et la machine, le comportement de Jacques s'explique mieux; Jacques malade est comme une mécanique* >> in **Émile Zola, Le Réalisme Symbolique**, op. cit. p. 60.

[159] **Ibidem**, Claude Seassau groups *le cheval, la fourmi* and *les insectes humains* in a single class, that of the labouring beasts, which are victims of a determinism or are a symbol of humans exploited or enslaved by their fellow human-beings, op. cit. p. 57.

[160] Geoff Woollen: *Des brutes humaines dans* **La Bête Humaine** in **Zola: La Bête Humaine: Texte et Explication**, Colloquium of the Centenary in Glasgow, edited by Geoff Woollen, Glasgow, University of Glasgow French & German Publications, 1990, pp. 150-168.

in-law, Françoise. This infernal couple also receives the attributive figures of << *bêtes dévorantes* >> and that of << *vampires* >>. As such, their traits can be broken up in the following new revealing concatenation: /+ cannibals/, /+ bloodthirsty/, /+ dead corpse-eater/, /+ gluttons/, /+ demonic/, /+ dark/. We can understand why they never back down in the face of horrific deeds because they kill and roast the father, Fouan, just to steal his purse! Later on, after Françoise's rape - which Lise took part in by helping Buteau to overpower the poor victim - in a senseless rush for crime, Lise shoves a scythe into her sister's huge baby bump. The eight-month-old fetus is perforated and the mother bleeds like an ox, thus justifying the vampirism of the attacking couple. The motive of their crime was the recovery of her inheritance in agricultural land that the deceased would leave behind. Both murders had a common denominator: greed. This shows that for these lawless criminals, only money matters and no matter how it is made, especially if it is enhanced by sexual gratification[161]. Lower social classes also take a resounding blow in **Les Rougon-Macquart** because, at the time of the industrial revolution, man had lost his humanity, and was driven only by the fiduciary value of things. In Zola's fiction world, money is the new god that governs the decadent world of the Second Empire.

This study of the seme *animality* here is not exhaustive, far from it. But it has allowed us to make two observations: firstly, it puts sexuality in an intertextual context and, secondly, on the semantic axis called *sexuality*, it establishes a relationship of opposition between the semes << *life* >> and *desire* - Eros - and *death* - Thanatos. At the intertextual level, it can be seen that the Zolian narrator has used a polymorphic hypotext that mixes myths, fables and sacred biblical tales to construct his romantic hypertext. In his novels we also find animal figures that he did not invent but rather that he borrowed them from other forms of stories and authors who existed before him[162]. The presence of those figures is a factor of predictability and readability of Zola's fiction[163]. Indeed, depending on whether the protagonist is be dubbed << *une chatte* >> or << *une vipère* >>, the reader will expect a sensitive, an endearing, a sentimental and a debauched sexual subject, or a sexual subject who will destroy all their sexual objects, given their a priori venomous and deadly character. The novels will corroborate those primary narrative programmes as the reader goes through the different pages of each of the titles in the **Rougon-Macquart** series. In addition, this process has an undeniable caricatural and a satirical value[164] since

---

[161] David Baguley considers that sex and money are the social ferment in Zola's works; for further reading on this please refer to **Naturalist Fiction. The Entropic Vision**, op. cit. p. 210.

[162] Maarten Van Buuren studies the pedagogic role of intertextuality in Zola's literature when he considers the intervention of specialists (doctors, priests) at the start or at the end of chapters within novels or indeed, of the novels themselves. For further reading on this, refer to **Les Rougon-Macquart d'Émile Zola. De la Métaphore au Mythe**, op. cit. p. 36.

[163] **Ibidem**, Maarten Van Buuren writes : << *Zola n'invente pas ses métaphores. Il les puise dans un réservoir d'images transmises de génération en génération et dont l'origine se perd dans la nuit des temps* >>, pp. 36-37.

[164] Claude Seassau also writes : << *Le bestiaire des personnages est d'une importance capitale, il soutient la vision imagée que Zola a du monde. Il est la traduction en images de la réalité de*

it makes it possible to highlight both an atrophy or a hypertrophy, or even a shortage of the vital forces or energy in the animalised characters. For Philippe Bonnefis, << *Elle* [l'animalisation] *est aussi l'instrument d'une satire, parce qu'elle sanctionne les ridicules d'une humanité au sang pauvre [...], et sclérosée par le labeur, la lâcheté ou l'inintelligence* >>[165].

Bonnefis, assuming that animalisation is first and foremost a dehumanisation, goes as far as to admit to a << *fatalité biologique* >> in the sense that << *le taureau* >> represents the government, << *les chiens* >> being the bourgeois, << *les rapaces* >> being the financiers and the people, << *le troupeau* >>, which shall be led to the slaughterhouse[166] in **La Débâcle**[167]. Generally-speaking, we can also agree with David Baguley for whom animalisation is certainly the mark of a regression because << *les personnages ''régressent'' pour sombrer dans la poursuite de leurs instincts, de leur animalité* [...] >>[168]. This increasing regression ultimately ends with death. In Zola's works, humanity is headed for doomsday and one of the instruments leading to that inevitable tragedy is sexuality, for sex gives both life and death[169].

In addition to benefiting from an animalistic approach, sexuality is also presented in a diabolical and satanic way in **Les Rougon-Macquart** series.

4. THE DIABOLICAL AND THE SATANIC APPROACH TO SEXUALITY

Satan or the devil, from a religious point of view, is a fallen angel. Opponent and enemy of God, he is the prince of all demons whose assignment is to bring down humanity by pushing it to commit sin against God. I will study here the diabolical approach to sexuality in this religious understanding starting with *the poetic function* that will study the purely metaphorical aspect of sexuality. I will then go on to study *the metalinguistic function* which is all about the referential Christian myths related to sexuality.

The demonising metaphors include the following figures: << *la chatte* >>, << *le chat* >> in **Nana** and << *le serpent* >> in **Nana** and in **La Curée**. In the opposite direction, there are some direct and immediately significant references such as : << *les damnés de Rognes* >>, << *les flammes* >>, << *le dieu cochon* >> in **La Terre**, << *les braises* >> and << *le feu* >> in **La Curée, La Faute de l'Abbé Mouret** and in **Nana**.

---

chaque individu, il est un moyen expressif de dévoiler la vérité de façon saisissante >>, in **Émile Zola, Le Réalisme Symbolique**, op. cit. p. 53.
[165] Philippe Bonnefis : *Le bestiaire de Zola : valeur et signification des images animales dans son œuvre romanesque,* in **Europe : Zola**, April-Mai 1968, op. cit. p. 99.
[166] **Ibidem**, p. 105.
[167] Émile Zola : [Napoléon III's dislocated army is a << *troupeau expiatoire qu'on envoyait au sacrifice, pour tenter de fléchir la colère du destin* >>, in **R. M. V**, op. cit. p. 460.
[168] David Baguley : **Zola et les Genres**, chapter III: *La Curée : la Bête et la Belle*, op. cit. p. 39.
[169] Chantal Bertrand-Jennings : **L'Éros et la Femme chez Zola**, op. cit. p. 13.

To what has already been said about << *la chatte* >> and << *le chat* >>, one must add that this animal symbolises the perverted feminine sexuality, lust and witchcraft. All these referents make it the servant of Hell according to the Greek mythology. Nana and Renée are therefore infernal agents whose job is to recruit new followers of Satan mainly in the Parisian space and under the reign of Napoleon III, which are clearly non-neutral narrative choices. They are two female figures who are always near a burning fire as if they were willful servants of hell[170]. Their victims are surely headed for hell. They are both incestuous, excessively debauched characters and in short, it is fair to argue that carnal sin is Nana and Renée's creed and their reason for living. Naturally, all the men who have the misfortune to fall in love with them inevitably descend to hell just like Count Vandeuvres, to shorten the fatal obituary list drawn up by Nana alone.

<< *Le serpent* >> is the animal that deceived Eve in the Garden of Eden according to the **Bible**, in chapter II of the book of *Genesis*. The serpent seduced the woman, convincing her to disobey God by eating the fruit of the forbidden tree. Consequently, man came to know of good and evil and became mortal. In **Les Rougon-Macquart** series too, the temptation comes from the woman. For she is the seductive power that drives her male companion into the whirlwind of evil and sin. Thus, Renée attracts Maxime to engage in incest. She also leads the unknown George into adultery, while Nana leads Count Muffat, a former fervent believer, in the meanders of debauchery and all the sexual perversions and aberrations he so fervently initially hated. She manages to stifle in him the voice of God that he had heard and venerated for the previous fifty years. Basically, in a narrative point of view, the woman is an open breach through which the devil creeps in and then goes on to rule the imperial society. The devil settles all the more easily in this imperial ground that it is indeed a space conquered by his messenger, the woman, who is the supreme temptation that ignores any resistance in this rotten world of the Second Empire, which is the ultimate breeding ground for sinners. As much the Emperor himself as the priest Mouret - in **Son Excellence Eugène Rougon** and in **La Faute de l'Abbé Mouret** respectively -, all the male protagonists can experience the fateful fall from grace inflicted on them by the so-called *"weaker gender"*[171].

There are, however, direct references to Satan and hell in the corpus. One of those references is the greenhouse, which represents the lair of Satan in **La Curée**. That greenhouse is penetrated by a << *flamme si lourde* >>[172]. This

---

[170] Chantal Bertrand-Jennings writes : << *[...] Zola entretint peut-être plus qu'aucun autre de ses contemporains [...] une vision infernale de la sexualité* >>, in **L'Éros et la Femme chez Zola**, op. cit. p. 9.

[171] Maarten Van Buuren shows that on the one hand the Paradou becomes hostile after abbé Mouret's fault with the animalistic metaphors applied to the sickly plants, and on the other hand, because of the preponderance of the images of the serpent, see **Les Rougon-Macquart d'Émile Zola. De la Métaphore au Mythe**, op. cit. pp. 141-142.

[172] Émile Zola: **R. M. I**, op. cit. p. 485.

overheated place is Renée's favourite space for the consumption of incest[173] in the arms of Maxime. The same goes for Nana about whom the narrator admits: << *Elle vint s'asseoir par terre, devant le feu. C'était sa place favorite* >>[174]. In both cases, the flame is reminiscent of the punishment awaiting the damned. Quite rightfully in **La Terre**, Father Godard thinks that << *le bon Dieu... enverrait tous rôtir en enfer, ces damnés de Rognes* >>[175]. Hell and the Devil are indeed constantly referred to in both **La Terre, La Faute de l'Abbé Mouret** and in **Nana**[176] as if the novelist were trying to convince the worshipers of the devil to redeem themselves while they still have a window of opportunity to do so. But the only voices of Abbé Godard, Brother Archangias and Monsieur Venot in the three novels are not enough to redeem the souls of all this multitude of hardened sinners. In Zola's universe, is it no easy task indeed to fall from Good into Evil and then somehow pull off the redemptive ascension that would bring anyone back from Evil to reach Good. Redemption is certainly a rare commodity in the naturalist fiction.

Notwithstanding, the situation of the sinners becomes desperate especially when they go on to gravely blaspheme against God. For example, in the face of the enormous damage caused by hail in the wheat fields, Buteau becomes furious and launches shamelessly: << *Sacré cochon de bon Dieu!* >>[177]. It should be noted that in the naturalist novel, the struggle between Good and Evil turns exclusively to the advantage of Evil so much so that any hope of redemption is ruined to the extent that sexual subjects become inexorably entangled into the sins of the flesh. The infernal drift goes so far as to equate men with devils in **Nana**, and even a child with the devil in **L'Œuvre**. That shows that the characters in question are entirely incarnated by the devil and are no longer simply tempted by him. Such a fusion between man and the devil expresses the forever damnation of the anthropomorphic protagonist in Zola's works.

Finally, when we read **Les Rougon-Macquart**, we realise that the boundaries are thin indeed between the human race and the divine; between the mythical and the diabolical; and between the human race and the animal species[178]. The blame for the weakened borders between the different species and reigns above

---

[173] Maarten Van Buuren shows in a decisive manner that *la mer de feu* in the greenhouse exacerbates the desire for incest in Renée far more than the vegetal monstruous growths. Refer to the above book for more on this, (pp. 142-143).

[174] Émile Zola: **R. M. II**, op. cit. p. 1272.

[175] Émile Zola: **R. M. IV**, op. cit. p. 860.

[176] For Roger Ripoll, there is no doubt that the images of hell have got a greater importance in **Nana** and in **La Curée** than in **La Faute de l'Abbé Mouret**. Refer to **Réalité et Mythe chez Zola**, op. cit. p. 96.

[177] Émile Zola: **R. M. IV**, op. cit. p. 696.

[178] That is similar to the *décloisonnement* in Maarten Van Buuren's terminology (**Les Rougon-Macquart d'Émile Zola. De la Métaphore au Mythe**, op. cit. pp. 180-181), which is to say the lack of frontiers between spaces like the church, the closed houses of prostitution, the beauty salons, the theatre and the *assommoir*. Such uniformity of spaces goes hand in hand with the uniformity of species and reigns.

is solely attributable to sexuality which remains an excessively unifying theme[179]. Sexuality, in **La Curée** – and likewise throughout the entire cycle - as shown by Alain Rochecouste, constitutes a vicious circle where these reigns move and interlock in a never broken concatenation.

Schematically, we can represent this vicious circle with Alain Rochecouste as follows[180] :

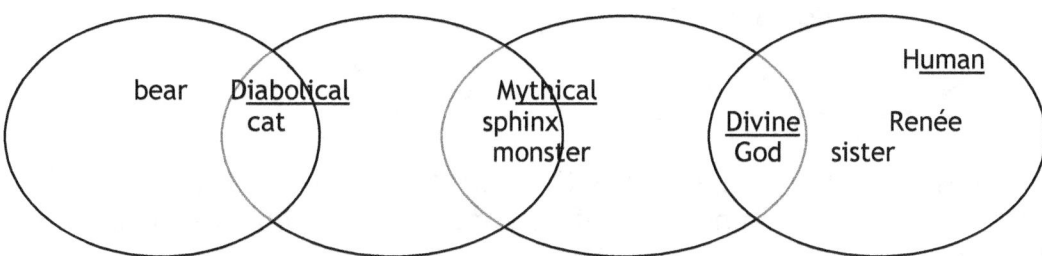

Let us understand, by exploiting this vicious circle, that in the theme of sexuality, there is no longer a hierarchy nor a scale of values. For example, in Buteau's mouth, *"God"* has become a mere *"pig"* and his action of destroying wheat fields is considered diabolical.

It is admitted in the collective consciousness that man was made in the image of God. This does not prevent Renée and Nana from having an *"animalistic"* side to them, a *"diabolical"* and a profound *"mythical"* side too. Their composite nature - Venus, goddess of Love, female cats, sphinxes, women, devils, etc. - is a hindrance to any inclination for spiritual elevation and redemption.

On the individual level, the vicious circle is maintained in Renée by her psychological evolution as represented by Anthony Zielonka in the following way[181] :

---

[179] David Baguley writes: << *In the most thorough thematic study of the **Rougon-Macquart** series, Auguste Dezalay has shown that Zola's novels most heavily charged with sexual themes, works like **La Curée** and **Nana**, deal fundamentally with such disappearing discriminations, recounting the assimilation of men and women with machines, plants, animals, and are characterised by mixture, mobility, flux, a promiscuity of states and forms* >>, see **Naturalist Fiction. The Entropic Vision**, op. cit. pp. 209-210.

[180] Alain Rochecouste : *Isotopie catamorphe*, in **La Curée de Zola ou << la vie à outrance >>**, Paris, SEDES, 1987, p. 47.

[181] Anthony Zielonka : *Renée et le problème du mal*, in **La Curée de Zola << ou la vie à outrance >>**, op. cit. p. 165.

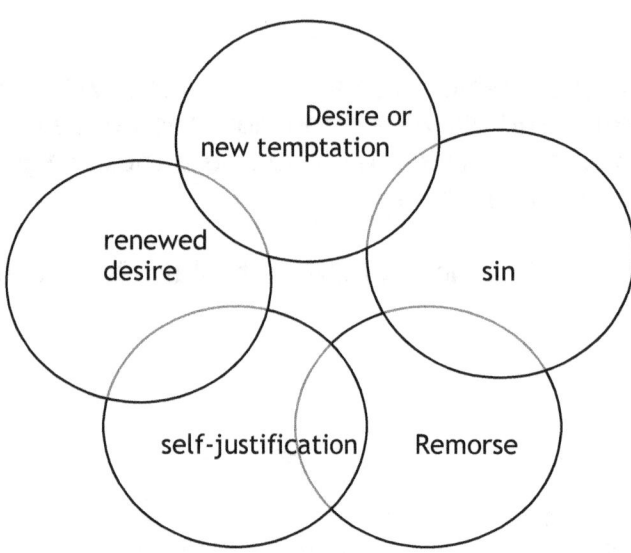

This picture must still be completed with a study of the characteristics of sexuality with the mythical component before concluding this chapter on a quite apocalyptic note.

5. THE MYTHICAL APPROACH TO SEXUALITY

The myths of sexuality that adorn Zola's fiction works are essentially of pagan and Christian origins[182]. However, they will not be studied in detail here since I will thoroughly study them in the following chapter III. For now, one can simply remember that the return of the ancient myth in the modern novel works as a restriction of the freedom of the narrator first, then of the protagonists. As a pre-established narrative program, the ancient myth imposes itself on the novelist, the creator who cannot award himself the freedom of renovating it sufficiently enough for he would risk counterfeiting the whole story. In the same way, the character identified or compared to a mythical hero will suffer the ascendancy and influence of the latter. They would have no choice but to assume entirely the destiny of their mythical referent, as tragic as it might be[183]. This is probably one of the reasons why Philippe Hamon claims that the Zolian character is << *prédéterminé* >>[184]. It is therefore necessary to agree that it is almost impossible to achieve pure naturalism through a work of fiction, that is to say a writing that would escape all the avatars of imagination and artistic

---

[182] We'll get back to the vocabulary of the so-called *origine gréco-latine* and of the *origine judéo-chrétienne* in Roger Ripoll's **Réalité et Mythe chez Zola**, op. cit. p. 60.

[183] Roger Ripoll, in **Réalité et Mythe chez Zola**, op. cit. writes : << *Les dieux sont les forces qui défient tous les interdits; les êtres humains, en transgressant ces interdits, se font semblables aux dieux pour un temps, mais pour un temps seulement, car ils ne peuvent incarner ces forces effrénées sans se détruire* >>, p. 83.

[184] Philippe Hamon : **Le Personnel du Roman. Le Système des Personnages dans Les Rougon-Macquart d'Émile Zola**, op. cit. p. 38.

creation. Faced with such constraints, the novelist is merely reduced to aspiring to naturalism instead of realising it[185].

For example, sexually connoted myths[186] associate Nana to *"Vénus"*, to *"Jupiter"*, to *"Mars"* and to *"Vulcain"*. From the first chapter of the novel, Nana, playing the main role in **La Blonde Vénus** at the Variety Theater, paralyses and electrifies the crowd by means of her power of seduction[187] and this, despite her poor talent as an actress. Never again would Paris be able to resist her. For Philippe Hamon, if the crowds chant in chorus the actress' name, it is because she would find herself later on << *dans tous les lits* >>[188]. *Vénus* - whose Greek denomination is Aphrodite - was the goddess of Love, capable of inflicting a stormy passion on her victims like Phaedrus. At the beginning of the novel, this mythical episode aims to warn the reader of the character's seductive power, and her capacity for destruction as well. That is why David Baguley wrote : << *Cette scène d'ouverture, qui se joue dans la salle du théâtre des Variétés, est extraordinairement* programmatique >>[189]. This is to say that the reader should not be surprised to see Nana subjugating Count Muffat until she leads him to his social, financial, moral and political downfall. Other victims of Nana can be consumed literally and figuratively by fire - see Part II. This first appearance of Nana, according to the word of Baguley, also marks the frenetic pace in the novel: << *Le mouvement de cette première scène annonce déjà le rythme de plus en plus accéléré, un rythme furieux, frénétique, frémissant [...]* >>[190].

The second *mise en abyme*, still in chapter I, puts *Vénus* and *Vulcain* - Aphrodite and Hephaestus face to face. This poorly matched couple[191] - the most beautiful of the goddesses and her husband, the ugliest of the gods, the wobbly and the disabled but strong blacksmith god, is represented by Nana and her lover Fontan,

---

[185] For Roger Ripoll, myths are flouting the exactness that Zola claims, see the book above, p. 62. Maarten Van Buuren does not say anything else when he asserts that Zola's scientism is undermined by the myth to the point that the actual thematic content is opposed to the mythical metaphorical content, see **Les Rougon-Macquart d'Émile Zola. De la Métaphore au Mythe**, op. cit. p. 15.

Claude Seassau seems to agree with Van Buuren on this point in his **Émile Zola, Le Réalisme Symbolique**, op. cit. p. 320.

[186] Roger Ripoll remarks that: << *Les noms qui reparaissent le plus souvent, bien plus souvent que tous les autres, sont ceux de Vénus et des Amours ; viennent ensuite les satyres et les faunes. Cette fréquence est déjà instructive : on trouvera souvent un rapport établi entre les mythologies et les puissances de la sexualité* >>, in **Réalité et Mythe chez Zola**, op. cit. p. 61. Further along, on page 80, Ripoll goes so far as to concede that the peculiarity of the Zolian myth is pagan eroticism.

[187] Maarten Van Buuren mentions the *pouvoir royal* of Nana in **Les Rougon-Macquart d'Émile Zola. De la Métaphore au Mythe**, op. cit. p. 156.

[188] Refer to Philippe Hamon, in **Le Personnel du Roman. Le Système des Personnages dans Les Rougon-Macquart d'Émile Zola**, op. cit. p. 149.

[189] David Baguley: **Zola et les Genres**, chapitre VI : *Nana, roman baroque*, op. cit. p. 66.

[190] **Ibidem**, op. cit., p. 66.

[191] This couple represents universal harmony because it combines strength with beauty, according to Roger Ripoll in **Réalité et Mythe chez Zola**, op. cit. p. 74.

the ugly actor. The important thing to note here is the cuckold, the adulterous relationship between Venus and Mars, which provoked the wrath of their legal partners - Vulcan and Athena. In the fictional narrative, Nana and Fontan operate a slip that delivers them from the rigidity of the mythical narrative and allows them to live a true relationship. If nobody comes to persecute them from the outside, Fontan, on the other hand, martyrises his beautiful girlfriend in a combination of obvious sadism and masochism. One takes pleasure in dominating and making suffer his partner who, in turn, likes to find herself in this position of a scapegoat to her lover. Nana thus acquires the experience of the woman who enjoys sex while she is being beaten up and abused. It is then that she reinvents herself as another self, transformed by love, as Valerie Minogue has so well pointed out: << *On a less trivial level, it is the 'regard de femme enceinte qui a envie de manger quelque chose de malpropre' which she directs at Fontan that introduces the episode of Nana's infatuation with the actor, in which we see Nana, the queen and goddess who subjects men to her every whim, striving after housewifely property, and herself subjected and enslaved* >>>>[192].

The play titled **La Blonde Vénus** also mentions << *Jupiter* >> - Zeus - known for his sexual ramblings. While the narrator does not say who plays his part in the play, Greek mythology shows the extent of his infidelities that constantly annoy his partner, goddess Juno.

The last pagan myth worthy of study is also of Greek origin since it is that of the *"Monster"*. We find it in Chapter IV of **La Curée** where Renée is metaphorically associated with a *"monster"*. From that moment on, she loses her humanity and wins a seat at the table of animals and hybrid creatures. Renée is negatively charged because the monster is involved in the tragic death of Hippolyte represented by the mirror-loving and self-obsessed Maxime. Let us recall that Maxime had identified his mistress as a *"monster"* in the overwhelming heat of the greenhouse and that, without realising that he himself was Hippolyte. From those references, we can expect the death of Maxime caused by his monstrous mistress. Of course, that does not seem right from the outset in **La Curée**; for Renée meets her death within that novel while Maxime survives her about twelve more years, before dying in **Le Docteur Pascal**, in his thirty-third year. But, if we take into account that in Zola's works, premature sexuality and debauchery cause early death, we can admit that because incest was so abundantly consumed in the arms of Renée, it led to the shortening of Maxime's life expectancy[193]. For in Zola's world, sin is a serial killer.

To conclude this chapter, we must remember that myths place the protagonists most often in a pagan or rather in a polytheistic world. But we do know that God - the only God in **the Bible** - does not exist in such a world marred by all

---

[192] Valerie Minogue: *Venus Observing, Venus Observed: Zola's* **Nana** in **Émile Zola Centenary Colloquium: 1893-1993**, edited by Patrick Pollard, London, The Émile Zola Society, 1995, p. 59.
[193] This is what Roger Ripoll calls the creative power of Zola from the myths borrowed, see **Réalité et Mythe chez Zola**, op. cit. p. 111.

types of sexual vices and the most disgusting sexual aberrations. The world of the **Rougon-Macquart**, in Zola's understanding, is amoral and predisposed to total disappearance[194] as soon as the divine wrath falls on it. Such is, in any case, one of the most significant dimensions of the many elements of paganism in the corpus. This sentence will be verified with the semiotics dimension in the following paragraph and with the psychocritical approach in chapter III of the second part. The return of such elements of Western cultural heritage in the **Rougon-Macquart**[195] reminds us, if need be, that no writer can create ex-nihilo since it is impossible to make a clean sweep of one's own culture especially in the course of producing a fiction work. From everything I mentioned above, it is easy to guess the crumbling fate awaiting the world of the **Rougon-Macquart**.

6. THE APOCALYPTIC APPROACH TO SEXUALITY

The last book of **The Bible** is about the apocalypse or the end of time - and of the world-, which is characterised by terrible and catastrophic events unfolding. The least I can say is that the corpus is not short of such situations. Only two giant fires and two major train crashes both caused by jealousy will suffice to demonstrate the apocalyptic approach to sexuality in the corpus.

The first of these fires comes to ruin the house of Mouret in **La Conquête de Plassans**. That space of sexual frustration is thus purified by fire by the hands of its rightful owner, François Mouret. It is a purifying fire[196] which consumes himself because he preferred that new fate decided by him alone. Indeed, Father Faujas had invested his space and had deprived François of it, sending the homeowner to a mental institution. The house was therefore seen in his eyes as a space of felony and betrayal to the point where only fire could cleanse and purify[197] it. The connection between sexuality and death had been referred to by Jean Borie as an << *interpénétration de la libido et de la mort* >>[198]. Throughout the **Rougon-Macquart** series, this interpenetration will never be denied.

---

[194] Roger Ripoll highlights: << *La dégradation que subissent les dieux symbolise la décadence de toute valeur et la corruption de toute une société ; au second acte de la* **Blonde Vénus**, *Nana salit le mythe même qu'elle incarne [...]. La fin du roman, poussant à l'extrême ce rabaissement de la divinité, traduit brutalement cette corruption d'un monde :* << *Vénus se décomposait* >>>>, **ibidem**, p. 75.

[195] As Roger Ripoll puts it, the recovery of hypotextual myths is a proof of culture, if not cultural mix up, see **Réalité et Mythe chez Zola**, op. cit. volume II, p. 926.

[196] Maarten Van Buuren opposes *le feu destructeur* to *le feu vital intérieur,* in **Les Rougon-Macquart d'Émile Zola. De la Métaphore au Mythe**, op. cit. 254. He then establishes the destructive or organic fire paradigm as follows: *flamboyer 392* times, *brûler 366, ardent 227, allumer 191, feu 110, chaud 76, braise 34* times (p. 255).

[197] Claude Seassau suggests that: << *La destruction nihiliste a un aspect mystique, seuls le sang et le feu peuvent purifier la terre comme dans les rites purificateurs* >>, in **Émile Zola, Le Réalisme Symbolique**, op. cit. p. 251.

[198] Jean Borie : **Zola et les Mythes, ou de la Nausée au Salut**, op. cit. p. 63.

Such a huge fire devastated the Borderie in **La Terre**, in chapter V, when Tron, dumped by his mistress, Jacqueline Cognet known as La Cognette, came back to set it on fire after having killed his rival, M. Hourdequin. It can be noted in all these cases that the sexually frustrated subject – because of the separation from their wife or mistress – takes revenge by setting fire to the space of their betrayal and frustration. These flames are reminiscent of those mentioned in the book of the apocalypse. However, if Baguley grants to all the violent deaths that enravel in **La Terre**, a << *notion tragique ou catastrophique* >>; he also believes that he can see in them the << *renouveau perpétuel du cosmos* >>, and the << *retour éternel de la nature* >>[199] throughout that novel. It is well-known that in Zola's works, scenes of death often take place when, symmetrically, a birth takes place. Zola seems to say that one is calling the other and that at the bottom of all this, life never stops since it only changes its shapes and forms.

In addition to that, two other catastrophes occur in **La Bête Humaine**, respectively in chapters X and XII. These are two train crashes deliberately caused by man. Firstly, it is a planned derailment executed by Flore in cold-blood when she is disappointed in being neglected in favour of a love rival. To split Jacques and Séverine up, she puts the lives of all the passengers of the Lison in danger without worrying about the hecatomb she would be responsible for. According to the narrator, the train of seven carriages was reduced to this: << *Les trois premiers* [wagons] *étaient réduits en miettes, les quatre autres ne faisaient plus qu'une montagne, un enchevêtrement de toitures défoncées, de roues brisées, de portières, de chaînes, de tampons, au milieu de morceaux de vitres* >>[200].

Pecqueux is also led by such a desire to mass murder so many people if necessary, in order to get rid of a single love rival in the last chapter of the novel. He wanted to kill Jacques Lantier because of his affair with his beloved Philomène. Regardless of the lives of hundreds - or thousands – of soldiers that were being carried to the front lines of the French-Prussian war of 1870, Pecqueux causes a double fall where both men are shredded. Meanwhile, the driverless train was launched at full speed in the dark night, offering a totally apocalyptic[201] vision, especially since that happens to the explicit of the novel. The suspense is reinforced by the fact that the narrator closes his story on such a dark picture,

---

[199] David Baguley : **Zola et les Genres**, chapter IX : *le réalisme grotesque et mythique de* **La Terre**., op. cit. p. 100.
[200] Émile Zola: **R. M. IV**, op. cit. p. .1260.
[201] It must be remembered that this same cataclysmic idea related to the machine is found in Jacques Noiray's book: << *Que ce soit directement, comme machine meurtrière, ou métaphoriquement, la machine apparaît toujours comme un instrument ou une image de mort. On dirait même que, pour Zola, la présence de l'objet technique est indissociable d'une représentation de la mort : c'est en tant que machine, c'est-à-dire sujet au détraquement, que le corps humain se révèle fragile et mortel ; c'est comme corps mécanique érotisé que la machine développe avec l'homme ou la femme des rapports pervertis et finalement meurtriers ; c'est comme incarnation des instincts de mort qu'elle trouve à la fois sa suprême puissance et sa fin cataclysmique* >>, see **Le Romancier et la Machine. I. L'Univers de Zola**, op. cit. p. 448.

leaving to the imagination of his readers to guess the outcome of the expected final crash. The narrator seems to be reluctant to take responsibility for the umpteenth inevitable railway disaster. The reader is helplessly mystified in the face of that forever present train crash, which is forever hanging over like a real sword of Damocles that no-one can prevent from falling harply on the heads of those innocent victims. It is true that for Zola, these soldiers were just like a herd of sheep heading to the slaughterhouse under Napoléon III's watch.

The sexually frustrated subject is a formidable nihilist in Zola's fiction works and it is better not to find oneself in their line of fire, hence McLynn's admission of the presence of a concatenation of chaos in that novel: << *There is, it seems, chaos within chaos, the aleatory within the contingent* >>[202].

In total, with regard to accidents, the narrator in Zola's novels warns us against the avatars of the technical progress that can, in the long run, harm mankind in very disturbing proportions even if sexuality is incriminated as being the main cause for the disasters spelled out here. Beyond that point, those disasters are a harbinger of the collapse of the whole society of the Second Empire and It is fair to conclude this point with McLynn for whom: <<*The world of* **La Bête Humaine**, *set in 1869-1870, mirrors the descent of the Second Empire itself into the darkness of the chaos world* >>[203].

There is, in Zola's works, a phobia and an obsession for sex[204] that is considered to be an instrument responsible for so much human suffering. Whether it be mythical or naturalistic, sexuality always presents itself in Zola's works in a diabolical and a catastrophic way. Yet, Zola has the courage not to avoid what he fears; he does not make it a taboo either. On the contrary, he confronts his fears to analyse them, to explain them and, if necessary, to exorcise them with lucidity: << *Or, sortir des enfers, c'est précisément le sens de l'entreprise de Zola, de son difficile nettoyage du corps et du monde* >>[205]. Because his characters lack such lucidity, they are swept away by the whirlwind of their invading morality-free libido. It can be postulated that although the author of the **Rougon-Macquart** series did not pioneer the introduction of the theme of sexuality in literature in general and in the novel in particular, it is nevertheless obvious that he showed an irrefutable originality[206] in that particular area.

---

[202] Pauline McLynn : *Human Beasts ? Criminal perspectives in* **La Bête Humaine**, in **Zola, La Bête Humaine : texte et explication**, Geoff Woollen (éd), op. cit. p. 133.
[203] **Ibidem**, p. 133.
[204] We can read in Jean Borie's book : << *Zola est vraiment obsédé par le corps et par la malédiction de l'ordure* >>, dans **Zola et les Mythes, ou de la Nausée au Salut**, op. cit. p. 36.
[205] Jean Borie: **Zola et les Mythes, ou de la Nausée au Salut**, op. cit. p. 38.
[206] Claude Seassau believes, **in Émile Zola, Le Réalisme Symbolique**, that one of Zola's originalities resides in the tension that exists between myth and reality, op. cit. p. 320 and on page 215, that the Zolian universe consists of a creative imagination with its original myths.

Roger Ripoll abounds in the same way in **Réalité et Mythe chez Zola**, by stressing that Zola proceeds to a renewal of the myths that he recovers, and that one of the originalities of the

Through these two chapters, we have seen that sexuality is the central theme of Zola's naturalism, the essential element around which everything gravitates. The denomination and the qualification of the character both depend on their sexuality as much as their being and their deeds. Man is primarily a sexual being in Zola's mind and it is his sexuality that dictates his general behaviour in society. Sexuality is therefore the true nature of man – both physiologically and psychologically - since it justifies and highlights the inherent violence in man; violence that turns him into the human beast[207]. Violence, however, takes different semantic paths such as sadism, masochism, passionate murder, pyromania, paedophilia, etc. The Zolian worldview is that of an irreversible fatality linked to sexuality. If being a hermaphrodite or an asexual character is a serious degeneration in the author's view, having a 'normal' sexuality is also the source of an atavistic violence. Sex is used to give life and, inevitably, it is a vector of death in the naturalistic novel, just like it was the tool of the original sin in the Garden of Eden. Likewise, the characters in the corpus who represent the imperial society have also sinned through sex between Aunt Dide and the poacher Macquart, for Aunt Dide is the new mythical Eve who committed sin by getting involved with the new devil, Macquart. Aunt Dide has committed an unforgivable sin in Zola's view and all her descendants will pay a hefty price for it by means of curses and bad omens. They will all be hit hard by the crack.

This is the time to take our investigation in the direction of another capital component of the story, namely the characters' study. I shall attempt to apprehend them in their being, in their appearance and through their different deeds and their future in the exclusive framework of sexuality.

---

treatment of the myth in the author's works is certainly << *l'accent mis sur le côté érotique du paganisme* >>, op. cit. p. 65 et p. 80.

[207] Émile Zola writes: << *Il y a un fonds de bête humaine chez tous, comme il y a un fonds de maladie* >>, in **Le Naturalisme au Théâtre** in **Le Roman Expérimental**, in **Œuvres Complètes**, volume 9 : **Nana 1880**, op. cit. p. 379.

SECOND PART: THE SEXUAL AGENTS FACING THE QUESTION OF FATALITY

THE GENEALOCIAL TREE OF THE ROUGON-MACQUART

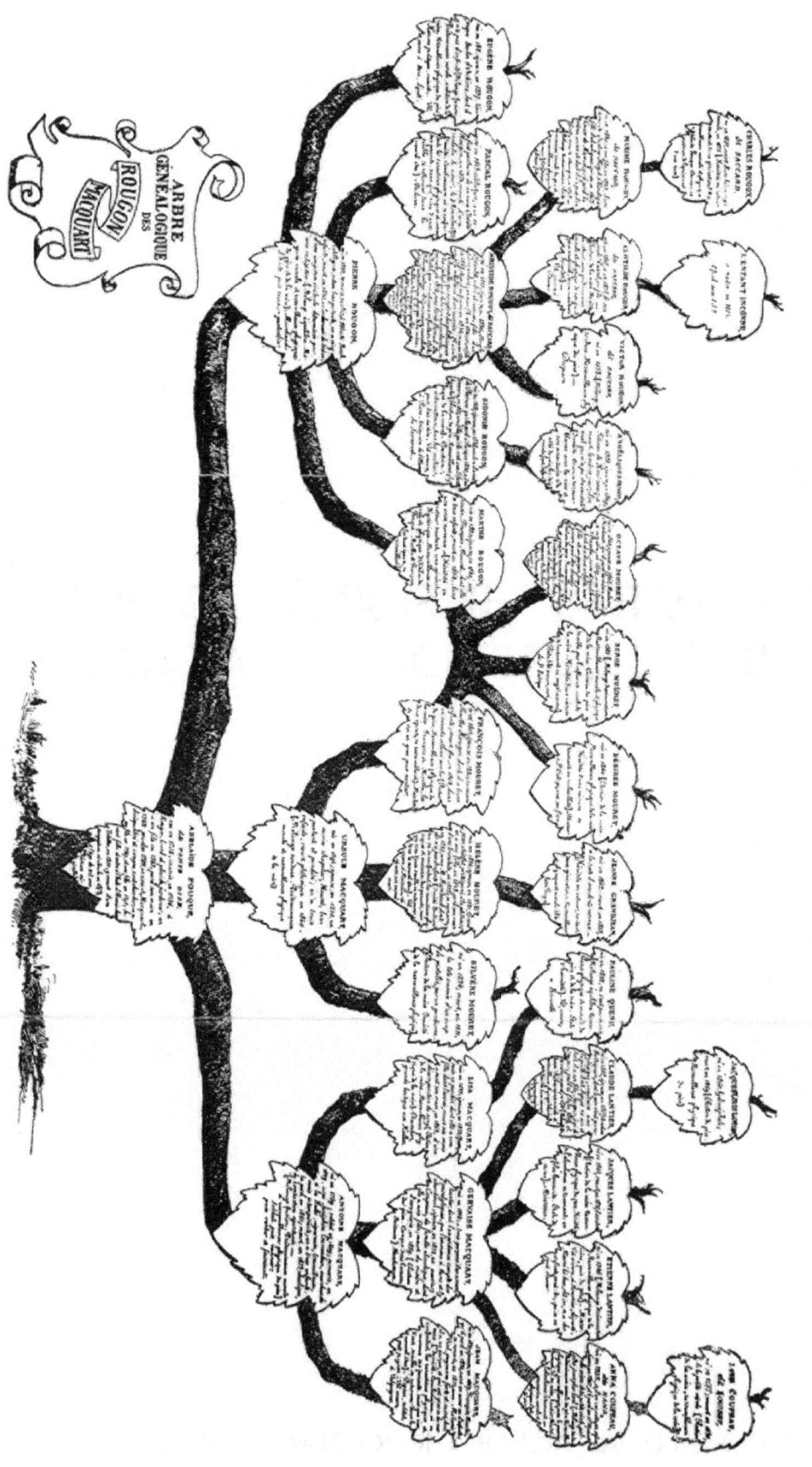

This study will try first to apprehend the characters, the most compulsory and the most eminent elements of any story. They constitute, according to the word of Roland Barthes, << *la grammaire du récit* >>[208]. Just like the verb is the compulsory constituent of the verbal phrase, or the subject noun commands the sentence, the character constitutes the first element of legibility of the narrative. This crucial importance of the character in relation to the narrative was rightly depicted by Barthes for whom it remains the irreducible element of any narrative for there are no narratives in the world that are able to do without it. Meanwhile, one can very well make a narration for example without mentioning neither the time nor the referential space[209] in which the story unfolds.

Nonetheless, I will try to grasp the characters in the corpus in the referential time and space in which they move. I will use the term of *actant*[210] following in Greimas' footsteps to designate not the traditional anthropomorphic character, but any entity that plays a fundamental actantial role in the story, either as a subject or an object, a giver or a recipient, or as an adjuvant or an opponent. I will add the epithet *"sexual"* to specify the type of agent that interests me. That is because those who come out of this theme will not be included in my analysis.

The character, first of all, has a name, a social status and can be attributed qualifiers. I will call the *being* of the character any information of this type which is aimad at identifying them.

CHAPTER I: THE BEING OF THE CHARACTERS OR THE EXPANSION OF PUPPETS

Characters, in a fiction work, are unique in the sense that they are not real. They are indeed fictional creatures that have only a virtual existence. They live only on pages, through ink and paper. Paul Valéry summed up the situation of the character in these words: << *Superstitions littéraires - j'appelle ainsi toutes croyances qui ont de commun l'oubli de la condition verbale de la littérature. Ainsi existence et psychologie des personnages, ces vivants sans entrailles* >>[211]. The study of the character, the now famous << *être de papier* >>[212], is exciting in many ways. Although I will not study here each of the two thousand anthropomorphic characters that abound in **Les Rougon-Macquart**, I intend to

---

[208] Roland Barthes : *Introduction à l'Analyse Structurale des Récits,* in **Communications, 8 : L'Analyse Structurale du Récit**, Paris, Seuil, 1982, p.10 et p.18, (1 ère Édition, Paris, Com, 1966).
[209] **Ibidem**, p.15.
[210] A. J. Greimas : **Du Sens II : Essais Sémiotiques**, chapter 1 : Structures Narratives, agents *et Acteurs,* Paris, Seuil, 1983, pp. 49-55.
[211] Paul Valéry : **Tel Quel**, Volume 2, Paris, Gallimard, 1960, p. 61.
[212] **Ibidem**, p. 61.

focus exclusively on the most important among them on the thematic axis of sexuality. Non-anthropomorphic agents will not be left out either once they become redundant or when they have a decive influence on the sexuality of their anthropomorphic counterparts.

According to the semioticians of the Groupe d'Entrevernes, a narrative sequence obeys a logical organisation as follows: from a phase of *manipulation* or *faire-faire*, a *destinateur* enters into a relationship with a *sujet-opérateur* with a view to make them acquire a *compétence* or an *être du faire*. That second phase puts the subject-operator in relation with the **modal objects** necessary to carry out their quest. Once **competent**, the **subject-operator** must relate to the value-object to establish a **performance** or *faire-être*. At the end of the chain, there is again a relationship between the addressee – or the beneficiary - and the subject-operator in order to stop the *sanction* or *l'être de l'être* and that consists in interpreting and evaluating the result of the quest undertaken by the latter. I will try, throughout this second part, to see how these four moments of the narrative programme are treated in the corpus.

1. THE MANIPULATION OR L'ÊTRE DU FAIRE

1.1. The author and his characters

We owe the very first manipulation to the author who, on July 1st, 1871, in Paris, wrote about his characters, in the general preface to the **Rougon-Macquart** series: << [...] *ils racontent ainsi le Second Empire à l'aide de leurs drames individuels, du guet-apens du coup d'État à la trahison de Sedan* >>[213]. The fiduciary contract was therefore tacitly written between a sender - the author, Zola himself - and his characters to whom he granted a desire to begin the quest for an object-value - the denunciation of a political regime.

It would still have been necessary to give them some skills in order to carry out the search for the object. Such operation whereby the character is granted the necessary skills is called competence. The competence of Zola's characters was never in doubt for it was so explicit in the preface mentioned above: << *Les Rougon-Macquart, le groupe, la famille que je me propose d'étudier, a pour caractéristique le débordement des appétits, le large soulèvement de notre âge qui se rue aux jouissances. Physiologiquement, ils sont la lente succession des accidents nerveux et sanguins qui se déclarent dans une race, à la suite d'une première lésion organique, et qui déterminent, selon les milieux, chez chacun des individus de cette race, les sentiments, les désirs, les passions, toutes les manifestations humaines, naturelles et instinctives dont les produits prennent les noms convenus de vices et de vertus. Historiquement, ils partent du peuple, ils s'irradient dans toute la société contemporaine, ils montent à toutes les*

---

[213] Émile Zola: **R. M. I**, op. cit p. 3.

situations [...]>>²¹⁴. Therefore, the primary concern for Zola was to tell the tale of the Second Empire. The "paper beings" that would help him depict the era of the Second Empire were victims of their inheritance from the outset. That was so blatant that Zola did not hesitate to proclaim that << *L'hérédité a ses lois, comme la pesanteur* >>²¹⁵. One can say, like Philippe Hamon did, that : << *Le personnage zolien, posons-le ici tout de suite, sera un personnage lisible et délégué à la lisibilité. [...] Lieu et objet de lisibilité, il sera aussi opérateur de lisibilité* >>²¹⁶.

Although the contract between the author and his characters was concluded, one must remember that the phase of *manipulation* had not yet been completed.

1.2. The identification and the categorisation of the sexual agents

Following Philippe Hamon, we can distinguish the *anthropomorphes* characters from the *non-anthropomorphes*²¹⁷. For this theoretician, the term *anthropomorphe* applies to a literary character in human form. Hamon distinguishes three categories of anthropomorphic characters as follows:

1) The *anaphore* characters, meaning the ones that are specific to a given creative work: in this context, it means all the characters whose last name²¹⁸ is Rougon, Macquart, Lantier and Mouret. They are the initial family that Zola intended to study in the series.

2) The *référentiel* characters, meaning those of historical essence that are not purely of a fictional type, like Napoléon or Bismarck.

3) The *embrayeur* characters, finally, are those who constitute a choir next to the anaphoric characters since they have a phatic function like Watson, this kind of Sherlock Holmes' shadow in Conan Doyle's works. Among them are the Fouan in **La Terre**, who are not part of the original family but who, however, have a particular narrative interest.

1.2.1. The anthropomorphic characters

1.2.1.1. The anaphoric characters

---

²¹⁴ Émile Zola: **R. M. I**, op. cit. p.3.
²¹⁵ **Ibidem**, p. 3.
²¹⁶ Philippe Hamon : **Le Personnel du Roman. Le Système des Personnages dans les Rougon-Macquart d'Émile Zola**, op. cit. p. 38.
²¹⁷ Philippe Hamon: *Pour un Statut Sémiologique du Personnage* in **Poétique du Récit**, op. cit. p. 125.
²¹⁸ Maarten Van Buuren asserts that << *L'unité du cycle est assurée en grande partie par la famille dont les membres se retrouvent dans chaque roman* >> in **Les Rougon-Macquart d'Émile Zola : De la Métaphore au Mythe**, op. cit. p. 13.

All the children born from Adélaïde Rougon - born Fouque – are anophoric characters. Adélaïde Rougon is cracked from the first volume, **La Fortune des Rougon** published in 1871. For Zola, *la fêlure* is *la tare originelle*, the seed of madness transmitted to Adélaïde Fouque by her father. That crack spread inexorably into her offspring of thirty-five individuals distributed in the twenty novels of the **Rougon-Macquart** series. Like a virus, the crack infects each member of the family by manifesting itself differently according to the temperament of each of them and according to their social class and environment. The anaphoric characters are thus catalogued and none of them - with the exception of Clotilde Rougon as I showed above - will be able to shake off that genetic condition and to get rid of << *la pesanteur* >> which is << *la fêlure* >>. That is why Hamon is probably not wrong in saying that << *Avant d'être déterminé par une hérédité, des influences, des milieux, etc., le personnage zolien est donc prédéterminé, ce qui n'était peut-être pas évident a priori pour un personnage relevant de l'esthétique réaliste-naturaliste* >>[219].

For example, the Rougon[220] who make up the legitimate branch are *sanguins*. In Zola's theory, this produces in them an evident << *appétit violent* >> that leads them << *à monter à toutes les situations* >>: Aristide is a banker; Eugène is a lawyer and then a Cabinet minister; Pascal is a doctor and Sidonie is a businesswoman, to name but a few. On the contrary, the Macquart[221] who constitute the illegitimate branch, are *nerveux* and such temperament, in the Zolian understanding, renders them alcoholic and dissipated characters. They are poor overall, manual workers, peasants, soldiers, poachers, drunkards and debauched characters, in short, they are branded << *canailles* >>.

Then, through the game of alliances by means of weddings in particular, two other branches arise. The first is that of Mouret which is straddling the two initial branches above. Ursule Macquart, by marrying the hatter Mouret, begot François Mouret, the future husband of Marthe Rougon. As a result, the Mourets inherited both the *sanguin* temperament of the Rougons in the image of Octave Mouret - who thus becomes a successful dealer of novelties - and the *nerveux* temperament of the Macquarts, which emerges for example in François Mouret - who becomes a madman[222] with suicidal thoughts in the latter stages of his life. The same goes for Silvère Mouret, a little handyman deprived of the slightest

---

[219] Philippe Hamon : **Le Personnel du Roman. Le Système des Personnages dans les Rougon-Macquart d'Émile Zola**, op. cit. p. 55.

[220] For Maarten Van Buuren, the Rougon are nothing but *arrivistes*, pushy and upstart. They seem to be "blessed" in every way possible, see **Les Rougon-Macquart d'Émile Zola. De la Métaphore au Mythe**, op. cit. p. 13.

[221] **Ibidem,** for Maarten Van Buuren again, on the other hand, the Macquart are always *des souffrants*, as if they were cursed with *suffering* and tribulation, op. cit. p. 13.

Claude Seassau for his part, stresses that the Macquart branch of the family is characterised by a strong heredity in **Émile Zola, Le Réalisme Symbolique**, op. cit. p. 18

[222] We do remember that according to Roger Ripoll, Zola was largely inspired by Lucas' theory of heredity, which stipulated that drunken parents were likely to beget crazy children, see **Réalité et Mythe chez Zola**, op. cit. p. 169.

aptitude for the things of the spirit and the intellect. The second branch is that of the Lantier born from Gervaise Macquart. Those ones all belong to the *nerveux* temperament and, therefore, they are as crazy and as mad as Jacques Lantier[223]; lower miners or factory workers like Étienne Lantier or talentless artists that are devoid of any genius like Claude Lantier.

The anaphoric characters do experience various sexual fortunes. If we take the example of Eugène Rougon, we can see that he is asexual both in **La Curée** and in **Son Excellence Eugène Rougon** and in **La Fortune des Rougon** too. The same remains true for his younger brother, Pascal Rougon, in the latter novel. As for Aristide Rougon dit Saccard, he << *avait partagé sa femme (Renée) avec son fils, vendu son fils, vendu sa femme, vendu tous ceux qui lui étaient tombés sous la main [...]* >>[224]. It is interesting to remember that Aristide chose himself a new surname, Saccard. Philippe Hamon has already very beautifully revealed the crucial importance of this change of identity in writing: << *Le nom peut renvoyer à tel ou tel contenu moral, esthétique, caractériel, idéologique, stéréotypé [...]. Les cas les plus intéressants à étudier seront sans doute ceux où l'on voit, dans un texte, un personnage s'inventer lui-même un nom ou un pseudonyme. Par exemple, dans **La Curée** de Zola, nous voyons le financier et spéculateur Aristide Rougon se choisir un nom de << guerre >> (où l'on reconnaît << sac >> (d'or) + le suffixe – ard ; << Saccard ! – avec deux c ... hein ? Il y a de l'argent dans ce nom-là ; on dirait que l'on compte les pièces de cent sous [...] >>, << Oui, un nom à aller au bagne ou à gagner des millions >> (lui répondit son frère Eugène). De tels noms << transparents >> fonctionnent comme des condensés de programmes narratifs, anticipant et laissant préfigurer le destin même des personnages qui les portent* >>[225].

Maxime Rougon dit Saccard << *cet être neutre, hermaphrodite étrange venu à son heure [...] devenait une femme aux bras de Renée* >>[226]. David Baguley summed up this character into a simple formula, believing that Maxime << *figure le prince trop charmant, dépourvu de la moindre trace d'énergie héroïque* >>[227]. As Maarten Van Buuren notes, the image of the effeminate man is always unfavourable in Zola's view [228].

---

[223] Roger Ripoll: **Réalité et Mythe chez Zola**, op. cit. p. 169.
[224] Émile Zola: **R. M. V**, Paris, Gallimard, 1967, p. 221.
[224] Émile Zola: **R. M. I**, op. cit. p. 485-486.
[225] Philippe Hamon : *Pour Un Statut Sémiologique du Personnage* in **Poétique du Récit**, op. cit. p. 150.
[226] Émile Zola: **R. M. I**, op. cit. p. 485-486.
[227] David Baguley: **Zola et les Genres**, *chapter III* : **La Curée** : *La Bête et la Belle*, op. cit. p. 38.
[228] Maarten Van Buuren : **Les Rougon-Macquart d'Émile Zola. De la Métaphore au Mythe**, op. cit. p. 186.

For Zola, Sidonie Rougon[229] is << *cet hermaphrodisme étrange de la femme, être neutre, homme d'affaires et entremetteuse à la fois* >>[230]. She joins her nephew, Maxime, in latent hermaphroditism and in the sexual inversion.

Marthe Rougon, wife of Mouret, loves Father Faujas and religion with ambiguity in **La Conquête de Plassans** while she abandons her true husband, François. She is a victim of what Bertrand-Jennings calls feminine hysteria manifested on the one hand by occultism and mystical superstition, and on the other hand by sexual deviation[231].

Ursule Macquart is rather tempered in **La Fortune des Rougon** unlike her brother, Antoine, who begets three babies one after the other with his wife, Josephine Gavaudan.

Gervaise, the second born of the couple, is strongly attracted to boys and men[232] and she brings forth two *"bastards"* with her lover, Lantier, respectively at the tender age of fifteen and eighteen, in the same novel. Their son, Claude Lantier, is a firebrand because he manifests << *de ces brusques poussées de colère dont il était coutumier* >>[233] and with a << *rage impuissante de création* >>[234], while his son is << *si laid, si comique* >> and who, moreover, << *devient idiot* >>[235] over time. Claude's younger brother, another Jacques, suffers from a double personality. He suffers indeed << *une abominable faim d'égorgement* >>[236] and he is *"la bête humaine"*[237]. Their youngest son, Étienne Lantier, has the dull anguish of the crack to the point where he would experiment << *un de ces besoins de tuer où il voyait rouge* >>[238]. As a general rule, it can be said that violent jealousy is the single reason for killing sprees and senseless murders in **Les Rougon-Macquart**[239].

---

[229] Claude Seassau writes indeed: << *Zola semble avoir été fasciné par la dualité de l'individu et particulièrement par la faculté pour un être donné de présenter les caractéristiques du sexe opposé simultanément à celles de son propre sexe* >> in **Émile Zola, Le Réalisme Symbolique**, op. cit. p. 39.
[230] Émile Zola: **R. M. I**, op. cit. p. 373.
[231] Chantal Bertrand-Jennings : **L'Éros et la Femme chez Zola**, op. cit. p. 50.
[232] Claude Seassau writes in the above book: << *Après l'acquisition de la boutique, Gervaise enrichie ne songe qu'à manger* << *comme une chatte* >>, *l'image de la chatte sous-entend que la faim réelle n'est que l'apparence d'une autre faim, sexuelle, que Gervaise apaise symboliquement en allant à la forge de Goujet* >>, op. cit. p. 56.
[233] Émile Zola: **R. M. IV**, op. cit. p. 21.
[234] **Ibidem**, p. 342.
[235] **Ibidem**, p. 217.
[236] **Ibidem**, op. cit. p. 1123.
[237] Claude Seassau notes in **Émile Zola, Le Réalisme Symbolique**, op. cit. (p.60), that La Lison and Jacques are both also assimilated to the boar and to the human beast, hence the degradation suffered by the mechanic: humanisation, animalisation and mechanisation.
[238] Émile Zola: **R. M. III**, op. cit. p. 1246.
[239] Also refer to Claude Seassau on this point in the work mentioned above, p. 199.

Finally, let us complete this paragraph on the anaphoric characters with Victor Rougon dit Saccard, who is a real << *monstre* >> [240] and rather an << *enfant mûri trop vite* >>[241] because of the << *appétits exaspérés de sa race, une hâte, une violence à jouir* >>[242]. In short, Victor is a real << *boue humaine* >>[243].

From all the data above, we can conclude that the anaphoric characters are sexual agents that are globally unbalanced because of the weight of their heavy genetic inheritance. They carry deep within the seeds of an inverted or a perverted sexuality[244], which is sometimes aberrant and/or neurotic, as the study of the characteristics of sexuality in the first part has shown.

2.1.2. The clutch characters or the ''*personnages embrayeurs*''

They are the numerous engaging characters in **Les Rougon-Macquart**. That is why I will study among them only those who have a keen and a determining interest on the paradigmatic axis of sexuality. At this game, Nana is the most decisive agent in this category and she is arguably the most complex one. As the heroine of **Nana**, the novel that bears her name, Nana has the ambiguous status of a << dedans-dehors >>, for if she is the daughter of Gervaise Macquart, she is also the daughter of Coupeau. She enjoys a form of miscegenation that makes her the product of an anaphoric character – her mother Gervaise Macquart - and a clutch character, her father Coupeau. She is therefore not fully an anaphoric character, nor strictly speaking a clutch character either, hence her ambiguous << dedans-dehors >> status. Nana is a true << *chienne en chaleur* >>, a << *femme-empire* >>, a << *chatte* >>, << *une mouche d'or* >>, << *une couleuvre* >>, << *un monstre* >>, << *un fauve* >> in << *sa folie de destruction* >>[245]. All those metaphors[246] expose the bestial and the satanic character[247] she is, reinforcing the predictability of her input in the narrative. In this regard, Roger Ripoll showed that if Nana was assimilated to the devil from the Draft of the novel, her identification with a goddess - Venus - intervened much later on[248] in the process of carving out the novel **Nana**. The onomastic exploitation of the semic features of this particular sexual agent as a maleficent goddess reveals a rich narrative programme as I pointed out in the previous section.

---

[240] Émile Zola: **R. M. V**, op. cit. p. 152.
[241] **Ibidem**, p. 157.
[242] Émile Zola: **R. M. V**, op. cit. p. 157.
[243] Jean Borie : **Zola et les Mythes, ou de la Nausée au Salut**, op. cit. p. 160.
[244] David Baguley thinks that perversion and inversion constitue the sexual normality in Zola's works, in **Naturalist Fiction. The Entropic Vision**, op. cit. p. 210.
[245] Émile Zola: **R. M. III**, op. cit. p. 1157, p. 1267, p. 1269, p. 1271.
[246] Philippe Bonnefis claims that Nana suffers 78 successive mutations for 17 animal incarnations in *Le bestiaire d'Émile Zola : valeur et signification des images animales dans son œuvre romanesque*, in **Europe : Zola,** no. 468-469, op. cit. p. 106.
[247] Maarten Van Buuren identifies her with pagan god, Moloch, because she is a maneater in **Les Rougon-Macquart d'Émile Zola. De la Métaphore au Mythe**, op. cit. p. 156.
[248] Roger Ripoll : **Réalité et Mythe chez Zola**, op. cit. p. 76.

Nevertheless, let us add that for Neide de Faria, << *Nana est le symbole le plus puissant du sexe dans Les Rougon-Macquart*>>[249], that is to say a << *femme fatale* >>[250] according to the terminology of Chantal Bertrand-Jennings: << *Nana, il va sans dire, détient les records de tous les maléfices féminins [...]. Dans une sorte de cannibalisme sexuel qui s'apparente à la mante religieuse, elle massacre ses amants ou cause leur mort indirectement* >>[251].

Next comes Renée Béraud du Châtel, Mrs Rougon. Having left the old moral France that her father embodies[252], she is also a chilly[253] << *bête amoureuse* >>, << *monstre* >>, << *sphinx* >>, << *sœur blanche du dieu noir* >>[254] without ceasing to be << *Vénus* >>[255]. She is also a femme fatale who attacks and forcibly possesses Maxime. The reader must remember, though, that all those significant ambiguities were noted and studied above. It is worth mentioning here still that there is an obvious encounter between the story and the history of the Second Empire around sexual subjects such as Laure d'Aurigny et Blanche Muller in **La Curée**. Professor Henri Mitterand noted in this regard that: << *Le nom de Laure d'Aurigny est le croisement d'un prénom à la mode et du nom de Blanche d'Antigny, actrice qui, en janvier 1870, avait eu des démêlés avec son bijoutier pour n'avoir acquitté que 800 F sur les 13.000 F que coûtaient ses diamants* >>[256]. Like her model from reality, Laure is associated with gold that rings in her name; she eats up men's fortunes and ruins her lovers including the Duke of Rozan. Blanche Muller follows the same pattern.

Apart from the ***anaphoric*** characters, however, all other sexual characters can be grouped under the following thematic axes:

1.2.1.2.1. The animalisation of the clutch characters

All the other sexual agents in the corpus can be found in the same dialectic of animality - or bestialisation if one prefers - and of a triumphant sexuality. I can mention among them:

---

[249] Neide de Faria : **Structure et Unité dans Les Rougon-Macquart de Zola (la poétique du cycle)**, Paris, Nizet, 1977, p. 282.
[250] Chantal Bertrand-Jennings : **L'Éros et la Femme chez Zola**, op. cit. p. 61.
[251] **Ibidem**, p. 63.
[252] For Van Buuren, in **Les Rougon-Macquart d'Émile Zola. De la Métaphore au Mythe**, op. cit., when Renée leaves her father's Paris for Saccard's, she can only suffer the harmful influence of this corrupt Paris (p.145). In fact, the social developments under the Empire would have led to an excess of sensations (or fever): fever of expenditure; fever of speculation and still, many other forms of fever (196 occurrences).
[253] Émile Zola: **R. M. I**, Renée is described as a << *fleur de serre* >>, op. cit. p. 145.
[254] **Ibidem**, p. 485.
[255] **Ibidem**, p. 544.
[256] **Ibidem**, pp. 1584-1585.

In **La Bête Humaine** : Séverine[257], Flore[258], Cabuche[259], Tante Phasie[260] and Président Grandmorin[261] ; in **La Curée** : M. de Saffré, Laure d'Aurigny, Blanche Muller, Sylvia and Mme Michelin ; in **La Faute de l'Abbé Mouret** : Albine, La Rosalie, Fortuné, Vincent and Catherine ; in **Nana** : Le comte Muffat, le marquis de Chouard, Vandeuvres, Satin, Mme Robert, Steiner, Georges and Philippe Hugon ; in **L'Œuvre** : Dubuche, Irma and Christine[262] ; in **La Terre** : Hilarion, Palmyre, La Trouille, La Bécu, Buteau, La Cognette[263], Les Charles, Tron, Hourdequin and Lise, and finally, in **Germinal**, let's mention Maigrat, Chaval, Catherine Maheu, La Mouquette[264], Négrel and Mme Hennebeau.

Once animalised, those sexual agents become some << *chiens* >>, << *chiennes* >>, << *cochons* >>, << *chattes* >>, << *singes* >>, << *boucs* >>, << *chèvres* >>, << *godiches* >>, << *vaches* >>, << *taureaux* >>, << *chevaux* >>, << *fauves* >>, << *bêtes féroces* >>, << *loups* >>, << *carnassiers* >>, << *brutes* >>, << *serpents* >>, << *grandes bêtes* >>, etc., or even mythical types of hybrid creatures : << *monstres* >>, << *centaures* >>, << *sphinx* >>. The rapacity, the filth and the lust that are contained in all those semes have already been studied in the first part of this

---

[257] In **Émile Zola, Le Réalisme Symbolique**, Claude Seassau believes that Séverine plays the male role of the seducer and Jacques, the female role of being seduced. He also believes that the vision of sexuality is nightmarish in the perspective of heroines like Gervaise Macquart, Catherine Maheu and Séverine Roubaud, op. cit. p. 207 and p. 211.

[258] **Ibidem**, Claude Seassau agrees with the duality of the character of Flore who receives the two metaphors of the wolf and of the goat, p. 59.

[259] **Ibidem**, Seassau admits that sometimes the name has an ironic value that would deliberately mislead the reader (p.36) and that this applies to Cabuche meaning "*empty*" "*caboche*", that is to say a simple character without malice, a human beast in fact, whereas in reality, Cabuche remains the only sensible and harmless being in the novel (p.38).

However, in his article *Des brutes humaines dans* **La Bête Humaine**, published in **Zola, La Bête Humaine: Texte et Explication**, Geoff Woollen (éd.), op. cit., Geoff Woollen sees Cabuche, as a puerile being, a real brute whose mental development has remained at the infant stage, p. 168.

[260] Claude Seassau, in the above book, op. cit. p. 38, in the same ironic principle, notes that Phasie means "*who has the faculty to speak*" while this character is secretive to the point of allowing herself to die slowly rather than give away to her husband, Misard, the secret hiding place of her fortune of 1,000 francs.

[261] Claude Seassau establishes that this name gives grand + morin (moor / more = to be black), meaning a fundamentally dark character; an immoral character whose country house, the Croix-de-Maufras, means "*ce qui fait mal*", **ibidem**, p. 55.

[262] For Chantal Bertrand-Jennings, Christine is part of the class of the infamous nymphomaniacs like La Cognette. However, they belong to the subgroup of the dried-up women alongside Gasparine in **Pot-Bouille**, Philomène in **La Bête Humaine** and La Sandorff in **L'Argent**. This subgroup is opposed to that of the appetising curvy women that are Nana in **Nana**, Renée in **La Curée** and Clorinde in **Son Excellence Eugène Rougon**, refer to **L'Éros et la Femme chez Zola**, op. cit. p. 61.

[263] **Ibidem**, p. 61: La Cognette is another skinny and infamous nymphomaniac.

[264] It is easy to classify La Mouquette in the group of the infamous nymphomaniacs, the curvy and appetising ones although Bertrand-Jennings fails to name her in **L'Éros et la Femme chez Zola**, op. cit.

book. In addition to being animalised, the clutch characters that are sexual agents can still suffer the phenomenon of reification.

2.1.2.2. The reification of the clutch and the anaphoric characters

<< *Les passages précédents fournissent suffisamment d'exemples d'un phénomène que Marx avait dénoncé, une dizaine d'années avant la publication des* **Rougon-Macquart**, *en le baptisant de réification. Selon Marx, la société capitaliste réduit l'homme au statut d'un objet qui représente une certaine quantité d'argent : il est << réifié >>>>*[265]. In **Les Rougon-Macquart** series, the sexual agent that functions as a clutch character undergoes an amazing reification that makes them a << *Torchon* >> as it is the case for Adèle in **Pot-Bouille**. This reification becomes relevant when the proper name of the sexual agent is precisely that of a specific object, exactly as an epithet that remains attached to the name. Thus, Adele is designated by the narrator by the following nominal groups: << *Ce torchon d'Adèle* >> and << *La Torchon* >>. Those designations are transparent from the outset because they predict that Adèle will be a dirty and vile girl; this thing that men will use to *"wipe their behinds"* before throwing it with disdain like a mere toilet paper. La Cognette is a small instrument that knocks[266] people over, and who knocks men down in **La Terre**. La Rosalie is a rose soiled by debauchery in **La Faute de l'Abbé Mouret**. The name is therefore an eminently revealing element of the particular narrative programme of the character who bears it because. << *Zola n'a pas laissé au hasard noms, prénoms et surnoms de ses personnages, ceux-ci ont été créés selon deux impératifs précis, leur valeur phonétique et leur valeur sémantique* >>[267], writes Seassau. The same goes for La Mouquette - in **Germinal** - which sounds like a /Carpet / with her huge bum which works as a supple and a comfortable sofa, where men would love to come and bask in. The name of this particular character is already a programmed debauchery and an invitation for men to have sleepovers and one-night stands. At the interpretive level of the character's being, bestialisation dehumanises the sexual agent[268] that suffers it. Then reification indeed takes away their status of animated character[269], that is

---

[265] Maarten Van Buuren : **Les Rougon-Macquart d'Émile Zola. De la Métaphore au Mythe**, op. cit. p. 175. The passages to which the author refers are found in Émile Zola : **R. M. V**, p. 252 et **R. M. I**, pp. 574-575, where it is said that Saccard tattooed advertising slogans on the buttocks of girls before sending them << *dans la circulation* >>, then the one which clearly assimilates Renée to a mere << *enjeu* >>, << *une mise de fonds* >>, << *un louis tombé dans la poche du spéculateur* >>, << *une valeur dans le porte-feuille* >>, << *un métal précieux* >>, etc.

[266] Philippe Hamon perceives indeed the << *cognée* >> in her name, see **Le Personnel du Roman. Le Système des Personnages dans les Rougon-Macquart d'Émile Zola**, op. cit. p. 125.

[267] Claude Seassau : **Émile Zola, Le Réalisme Symbolique**, op. cit. p. 28.

[268] **Ibidem**, Seassau thus justifies the descending grading of which Jacques is a victim when he is animalised as a boar, then mechanised as a machine, p. 60.

[269] In **Naturalist Fiction. The Entropic Vision**, David Baguley believes that the assimilation of men and women to animals, plants and machines is a solid proof of the promiscuity of states and forms, op. cit. p. 210.

to say, their vital energy. From the [+ human] trait of their initial state, the anthropomorphic character moves on to the traits [-human, + animated] and then slips away until the denouement where they are reduced to only being [-animate, -human]. This decadence – or degenerescence - ultimately sets up the stage for their inevitable death.

When it comes to the anaphoric characters, one can note the beautiful self-reification of Clotilde Rougon who would like to become a mere << *chose* >> that belongs to Pascal, her uncle and her lover: <<*Tu entends! Maître, que je sois un bouquet vivant, et que tu me respires ! Que je sois un jeune fruit délicieux, et que tu me goûtes ! Que je sois une caresse sans fin, et que tu te baignes en moi ! [...]. Je suis ta chose, la fleur qui a poussé à tes pieds pour te plaire, l'eau qui coule pour te rafraîchir, la sève qui bouillonne pour te rendre une jeunesse* »[270]

Despite this reification process, Clotilde embodies << *la rédemptrice* >>, << *la femme idéale* >>[271] in David Baguley's view. She represents the strength of revival against the forces of degeneration represented by her brother Maxime, her nephew Charles and her great-grandmother, Tante Dide[272]. This revaluation is due to the birth of her son, the unknown child.

What happened then between the disturbance - the transmission of the crack, the original taint - and the outcome? That question will be answered in depth in the following chapter II, which aims to analyse the performance and the sanction of the sexual agent in **Les Rougon-Macquart**. For the time being, I have already noticed that, in the end, the final state of this narrative diagram is total oblivion; the fatal outcome of the process initiated since the acquisition of the hereditary crack. Going slowly but inexorably, the anthropomorphic character degenerates, they lose all vivifying substance and they ultimately and fatally suffer an untimely death. All this takes place between 1787 - which marks the marriage of Adélaïde Fouque to Rougon in **La Fortune des Rougon** - and 1870 - which marks the end of the Second Empire with its crushing defeat at the hands of Bismarck's Prussia in **La Débâcle**.

2.1.3. The referential characters

The last type of characters I will mention here is that of the historical or referential characters. They are not very many in the corpus with good reason. Their profusion in a literary work, moreover in a novel, would take away its fictional value, the very same essence that makes the charm of the genre. Roland Barthes writes: << *C'est précisément ce peu d'importance qui confère au personnage historique son poids exact de réalité, ce peu est la mesure de l'authenticité [...]. Les personnages historiques réintègrent le roman comme*

---

[270] Émile Zola: **R. M. V.** op. cit. p. 1129.
[271] Chantal Bertrand-Jennings : **L'Éros et la Femme chez Zola**, op. cit. p. 69.
[272] David Baguley : **Zola et les Genres**: chapter XI: *Du naturalisme au mythe: l'alchimie du* **Docteur Pascal**, op. cit. p. 124.

famille, et tels des aïeuls contradictoirement célèbres et dérisoires, ils donnent au romanesque le lustre de la réalité, non celui de la gloire ; ce sont des pendants superlatifs du réel >>[273].

In the **Rougon-Macquart** series, it is essentially the Emperor, Napoléon III, and Chancellor Bismarck that make up this category of referential charcters. The first one appears episodically in **La Curée** and in **Son Excellence Eugène Rougon**. He lets himself be visibly subjugated, first by Renée, then by Clorinde, despite both being married women. He is portrayed as everything but a handsome man, small in stature and amorphous. He does not gather enough narrative importance even if he plays a marginal role in the overall action in **Son Excellence Eugène Rougon**: he sleeps indeed with Clorinde and names her husband, Délestang, Minister of the Interior after sacking Eugène Rougon. This little importance of the referential character in the novelistic plot is probably justified by the specificity of the field of fiction that differs from that of a documentary and/or a report. Thus, although according to the other agents the monarch is guilty of two acts of adultery in each of the above novels, Napoléon III does not earn an effective classification in the category of characters who actively participate in the plot as essential components of the fiction. In short, he is not an agent. For Philippe Hamon: << *Citer un nom historiquement << plein >> de sens (Napoléon, Bismarck...) ; mais vide de signifié narratif (il ne << participe >> pas au récit, à l'intrigue, aux aventures des personnages), forme donc, dans le discours réaliste, le pendant superlatif de la promotion du << détail insignifiant >>>>*[274].

As I showed elsewhere[275], in Chapter III of **La Curée**, the exquisite beauty of Renée cast a spell on Napoléon III while the reader is informed that he spent one night with the Duchess of Sternich. The Emperor would therefore have the same sexual vices as his subjects, showing that the whole political system of the third Empire was rotten from top to bottom. The fact that Renée finds him somewhat aged, symbolises the end of the regime he embodies and spearheads[276].

The second referential character is mentioned in **Nana**. He is not seen taking part in anything, plot-wise, but he is supposed to be ugly, cold and having a mistress in Paris. The reasons for his apparent effacement are the same as for Napoléon III.

Beside the anthropomorphic characters, there are some non-anthropomorphic characters that deserve to be studied for their capital role in the inevitability of sexuality in our corpus.

---

[273] Roland Barthes: **S/Z**, Paris, Seuil, 1970, pp. 108-109.
[274] Philippe Hamon : *Un discours contraint* in **Littérature et Réalité**, Paris, Seuil, 1982, p. 175.
[275] Famahan Samaké : **Procès du Second Empire dans La Curée d'Émile Zola**, Abidjan, Masters Degree Dissertation in Arts – French literature -, Université de Cocody, Abidjan, March 1995.
[276] **Ibidem,** p. 46.

2.2. The non-anthropomorphic characters

I will have to classify them into two distinct categories according to whether they be natural or unnatural.

2.2.1. The natural non-anthropomorphic characters

2.2.1.1. The Earth

In **La Terre**, if there is one heroine in the structuralist meaning of the word, it is the earth itself, which is moreover the eponymous character here. She is portrayed as being << *indifférente et ingrate*[277] >>, immense, insatiable and frivolous to the point where she exhausts systematically her male lovers - the peasants - in all their work, laminating the first one before moving on to the following ones. That connotation of devouring men is attributed to the earth in both **La Terre** and in **La Faute de l'Abbé Mouret**. The land is indeed a man-eater with the trait [+ sexual], [- animated] in this novel to the point where its possession - even that of a small piece of land - is lived by the peasant as a rare orgasm, with ambiguous chills related thereto. That is why when Buteau inherits the lands of Françoise, it feels like a compelling sexual impulse that he can neither control nor repress. His psychosomatic state is thus translated: << *Toute sa chair s'était mise à trembler de joie, comme au retour d'une femme désirée et qu'on a crue perdue. Un besoin immédiat de la revoir, dans sa crainte folle que l'autre (Jean Macquart) pouvait l'emporter, lui tourna la tête*[278] >>. Such depiction of the carnal relationship between the land and the farmer also appears in **La Faute de l'Abbé Mouret** where the narrator tells his readers that << *Les Artaud, en plein soleil, forniquaient avec la terre, selon le mot de Frère Archangias* >>[279]. For Maarten Van Buuren, it is however an incestuous relationship because << *la terre est une mère. Elle met au monde l'homme qui, devenu adulte, devient son amant* >>[280].

If the earth is able to arouse as much the anthropomorphic sexual agent, if it never turns down their advances, it still never allows itself to be controlled by any of them. The earth is indeed a capricious mistress, which always leaves her lovers in tatters after exhausting them, both physically and emotionally. This was the case for Fouan, who << *y avait épuisé les muscles de son corps, il s'était donné tout entier à la terre, qui, après l'avoir à peine nourri, le laissait misérable, inassouvi, honteux d'impuissance sénile, et passait aux bras d'un autre mâle, sans pitié même pour ses pauvres os, qu'elle attendait* >>[281].

---

[277] Émile Zola: **R. M. IV**, op. cit. p.434.
[278] **Ibidem**, p. 777.
[279] Émile Zola: **R. M. I**, op. cit. p. 1240.
[280] Maarten van Buuren : **Les Rougon-Macquart d'Émile Zola. De la Métaphore au Mythe**, op. cit. p. 266.
[281] Émile Zola: **R. M. IV**, op. cit p. 434.

In all, the earth is a debauched mistress, a nymphomaniac and a necrophilic man-eater. That is why I do not share the point of view of Philippe Hamon when he argues that Nature - just like Paris and the machine - is an asexual entity[282]. In Zola's naturalism indeed, everything lives, and everything is sexual. In this, Zola was maybe ahead of his time by painting pansexuality in his fiction works over a Century before the concept was formally accepted. The omnipotence of the earth is largely explained by its status as a natural and an eternal element[283]. Indeed, how could the fleeting anthropomorphic sexual agent triumph over such a huge non-anthropomorphic and eternal sexual character?

In the corpus, the closest element to the earth is the vegetation that sits on it.

2.2.1.2. The Woods

In Zola's fiction works, the woods are sexual agents that are directly attached to the land of which they constitute the hairy and fragrant crown. In the corpus, their names are, the Bois de Boulogne in **La Curée**, and the Paradou in **La Faute de l'Abbé Mouret**. The pungent smell of the woods is so penetrating that it suggests the alcove and it is a vibrant invitation to engage in sexual intercourse. The woods have got the seductive powers that Aphrodite used to have in the Greek mythology. In **Les Rougon-Macquart**, when the woods are natural, they are beautiful and they rise to the rank of sexual agents in the same way as their anthropomorphic counterparts with whom they enter in conjunction.

Indeed, the Bois de Boulogne promotes incest by raising the idea of this perversion in Renée's mind. Furthermore, it leads the Parisians to engage in large-scale adultery[284] while the Paradou literally pushes Abbé Mouret into Albine's arms. The woods are not only an accomplice in the theme of sexuality, they are rather active sexual agents in their own right. We must therefore recognise their quality as adjuvants, even as recipients[285], given their complicity in the search for the anthropomorphic sexual object. As an example, in **La Faute de l'Abbé Mouret**, the narrator, explaining the fault of the priest and Albine, confesses insistently: << *C'était le jardin qui avait voulu la faute [...]. Maintenant, il était le tentateur dont toutes les voix enseignaient l'amour* >>[286].

---

[282] Philippe Hamon : **Le Personnel du Roman. Le Système des Personnages dans les Rougon-Macquart d'Émile Zola**, op. cit. p. 200.
[283] Henri Mitterand presents the earth as being the << *Alma mater, puissante vivante, femelle dominatrice et indifférente, la terre changeante et éternelle* >>, in Émile Zola : **R. M. IV**, op. cit. p. 1514.
[284] For Maarten Van Buuren, in **Les Rougon-Macquart d'Émile Zola. De la Métaphore au Mythe**, op. cit. p.179, people go to the Bois de Boulogne to see (others) and to be seen, for the the promenade is a spectacle.
[285] Philippe Hamon: **Le Personnel du Roman. Le Système des Personnages dans les Rougon-Macquart d'Émile Zola**, op. cit. p. 250.
[286] Émile Zola: **R. M. I**, op. cit. p. 1407.

One could easily agree with Philippe Hamon, who writes : << [...] *telle est la Nature, construisant dans le Paradou, pour Serge et Albine, un itinéraire implacable menant à la faute* >>[287].

Non-natural woods are also in a conjunctive relationship with the anthropomorphic sexual agents and that is why the greenhouse becomes the favourite space where incest is enjoyed[288] by Renée and Maxime as noted above. More than just a space, the greenhouse is a real adjuvant or enabler for Renée and Maxime. It warms their chilly nights of winter while offering them the opaque veil necessary to conceal their reprehensible antics. Assuming that the woods constitute the hairy crown of the earth, they take on a psychoanalytic dimension in the theory of Sigmund Freud, who established the evocative and the seductive power of the hair, the fragrant part of what he named sexual *fétichisme*. For him, the hair awakens the sexual desire in the libidinal subject by the sole olfactory excitation[289]. Neide de Faria also emphasised the importance of odours in the process of seduction in **Les Rougon-Macquart**[290] in particular. The greenhouse, to borrow a word from Jean-François Tonard, represents << *la dégénérescence de la nature* >>[291].

Nevertheless, the non-anthropomorphic sexual agents also register in their ranks the city of Paris.

1.2.2.1.3. Paris

Analogue to the woods, Paris is a character of << *folie et de honte* >>[292], covering up the << *orgies* >>[293]. It is a giant character who occupies the position of a sender pushing other sexual agents to engage in debauchery overwork. It thus appears in **La Curée**, in **L'Argent**, in **L'Œuvre**, in **L'Assommoir**, in **Nana**, in **Pot-Bouille** and in **La Bête Humaine**; to name just a few typical examples in the corpus. From page 8 of **La Débâcle**, the narrator denounces << *Paris dévorateur* >> where Maurice Levasseur and many others throw money into the fire if not at women. This image of the devouring Paris[294] and as the theatre of excessive

---

[287] Philippe Hamon : **Le Personnel du Roman. Le Système des Personnages dans les Rougon-Macquart d'Émile Zola**, op. cit. p. 231.
[288] Chantal Bertrand-Jennings calls the greenhouse << *un aphrodisiaque* >>, in **L'Éros et la Femme chez Zola**, op. cit. p. 65.
[289] Sigmund Freud: **Trois Essais sur la Théorie de la Sexualité**, op. cit. p. 67.
[290] Neide de Faria: **Structure et Unité dans Les Rougon-Macquart de Zola (la poétique du cycle)**, op. cit. pp. 282-284.
[291] Jean-François Tonard: **Thématique et Symbolique de l'Espace Clos dans le Cycle des Rougon-Macquart d'Émile Zola**, op. cit. p. 67.
[292] Émile Zola: **R. M. I**, op. cit. p. 326.
[293] **Ibidem**. 326.
[294] In Maarten Van Buuren's book, on the one hand we find Paris as a city that is both << *coquette* >>, << *dangereuse* >> and << *frivole* >>; then, on the other hand, as a << *monstre dévoreur* >> and an << *amante soumise* >>, in **Les Rougon-Macquart d'Émile Zola. De la Métaphore au Mythe**, op. cit. p. 72 et p. 74.

prostitution never leaves **Les Rougon-Macquart** and the examples are infinite. That is why Clotilde Rougon testifies to her gratitude toward her uncle, Pascal, for having taken her away from that corrupt milieu of Paris for La Souléiade in Plassans, a milieu of truth and love. She believes that that transfer corrected her heavy heredity: << *Comme tu l'as répété si souvent, tu as corrigé mon hérédité. Que serais-je devenue, là-bas, dans le milieu où a grandi Maxime ? [...]. Oui, si je vaux quelque chose, je le dois à toi seul, à toi qui m'as transplantée dans cette maison de vérité et de bonté* >>[295].

Overall, there is no other single space in the corpus that is as scary as Paris. The capital city is painted as a place of perdition that must be removed as it is unfit to be considered as a social environment in which children should be brought up. That is the reason why Pascal chose to transplant his niece Clotilde from there to Plassans. It is precisely for that reason that their child escapes from the grip of the hereditary defect known as the *fêlure*. As Van Buuren sees it, the return to the countryside, to nature, is a source of renewal in the works of Zola[296]. Without a doubt, the cases of Clotilde and Jean Macquart in **Le Docteur Pascal** seem to validate such statement, although the same does not go for the Fouans in **La Terre** nor for the Artauds in **La Faute de l'Abbé Mouret**[297]. For those ones indeed, the earth remains a devourer, an ungrateful, an anthropophagus and a cannibalistic lover. What then can be said about non-anthropomorphic sexual agents?

2.2.2. The unnatural non-anthropomorphic character

This is essentially about the painting that is presented in **L'Œuvre** - named *künstlerroman à thèse* by David Baguley[298] - and like << *une rivale terrible* >>[299] and << *une assassine* >>[300], according to Christine, Claude Lantier's wife. For Van Buuren : << *La peinture/maîtresse se métamorphose en une peinture/monstre qui finira par le [Claude] dévorer* >>[301]. In truth, the two sexual agents, the anthropomorphic (Christine) and the non-anthropomorphic (the painting), compete for the love of the same husband (Claude Lantier), who lives a real-life situation of bigamy on the brink of tragedy : << *Dans ce genre ''phallocentrique''* [künstlerroman], *le génie est toujours mâle, la Muse femme et le choix qui s'offre à l'artiste, ne peut être qu'entre deux maîtresses : l'Art*

---

[295] Émile Zola: **R. M. V**, op. cit. p. 1154.
[296] Maarten Van Buuren in **Les Rougon-Macquart d'Émile Zola. De la Métaphore au Mythe**,, op. cit. p. 140.
[297] Please refer back to, 1.2.2.1.1. The Earth
[298] David Baguley opposes the *künstlerroman* (the novel of the artist) to the *bildungsroman* (the apprenticeship novel), in **Zola et les Genres**, chapter VIII: *l'Œuvre, künstlerroman à thèse*, op. cit. p. 82.
[299] Émile Zola: **R. M. IV**, op. cit. p. 153.
[300] **Ibidem**, p. 344.
[301] Maarten Van Buuren : **Les Rougon-Macquart d'Émile Zola. De la Métaphore au Mythe**, op. cit. p. 60.

et la Femme. Celle-ci, manifestation de la vie, peut être la source de l'inspiration de l'artiste, mais elle peut devenir aussi la source de sa perdition selon le fonctionnement inexorable de cette loi du vampirisme qui semble dicter la vie sentimentale de l'artiste [...] >>[302]. And it is precisely for being unable to avoid being torn between those two lovers, Christine and the painting, that Claude ends up losing his mind and that he ends up hanging himself in front of his large unfinished canvas at the end of the very last night he spent in the arms of the woman of flesh : << *Leur ardente nuit d'amour sera parvenue à couper les derniers liens qui rattachent Claude à la peinture ; mais, au matin, elle le conduira au suicide devant sa toile inachevée. La femme a été pour lui un mauvais ange qui a réussi à anéantir son génie créateur. L'épisode du suicide de Claude entérine la victoire du corps sur l'esprit déjà annoncée par* **Nana**, *celle du principe féminin maléfique sur le personnage masculin bénéfique* >>[303].

Whether they be natural or not, anthropomorphic or not, the sexual agents in **Les Rougon-Macquart** always have a suspicious sexuality. Before doing anything further, the agent must fulfill the conditionality of the competence.

2. THE COMPETENCE OF THE SEXUAL AGENT

The competence of an agent implies a *devoir-faire*, a *vouloir-faire*, a *pouvoir-faire*, and lastly, a *savoir-faire*[304]. The agent can acquire those skills directly from the narrator, therefore innately. Thus, I shall study next some innate sexually competent agents whose creator god has assigned to them the so-called competence from the beginning, meaning from their designation or naming process.

2.1. The decomposition of the nominal lexemes

Let us approach this point from an isotopic angle. By isotopy, I mean << *ce qui garantit l'homogénéité d'un message ou d'un discours* >>[305]. More precisely, I will proceed by semiological isotopy, that is to say an isotopy provided by the redundancy and the permanence of the nuclear categories or semes. Such an onomastic study of the Zolian character is so important that Philippe Hamon speaks of an << *isotopie sonore* >>, and better still, of << *agents phoniques* >> [306]. Meanwhile, Claude Seassau believes that the name reinforces the meaning and the coherence of the character[307]. I will take care, first of all, of the decomposition of the absolute proper names, then of those which are accompanied by an article or an adjective epithet.

---

[302] David Baguley, in **Zola et les Genres**, op. cit. p. 86.
[303] Chantal Bertrand-Jennings : **L'Éros et la Femme chez Zola**, op. cit. p. 63.
[304] Le Groupe d'Entrevernes : **Analyse Sémiotique des Textes**, op. cit. p. 61.
[305] **Ibidem**, op. cit. p.123.
[306] Philippe Hamon : **Le Personnel du Roman. Le Système des Personnages dans les Rougon-Macquart d'Émile Zola**, op. cit. p. 116.
[307] Claude Seassau : **Émile Zola, Le Réalisme Symbolique**, op. cit. p. 27.

2.1.1. The absolute names

<< *Qu'il soit transparent ou plus opaque, le système onomastique à valeur symbolique est un facteur permettant une connaissance plus profonde du personnage, contribuant à donner un sens à son rôle ; c'est un élément important mais qui ne saurait remplacer l'analyse des traits constitutifs des personnages* >>, Seassau[308] writes. I will limit my analysis to the transparent names only, that is to say those which are *sexuellement pleins* such as Madame Lerat and Nana in **Nana**; M. Lequeu, Tron and Buteau in **La Terre**; Renée, Phèdre, Narcisse, Hippolyte and Écho in **La Curée**; Macquart and Miette in **La Fortune des Rougon**; Séverine and Flore in **La Bête Humaine** and Dubuche in **L'Œuvre**.

The decomposition of Mrs. Lerat gives /le/ + /rat/, rodent animal living in the sewers and responsible for the pandemic plague of the old times. In the English tradition, the rat is associated precisely with sexual felony. With such an agent, the reader can expect to deal with a corrupt sexual agent and a potential destroyer of the Parisian society.

Nana is decomposed in the following way: /Anna/ whose anagram /Nana/ recalls the infantile language. Nana, in today's language, is also the generic family name for beautiful girls[309]. She will therefore not be married and will remain young and beautiful for the purpose of prostitution. But above all, Nana remains a big child throughout the novel in addition to being the goddess of love. As Valerie Minogue writes so well, she is the symbol of the lost innocence of humanity, hence her tragic greatness: << *Pursuing the alteration of Nana observing and observed in the context of the child/seductress duality carries us into the heart of Zola's vision, for the persistence of the child in Nana represents not only Nana's lost innocence, but, in the epic dimension of Zola's imagination, the lost innocence of humanity at large. It is this extra dimension that endows the figure of Nana with a certain tragic grandeur* >>[310]. As a child, she is never inhabited by wisdom. Moreover, when she becomes a mother, she gets rid of her son, Louiset, whom she gives away to her aunt, precisely because a child cannot assume the education and the upbringing of another child. For Jean Borie, Nana sums up alone, Dalila, Circé and Salomé and if she is hairy, it is to emphasise her devouring animality, that of the Medusa[311].

---

[308] Claude Seassau : **Émile Zola, Le Réalisme Symbolique**, op. cit. p. 38.
[309] This interpretation is certainly anachronistic since Zola forged the name nearly seventy years before the noun "Nana" started being informally used to designate beautiful and seductive young women. However, that does not prevent my interpretation from being receivable. Moreover, it is plausible that the success of Zola's **Nana** was at the origin of this current use of "*Nana*" in popular language.
[310] Valerie Minogue : *Venus Observing – Venus Observed : Zola's Nana*, in **Émile Zola Centenary Colloquium: 1893-1993**, Patrick Pollard (éd.), op. cit. p. 62.
[311] Jean Borie : **Zola et les Mythes, ou de la Nausée au Salut**, op. cit. pp. 48-50.

Her lover Muffat is a /museau/ or a /muzzle/, which is a mammal's snout. He will therefore be stupid, unpleasant, ill-mannered, rude and indelicate. Despite his honourable rank of a chamberlain[312], he will play the horse and the dog at Nana's house. His debauchery sounds the death knell of what Minogue calls << *The supposedly devout aristocracy* >>[313].

Buteau Fouan will be a /butt/ or an instrument to /kill/, to /bump someone off/[314]. This is reminiscent of his peasant status and his particularly stubborn nature. He is also a /crazy/ + /ant/ by his last name. The prefix /fou/ indicates the psychic lesion that strikes him while the suffix /ant/ recalls the ending of the present participle which places his madness in the perspective of an engaged yet an unfinished process. At the phonetic level, /Fouan/ conveys the idea of what stinks like a fart and produces a lot of noise. All in all, he is a character devoid of morality and conscience. Therefore, he is all about instincts - libidinal and homicidal instincts - and excrement. In spite of all that, according to Bertrand-Jennings, he remains undoubtedly the only sinner who escapes from any sanction whatsoever because he is the: << *seule brute humaine que ne semble pas effleurer la notion de faute. Mais son appartenance à la race des conquérants explique sans doute cette impunité* >>[315]. Such explanation seems debatable since Bertrand-Jennings also grants the status of conquerors to Eugène Rougon, Brother Archangias and Abbé Faujas, all of whom have been severely punished. It seems to me that Buteau is rather spared from any punishment solely because he represents the ultimate alpha male: his extraordinary virility and fertility spare his blushes. Moreover, of all the descendants of Father Fouan, he remains the only one able to labour the lands bequeathed by the patriarch. He is the only descendant of the patriarch capable of making the lands yield profit again. Overal, he symbolises hope, hard work and sustainability of the Fouan breed. One must refer to the last chapter of this book to convince oneself of the importance of the notions of work and fertility[316] in Zola's philosophy.

M. Lequeu gives /le/ + /queue/, indicating that which is held only by their tail. This familiar rudeness denounces his incontrollable interest for sex, which is his only reason to live.

---

[312] For Maarten Van Buuren, if Nana makes Muffat spit on his official outfit, as if to take revenge on his social class and destroy it, it remains obvious that this self-absorption has a beneficial effect on the character since it frees him from his Catholic coldness and makes him enjoy greedily his teenage years, see **Les Rougon-Macquart d'Émile Zola. De la Métaphore au Mythe**, op. cit. p. 231.

[313] Valerie Minogue : *Venus Observing – Venus Observed : Zola's **Nana***, in **Émile Zola Centenary Colloquium: 1893-1993**, Patrick Pollard (éd.), op. cit. p. 57.

[314] Philippe Hamon seems to hear the sounds << *fouir* >> and << *enfouir* >> in the surname Fouan, in his book **Le Personnel du Roman. Le Système des Personnages dans Les Rougon Macquart de Zola**, op. cit. p. 123.

[315] Chantal Bertrand-Jennings: **L'Éros et la Femme chez Zola**, op. cit. p. 27.

[316] See the IVth Part, chapter 2, I.1. A natalist? Yes, but a socialist?

Tron is a /tronc (trunk)/, and is therefore solid like a tree. He symbolises manhood because he recalls both Apollo and Priapus. It is for this reason that La Cognette harasses him and takes him for her lover. Alas Tron, because he is a trunk, will have no more brains or morals than a tree. He is the victim of an exacerbated jealousy coupled with a homicidal madness.

As for Renée, she has the masculine trait /René/ and the feminine /-e/ trait. She is therefore a phallic woman. She loves men and plays the man when she falls on an effeminate lover like Maxime. Her masculine character is first and foremost the sign of the initiative she takes when it comes to having sexual intercourse before it becomes a sign of degeneration, for in Zola's understanding, the Empire has achieved the feat of turning men into women and women into men. When becoming Phaedrus by analogy, Renée acquires the traits [+ mythical], [+ incestuous], [+ victim of the gods][317], [+ chastised]. While she's playing the Nymph Echo, she becomes [+ mythical], [+ unsatisfied], [+ disdained] and [+ consumed]. The different associations of Renée with many mythical figures make this novel << *De tous les romans de la série des* **Rougon-Macquart**, **La Curée** *est peut-être celui qui exhibe le plus de relations transtextuelles* >>[318] according to Baguley's word. Renée belongs naturally to the class of the << *femmes fatales* >> of Bertrand-Jennings and she will be struck by the implacable fatality that kills the dissipated heroes in the works of Zola.

At the same time, Maxime, by playing Hippolyte, acquired the traits [+ mythical], [+ victim of Phaedrus], [+ innocent]. His role as Narcissus then added the traits [+ mythical], [+ dandy], [+ self-absorbed] and [+ fatal destiny]. The destinies of those two sexual agents are intimately related as it can be seen from the comparison of their specific traits above. Therefore, they will be doomed to the same fate as David Baguley writes: << [...] *Renée se délecte de son narcissisme et son être se désagrège* >>. What goes for her, goes for him too since the decadence and the degeneration that hit this latent hermaphrodite have already been shown in this book.

Macquart[319] is a / + macaque /, a /+ monkey/, for a macaque is a particularly ugly monkey. But this character's ugliness will also be moral with his drunkenness and his laziness. The words of his nephew, Pascal Rougon, confirm this state of affairs : << [...] *ce vieux bandit d'oncle, qui a mené, mon Dieu ! on*

---

[317] Émile Zola, however, did not seem to be content with the mythical dimension of Phaedrus. His ambition was rather to dissect her, that is, to inflict on her a naturalistic treatment: << *Justement, nous voulons recommencer* Phèdre. *[...]. Nous trouvons que le terrain métaphysique cédant la place au terrain scientifique, la littérature théologique et classique doit céder la place à la littérature naturaliste. [...]. Phèdre est malade, eh bien ! voyons sa maladie, démontons-la, rendons-nous-en les maîtres, s'il est possible [...]* >>, À M. Charles Bigot, controversial article included in **Le Roman Expérimental** in **Œuvres Complètes**, volume 9 : **Nana 1880**, op. cit. p. 454.
[318] David Baguley : **Zola et les Genres**, chapter III : ***La Curée*** : *la Bête et la Belle*, op. cit. p. 35.
[319] In **Les Rougon-Macquart d'Émile Zola. De la Métaphore au Mythe**, Maarten Van Buuren points out that Macquart is characterised by the metaphor of the wound, op. cit. p. 172.

peut le dire à cette heure, une existence peu catholique >>³²⁰. In addition to that, Philippe Hamon has already noted the idea of the jaw and that of chewing in the name, Macquart, and in its termination / -ard /, which is both pejorative and popular. What is more, it remains the << *leitmotiv onomastique de nombreux personnages négatifs* >>³²¹, like Misard, Bachelard, Chouard and Péchard. For Zola indeed, Macquart is the prototype of the bastard, that is to say the one who, from their conception, was already a fault, a mistake and a failure.

Miette is both an incomplete, a scattered and an unfinished business because she is only the fragment of a human being, a / + crumb/, a tiny bit of a human being. With Philippe Hamon, we can agree that such a diminutive qualification of the character << *diminue l'héroïne ou le héros* >>³²². She cannot therefore survive on the earth for long, especially since her full name, Marie, is that of a dead woman. She will always be haunted by death³²³.

Flore is a /flora/, the savage that lacks education and therefore cannot differentiate right from wrong³²⁴. Having grown naturally and freely like mere grass, she will have as much intellect as a tree or as grass. It seems that the benefit of her proximity to nature has been compromised by the other proximity: that of her family home with the railway, a symbol of the decadent industrial society. In the words of Bertrand-Jennings, she is a << *vierge invaincue* >>, a << *danger* >> and << *un monstre* >>³²⁵.

Séverine is /severe/, better still, the suffix /-ine/ gives her the quality of a chemical substance that could have severe consequences on all those who rub shoulders with her, like Roubaud, her husband, and Jacques, her lover³²⁶. *Femme fatale*, she will push those two agents to kill for her beautiful eyes. However, she herself becomes the victim of the murderous madness of the latter, becoming the slayer killed by a peculiar return of things. In total, vice, perversion and crime form vicious circles in **La Bête Humaine** and that is why, although Jacques has killed once, he continues to manifest murder impulses soon after, as if the urge to slaughter women were an irresistible libido-like urge. The

---

[320] Émile Zola: **R. M. V**, op. cit. p. 1097.
[321] Philippe Hamon : **Le Personnel du Roman. Le Système des Personnages dans Les Rougon-Macquart de Zola**, op. cit. pp. 115-116.
[322] **Ibidem**, p. 119.
[323] Starting from the positive value of the Virgin Mary in Zola's works, Roger Ripoll points out the similarity between Miette of **La Fortune des Rougon** and Marie in **La Confession de Claude**: << *Vierge condamnée à la mort, comme Miette. Le choix même du prénom est significatif, Zola tenant à préciser que Miette est un diminutif de Marie* >>, in **Réalité et Mythe chez Zola**, op. cit. p. 107.
[324] Let us recall that Claude Seassau had noted the duality of Flore both as a << *louve* >> and as a << *chèvre* >>, in **Émile Zola, Le Réalisme Symbolique**, op. cit. p. 59.
[325] Chantal Bertrand-Jennings: **L'Éros et la Femme chez Zola**, op. cit. p. 39.
[326] Claude Seassau asserts in **Émile Zola, Le Réalisme Symbolique**, op. cit. p. 210-211, that a nightmarish light is shed on sexuality in the Roubaud-Séverine affair, while sex is a fatality and a habit from the perspective of Séverine alone.

other persona that dwells in him – the demon - demands blood, the hot blood of the women Jacques is attracted too.

Finally, let us come to Dubuche that can be broken down in /du/ + /buche/, the gentleman who burns like a dry log of wood in contact with his sickly wife, the Margaillan girl, the rotten and the infectious *"race"*.

In spite of the fact that the proper nouns form a highly signifying semiotic isotopy at times, they are not the only ones that should be taken into account since there are also, in the corpus, some rather curious names that start with a definite article.

2.1.2. Names accompanied by an article or an adjective.

It is necessary to study in this paragraph, La Tricon in **Nana** ; La Torchon in **Pot-Bouille** ; La Mouquette in **Germinal** ; La Cognette and La Trouille in **La Terre** ; Le beau Narcisse and La Nymphe Écho in **La Curée** ; La Rosalie in **La Faute de l'Abbé Mouret** and, lastly, La belle Normande in **Le Ventre de Paris**.

While breaking down La Tricon, we get /la/ + /tri/ + /con/, a vulgarity which is supposed to sort out the *"cons"* or *"pussies"*. She will therefore be the living symbol of excessive debauchery. The Cognette, La Torchon and La Mouquette have already been broken down into minimal constituents and features. La Trouille sows /la/ + /trouille/ by being precocious and nymphomaniac. Rognes and its inhabitants are constantly being laid by La Trouille, night and day. For her father, who is ironically named Jésus-Christ - the parodic dimension of that designation clearly shows Zola's lack of esteem or respect for the Christ and Christendom – La Trouille is a << *bougresse* >>. Yet, as Seassau writes: << *le mot << bougresse >> cache le mot derrière, car bougre, qui donne au féminin bougresse, signifie à l'origine hérétique et sodomite* >>[327]. Because of that connotation, she will always be laying on her backside with boys on top of her, if not standing on all fours, offering her bottom to them.

In contrast, Le Beau Narcisse shows a stiff resistance to the ardour of female sexual agents. This is a chaste character because this /+ Beau or handsome/ man is a /+ dandy/. The epithet alone is a pledge of seduction and the definite article / le/ specifies him and identifies him absolutely with that aesthetic value. For Baguley, Le Beau Narcisse << *figure le prince trop charmant* >>[328] but any excess is a flaw, not an asset. This agent, on a metalinguistic level, is of mythical essence and, on a referential level, he combines with Maxime who plays his own role in the play. On a poetic level, the name represents metaphorically the same Maxime who shows an exacerbated dandyism in **La Curée**. Likewise, La Nymphe Écho is the metaphor for Renée, an inferior goddess dwelling in the woods. We

---

[327] Claude Seassau : **Émile Zola, Le Réalisme Symbolique**, op. cit. p. 217.
[328] David Baguley : **Zola et les Genres**, op. cit. p. 38.

must therefore take Renée and Maxime together insofar as their destinies are intimately intertwined on both the mythological plan and on the narrative plan. Both have the traits [+ mythical], [+ lovers], [+ metamorphosis], [+ victim of fatality] and [+ reified]. The difference between them is in the sense of their sexuality. Indeed, in appearance, Narcisse is [+ inverted] while Renée is [+ extrovert]. Through the play of mirrors, Renée will also become a female Narcissus and will be hit by the same fate as Narcisse.

La Belle Normande in **Le Ventre de Paris**, with the definite article /la/, is unique in her kind because the epithet /belle/, which is an integral part of the noun phrase that designates her, works as a call for love. Then, the noun /Normande/ designates in principle anyone that is from the region of Normandie[329], extreme North-West of France. If her name is totally blotted out for the benefit of that of her entire native region by means of periphrasis, that means that she is a worthy representative thereof, a kind of Miss Normandy, for example. Nevertheless, her great beauty is a frightening reality in Florent's eyes.

On the other hand, La Rosalie is a /rose/ made /dirty/ by the big Fortuné in **La faute de l'Abbé Mouret**. Tall and robust, she would probably be a good lady if she had not been seduced too soon by her rogue future husband. And it is appropriate to read here the term seduce in its strongest sense : << *La séduction de l'homme retrouve chez Zola son sens étymologique : séduire, c'est-à-dire << se-ducere >>, signifie, conduire à soi, amener à soi, donc détourner l'autre de sa voie, l'amener à l'écart >>*[330]. The fruit of their debauchery is too corrupt later on to live more than three months on earth because in Zola's works, the ground of debauchery is not fertile, and every child born of a dissipated woman is condemned to a rapid degeneration and, ultimately, to an early and an untimely death[331].

All the metalinguistic and the intertextual references mentioned here are likely to accentuate the predictability of the sexuality of the agents concerned while considerably reducing their autonomy in the fiction works. They seem to walk on the flowerbeds of their mythical or intertextual referents so that they undergo the destiny of those[332]. The reference to a myth, to a story *already written* and *too well-known*, restricts both the freedom of the novelist as a creator and that of the character associated with a mythical hero. By these sad times of impoverishment of the blood – that is called degeneracy in Zola's views - whichever character that intends to rise to the rank of the gods is already

---

[329] Maarten Van Buuren remarks in **Les Rougon-Macquart d'Émile Zola. De la Métaphore au Mythe**, that she is associated with a goddess, and at the same time as an idol of immolation and cannibalism, op. cit. pp. 154-155.
[330] Claude Seassau : **Émile Zola, Le Réalisme Symbolique**, op. cit. p. 204.
[331] This fatum explains the sad fate of Louiset, son of Nana, in the novel that bears her name.
[332] Roger Ripoll claims in **Réalité et Mythe chez Zola**, op. cit. p. 83 that: << *Les images des dieux portent en elles l'énergie primitive d'une sexualité dévorante* >> and that's why the characters that identify with gods (or mythical heroes) run to their own destruction.

defeated, because the Second Empire is not the Ancient Greece. The breed of the demi-gods has died out, and this is the time of the dwarves that are no longer great, except for their pride and their corruption. When the novel refers to the myth or is indeed invaded by mythology, what it loses in unpredictability and in suspense is probably gained in referential illusion.

Now is the time to take a look at the being of the characters to question whether it is consistent or contrary to their appearance. This approach is likely to establish any possible cases of truth, falsehood, secrecy and lies.

2.2. The /Being/ versus the /appearance/ or the category of truthfulness

According to the semioticians of the Groupe d'Entrevernes: << *Le discours construit et dispose sa propre vérité. Et l'une des tâches de la sémiotique est de rendre compte de cette disposition* >>[333]. As such, one opposes manifestation and immanence or /to appear/ versus /to be/. In detail, there are four possibilities in the context of truthfulness:

/to appear/ + /to be/ = true
/not-appearing/ + /not-being/ = false
/not-appearing/ + /being/ = secret
/appearing/ + /not being/ = lie

The agents who appear what they are, are in the truth in the image of Venus, like Renée and Nana, who both appear to be, and truly are goddesses of love. But this appearance becomes a lie since instead of being carriers of true and pure love, Renée and Nana are sexual << *monstres* >>, << *sphinx* >> and << *serpents* >>, some << *chattes* >> and a << *mouche d'or* >>, killing and polluting all around them. This is how they fall into the phenomenon of lies: they are really not what they appear to be. For Bertrand-Jennings, they are << *infâmes nymphomanes* >>,[334] which means that they are potentially more dangerous for men than << *les hystériques* >>.

The secret comes out when the protector Grandmorin is actually what he does not seem to be: the abuser of Séverine[335] in **La Bête Humaine**, a << *cochon* >>, a << *misérable* >> drenched in execrable businesses just like Baron Gouraud, in **La Curée**, whose red ribbon of senator does not free him from his seedy and sleazy morals.

---

[333] Le Groupe d'Entrevernes : **Analyse Sémiotique des Textes**, op. cit. p. 45.
[334] Chantal Bertrand-Jennings : **L'Éros et la Femme chez Zola**, op. cit. p. 61.
[335] If we should take from Président Grandmorin, who benefits from his position of << *paternité* >> to sexually abuse Séverine, << *sa fille* >>, we can agree with Maarten Van Buuren who concludes that fraternity is the only family tie that always remains positive and disinterested in Zola's works, see **Les Rougon-Macquart d'Émile Zola. De la Métaphore au Mythe**, op. cit. p. 184.

The deceitful type in this last novel is also suitable for the pederast Baptiste, who appears to be devoid of sexuality. He appears at the same time to be the only one in the novel who does not seem to feel anything for women. In fact, he passes for an absolute chaste, whereas in reality, the grooms – the stable boys – are the victims of his paederastic practices. This backwards sexual activity of sodomy is an ignominy in Zola's world. Therefore, Baptiste becomes a false chaste, a liar and an impostor[336].

The last two possibilities in the category of truthfulness are << *le vrai* >> and << *le faux* >> represented on the one hand by Buteau, and on the other hand, by Eugène Rougon. Buteau seems brutal, even bestial in his triumphant and immoral sexuality. He is in *le vrai* especially since his appearance is in absolute conformity with his being; for he brutally rapes his sister-in-law and savagely commits parricide on Fouan. On the other hand, it is obvious that Eugène Rougon is a false sexual agent because he does not seem interested in sex and in reality, he is not sexually active. His chastity, however, makes him a fake in the category of sexual agents since his libido seems to have changed and turned into a fierce love for power. He only enjoys the domination and enslavement of others[337] in **Son Excellence Eugène Rougon**. As a fake, his being is different from his appearance.

In the end, the designation of Zola's characters announces their << *programme narratif global* >>[338], thus giving the sentiment of << *un déjà-écrit* >>[339], as it is characterised by its multiplicity. Hwever, it is a conjunctive diversity that is laid in the same final mold: that of decline and of fall[340]. The diversity of their designations is explained by the disjunction between their appearance and their being: they are impostors, better still, mutants of a new breed. When they look kind, even goddesses of love, they really are demons or monsters. When they appear human, they never stop being animals, hybrid creatures, fabulous or mythical beings. This gives the **Rougon-Macquart** their new status, the true **Métamorphoses**, except for the fact that their heroes have degenerated into mere derogatory dwarves.

---

[336] Maarten Van Buuren calls metaphor of drama the discrepancy between the being – *l'être* - and the showing off -*le paraître*, in **Les Rougon-Macquart d'Émile Zola. De la Métaphore au Mythe**, op.cit. p. 171.

[337] Philippe Hamon calls this particular type of pleasure << *libido dominandi* >>, in **Le Personnel du Roman. Le Système des Personnages dans Les Rougon-Macquart de Zola**, op. cit. p. 236.

[338] **Ibidem**, op. cit., p. 108.

[339] **Ibidem**, p. 147.

[340] **Ibidem**, Philippe Hamon admits that Zola's characters are condemned to a cyclothymia, meaning the succession of << *hauts* >> - highs - and << *bas* >> - lows, p. 176.

David Baguley also notes: << *In naturalist works, however willing the spirit, the flesh is far too strong, for there is a kind of primitive 'nature', an irresistible, universal, depersonalized, instinctive (Schopenhauerian) Will that rises to the surface, saps the individual's sense of human values and brings about the decline* >>, in **Naturalist Fiction. The Entropic Vision**, op. cit. pp. 212-213.

Nevertheless, until now, the sexual agents have been approached only from an individual angle, on a case-by-case basis. Truth be told, the literary character is not isolated in the narrative since they integrate a class of agents that must be determined in order to better grasp their actual functionality, a fact that emerges in what is known as the actantial diagram.

3. THE ACTANTIAL DIAGRAM ON THE AXIS OF SEXUALITY

Inspired by Vladimir Propp, Souriau[341] established six *fonctions* of the character on three axes. On what he calls *"l'axe du vouloir"*, he opposes *"le sujet"* to *"l'objet"* of its quest, whereas on the *"axe du pouvoir"*, *"les adjuvants"* contradict de facto *"les opposants"* to the subject. This whole process is triggered on what he calls *"l'axe de la communication"* by *"un destinateur"* which mandates the subject to seek the object of which the beneficiary is *"le destinataire"*, the opposite instance to the *"destinateur"* or sender. The actantial diagram established from these six essential functions allows us to grasp as a whole and in a synthetic way, the sum of the interpersonal relationships in a narrative. It visualises for example the major oppositions or conflicts of interest between two or more agents, or the alliances between them. The sponsors of the actions and their beneficiaries do not escape either from the actantial diagram.

Generally speaking, in **Les Rougon-Macquart**, each of the characters becomes a sexual subject at some point or another, desiring a sexual object that can be any other sexual agent in the corpus, be it anthropomorphic or not. Let us put it this way: Zola's character is sexually motivated from their designations as well as from their qualifications. This is why any segregation between Zola's characters in relation to sexuality would be unfortunate and unjustified. In this perspective - where every agent has the capacity to become a sexual subject from one moment to another -, the function of the primary sender is attributed to the main narrator who is the supreme *"force vectorielle"* in the view of Claude Bremond[342]. The Zolian narrator, like a rancorous Greek god, breathes a stormy and a devastating passion into Phaedrus, the symbol of all sexual subjects and pushes her to begin a quest to tame one or more sexual objects. The recipients are sometimes the selfishness of the sexual subject itself or their desire to become rich. Sometimes the goal is the satisfaction of some reprehensible sexual instincts or simply the justification of the theory of heredity elaborated by Zola. The adjuvants are the historical era of the Second Empire, the narrative times and spaces, the passivity of the parents and/or the spouses of the sexual object. In front of such panoply of adjuvants, one observes only a few rare forces likely to obstruct them on the way to the satisfaction of their excessive and rampant sexuality.

---

[341] Michel Raimond borrows that theory of the narrative fonctions from Claude Bremond and Souriau, in **Le Roman**, Paris, Armand Colin, 1989, p. 86.
[342] Claude Bremond : *La Logique des Possibles Narratifs* in **Communications, 8**, op. cit. p. 68.

There are still a few opponents in the corpus. Naturally, the function of opponents in the field of sexuality in the novels of Zola is reduced to the tiniest portion. Only the priests - and often the jealousy of the spouses of the coveted sexual objects - do furnish the category of opponents. It goes without saying that they do not constitute any real counterweight which could annihilate the inclinations of the vast coalition of the very many adjuvants.

For example, in **La Curée,** the corrupt environment of Paris[343], plus the no less corrupt era of the Second Empire[344], are fertile grounds for the consumption of incest between Renée and Maxime especially since the husband - and father – Aristide, shows no jealousy[345] whatsoever, nor does he exercise any control over his wife. Céleste and Mrs. Sidonie firmly stand together with the incestuous as their accomplices and suddenly, there is no real opposition body that can - or is willing - to confront the lovers. To that end, one can draw a general and canonical actantial diagram which encompasses the whole theme of sexuality in **Les Rougon-Macquart:**

Diagram n°. 1

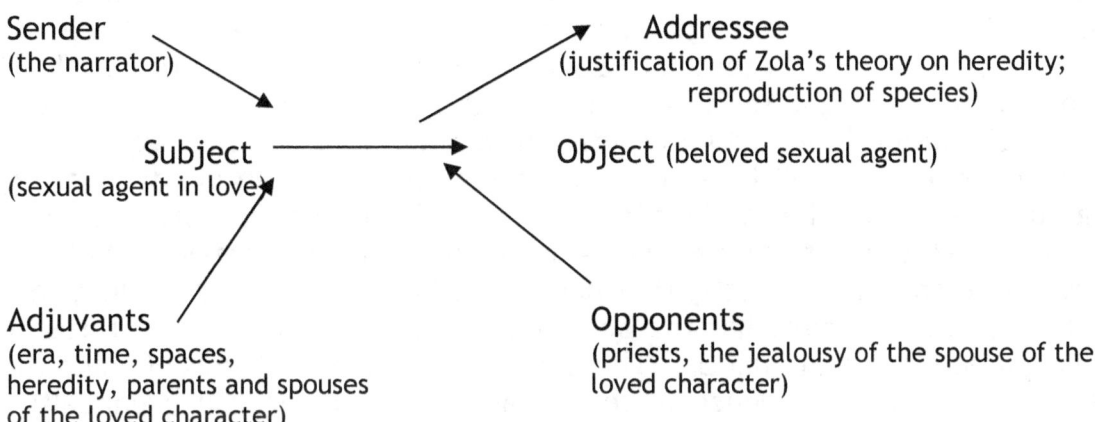

This first diagram shows that in Zola's novels, the narrator is not neutral. On the contrary, he is the bearer of both a political and a literary ideology because he holds the Second Empire responsible for the outrageous debauchery that was shaking France at the time. In any case, we can agree with Bertrand-Jennings who perceived that **Nana** in particular was an allegory for the whole Second Empire regime: << *C'est volontairement que Zola a fait de Nana l'allégorie de*

---

[343] Maarten Van Buuren : **Les Rougon-Macquart d'Émile Zola. De la Métaphore au Mythe**, op. cit. pp. 72-73.

[344] **Ibidem**, p. 144, Maarten Van Buuren writes : << *La serre évoque la société sous le Second Empire en raccourci. C'est un symbole particulièrement puissant parce qu'il présente le progrès industriel, la révolution bancaire, l'altération des relations humaines comme le résultat d'une culture épuisante qui, aux yeux de Zola, doit mener inéluctablement à la dégénérescence des organismes sociaux* >>.

[345] In this, Saccard is diametrically opposed (and ironically enough) to Thésée according to Roger Ripoll, in **Réalité et Mythe chez Zola**, op. cit. p. 73.

l'Empire, et de son roman sur la courtisane, la geste de la décomposition d'une société et d'une civilisation par la contagion du vice et de la débauche. Née avec le Second Empire, Nana mourra en 1870 avec lui, alors que la foule dans la rue hurle << À Berlin ! >>>>[346].

The theme of sexuality also allowed Zola to elaborate and justify the theory of heredity that was the foundation of his novelistic aesthetics: naturalism. The omnipotence of heredity in the corpus also marks the victory of biology over culture as expressed by McLynn: << [...] *in this world there is no moral agent available to mediate the demands of culture and biology. Family, religion and all other agents of cultural formation seem absent, so that biology triumphs* >>[347]. This triumph of biology is nothing but the fatality of sexuality.

Sometimes it happens that characters become the occasional recipients of the sexuality of other characters, including their parents. That is when marriages for sale occur in the corpus. For example, Mr. de Mareuil "buys" a husband - Maxime Rougon dit Saccard - for his daughter, Louise de Mareuil, in **La Curée**. It can also be mentioned the reverse narrative episode that happens when Aristide Rougon dit Saccard "sells" his son, Maxime, to Louise de Mareuil because of the enticing dowry of one million francs offered by her father. That type of fiduciary contract is also present in **L'Œuvre** when the Margaillans literally "buy" Dubuche for their daughter, Estelle. It should be noted that the two sexual agents, Louise and Estelle, similarly suffer from lung disease. The degradation of their physique – or shall I say their degeneration – and the lung disease are two factors that justify the need for them to "*buy themselves healthy spouses*". In **Les Rougon-Macquart**, money makes up for ugliness and disease[348] but the healthy sexual object is so costly that one has to be rich to afford it. In Zola's view, the industrial society has the peculiarity to reduce man to the status of mere vulgar goods sold at auction. This translation of man in terms of value for money is the ultimate evidence of the decadence of society since unhealthy wives will soon spread degeneracy within the entire society by means of contagion.

The recipients are therefore not only the nubile but sick young girls, but also and above all, the selfishness and the vanity of their parents, and, to a lesser degree, the healthy spouses. The first category aspires to live a flourished sexuality in the arms of healthy young men full of life. The second wants to satisfy their vanity by marrying their sick and ugly daughters to the most eligible and the most handsome bachelors in town. The latter simply sold their health to the highest bidder.

---

[346] Chantal Bertrand-Jennings: **L'Éros et la Femme chez Zola**, op. cit. p. 72.
[347] Pauline McLynn: *Human Beasts ? Criminal perspectives in* **La Bête Humaine** in **Zola, La Bête Humaine : Colloque du Centenaire à Glasgow, texte et explication**, Geoff Woollen (éd.), op. cit. p. 133.
[348] On the links between money and sexuality, please refer to Maarten Van Buuren's **Les Rougon-Macquart d'Émile Zola. De la Métaphore au Mythe**, op. cit. p. 175.

The following actantial diagrams 2 and 3 will illustrate such narrative statements:

Diagram n°. 2 :

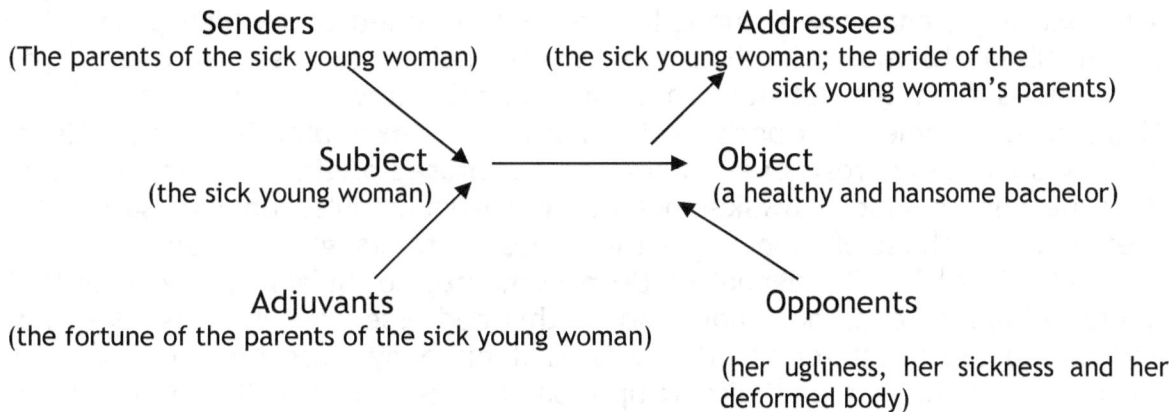

Diagram n°. 3 :

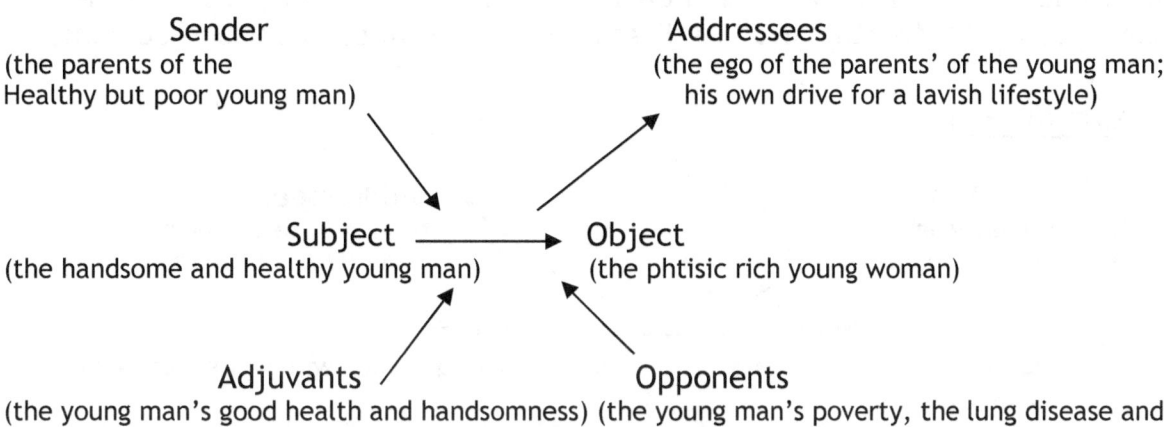

Thus, in **Les Rougon-Macquart**, sexuality squarely belongs to the field of transactions and business[349], in the purely economic sense of the word. It must be pointed out that all those actantial diagrams have got one thing in common: selfishness. It is all about selfishness and covetousness in the end to the point where there are no borders nor differences between the categories of the sender, the addressee, the adjuvants and the opponents. They are all the same as they only get married in order to satisfy their greed. Only the subject and the

---

[349] David Baguley, taking interest in the absence of affection of any kind between Saccard and his wife, Renée, wrote: << *Et le seul baiser qu'il lui donne dans le roman, "le baiser sur le cou", devient "peu à peu la révélation de toute une nouvelle tactique" d'agiotage. C'est la curée qui "bénit" leur mariage* >>, in **Zola et Les Genres**, op. cit. p. 37.

In the same line of argument, please refer also to, **Les Rougon-Macquart d'Émile Zola. De la Métaphore au Mythe** by Maarten Van Buuren, op. cit. pp. 174-176.

object are different and are the complete opposite of each other. In **Les Rougon-Macquart**, money buys love and spouses so to speak.

Further along, it must be pointed out that sexuality often depends on another type of factor, for example the neuroses and the normal or the instinctive sexual drive. In the perspective of neuroses, the function of the receiver is held by a paradoxical instance that cannot be precisely grasped and which pushes the sexual subject to undertake their quest to take hold of their sexual object. The recipient is then the satisfaction of a homicidal drive, a desire to kill[350] - Thanatos -, or some other perverse inclination. For example, Jacques Lantier is disturbed by the neurosis of a distant and a confused origin, the demon within. He experiments sudden awakenings of his sexual impulse only to satisfy his overwhelming thirst of blood. He then goes on to slaughter a female with a white cleavage[351]. Throughout **La Bête Humaine**, he suffers the diktat of that sender whom he does not know and of this addressee of whom he does not understand the thirst for blood. It is as if his body were hosting two alien personalities; one of them building up a peculiar sexual appetite and the other bringing about the impulse for murder - known today as *féminicide*. Their heavy influence always clashes with his own personality in terms of terrible suffering - migraine - and self-incrimination each time he is defeated by his other self[352]. Let us draw this fourth narrative diagram to represent such episode demonic:

Diagram n°. 4:

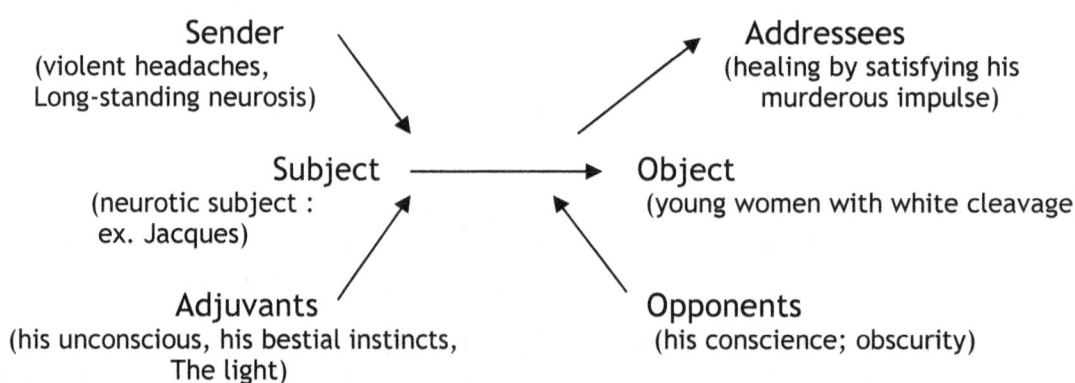

It is easy to see here that the consciousness and the unconscious of the sexual subject engage in a fierce battle for the control of the subject at the inner level.

---

[350] The book of Maarten Van Buuren asserts the same: **Les Rougon-Macquart d'Émile Zola. De la Métaphore au Mythe**, op. cit. p. 192.

[351] Claude Seassau thinks that: << *Le personnage le plus proche de la bête est Jacques Lantier : en tuant Séverine il a un << grognement de sanglier >>. Dans la symbolique chrétienne le sanglier est le symbole du démon. Jacques, à cause de sa maladie, semble habité par un démon dont l'action se traduit par l'obsession de tuer une femme* >>, in **Émile Zola, Le Réalisme Symbolique**, op. cit. pp. 59-60.

[352] On the question of the superiority of the "*ça*" on the "*moi*" in humans, please read the book by Maarten Van Buuren, cited above, op. cit. pp. 60-61.

On the outer level, darkness and light are also fighting each other. The former stifles the impulse for murder while the latter awakens and exacerbates it. That is why Jacques Lantier persists in making love only in total darkness like a modern wizard or a vampire. Darkness is the only way for him to suppress his drive for murder and to keep it in check. Symbolically, the association of this subject's consciousness with darkness is undoubtedly a phenomenon of demonisation that condemns him forever[353] as a prince of darkness. That is why Jacques is both an ambiguous, an enigmatic, a paradoxical and a diabolical sexual subject at the same time.

Finally, the ordinary sexual drive as a recipient leads to the search for the sexual object in certain subjects in order to satisfy their instincts or simply for the purpose of procreation. Adjuvants are then very numerous at the expense of the few - and often too weak - opponents to support the power of adversity. The reader can therefore foresee a strong debauchery[354] in **Les Rougon-Macquart** from this categorisation of characters that emerges in this fifth actantial diagram:

Diagram n°. 5 :

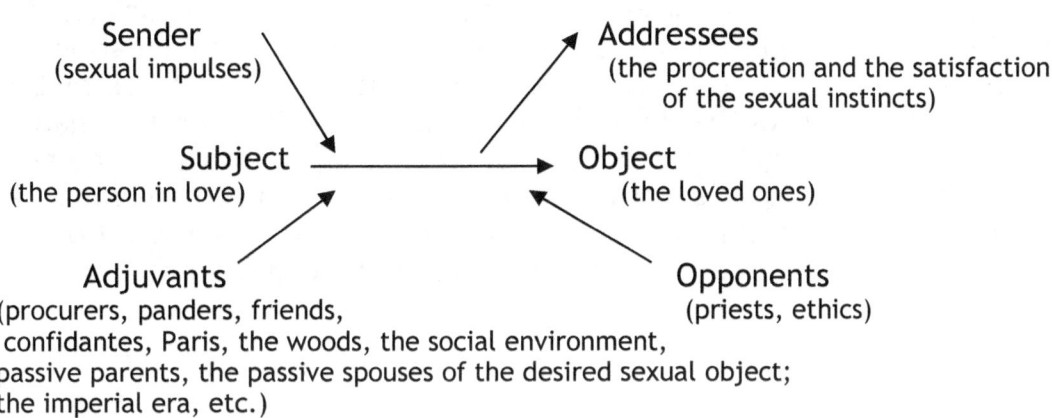

This study of the being of the characters has shown that they are all sexually determined. That determinism is valid for both the anthropomorphic and the non-anthropomorphic sexual agents - contrary to what has been argued by Philippe Hamon[355]. Indeed, it has been shown that nature could be a real destinator, a sexual object and subject at the same time. Similarly, extremely important male sexual subjects have been revealed throughout this chapter,

---

[353] Jacques Noiray points out that: <<Les ténèbres sont donc pour Zola, dans leur opacité liquide, un élément menaçant qui submerge et qui tue>>, in **Le Romancier et la Machine, I : L'Univers de Zola**, op. cit. p. 303.
[354] David Baguley argues that adultery is an eminently literary theme, and that it is preponderant in naturalist writers's works in general, in **Naturalist Fiction. The Entropic Vision**, op. cit. p. 207.
[355] Philippe Hamon amazingly assured, in **Le Personnel du Roman. Le Système des Personnages dans Les Rougon-Macquart d'Émile Zola**, that Paris, Nature and the Machine were non-sexual entities, op. cit. p. 20.

such as Cabuche, Grandmorin, Jacques and Claude Lantier, or Octave Mouret and Florent. This reinforces my position in favour of a fairer treatment of the characters in the field of sexuality and against any segregation in favour of the female gender[356] only. I can therefore make the following statement: any study that does not take into account the mythical dimension of Zola's characters would be incomplete like the one that Philippe Hamon did. To sum things up, the being of Zola's character is first of all about their sex or gender; which is at the origin of their birth; which is often transparent in their name, in their qualifications, and which motivates their relationships with their fellow characters. Sex is therefore for the character in Zola's works as a burden which they cannot get rid of; and which can lead them to destroy others or to self-destroy. At the end of the day, sex appears to be the social ferment that poisons the world of the Second Empire and that which will ultimately bring about the downfall of Napoléon III's regime.

After the superposition of the texts of the corpus, which constitutes the first of the four main operations with regard to the psychoanalytic method, it is necessary to examine in depth the interpersonal relationships which constitute the last stage of the analysis of the character in the understanding of the structuralists. The sexual relationship is, in fact, reflexive - for the inversions -, reciprocal - for the accepted norm - and neurotic, as far as the sublimation and the neuropsychic transfer of the beloved one are concerned. All those factors put sexuality at the heart of the field of psychoanalysis. This is why my analysis in the following chapter will be profoundly marked by the psychocritical method, especially with Sigmund Freud's works. It will also equally be strongly marked by semiotics in the sense that it is necessary to study the manifestations of sexuality in the specific textual space of the **Rougon-Macquart** series.

---

[356] This is the main weakness of the study by Chantal Bertrand-Jennings in **L'Éros et la Femme chez Zola**, op. cit. Let us reiterate that Philippe Hamon had also had the same tendency when working on the sexuality of Zola's characters in his book **Le Personnel du Roman. Le Système des Personnages dans Les Rougon-Macquart d'Émile Zola**, op. cit. p. 191.

CHAPITRE II : THE DEEDS AND THE BECOMING OF THE CHARACTER OR THEIR PERFORMANCE AND THEIR SANCTION

The whole of this following chapter will be treated in the light of the semioticians of the Groupe d'Entrevernes' theory, which is all about *"le faire-être"* of the character or their performance, then *"la reconnaissance"* or *"la sanction"* of the character. In other words, what do the sexual agents do and what is the consequence of doing so? Are they rewarded or blamed for their various performances related to the satisfaction of their sexual instincts? What is the fatal consequences that is awaiting them at the end of their sexual performances?

I. THE *"FAIRE-ÊTRE"* OF THE CHARACTER OR THEIR PERFORMANCE

The *"être-être"*, in the semiotics approach, represents everything the character does in the narrative. It will be studied in its various components for I am attempting to shine a light on the networks of interpersonal relationships and the system of operations which constitute the deep level in the semiotics analysis of the narrative.

1.1. The system of operations related to sexuality

It has been shown above, in the onomastic exploitation of the characters, that they were bestialised or mythified in order to accentuate the predictability of their bestial, or monstrous, or even diabolical sexuality. Sexual subjects are arranged in a dichotomous way in the corpus. Indeed, when a subject-operator wants to enter into a relation of conjunction with any given value-object, there is also another subject-operator who covets that same value-object. From there arises the phenomenon of jealousy which is very common[357] in **Les Rougon-Macquart**.

The relation of conjunction between a subject-operator and its value-object is noted (S∧O), and the relation of disjunction, (SVO). I will use those symbols following the semioticians of the Groupe d'Entrevernes. Let us recall from the outset that there is a conjunction when a subject enters into possession of their value-object and, conversely, the disjunction indicates that they have lost that value-object.

1.1.1. Conjunction and disjunction

---

[357] For further reading on this topic, please refer to Claude Seassau: **Émile Zola, Le Réalisme Symbolique**, op. cit. pp. 198-199.

Thus the (S1∧O) is opposed to (S2VO), or, globally, we obtain: (S1∧OVS2). This doubling down of the statement of enounciation indicates that the sexual-value-object acquired by the subject (S1) is de facto lost by subject (S2). For example, in **La Curée**, when Maxime earns Renée's love, her former lovers - such as M. de Mussy or M. de Saffré - lose her de facto as a sexual value-object because she finds them << *assommants* >>[358] from that point on and dumps them for good.

But the acquiring subject may lose their acquisition also in different circumstances such as death, madness, loss of sex drive, etc. Those relationships of disjunction show that the sexual acquisition is fragile and not sedentary by any means. The reader thus sees in **La Bête Humaine**, Roubaud (S1), who adores and marries Séverine (O), to establish the following conjunction (S1∧O), before abandoning her following the murder perpetrated on Président Grandmorin, his rival, thus establishing a disjunctive state of transformation (S1∧OVS1). In **La Conquête de Plassans**, Mouret (S1), locked up by Father Faujas, ''loses'' his wife, Marthe Rougon (O)[359], in a transitive operation or dispossession. The disjunctive performance realised here by the priest (S2), is a dispossession of which François Mouret is the victim. That is why he returns home to take revenge by setting the family home ablaze:

(S1∧O) ⟶ (S1VO), which can also be noted as (S1∧OVS1). I will come back to this narrative statement in Chapter II of Part Three.

It may happen, however, that a sexual subject voluntarily surrenders their sexual value-object to another competing sexual subject. I will call such operation a gift.

1.1.2. The gift

Some cases of gifts are available in Zola's works but it is useful to define what is meant by ''test'' and ''donation or gift'' before giving a few examples. The term *épreuve* – or test - refers to the concomitance of appropriation and dispossession while the gift or donation is the concomitance of renunciation and attribution. The latter takes place in a peaceful background and the former in a conflictual background. Specifically, in **La Bête Humaine**, the attitude of abandonment of Séverine by Roubaud is a renunciation or a surrender[360]. The adultery between her with Jacques Lantier is an attribution since the legitimate

---

[358] Émile Zola: **R. M. I**, op. cit. p.327.
[359] Refer to Chantal Bertrand-Jennings' argument on female hysteria and the sexual deviation based on the examples of Marthe Mouret and Clotilde Rougon, in **L'Éros et la Femme chez Zola**, op. cit. p. 50.
[360] For Philippe Hamon, in **Le Personnel du Roman. Le Système des Personnages dans les Rougon-Macquart d'Émile Zola**, the ludic activity renders sexuality non-existent in Zola's works, op. cit. p. 204. Indeed, when Roubaud gets heavily involved in gambling, he appears to have surrendered all of his sexual urges, and even his very virility to gambling to the detriment of his flesh.

husband, Roubaud, is consenting to the affair to the point where he puts the lover of his wife on guard against the actions of another suitor who could dispossess him of his mistress! Between Roubaud and Jacques, there is therefore an operation of donation or of renunciation.

In **Nana**, on the other hand, Count Muffat, by securing Nana as a sexual value-object, dispossesses the banker Steiner to the great displeasure of the latter. This means that Count Muffat has put his rival to the test, a test he could not pass. The conflictual background of the test only disappears when the two rivals agree to exchange their valuables.

1.1.3. The exchange or the contract

Thus, emerges the phenomenon of exchange which turns out to be a double performance of gift; for if subject S1 enters into conjunction with an object O1, it is on the one hand - concomitantly - in disjunction with an object O2:

$$(S1 \wedge O1) \longrightarrow (S1 \vee O2).$$

On the other hand, the object O2 is in conjunction with a subject S2: (S1) and (S2) then execute an operation of exchange. It is in this dialectic that one must read the marriage of Maxime (S1) and Louise de Mareuil (S2) in **La Curée**. Their value-objects, respectively (O1) and (O2) were on the one hand the money to be gained in terms of dowry, the health, the beauty and the love to be obtained on the other hand. The case of Dubuche and Estelle de Margaillan, in **L'Œuvre**, is analogous to that of Maxime and Louise de Mareuil in every respect.

Schematically, we can establish the following diagram: State 1: $(O1 \wedge S1 \vee O2)$ vs $(O1 \vee S2 \wedge O2)$. But the transformation of the performative deed or exchange operation gives the following line:

$$F(S) \longrightarrow [(O1 \vee S1 \wedge O2) \longrightarrow (O1 \wedge S2 \vee O2)].$$

However, this operation is done according to a fiduciary contract, that is to say on the basis of an agreement on the value of the *"objects"* exchanged. So, the handsome and *"healthy"* Maxime sells those qualities of his that are well worth the ugliness, the chronic disease and one million francs of Louise. The former who was in disjunction with wealth and in conjunction with health, handsomeness and hence with love. He ended up entering into conjunction with the much-desired wealth by getting married to Louise. Still, he goes on to lose his health while in contact with that sickly woman who poisons him slowly. As for Louise, she loses a million francs by marrying Maxime but, in return, she gets the love she was desperately seeking. She secures a relative health and happiness by getting married to a handsome and healthy young man. This narrative diagram is also valid for Estelle - who mirrors Louise - and for Dubuche - who mirrors Maxime.

This is the place to point out that in Zola's fiction, the subject-operator is often subjected to the pressure of the modaliser or the recipient. For example, still in **La Curée**, it is Aristide Saccard, as a modaliser, who convinces his son, Maxime, so that he agrees to marry Louise, although he is not really in love with her. Let us remember, nevertheless, that the subject-operator could do nothing without the acquisition of different modal values or competence. This acquisition is made during the *"modalités de la virtualité"*, of *"l'actualité"*, of *"la réalité"*, or simply in a *"système de modalités"*.

1.1.4. The virtuality

As far as virtuality is concerned, one must distinguish the subject-operator from the addressee. Indeed, the subject-operator wants to do or must do something, like Renée who seeks << *une jouissance rare* >> that she conceives as an irreducible need. The sender, or whoever communicates << *le désir de l'inceste* >> to her, is nothing but << *l'ennui* >>, or what Baudelaire named << *le spleen* >>. There is virtuality in Chapter I of **La Curée** when Renée puts into perspective a fact - not yet actualised - yet it is a fact which is specified by the discovery of her love for Maxime and leading up to the full consumption of the incest:

$$F(S) \longrightarrow [(S1 \vee Om) \longrightarrow (S1 \wedge Om)].$$

The subject (S1), Renée, who has not yet conquered her modal object (Om), the incest, initiates a process of virtual accomplishment of that incest. But the attribution performance of the modalities of virtuality or a *"contrat de manipulation"* that is subdivided into a *"communication transitive"* or reciprocal feeling such as boredom, as in the case of Maxime and Renée, and in a *"communication réfléchie"*, like in the case of Dubuche, who alone combines the roles of the sender and that of the subject-operator. Indeed, no other character asks him to marry Estelle de Margaillan if not his own will to free himself from his poor living conditions to reach the bourgeoisie. As a result, he remains a subject-operator engaged in a quest motivated by himself. At the antipodes of virtuality lies the actuality.

1.1.5. The actuality

The modalities of the actuality, unlike the /must-do/ and the /will-do/ virtuality, are a /power-to-do/ and a /know-how/. The qualifying performance of the /know-how/ or the /power-to-do/ is transformed into the qualifying modalities, which are narrative progresses when we move from the virtuality to the actualisation or realisation. In **L'Œuvre**, such is the neurotic libidinal relationship that unites Claude Lantier with his painting /know-how/ - or his *techné* - and an effective /power-to-do/. Knowing how to paint, he creates paintings to which he devotes all his love to the detriment of his legitimate wife[361], thus falling into sexual fetishism. The bridge between actuality and reality is easy to cross though.

1.1.6. The reality

With regard to the modality of reality - *"le faire"*, it is neither more nor less than a deed in its raw state, or if one prefers, the realisation of a performance by a subject-operator. In this respect, let us mention, among other things, the incest between Renée and Maxime. Renée establishes such a modality of reality when she conquers Maxime's effective love after the dinner at the Café Riche. In **Nana**, Nana and the brothers Georges and Philippe Hugon, Nana and Count Muffat - and his son-in-law Daguenet - and then with the Marquis de Chouard - the one who is spoiled or who falls apart[362] -, or the incest between Dr. Pascal Rougon and his niece, Clotilde Rougon, in **Le Docteur Pascal**, or even the incest between Buteau and his sister-in-law, Françoise, the incest between Hilarion and his sister, Palmyre, then his attempted rape on his grandmother, La Grande, in **La Terre**, are all examples of realities in the context of incest alone. It must be understood that the examples are legion too when it comes to other sexual aberrations. All this shows that sexuality is a widespread phenomenon in **Le Rougon-Macquart** and especially that it is realised or consumed very often without the slightest regard for social morality nor for religious morality. The literary world of Zola is that of sexual depravity on a gigantic scale.

By extension, I must stress that there is an abundant cruelty inherent to sexuality[363] in Zola's works of which there are numerous examples in **La Curée** with the brutal rape of Renée in the country; the rape and murder of Françoise[364] in **La Terre**. The murders of Séverine, of Grandmorin, of Aunt Phasie, of Jacques Lantier and Pecqueux, the murder of twenty passengers of La Lison, then the

---

[361] According to Philippe Hamon in **Le Personnel du Roman. Le Système des Personnages dans Les Rougon-Macquart d'Émile Zola**, Claude wastes his sexuality on his art – painting – and on the virtual women he has painted, op. cit. p. 88.

We can also read in David Baguley's **Zola et les Genres**, that Claude sacrifices himself to the ideal woman, op. cit. p. 88.

For Neide de Faria, *la Femme* (represented onto a canvas) eats up the life of Claude, see **Les Rougon-Macquart d'Émile Zola (la poétique du cycle)**, op. cit. p. 262.

[362] Chantal Bertrand-Jennings thinks that: << *Dans* **Nana** *le principe de mort est représenté par le vieux marquis de Chouard,* << *ce coin de charnier* >> *venu échouer dans le lit de la courtisane* >>, in **L'Éros et la Femme chez Zola**, op. cit. p. 17.

[363] On the extreme sexual violence (of which the greedy consumption would be the cardinal image), please refer to **Émile Zola, Le Réalisme Symbolique** by Claude Seassau, op. cit. pp. 187-260.

[364] I can agree with Jacques Noiray's argument in **Le Romancier et la Machine, I : L'Univers de Zola** for whom Flore's suicide is no less than a rape and a loss of virginity, op. cit. p. 423 ; one might even consider that rape is again the true loss of virginity as far as Françoise is concerned in **La Terre**, since she has never had any orgasm nor even the slightest sexual pleasure with her husband, Jean Macquart, neither when he took her virginity nor during the course of their marriage. Nonetheless, when Buteau rapes her, Françoise experiences orgasm for the very first and only time in her life.

suggested mass murder of hundreds – or thousands, maybe - of soldiers whose fate is unknown in **La Bête Humaine**. All those tragedies have a common denominator: jealousy. That is why that novel is the one << *où la bête humaine est vraiment déchaînée* >> according to Neide de Faria[365]. Vandeuvres and Georges Hugon's suicide in **Nana**; the pyromania of Tron, the murder of Hourdequin in **La Terre**; finally, the pyromania and the suicide of Mouret in **La Conquête de Plassans**, are so many reasons to persuade Bertrand-Jennings that certainly: << *on ne jouit donc jamais impunément dans les romans zoliens où les personnages vivent comme Renée Saccard dans la crainte que* << *le mal fût puni tôt ou tard* >>>>[366]. All those occurrences give credit to the negative remark made a moment ago. And, as if that were not enough, premature sexuality is added to that already very long list of sexual depravations and wickedness.

One can also observe cases of sexual premature characters especially in **La Fortune des Rougon** with Miette, Silvère[367] and Gervaise; in **L'Argent** with Victor Rougon dit Saccard; in **La Curée** with Maxime and Renée; Georges Hugon in **Nana**, Nana in **L'Assommoir**; Delphin, Nénesse and La Trouille in **La Terre**; the maids in **Pot-Bouille**; Catherine Maheu in **Germinal**, etc. But it must be remembered that in Zola's fiction works, premature sexuality calls for an early death as part of the system of modalities.

1.2. The system of modalities

That system is divided into an *"obéissance active"* - /devoir-faire/ + /vouloir-faire/ -, in an *"obéissance passive"* - /ne pas devoir-ne pas faire/ + /ne pas vouloir-ne pas faire/ -, in a *"résistance active"* - /devoir-faire/ + /vouloir ne pas faire/ - and lastly, in a *"résistance passive"* - /ne pas devoir-ne pas faire/ + /ne pas vouloir-ne pas faire/. Sexuality is dominated by attempts at seduction, persuasion or conversion. It is the domain par excellence of the system of modalities. In details, I will move from the obedient sexual agents to those who are resistant, with, of course, both the passive and the active variants in each case.

1.2.1. The Passive obedience

Applied to the corpus, this study reveals that on the axis of passive obedience, there is an incredible amount of sexual agents among which one can mention only Duveyrier, La Torchon d'Adèle, Clarisse and all the sexual conquests in **Pot-Bouille**; Claude Lantier and Séverine in **La Bête Humaine**; Adélaïde Fouque,

---

[365] Neide de Faria : **Structure et Unité dans Les Rougon-Macquart de Zola (la poétique du cycle)**, op. cit. p. 84.
[366] Chantal Bertrand-Jennings : **L'Éros et la Femme chez Zola**, op. cit. p. 13.
[367] Bertrand-Jennings considers that Miette and Silvère experience the << *désir du néant, de la mort* >>, just like Serge Mouret and Étienne Lantier in: **L'Éros et la Femme chez Zola**, op. cit. p. 34.

Macquart, Miette[368], Silvère, Antoine and Fine, Gervaise[369] and Lantier in **La Fortune des Rougon**; Nana and her many lovers in **Nana**; Hélène Grandjean and the Doctor Deberle in **Une Page d'Amour**; La Cognette and her many lovers in **La Terre**; la Mouquette and hers, Maigrat and the wives of the miners in **Germinal**, to quote only those few. Let us note that the passive obedients are the agents who undergo the sexual assaults of their counterparts without trying any real resistance, even if their own sexual appetite does not attract them to their assailants. For example, Nana, who does not like Count Muffat, passively becomes his mistress only because she needs his money. Like a prostitute, she does not choose the figure of her client. The same goes for the wives of the miners who sleep with the trader, Maigrat, for foodstuff and other items that they could not buy otherwise because they were made destitute after a long strike[370]. The passive obedient is therefore an agent who is not necessarily in love with their partner. Consequently, they are sexually exploited for a certain interest – money or food. Yet, in the corpus, active obedients are by far the majority when it comes to sexuality.

1.2.2. The Active obedience

At one point or another, all agents rush to assault their sexual objects with one motto: climax the most, climax at all costs! Thus, the active obedience on the axis of sexuality shows that the characters in the **Rougon-Macquart** series are almost all willing to engage into debauchery: paedophilia - Baron Gouraud in **La Curée**, Grandmorin in **La Bête Humaine** -, paederasty - Baptist in **La Curée** -; lesbianism - Satin and Mme Robert in **Nana**; Suzanne Haffner and Adeline d'Espanet in **La Curée**; sexual morbidity - Jacques and Cabuche in **La Bête Humaine** and Claude Lantier in **L'Œuvre**; hermaphroditism - Maxime, Renée and Mme Sidonie in **La Curée**; Miette and Fine Macquart, née Gavaudan in **La Fortune Des Rougon** and Flore in **La Bête Humaine**; and excessive adultery throughout almost the entire corpus - especially with Octave Mouret and Mme Berthe Vabre and Marie Pichon[371] in **Pot-Bouille**; Jacques and Séverine, Pecqueux and

---

[368] Chantal Bertrand-Jennings, suggests that Miette attracts and seduces Silvère, leading him to commit sin, in **L'Éros et la Femme chez Zola**, op. cit. p. 54.

[369] In **Émile Zola, Le Réalisme Symbolique**, op. cit. pp. 208-212, Claude Seassau distinguishes a trio of young girls (Gervaise, Catherine and Séverine) who undergo sexual intercourse without pleasure, at least during their tender age.

[370] Claude Seassau admits that << *Maigrat fait chèrement payer ses marchandises,* [and that] *il ne consent à faire crédit au mineur qui ne peut payer qu'à la condition que la femme ou les filles du mineur acceptent ses avances, afin d'abuser d'elles. Maigrat est un oppresseur et un exploiteur, tout autant que le capital (et les mineurs en révolte s'attaqueront à lui) ; il s'apparente aux riches, à ceux qui sont gras, que le mot maigre tente de cacher dans << Maigrat >>*, in **Émile Zola, Le Réalisme Symbolique**, op. cit., p. 37.

[371] For Philippe Hamon, in **Le Personnel du Roman. Le Système des Personnages dans Les Rougon-Macquart d'Émile Zola**, she is a victim of << *une enfance prolongée* >>, just like Saturnin Josserand, Désirée Mouret, Cabuche, Flore, Colomban, Rosalie and Quenu, op. cit. p. 202.

Philomène, Séverine[372] and Grandmorin in **La Bête Humaine**; Maxime and Renée, the unknown Georges, Renée and M. de Saffré, M. de Mussy, the US Embassy employee, Ms. Michelin and Baron Gouraud in **La Curée**; Rose Mignon and her lovers, then Nana and hers in **Nana**; Aunt Dide and Father Macquart in **La Fortune des Rougon**; Buteau and Françoise, La Bécu and Jésus Christ - this is Zola's fornicating Jesus, ultimate blasphemy and supreme rejection of the vow of chastity advocated by the Catholic Church -, La Trouille and her young lovers, La Cognette and hers in **La Terre**. But I will stop there for the sake of concision. In such an atmosphere, what would be the extent of a possible resistance if it ever existed?

Although weak and sporadic, resistance to sexuality exists in the corpus in two forms, one passive and the other active.

1.2.3. The passive resistance

On this axis, there stand Françoise, who passively resists Buteau in **La Terre**; Séverine does as much before Cabuche and Jacques Lantier before Flore in **La Bête Humaine**. Finally, Baptiste resists women in **La Curée**. The low abundance of sexual agents on this axis is a clear proof that the characters in the corpus are almost all dependent on their libido and that they are no masters of their primary instincts. In addition to the passive resistant characters, there are some active resistant ones who will be questioned before we draw a conclusion on the system of modalities.

1.2.4. The active resistance

This last component of the system of modalities is furnished only by a minority of sexual agents, including Louise in front of Grandmorin in **La Bête Humaine**; the priest Faujas in front of Marthe Mouret in **La Conquête de Plassans**; and Florent[373] fiercely resists La Belle Normande in **Le Ventre de Paris**. So, in total, there are three active sexual resistant agents in front of their stalkers. That shows that resistance to temptation is no easy task in Zola's works. However, an ambiguous case can be mentioned in this category, namely the Cabinet Minister Eugène Rougon, the Home Secretary who has little interest in women despite his actual presence in four of the **Rougon-Macquart** novels. Nonetheless, he excludes himself from the category of active resistance because of his libidinal and intellectual relationship with the political power he regards *"amoureusement"*. He ends up sleeping with Clorinde, a weakness that signalled

---

[372] Chantal Bertrand-Jennings believes that sexuality is imposed on certain characters as a fatality from the outside; outside their own will or their personal dissipation indeed. They are mainly Étienne Lantier, Catherine, Jean, Françoise, Séverine, Cabuche, Louisette, Goujet and Gervaise, see **L'Éros et la Femme chez Zola**, op. cit. p. 30.

[373] According to Philippe Hamon in **Le Personnel du Roman. Le Système des Personnages dans les Rougon-Macquart d'Émile Zola**, Florent wastes his sexuality too by living in utopia and daydream, p. 204.

his political disgrace and downfall for there is no room for both politics and women in his love life. By giving in to a woman, he sacrificed his political fortunes and got sacked from the Cabinet.

Similarly, abbé Faujas[374] can be excluded from this category because he is so pushy and bossy that he manages to take over wherever he goes, including in other people's homes. By voraciously imposing himself on others, as if he found there a particular enjoyment, is he not achieving that way another type of libidinal satisfaction?[375] On the other hand, Florent's resistance is a curious case of sex phobia. But the sex phobia is a sin in the eyes of Zola since it supposes the refusal of fertility and reproduction. It is, in a word, a form of death.

For the sake of clarity, the system of modalities can be drawn as follows:

The terms on the same axis or on the same line are antithetical and are mutually and logically implied. Chiasmatic arrows have the same character of logical implication. It must be understood that all the characters mentioned above necessarily belong to one of the categories represented in those two diagrams. The performance, or the deed of the being that is the character manifests itself by means of total sexual bulimia, an excess of vice and litter that will cause the loss of the Second Empire: << *le thème majeur – thème prétexte, sans doute, mais qui a son importance – des* **Rougon-Macquart**, *c'est l'épopée d'un régime décadent et corrompu qui court à la catastrophe finale en causant tous les maux* >>[376]. The remark that arises from that is that in Zola's novels, adultery and other sexual vices are a regular and a highly iterative theme, as if the author were the unconscious victim of an obsession in the field of the libido[377].

---

[374] One can consider that he belongs to the category of what Philippe Hamon calls *la libido dominandi,* in **Le Personnel du Roman. Le Système des Personnages dans les Rougon-Macquart d'Émile Zola**, op. cit. p. 236.

[375] Chantal Bertrand-Jennings points out in **L'Éros et la Femme chez Zola,** that Eugène falls out of favour with the Emperor when he becomes weak in front of Clorinde, op. cit. p. 81.

For Maarten Van Buuren, Clorinde, Eugène Rougon and abbé Faujas are simply some << *personnages blindés, forts, impassibles* >>, who resist efficiently to the urges of the flesh, see **Les Rougon-Macquart d'Émile Zola. De la Métaphore au Mythe**, op. cit. p. 232.

[376] Chantal Bertrand-Jennings: **L'Éros et la Femme chez Zola**, op. cit. p. 73.

[377] Let us recall that according to Claude Seassau, in **Émile Zola, Le Réalisme Symbolique**, this is more of a controversial and of a satirical intention than a realistic and a truthful painting of the imperial society, op. cit. p. 203.

This is the time to take a look at some sexual performances in **Les Rougon-Macquart**.

1.3. Studying some specific performances

This is about studying the cases of the chaste and the virtuous sexuality before approaching those that are tainted by perversion and incest.

1.3.1. The "virtuous and chaste" characters

The use of quotation marks is justified here inasmuch as this chastity and virtue are quite relative and contextual because the reality is that no character in Zola's universe is exempt from reproach on the thematic axis of sexuality. As a result, these two qualities become rather semblances of quality since the "virtue" in question is really positioned as a deviation or a sexual inhibition, or even as the result of a proper neurosis.

In addition to that, the characters who can claim to fit in this category are very few in the corpus. In **La Fortune des Rougon**, for example, the only sexually "chaste" and "virtuous" characters are Pierre Rougon and Félicité Puech[378], those spouses who do not commit any adultery in the novel. One can thus understand Pierre's anger before the misconduct and "adultery" of his mother, Aunt Dide. Their son, Eugène, also shows chastity as if he inherited it from his parents since he was their first born. If he dodges the female contact – just like the abbé Faujas[379] in **La Conquête de Plassans** -, it is because he wanted to remain a << *conquérant* >>, according to Bertrand-Jennings. But the truth is that Eugène Rougon's only love is for politics, this other mistress that he worships. Philippe Hamon had just classified **La Conquête de Plassans** in a trilogy of the libido, with **Le Docteur Pascal** and **Nana**; trilogy that he named: << *Libido dominandi, libido sciendi, libido sentiendi* >>[380]. Eugène is a neurotic character who considers women as a destabilising factor; a species which would take away him manhood and his virility; a chasm capable of drowning and annihilating the male in him, or one which can compromise his political career. Is not the female sex associated with a << *poison* >> in **La Bête Humaine**[381], before the woman is associated with the << *monstre de l'Écriture* >>[382], with a << *fatal* >>[383] being

---

[378] In **L'Éros et la Femme chez Zola**, Bertrand-Jennings mentions a subgroup of women with a clear political intrigue; they are Félicité and Clorinde, op. cit. pp. 74-75. Political intrigues would represent for those women a source of a far higher pleasure – and climax - than sex can ever grant them.

[379] According to Maarten Van Buuren, man is like a malleable substance, which poses a threat to physical integrity and allows someone like Father Faujas to "*pétrir*" Marthe at will, in **Les Rougon-Macquart d'Émile Zola. De la Métaphore au Mythe**, op. cit. p. 230.

[380] Philippe Hamon: **Le Personnel du Roman. Le Système des Personnages dans Les Rougon-Macquart de Zola**, op. cit. p. 236.

[381] Émile Zola: **R. M. IV,** op. cit. p. 1019.

[382] Émile Zola: **R. M. II**, op. cit. p. 1271.

[383] **Ibidem**, p. 1269.

and << *un ferment de destruction* >>³⁸⁴, and finally somebody who is destined to << *l'enfer* >>³⁸⁵ ? Nana is, for example, according to the word of Neide de Faria, the << *vraie idole d'une secte païenne* >>³⁸⁶.

Practically, in the same context, I can mention Florent in **Le Ventre de Paris** for he dreads the advances of La Belle Normande as one would flee the plague. As much in his eyes as in those of Eugène, the woman remains an unfathomable abyss which one must refuse to explore. His exclusive camaraderie with Ms. François makes him look like a kind of virtual homosexual according to Naomi Schor: << *Indeed, Florent seems a model of male homosexuality as described by Freud in his article "Certain Neurotic Mechanisms in Jealousy, Paranoia and Homosexuality* >>³⁸⁷. Florent is indeed inhibited by the memory - or rather the spectre - of the woman killed on the barricades and whose body rested on him. This obsession becomes, in the terminology of Jean Borie, << *la nausée* >>³⁸⁸, and in that of Philippe Hamon, << *la repulsion* >>³⁸⁹, which is the opposite of the sexual << *pulsion* >>. Like Florent, Souvarine is haunted by the spectre of the woman hung during the Moscow revolution³⁹⁰ in **Germinal**. Jacques Lantier is haunted by the living woman in **La Bête Humaine**. Serge Mouret is also haunted by the Virgin Marie³⁹¹ while Claude Lantier is haunted by the virtual and the ideal Woman. Different phobias, of course, but with a common source, the woman, and a common victim, the man. Because in Zola's works, chastity is unnatural, it is the result of a psychic and a physiological disturbance because the human species is made to reproduce itself. Chastity is therefore to be fought against - as much as debauchery - because it is a harbinger of death.

Probably, the only true chaste in **Les Rougon-Macquart** is M. Béraud Du Châtel, the father of Renée, the heroine of **La Curée**. Mr. Du Châtel is the perfect example of the character who has come into disjunction with their space - Paris - because of the depravations, the debauchery and the multiforms of corruption that have taken place since the rise of the Prince-Président to power. That is why, throughout the novel, he is "seen" cloistering at home in his austere old

---

[384] Émile Zola: **R. M. II**, op. cit. p. 1435.
[385] **Ibidem**, p. 1410.
[386] Neide de Faria : **Structure et Unité dans Les Rougon-Macquart de Zola (la poétique du cycle)**, op. cit. p. 265.
[387] Naomi Schor: **Zola's Crowds**, op. cit. p. 32.
[388] Jean Borie : **Zola et les Mythes, ou de la Nausée au Salut**, op. cit. p. 62.
[389] Refer to **Le Personnel du Roman. Le Système des Personnages dans Les Rougon-Macquart de Zola** by Philippe Hamon for more on this, op. cit. p. 252.
[390] **Ibidem**, Philippe Hamon associates this with << *une nausée* >>, the subject Souvarine being rather governed more by << *l'abject* >> than << *l'objet* >>, op. cit. p. 252.
[391] **Ibidem**, p. 252.
  Maarten Van Buuren writes about the abbé Mouret: << *La vénération pour Marie est le premier signe de faiblesse qui préfigure son amour pour Albine* >>, in **Les Rougon-Macquart d'Émile Zola. De la Métaphore au Mythe**, op. cit. p. 173.

hotel, as if to escape the corrupt and the immoral new society that was imposed on him.

As far as **Nana** is concerned, there are two rather virtuous sexual agents that are somewhat powerless in the face of the widespread gangrene of the dissipation of the other protagonists. They are Madame Hugon and M. Venot, the Jesuit and friend of Count Muffat. In **La Faute de l'Abbé Mouret**, Brother Archangias is the negative replica of Mr. Venot. Madame Hugon openly and constantly condemns the excesses of Nana whose neighbourhood she loathes in the country. It is therefore naturally with rage that she hears of the relationship of the demi-mondaine with her two sons, Georges and Philippe. Her martyrdom becomes all the more untenable when her children fall into incest before she knows it. The climax of her suffering comes, however, when the youngest son tries to commit suicide at Nana's place. He was simply heartbroken to realise that his eldest brother, Philippe, shared the same lover as him. Despite Madame Hugon's virtue, therefore, this mother will have suffered in her flesh because of Nana the devourer [392] and the maneater for Nana represents the victory of evil over good, the triumph of the devil over Zola's god.

As for M. Venot, he remains the spokesman of a God of repentance and of redemption. It is he who tries to open his friend Count Muffat's eyes when the latter had fallen into debauchery in contact with Nana after fifty years of absolute piety[393]. As a first-rate moraliser, Venot's ambition is to save his dear friend from hellfire by removing him from the rotten environment in which he has gone astray. Brother Archangias, this other chaste and moralising character, discovers the absolute effective remedy that can uproot evil. For him, it is necessary to twist the necks of every baby girl for women's body is the dwelling place of the devil: << *Elles ont la damnation dans leurs jupes. Des créatures bonnes à jeter au fumier, avec leurs saletés qui empoisonnent ! Ce serait un fameux débarras si l'on étranglait toutes les filles à leur naissance* >>[394]. Naturally, the misogyny of Frère Archangias[395] arises to an anti-religious and an anti-naturalist level[396]. This man of God is the Antichrist and the symbolic true agent of death in Zola's view.

---

[392] She disorganises families and society at large according to Chantal Bertrand-Jennings, in **L'Éros et la Femme chez Zola**, op. cit. p. 65.
    Maarten Van Buuren goes on to say that she puts her lovers and society on fire, in **Les Rougon-Macquart d'Émile Zola. De la Métaphore au Mythe**, op. cit. p. 262.
[393] Van Buuren recalls << *la froideur catholique* >> of the count; this coldness probably calls upon the fire of Nana which will cure him in **Les Rougon-Macquart d'Émile Zola. De la Métaphore au Mythe**, op. cit. p. 231.
[394] Émile Zola: **R. M. I**, op. cit. p. 1239.
[395] In **Réalité et Mythe chez Zola**, Roger Ripoll recognises his symbolic role of a representative of the god of anger who must surprise Albine and Serge and curse them, op. cit. p. 95.
[396] Chantal Bertrand-Jennings points out that religion is the enemy of the couples in Zola's novels, in **L'Éros et la Femme chez Zola**, op. cit. p. 19.

On the whole, as much the chaste characters are scanty, as much they are not very effective either. They are even powerless before the omnipotence of vice. In fact, in the epic combat which opposes vice to virtue in **Les Rougon-Macquart**, the first triumphs over the second any day. Thus, one must take the devastating defeat of Madame Hugon who mourns the death of her youngest son at the same time as the imprisonment - another form of death - of the elder. With Bertrand-Jennings, we can say that: << [...] *Zola aborde le plus grand problème qui hante toute son œuvre : celui du mal lié à la sexualité et à la conscience morale* >>[397].

As for M. Venot, his victories over vice are quite fake and intermittent, for Count Muffat becomes receptive to his moralising speech only when he is overwhelmed with pain and jealousy. Muffat's resolution to follow the right path of God is always a decision taken in a negative and in an oppressive emotional state of mind. Such resolution does not stand up to the psychological "normalisation" process once he becomes lucid and forgiving towards his mistress, Nana. Like a drug addict, he then sinks deeper into debauchery with more fever than before. Must we therefore come to the conclusion that the devil is victorious over the Jesuit Venot? Without a doubt, and, it must be emphasised, that those alternative victories and defeats follow each other tirelessly until the count decides to ensure the final victory of the evil over good by remaining attached to Nana to the detriment of his friend Venot and of his own family. Brother Archangias is on the same wavelength as the Jesuit Venot since he proposes to bring the abbot Mouret back to the Lord. The only difference is that Archangias is rather more the spokesman of a God of punishment than a simple moraliser. He is also an absolute antinaturalist who strongly condemns carnal and reproductive relationships. That is why he gets no sympathy from the narrator whatsoever. His conduct is simply condemned when his diatribes cause the separation of Mouret from Albine, a drama amplified by the death of this poor girl and her unborn baby. Archangias, or an archangel descended on earth to fight nature - by substituting the laws of heaven to those of nature - is, in certain respects, responsible for this double homicide. Archangias thus departs from God and, by extension, from the author Zola, a fierce naturalist and a natalist. Moreover, despite the watchful eyes of Brother Archangias, Father Mouret managed to return to Albine's house in the Paradou, hopping over the large body of the *"gendarme de Dieu"* who barred his entrance. The body of Archangias thus becoming a physical obstacle, the border between good and evil, between paradise and hell, between religion and nature, between abstinence and carnal pleasure. Symbolically, to stride across someone or something is to ignore them, not to subscribe to their views, to disobey them. This step[398] by the young priest is therefore the symbol of his disobedience to God and the renunciation of his

---

[397] Chantal Bertrand-Jennings: **L'Éros et la Femme chez Zola**, op. cit. p. 25.
[398] We can paraphrase Philippe Hamon by saying that the wall that surrounds the Paradou marks the border between nature and culture, heaven and earthly hell, love and hatred, ease and discomfort. This contrast is inspired by Philippe Hamon's study of the wall separating the Rougon and the Macquart houses in **Le Personnel du Roman. Le Système des Personnages dans Les Rougon-Macquart d'Émile Zola**, op. cit. pp. 211-212.

Catholic church's principles, at least for a moment. Vice is imperious indeed, sin is irresistible and violent; it easily imposes itself onto the sexual agent with despotism[399] in Zola's universe.

1.3.2. The evil characters

The dictionary defines *"pervers"* as being << *les sujets caractérisés par une perversion des instincts élémentaires, et qui accomplissent systématiquement des actes immoraux, antisociaux* >>[400]. Perversion itself will be heard as a << *dépravation, une déviation des instincts, des tendances, dues à des troubles psychiques* >>[401]. This definition of the lexicologist is however too vague, especially as it does not specify the disorders that deserve to be classified in the context of perversion nor does it specify the trajectory from which instincts deviate, nor at which point such deviation occurs. For me, perversion is essentially sexual, and I mean all the sexual practices that are deemed reprehensible within society. Its paradigm include the following: << *la bestialité, l'exhibitionnisme, le fétichisme, le masochisme, la nécrophilie, le sadisme, etc* >>[402].

The evil characters in the corpus are, by and large, Claude Lantier, Renée Saccard, Baptiste, Aristide Rougon dit Saccard and Maxime Rougon dit Saccard, Jacques Lantier, Président Grandmorin, Misard, Flore and Cabuche, Hilarion and Buteau, and, finally, Nana, Satin and the Count Muffat. It is understood that each of these agents manifests their perversion in a specific way.

For example, Claude Lantier manifests his perversion in the form of a crazy and an ambiguous love for his paintings by devoting all of his libido to his paintings to the despair of his legitimate wife, one of his fleshly models. Claude gives all his love to the virtual women, which he represented on his canvasses. It is without doubt the only access to freedom offered to him because: << *Dans cette guerre entre l'Art et la Femme* [...] *la loi exige, semble-t-il que l'artiste transforme la femme en objet d'art ou bien périsse entre ses bras* >>[403]. For Neide de Faria indeed, in Claude's perspective, success means succeeding in painting the Woman[404].

---

[399] For more reading on the superiority of the "*ça*" on the "*moi*", please refer to Maarten Van Buuren in his **Les Rougon-Macquart d'Émile Zola. De la Métaphore au Mythe**, op. cit. pp. 56-60.
[400] **Le Petit Robert 1**, op. cit. p. 1413.
[401] **Ibidem**, p. 1413.
[402] Sigmund Freud: **Trois Essais sur la Théorie de la Sexualité**, op. cit. p. 39.
[403] David Baguley: **Zola et les Genres**, chapter VIII : **L'Œuvre**, *künstlerroman à thèse*, op. cit. p. 88.
[404] Neide de Faria: **Structure et Unité des Rougon-Macquart d'Émile Zola (la poétique du cycle)**, op. cit. p. 72.

As for Baptiste, he is what Sigmund Freud calls << *un inverti absolu* >>[405] because his sexual object is exclusively homosexual. As a result, he has a real aversion for the opposite sex, the woman. In Freudian terminology, Maxime Rougon must be seen as << *un inverti amphigène* >> or a psychosexual hermaphrodite whose sexual object can sometimes be homosexual and sometimes heterosexual. He is what one would call today a *"bisexual"* man. His father, Aristide, is a sadist who rapes a neighbour on the stairs while Grandmorin is an unrepentant rapist and a paedophile. He is both a pervert and a sadist. Misard is also a sadist who goes so far as to poison his wife in a struggle that means far more than the supposedly hidden fortune of his wife to put his hands on. Nelly Wilson sees in fact in that tragic episode a struggle of the male seeking a triumph over the superiority of his female companion: << *Obsession with his wife's inheritance of a thousand francs has more of a symbolic than the monetary value, representing the desire to reassert male domination over his physically and financially stronger female partner* >>[406].

Cabuche is a sexual immature character who takes objects that belonged to the beloved woman as sexual objects by substitution. He is a real brute in the sense that he has in Geoff Woollen's article, meaning savagery, roughness, incompletion, incomplete, regression, the primitive type[407]. His immaturity is similar to that of Saturnin Josserand[408] of **Pot-Bouille** who is in love with his little sister, Berthe, but who cannot materialise his neurotic and incestuous love into a physical love. As a result, he becomes friends with all his sister's lovers, sharing their sexuality and happiness, and becoming paradoxically very aggressive towards his sister's husband, Auguste Vabre, whom he considers his true rival. This makes him a virtual ripper, according to Geoff Woollen: << *Another prototypical ripper is Saturnin Josserand in* **Pot-Bouille** *[...]. He occasionally gets hold of a knife, whence threats such as ''Je vais leur ouvrir la peau du ventre'', ''parlait d'embrocher le monde'' and the final attempted bleeding of Auguste Vabre* >>[409].

Jacques Lantier does almost as much with his carnal love for La Lison, his locomotive that is maintained as a beloved mistress[410]. In Jacques' perspective,

---

[405] Sigmund Freud: **Trois Essais sur la Théorie de la Sexualité**, op. cit. p. 39.
[406] Nelly Wilson : *A question of motives : heredity and inheritance in* **La Bête Humaine**, Zola, La Bête Humaine: texte et explication, Geoff Woollen (éd.), op. cit. p. 185.
[407] Geoff Woollen : *Des brutes humaines dans* **La Bête Humaine**, Zola, La Bête Humaine: texte et explication, Geoff Woollen (éd.), op. cit. pp. 150-168.
[408] Saturnin Josserand, Victor Saccard and Florent are the social << *exclus* >>, according to Philippe Hamon, in **Le Personnel du Roman. Le Système des Personnages dans les Rougon-Macquart d'Émile Zola**, op. cit. p. 232.
[409] Geoff Woollen: *Jacques the Ripper* in **Émile Zola Centenary Colloquium: 1893-1993**, Patrick Pollard (éd.), op. cit. p. 75.
[410] In **Le Romancier et la Machine, I: L'Univers de Zola**, Jacques Noiray insists on the nature of the erotic relationship that exists between the machine and Jacques; the Lison being regarded as a soothing mistress first, then as a woman of flesh before becoming bad-tempered when Jacques takes a mistress of flesh, Séverine, op. cit. pp. 404-413.

this machine is nothing less than an adjuvant and a sexual object[411]: << *En plus, cette machine reçoit presque autant d'attributs que Séverine – la rivale humaine dont elle est << jalouse >> – en tant que première << maîtresse apaisante >> de Jacques >>*[412]. But Jacques is also a sadist and a masochist unique in his kind with this hereditary crack that tortures him and pushes him to achieve orgasm by spilling a female's blood. The sadism of Hilarion or Buteau leads to incest and murder, whether voluntarily or accidentally. Those are two rapists who choose their victims from their close relatives.

Nana and Satin are lesbians just like << *les inséparables* >> in **La Curée**, Adeline d'Espanet and Suzanne Haffner. While only Satin is an absolute invert, the others belong to the category of the amphigenic inversion or bisexuals. Like children, they have a sadistic conception of the heterosexual act. For Freud, indeed: << *Lorsque les enfants sont témoins à un âge aussi tendre, de rapports sexuels entre des adultes, ils ne peuvent manquer de considérer l'acte sexuel comme une sorte de mauvais traitement ou de violence et de lui donner, par conséquent, un sens sadique* >>[413]. Finally, those lesbians appear in Zola's works as sexual neurotic subjects.

Count Muffat is an indecrostable masochist who climaxes and delights in the suffering inflicted on him by his sexual object[414]. In this regard, we can read in **Nana** : << *Elle* (Nana) *le* (Muffat) *traita en animal, le fouailla, le poursuivit à coups de pieds [...]*.

Et lui aimait sa bassesse, goûtait la jouissance d'être une brute. Il aspirait encore à descendre, il criait :

-Tape plus fort [...]. Hou ! hou ! je suis enragé, tape donc ! >>[415].

One can only expect a paroxysmal exacerbation of sexual depravities in Muffat when he identifies himself as a rabid dog. Beyond all that has been shown above, this way of portraying sexuality in **Les Rougon-Macquart** constitutes the satire of a perverse and a vicious society. It is also Bertrand-Jennings' view that : << *Il ne fait aucun doute que la << normalité >> sexuelle est une des valeurs prônées par Zola, et que, tout comme le lesbianisme, l'homosexualité masculine se trouve être bafouée dans son œuvre. Chez les homosexuels des deux sexes il s'agit de dénoncer le décadentisme d'une société corrompue, chez les*

---

[411] In **Le Romancier et la Machine, I: L'Univers de Zola**, Jacques Noiray believes that the Lison is a << *substitut primitif de la femme* >>, just like **Le Bonheur des Dames**; those two – the Lison and the Departmemt store - are << *parfaites machines à jouir* >>, p. 410.

[412] Neide de Faria: **Structure et Unité dans Les Rougon-Macquart de Zola (la poétique du cycle)**, op. cit. p. 138.

[413] Sigmund Freud: **Trois Essais sur la Théorie de la Sexualité**, op. cit. p.25

[414] Maarten Van Buuren : **Les Rougon-Macquart d'Émile Zola. De la Métaphore au Mythe**, op. cit. p. 231.

[415] Émile Zola: **R. M. II**, op. cit. p. 1461.

lesbiennes, c'est avant tout à la rébellion contre un ordre établi masculin qu'on semble s'attaquer >>⁴¹⁶.

1.3.3. The vicious characters

Vice will be understood here as a serious sexual perversion where the sexual subject is incapable of giving up - in spite of the opposition of his conscience and that of social and religious morality. However, incest - which is arguably the most serious and the most significant form of perversion - will be addressed in a specific paragraph given its many occurrences and multifaceted treatment that defy all competition.

From the outset, let us note that all the evil characters mentioned here are all vicious. Thus, Maxime is "*un polisson*" and, at thirteen, he seems to fall in love with his father's young wife, Renée, who is forced to order him to watch out. Years later, Renée loves to play the man in their intimate moments, not to mention that as a child, she loved to look at men's naked belly.

Nana is a vicious and a capricious person who engages in lesbianism and prostitution. She is also vicious when she pushes for the marriage between Daguenet and the daughter of Count Muffat on the sole condition of being the first woman to bed the groom on the wedding night! Her vice goes so far as to force Muffat, count and chamberlain, to wear his official outfit and to show off in front of her. Shen then leads him to play the mad dog barking on all fours while she's beating him up rhythmically on his backside. **Les Rougon-Macquart**, overall, celebrate an upside down world, struck by the inevitability of sexuality and the overwhelming power of woman over men: << *L'inversion progressive puis la destruction des classes riches s'y fait par le truchement de la femme, et de la femme sortie du peuple* >>[417], writes Bertrand-Jennings.

Roubaud, because he became an accomplice of the adulteries of his legitimate wife, Séverine, puts himself on the fringes of morality. Grandmorin and Baron Gouraud are both vicious despite their respective high social positions as Chairman of the Board of Directors of the Railway Company and as a Senator. From then on, it appears that the imperial high society had no regard for morality, especially when comparing them to Count Muffat and the Marquis de Chouard[418] in **Nana**; then with the august character of the Emperor Napoléon III, who is guilty of a few adulteries and infidelities in the series. The children do not escape this pandemic of vice either because Delphin, Nénesse and La Trouille are vicious from their childhood. For Marcel Girard, those children are: << *les adolescents, les enfants, trois vicieux, tous corrompus par l'âpreté et la*

---

[416] Chantal Bertrand-Jennings : **L'Éros et la Femme chez Zola**, op. cit. p. 41.
[417] **Ibidem**, p. 68.
[418] **Ibidem**, Chantal Bertrand-Jennings states that << *Dans* **Nana**, *le principe de mort est représenté par le vieux marquis de Chouard,* << *ce coin de charnier* >> *venu échouer dans le lit de la courtisane [...]* >>, p. 17.

sensualité ambiantes >>[419]. Meanwhile, for Jésus Christ, father of La Trouille, his daughter is << *la bougresse qui me déshonore* >>[420]. In fact, since their thirteenth year, those children are sexually very active. The two kids are getting laid by the girl who looks nymphomaniac[421] from a young age as her exacerbated thirst for male companions is never quenched. The debauchery of those kids is therefore the symbol of a humanity that has lost its innocence by living too fast and too deep into sexual sins. La Trouille perfectly joins La Cognette in debauchery because the latter is unable to say no to a man. In fact, frivolity is erected as a binding law in her understanding. Not even the fierce jealousy of her master and official lover, M. Hourdequin, can dissuade her from dissipation. She even transforms all the spaces into alcoves, from the barn to the attic, through the fields, the stables, her master's house, the servants' rooms, and so on. La Cognette belongs to the category of women of the people who decay the high society[422] and bring about the downfall of the Second Empire.

Buteau's vice is one of the most original in the series for he is an unwavering villain who tirelessly harasses his sister-in-law without even bothering about the presence of his legitimate wife. He finally manages to rape Françoise with the help of Lise, his wife, who is the sister of the victim. Buteau's vice leads straight to the last type of vice announced a while ago.

1.3.4. The incestuous characters

Incest is by far the most widespread and the most immoral sexual vice in the fiction world of the **Rougon-Macquart**. Moreover, it has many variations ranging from the virtual or simulated incest to the real incest, passing of course by the symbolic or the allegorical incest. I must stress that I will address the theme of incest as all sexual relationships between a man and a woman belonging to the same family or that are allies to an extent that prohibits marriage between them. For many psychoanalysts like Sigmund Freud, going back as far as the Greek mythology, incest finds its explanation in what is known as the Oedipus complex. Only the << *sur-moi* >> can censor the incestuous tendencies we owe to the *ça*[423] as the subject progresses towards maturity, and that education shows him the absurdity of his unconscious desires.

---

[419] Marcel Girard: *Préface* in **La Terre** par Émile Zola, Paris, Garnier-Flammarion, 1973, p. 23.
[420] Émile Zola: **R. M. IV**, op. cit. p. 484.
[421] For Chantal Bertrand-Jennings, nymphomaniacs are worse than hysterics, in **L'Éros et la Femme chez Zola**, op. cit. p. 61.
[422] **Ibidem**, p. 68.
[423] From the works of Groddeck, Freud and Laplanche-Pontalis, Maarten van Buuren concludes that the "*ça*" is the home of innateness and repression, exactly what is non-personal in man. The "*ça*" is also the horse, or the superior force to which the "*moi*" - which is its opposite - is only the rider, in **Les Rougon-Macquart d'Émile Zola. De la Métaphore au Mythe**, op. cit. p. 54.

"*Le sur moi*" indeed regulates this vicious and perverse inclination[424] by confronting the subject with social realities and individual reason. However, according to Freud, the repression of the tendency to engage into incest, the struggle engaged by man against himself to stifle and suppress his incestuous inclination - can be wrong and thus lead the sexual subject to neurosis[425]. It can also prevent the subject from seeking to realise his tyrannical desire. For this study, cases of incest happen between the following couples: Renée and Maxime; Nana and Georges Hugon, Nana and Philippe Hugon; Palmyre and Hilarion; Hilarion and La Grande; Buteau and Françoise; Victor and mother Eulalie, and finally, the couple Pascal and Clotilde Rougon known as Saccard.

1.3.4.1. The pseudo-incest or incest by allegory

This designation will group the cases where the name of incest is inappropriate by definition since the sexual relationship existing between the incriminated characters is not befitting the concept, but which the narrator does not cease to consider as incestuous. As such, Victor Rougon dit Saccard and mother Eulalie commit a pseudo-incest in **L'Argent**. By collecting the child abandoned by his father and by bringing him up, Mother Eulalie becomes his adoptive mother. The age gap between the two protagonists approaching thirty years of age - 15 for Victor and over forty for Eulalie - reinforces the idea of a mother-to-son relationship. Their sexual intercourse scenes are therefore seen by the narrator as the manifestation of incest and a paedophile affair on top of that. Such a miseducation made the child Victor Rougon << *une boue humaine* >> according to Jean Borie[426]. Most of blame should fall on the despicable foster parent though.

An identical scenario occurs in Nana where Georges Hugon calls **Nana**, his mistress, << *maman* >>[427]. Moreover, she likes it that way by demanding that he calls her only by that name. Conversely, she calls him << *bébé* >>. While the age gap is negligible between Nana and George - 18 against 17 – the fact remains that the former is presented as an accomplished woman, a prostitute who is sexually very experienced while the latter passes for a toddler. If she gives into him, it is more out of charity than out of love. As Valerie Minogue says, Nana is very often presented as << *apitoyée* >> and << *attendrie* >>, a sentimentalism that is not unconsequential, as pointed out by Valerie Minogue: << *such*

---

[424] Maarten Van Buuren : **Les Rougon-Macquart d'Émile Zola. De la Métaphore au Mythe**, op. cit., p. 55.

[425] **Ibidem**, op. cit, Maarten Van Buuren believes that Serge suffered such a failure: << *L'observation rigoureuse des règles sacerdotales condamne Serge à une vie réglée et comme mécanique. Sous la poussée des forces passionnelles que Serge refoule, mais qui ne cessent de l'assaillir, cette mécanique se détraque* >>, p. 59.

[426] Jean Borie : **Zola et les Mythes, ou de la Nausée au Salut**, op. cit. p. 160.

[427] Maarten Van Buuren sees effectively in her a maternal woman in his book **Les Rougon-Macquart d'Émile Zola. De la Métaphore au Mythe**, op. cit. p. 205.

sympathetic feelings in fact often lead to her sexual capitulation >>[428]. The sexual relationship between them is nothing less than an incest in the eyes of the Zolian narrator. This poor boy, according to the same critic, runs to his own loss by going to Nana's house as soon as we see him << *taking the first step on a path that leads to his own death and his brother's disgrace* >>[429].

The fact remains that incest can take a proven form in the corpus.

1.3.4.2. The true incest

The sexual relationship between those two lovers becomes truly incestuous from the moment where Nana multiplies her sexual partners by adding to her long list of victims Philippe Hugon, Georges' eldest brother. Renée and Maxime belong to that same trend with a slight nuance: their incest reminds the reader of that of Oedipus and Jocasta. In **La Curée**, Renée, the mother, is the adored mistress of her son, Maxime, and like their illustrious predecessors from mythology, those two characters are severely punished for their fault.

Françoise and Buteau are first cousins and they commit an incest that could have been tolerable if Buteau had not been married to Françoise's elder sister, Lise. The triangular sexual relationship Françoise-Buteau-Lise in **La Terre** is reminiscent of the Georges-Nana-Philippe triangle denounced above. Nevertheless, it should be recognised that all those incestuous characters identified so far, with the exception of Hilarion, also experiment a so-called "normal" sexuality despite their perversion. Hilarion, in **La Terre**, is indeed the only one among them to only experiment sexual pleasure exclusively through his incestuous relationship with his elder sister, Palmyre. To this consanguineous partner, Palmyre, he certainly has tried and failed to add his grandmother, the octogenarian nicknamed La Grande. His problem, it seems, lies in his physical appearance which is reminiscent of Vulcan since he is as wobbly and as ugly as that mythical ancestor. His unattractive physique is a harbinger of his moral ugliness. As a recidivist rapist, the neurotic sexual subject that he is, falls back on his grandmother following the disappearance of Palmyre. As detestable as he might be in the eyes of moral people, Hilarion is nevertheless the most interesting sexual subject in the series because he is at the same time a neurotic and a sexual immature breed, a kind of sexual psychopath that is violent and bestial in the rut. It is therefore necessary to distinguish the two victims of his incestuous violence in the sense that Palmyre ends up being a consenting victim. Amazingly enough, she defends her predator against the sarcasms and other gossip of the dumbfounded neighbours. On the contrary, the grandmother cannot be counted as a consenting partner if we refer to the description of the circumstances of her rape. The narrator writes: << *[...] il (Hilarion) avait trop*

---

[428] Valerie Minogue : *Venus Observing-Venus Observed : Zola's* **Nana** dans **Émile Zola Centenary Colloquium: 1893-1993**, Patrick Pollard (éd.), op. cit. p. 59.
[429] **Ibidem**, p. 57.

jeûné depuis la mort de Palmyre, sa colère se tournait en une rage de mâle, n'ayant conscience ni de la parenté ni de l'âge, à peine du sexe. La brute violait, cette aïeule de quatre-vingt-neuf ans, au corps de bâton séché, où seule demeurait la carcasse fendue de la femelle. Et, solide encore, inexpugnable, la vieille ne le laissa pas faire, put saisir la cognée, lui ouvrit le crâne, d'un coup [...]. Hilarion ne mourut que le lendemain >>[430].

La Grande, by killing the male, joins La Brûlé in **Germinal**, Maigrat's emasculator, in the category of the << *figures mythiques de la mère castratrice* >> in Bertrand-Jennings' words[431].

About this emasculation precisely, Seassau believes that it shows that sometimes women are taken by a Dionysian delusion which makes them bacchantes and renders them the most violent and the most offensive characters[432] in Zola's works, although Maigrat was emasculated because of his lust[433].

Dr. Pascal enters in conjunction with his niece, Clotilde Rougon, in **Le Docteur Pascal**, to the point where he gets her pregnant[434]. Their son, << *l'enfant inconnu* >>, seems cleansed from the original crack and the lack of name for him works like the absence of all genetic marks. It is the new being who does not have to undergo the fatality of heredity, the one the narrator calls << *le messie que le siècle prochain attendait* >>[435]. Let us note here the perfect conjunction between the sexual subject - Pascal - and his sexual object - Clotilde - especially when, for the very first time, they have sex: << *Ce ne fut pas une chute, la vie glorieuse les soulevait, ils s'appartinrent au milieu d'une allégresse. La grande chambre complice, avec son antique mobilier, s'en trouva comme emplie de lumière [...]. Elle (Clotilde), éblouie et délicieuse, n'eut que le doux cri de sa virginité perdue ; et lui, dans un sanglot de ravissement, l'étreignit toute, la remerciant, sans qu'elle pût comprendre, d'avoir refait de lui un homme* >>[436].

That allusion to Pascal's newfound virility completes the hint on page 1030, which specified that when he returned from Marseilles, where he saw prostitutes, << *[...] il revint comme foudroyé, frappé de déchéance, avec la face hantée d'un homme qui a perdu sa virilité d'homme* >>[437].

However, despite the fact that incest is perceived here as a life-saving therapy in Pascal's perspective, and as an ecstasy for the two lovers, it remains a

---

[430] Émile Zola: **R. M. IV**, op. cit. p. 726.
[431] Chantal Bertrand-Jennings : **L'Éros et la Femme chez Zola**, op. cit. p. 45.
[432] Claude Seassau : **Émile Zola, Le Réalisme Symbolique**, op. cit. p. 254.
[433] **Ibidem**, p. 255.
[434] For Chantal Bertrand-Jennings, it is the child who exculpates the free and incestuous union of Pascal and Clotilde, see the book above, op. cit. p. 94.
[435] Émile Zola: **R. M. V**, op. cit. p. 1219.
[436] **Ibidem**, p. 1061.
[437] **Ibidem**, p.1030.

scandalous topic for gossip in Plassans where the lovers live. The eyes of others is ruthless: << *Et cela tournait au scandale, cet oncle qui avait débauché sa nièce, qui faisait pour elle des folies de jeune homme, qui la parait comme une sainte vierge* >>[438]. As we can see, Pascal is at the centre of all the criticism because he occupies the dominant position[439] as an uncle, a *"master"*, and above all, a foster father who had collected Clotilde from the age of five. He raised her personally until she reached twenty-five years of age when she offered him her virginity as a supreme reward! I entirely agree with Chantal Bertrand-Jennings on this: « *Les deux éléments du couple idéal zolien ne sont jamais égaux. Toujours beaucoup plus jeune, la femme se soumet à un maître qu'elle admire et dont elle se fait l'humble servante reconnaissante* »[440].

The characters, as part of the narrative syntagmas, after going through the phases of manipulation, skills and performance, deserve a sanction, the last phase of the narrative programmes that is still to be studied.

II. THE RECOGNITION AND THE SANCTION OF THE SEXUAL AGENT

According to the researchers from the Groupe d'Entrevernes, << *le destinateur évalue la véridication des états transformés, sanctionne (positivement ou négativement) le sujet-opérateur de la performance* >>[441]. I have shown in the first part of chapter I that the author, from his preface, posed as the true sender for he has granted his characters various skills. Having made them realise the above performances, he must then submit them to the phase of sanctions which will be spread over four main stages. I will not go back to the first of those stages, which is transcendental, since the character that suffers from it cannot get rid of it. We are referring to the initial crack or *"fêlure"* that comes from the character's all-powerful creator, the novelist Zola. This first sanction indeed is the crack, the first fatality, the original taint that strikes all the anaphoric characters as well as a number of clutching characters. The problem of the disjunctional and the conjunctional dichotomy of the Zolian character, a paper-being both disjunct with their space and then in conjunction with their historical social milieu, will not be discussed here either. That question will simply be the subject of further investigation in the third part.

2.1. The miscarriages

On the one hand, it is well known that in **Les Rougon-Macquart**, there are very few children. On the other hand, there are many adulterers and a large number of couples formed in the corpus. How can this be explained in the work of a naturalist, or even a natalist? In any case, with the exception of **La Fortune des**

---

[438] Émile Zola: **R. M. V**, op. cit. p. 1074.
[439] Chantal Bertrand-Jennings: in **L'Éros et la Femme chez Zola**, op. cit., p. 117.
[440] **Ibidem**, p.117.
[441] Le Groupe d'Entrevernes : **Analyse Sémiotique des Textes**, op. cit. p. 45.

Rougon where several births take place, all the other novels in the cycle narrate mostly miscarriages and stillbirths. However, this exception is easily explained by the fact that this first novel in the cycle, was dubbed by Zola himself: << *le roman des origines* >> or the novel of the foundations. It goes without saying that the author was obliged, for literary and doctrinaire purposes, to sketch the family tree[442] of his guinea pig family. Eighteen children are thus born successively in this first volume of the **Rougon-Macquart** and very quickly, Aunt Dide becomes a mother, a grandmother and a great-grandmother in the same diegesis. There are clear signs of a particular narrative acceleration that Zola will no longer practice in any of the later novels. It can be argued that it was a matter of quickly setting up the scenery for the << *scientifique* >> study that he was later going to carry out on that primary << *groupe humain* >>.

Apart from that volume, which marks the end of the reproductive process, all the following novels are characterised by a significant slowdown in the field of human reproduction. However, vices and perversions will be amplified over time in the next episodes. One might therefore be tempted to postulate that in **Les Rougon-Macquart** vices and perversions are incompatible with fertility and reproduction. It appears that in Zola's works, indeed, the most debauched characters have a very slim chance at enjoying motherhood or paternity, things they should normally expect in the real world. In **La Curée** for example, Renée miscarries after her rape in the country - her first experience with a man -; Nana also miscarries at eighteen in **Nana**. Françoise does not live until the birth of her baby in **La Terre** for she is murdered while eight months pregnant. This bad fatum strikes again Albine, who dies around her third month of pregnancy[443] in **La Faute de l'Abbé Mouret**.

Finally, the calf of the Mouche sisters' cow is lost during the parturition process in spite of La Frimat's science in **La Terre**. Even the most dissipated women like La Cognette, La Trouille, Laure d'Aurigny, Irma and many others experience virtually no pregnancy as if they were implicitly all barren. Bertrand-Jennings summarises such situation by postulating that many bad women are deprived of children in Zola's works and that only the good mother can be tolerated[444]. It can be argued that this is one of the sanctions for dissipation and debauchery in the corpus. Perhaps, when the time comes, I will investigate some possible psychoanalytic ties between the author and his characters on this. One could, for example, wonder if this apparent infertility in his characters was not the

---

[442] In **Les Rougon-Macquart d'Émile Zola. De la Métaphore au Mythe**, op. cit., Maarten Van Buuren emphasises the fact that the family tree, which alone is saved from the arson by Madame Félicité and Martine, is mythologically characterised by its deliberate qualification of << *relique sainte* >>, p. 159.

[443] Given the impressive number of orphans, adoptive parents and children who died in Zola's works, Philippe Hamon believes that << *La ligne généalogique* << *réelle* >> *du personnage, chez Zola, est souvent une ligne brisée* >>, in **Le Personnel du Roman. Le Système des Personnages dans Les Rougon-Macquart d'Émile Zola**, op. cit. p. 61.

[444] Chantal Bertrand-Jennings : **L'Éros et la Femme chez Zola**, op. cit. pp. 97-99.

result of a neurosis, or even a psychosis on the part of the author himself. In such case, the many miscarriages and barrenness could be seen as the emanation of his unconscious which would resurface in his work of novelistic creation, for they constitute elements formerly repressed in his unconscious. Chapter III will focus more on this specific point.

Roughly speaking, miscarriages are nevertheless a concatenation of significant narrative elements in the sense that they lead the **Rougon-Macquart** society to a brutal evanescence and to its painful death. Hence the menacing existential threat to the imperial society of which it is at least the allegorical representation. This is a barren and a devilish society that is doomed from the the word go. The verdict of Zola seems implacable: the one and the other, the virtual and the real world both head towards their disappearance, pure and simple, due to the lack of renewal of the population by means of natural reproduction. Zola's characters bear no seeds! Somehow the characters who succeed in reproducing[445] themselves have children who are victims of many forms of abnormality that are inherited diseases, physical and intellectual disabilities - which most often end up rushing them to an untimely death[446].

2.2. The hereditary diseases

It should be remembered from the outset that children born in the corpus are all hit with a hereditary fatality, except for << *l'enfant inconnu* >>. They all *"benefit"* from the original deficiency which is << *la fêlure* >>, also labelled *"la tare orginelle"* that Aunt Dide has spread all over the family tree. The crack, however, takes various forms and one of those forms remains the precarious and ill health. The most significant examples in this regard are undoubtedly those of Louiset, son of Nana, Alice and Gaston Dubuche, Miss Régine Margaillan and Jacques, the son of Claude Lantier, Charles, the son of Maxime, Louise de Mareuil and finally, Hilarion.

In general, those poor children all suffer from serious respiratory problems. Suffering from acute chest infections, they cannot stand fresh air which is paradoxically the essential natural food for all living beings. From this point of view, children appear in **Les Rougon-Macquart** as the least naturalistic agents, given their inability to adapt to the laws of nature. The disease that comes up most often - and which is called by name - is phthisis which is a kind of galloping pulmonary tuberculosis. We can notably mention Mademoiselle Régine

---

[445] In **L'Éros et la Femme chez Zola**, op. cit., Chantal Bertrand-Jennings asserts that: << *De fait, c'est sous le signe de la fertilité que se place une grande partie de l'œuvre zolienne* >>, p. 97. That seems rather paradoxical, because it would rather be difficult to explain why human reproduction is so rarely successful in Zola's works, even if the critic is quick to add that many bad women are deprived of children by the novelist, just like Renée, Clorinde and Thérèse Raquin, p. 97. It seems to me more accurate to say that Zola's works are placed under the sign of sterility and infertility.

[446] Chantal Bertrand-Jennings reaches a similar conclusion, **Ibidem**, p. 127.

Margaillan, Alice and Gaston Dubuche, then Louise de Mareuil, as the main phthisis sufferers.

Alice and Gaston Dubuche are presented by the narrator as play dough that are totally unable to move alone, to the point where their father: << *luttait heure après heure pour les sauver; les sauvant chaque matin avec l'effroi de les perdre chaque soir* >>[447]. The narrator goes so far as to assert, not without hyperbole, that they were so weak and so light that a strong wind would carry them away! Those poor devils thus pay a heavy price for the misconduct of their ascendants because of heredity. Their mother herself was already << *déplumée comme un oiseau malade* >>[448] before becoming << *un chat écorché* >>[449] according to the expression of the painter Claude Lantier. And the narrator does insist on the inherited disease passed on to the unfortunate offspring of the grandmother: << *Madame Margaillan, cette femme pâle, en lame de couteau, était morte phtisique ; et c'était le mal héréditaire, la dégénérescence, car sa fille, Régine, toussait elle-même depuis son mariage* >>[450]. The phthisis washes her away to the point of making her unable to continue to play her role as a wife and as a mother: << *Dubuche avait même laissé entendre que, sa femme ayant failli mourir à ses secondes couches et s'évanouissant d'ailleurs au moindre contact trop vif, il s'était fait un devoir de cesser tous rapports conjugaux avec elle. Pas même cette recreation* >>[451]. By comparing those three generations of characters, we realise that their decline is progressive and yet radical[452]. The children, who are the foliage of the family tree, are nothing more than yellow leaves, lacking any invigorating sap. All other characters called phthisic experiment the same fate of progressive extinction. Of course, the higher they are perched on this family tree, the greater their chances of dying at a young age. Their life expectancy will only be acceptable when they are closer to the roots. Beyond the phthisis, one can mention the sclerosis that strikes to death Dr. Pascal and the ataxia that nails Maxime in an armchair before killing him in **Le Docteur Pascal**.

2.3. The amorphous children

The whole class of children deprived of energy will be dubbed amorphous for they lack consistency as if they had been emptied of their bone marrow. It is obvious that the Dubuche children and their mother also belong to this class of agents. I will therefore not go back to their case. The other amorphous children are Maxime Rougon and his son Charles, his sister Clotilde, Louiset, Victor

---

[447] Émile Zola: **R. M. IV**, op. cit. p. 316.
[448] **Ibidem,** p. 151.
[449] **Ibidem,** p. 123.
[450] **Ibidem,** p. 313.
[451] **Ibidem,** p. 314.
[452] David Baguley speaks about a dynamic of disintegration, etiolation and liquefaction in **Naturalist Fiction. The Entropic Vision**, op. cit. p. 202 et p. 198.

Rougon, and finally, Hilarion and his sister Palmyre. Perhaps the most revealing cases are those of Maxime, Louiset and Charles.

I have already pointed out that Maxime is effeminate, degenerate, phlegmatic and a kind of strange hermaphrodite. For Maarten Van Buuren, the metaphor of disguise is a sign of corruption[453] and the degeneration of the Empire[454]. His son Charles - born from his early love with one of Renée's maids - is naturally another degenerate in the terminal state. He is quickly sent to the countryside by his grandfather, Aristide, as a precautionary measure to prevent him from contaminating the healthy members of the Saccard family on the one hand, and on the other hand, to slow down the process of his advanced degeneration. Charles' state of health is similar to that of the Dubuche children that was mentioned above. The narrator says about him that: << *On ne pouvait le toucher, sans que la rosée rouge perlât à sa peau : c'était un relâchement des tissus, si aggravé par la dégénérescence, que le moindre froissement déterminait une hémorragie* >>[455]. The child then becomes more stupid as he grows up and, inevitably, he dies at the age of fifteen as a result of a haemorrhage with no apparent cause. This is because the sap of Aunt Dide quickly dried up in him who belonged to the fifth generation of the Rougons.

As for Louiset, the son of a prostitute, he is hit hard by an implacable heredity, especially since his father's identity remains a great mystery. That complicates the diagnosis that the narrator would have liked to make of his ailment: << *le grand air* (le) *rendit malade* >>[456]. And the narrator finally makes the following statement: << *Le petit Louis* (avec) *ses plaintes tristes d'enfant rongé de mal,* (victime) *de quelque pourriture léguée par un père inconnu* >>[457]. Louis seems to be from an ancient race[458] for he's withered and so frail, with a sad and serious face like that of an adult.

---

[453] Maarten Van Buuren : **Les Rougon-Macquart d'Émile Zola. De la Métaphore au Mythe**, op. cit. p. 185.
[454] **Ibidem**, p. 187.
[455] Émile Zola: **R. M. V**, op. cit. p. 1094.
[456] Émile Zola: **R. M. II**, op. cit. p. 1404.
[457] **Ibidem**, p. 1452.
[458] Roger Ripoll recalls in **Les Rougon-Macquart d'Émile Zola. De la Métaphore au Mythe**, that according to Dr. Lucas, whose scientific theories had inspired Zola, degeneration is the inevitable fate awaiting families from the fifth generation. And indeed, Louiset belongs to the fifth generation from Adélaïde Fouque, hence the conformity of Zola's "*scientific*" conceptions with that of his *maître à penser*, op. cit. p. 168.

Zola's painting of heredity in the family of the Rougon-Macquart seems, in fact, in all aspects, to be reasonably aligned with the theories of the scientists of his time if one believes the book of the reknown scholar Professor Michel Foucault, who writes that in the second half of the nineteenth Century, innovations in sex technology << *s'articulaient facilement, car la théorie de la* << *dégénérescence* >> *leur permettait de renvoyer perpétuellement de l'une à l'autre ; elle expliquait comment une hérédité lourde de maladies diverses - organiques, fonctionnelles ou psychiques, peu importe - produisait en fin de compte un pervers sexuel (cherchez dans la généalogie d'un exhibitionniste ou d'un homosexuel : vous y trouverez un ancêtre hémiplégique, un parent phtisique, ou un oncle atteint de démence sénile) ; mais elle expliquait comment une*

In the corpus, there is another case of health issue similar to that of Louis. This case is about Jacques, the only son of Claude Lantier in **L'Œuvre**. The physical portrait of this poor lad is simply pitiful: << *Blême, la tête de l'enfant semblait avoir grossi encore, si lourde de crâne maintenant, qu'il ne pouvait plus la porter. Elle reposait inerte, on l'aurait crue déjà morte, sans le souffle fort qui sortait de ses lèvres décolorées* >>[459]. This is the place to stress that the character here reaches the bottom of the abyss even for the amorphous character's standard. Jacques owes his misfortune to his father, a Lantier, therefore a madman who has his share of the original crack as the great-grandson of Aunt Dide. Basically, we have to agree with David Baguley that the naturalistic child is characterised on the one hand by << *[...] the figure of the ugly, deformed or preformed child* >>[460], and on the other hand: << *the naturalist child incarnates the essential naturalist condition by its marginally human aspect, its brief, tenuous hold on human existence, its evident biological nature* >>[461].

Generally speaking, the amorphous characters pay the highest price for the debauchery and the perversions of their parents. They are ruthlessly sentenced to death as culprits for the sins of their parents. This treatment may seem unfair to those who consider them to be innocent children that pay a heavy for crimes committed by their parents. The fact remains that this hereditary ransom will turn into a double fatality with the addition of the influence of the milieu on them. However, in the understanding of the Zolian narrator, these considerations are irrelevant. What matters is dissipation, the consequences of which are as varied as they are enormous for the imperial society.

The sexual practices studied here are indeed the cause for such an implacable fatality[462].

2.4. The mad and/or crazy characters

---

perversion sexuelle induisait aussi un épuisement de la descendance – rachitisme des enfants, stérilité des générations futures. L'ensemble perversion - hérédité - dégénérescence a constitué le noyau solide des nouvelles technologies du sexe. Et qu'on n'imagine pas qu'il s'agissait là seulement d'une théorie médicale scientifiquement insuffisante et abusivement moralisatrice. Sa surface de dispersion a été large et son implantation profonde >>, in **Histoire de la Sexualité, I, La Volonté de Savoir**, Paris, Gallimard, Tel, 1976, pp. 156-157.

[459] Émile Zola: **R. M. IV**, op. cit. p. 258.
[460] David Baguley: **Naturalist Fiction. The Entropic Vision**, op. cit. p. 213.
[461] **Ibidem**, p. 213.
[462] Émile Zola sees in Maxime's femininity the decay of the Empire: << *Ce joli jeune homme, dont les vestons montraient les formes grêles, cette fille manquée, qui se promenait sur les boulevards, la raie au milieu de la tête, avec de petits rires et des sourires ennuyés, se trouva être, aux mains de Renée, une de ces débauches de décadence qui, à certaines heures, dans une nation pourrie, épuise une chair et détraque une intelligence* >>, in **R. M. I**, op. cit. p. 486.

There are three madmen in the real sense of the term in **Les Rougon-Macquart**; it is Father Fouque whom - << *mourut fou* >>[463]-, François Mouret, and lastly Aunt Dide who spends twenty-five years in the asylum in **Le Docteur Pascal**. But beside these three really mad individuals, there are many virtually "*crazy*" and broken characters even though they seem lucid. They are Claude Lantier, Jacques Lantier and Roubaud, Marthe Mouret, Buteau Fouan and Hilarion, Nana, Georges Hugon and Renée. The reader knows almost nothing about the madness of Father Fouque, the narrator having almost obscured this aspect in his narration. However, Adélaïde inherits her father's madness because she behaves in a strange way which most often defies all logic[464]. Her misconduct and hallucinations are legendary in the novel of the origins, **La Fortune des Rougon**. As the story unfolds in this first volume of the cycle, the reader realises that her crack is transmitted to each member of her offspring[465] and that it manifests itself differently in each individual. But a strong bond exists between them: the passion that Zola had named << *l'appétit* >> which eats them all up so ferociously.

This is how Marthe Mouret born Rougon, granddaughter of Aunt Dide, is disorderly, broken, hysterical in the terminology of Bertrand-Jennings, to the point of having an equivocal passion for the priest Faujas and for Divinity. She ends up devoting all her life to the priest: she neglects her husband; she gives up her home for the priest's sake; she gives away her fortune and she goes so far as to be an accomplice in the internment of her husband. Note that the husband, Mouret, got locked up under the instigation of the abbot[466]. Eventually, François Mouret, unjustly locked up with madmen, goes crazy[467] for real and turns into a criminal pyromaniac. He symbolises the unfortunate victim of sexual

---

[463] Émile Zola : **R. M. I**, op. cit. p. 41.
[464] According to Roger Ripoll, naive obedience to one's impulses is precisely the evident sign of Aunt Dide's imbalance, p. 477. Ripoll deduces from all the foregoing that the animal ferocity that is spreading among the Rougon-Macquart family is simply born of Aunt Dide, in **Réalité et Mythe chez Zola**, op. cit. p. 479.
[465] Roger Ripoll highlights the following: << *En Tante Dide, il faut reconnaître, malgré la différence d'âge, cette figure de femme fatale dominée par des puissances destructrices* >>, that is to say, the << *Figure de la fatalité* >>, **ibidem**, op. cit. p. 478.

For Françoise Gaillard, the initial adultery of Aunt Dide is the source of all crimes in the fictional cycle: << *Les crimes qui se sont gravés dans l'esprit désormais éteint de Tante Dide, ne sont jamais que la conséquence et la répétition d'un crime antérieur, jamais vraiment nommé, tout au plus, vaguement désigné comme étant l'adultère dont elle s'est rendue coupable autrefois, aux temps presque légendaires de la naissance de la famille Rougon-Macquart... Tous les crimes qui éclaboussent de sang la famille maudite, ne sont que la répétition de cet événement primitif qui est resté fixé dans la mémoire collective* >>, in Genèse et Généalogie (le cas du Dr Pascal), article published in **Romantisme XI**, 1981, p. 188.
[466] in **Le Personnel du Roman. Le Système des Personnages dans Les Rougon-Macquart de Zola**, Philippe Hamon believes that given the ideological importance of the topography, Father Faujas, by settling in Mouret's household, << *prend possession* >> indeed, and that his black cassock brings a spot of mourning in this previously peaceful home, op. cit. p. 223.
[467] See Naomi Schor who considers him a << *complacent bourgeois* >> and an << *institutionalized madman* >>, in **Zola's Crowds**, op. cit. p. 38.

frustration who becomes a dangerous criminal posing a serious threat to themselves and to the entire community.

The *"madness"* of Claude Lantier is, however, the most original in the series because it is characterised by his lucidity that defies madness itself. It is a madness of the unconscious, the foolish genius devoid of creative inspiration[468] and it manifests itself through his relationship with his artistic creation. As a professional painter, Claude is unable to complete a painting that he wishes to complete at all cost. He destroys all his unfinished canvases and commits suicide in front of that of the Ideal Woman that he cannot succeed in completing. Madness of destruction and of self-destruction, it manifests itself on a sexual level by its disastrousness, by his almost physical love for the women he paints but not for the living models that posed for him. In his psyche, there is such a confusion that he is no longer able to distinguish carnal love from intellectual and artistic love. He is also unable to differentiate the concrete and the abstract. For Philippe Hamon, Claude squanders his sexuality in his painting[469], or rather on painted women. According to Baguley, he sacrifices himself to the ideal woman when his artist friends prostitute their talent by giving into sensual women[470]. We must remember that Claude is the fruit of the debauchery of a drunken mother, Gervaise Macquart, and the brother of Nana, the high-class prostitute. In Zola's naturalistic theory, he cannot be purebred given such a family background. It is in this sense that Philippe Hamon speaks of the << *fonction mnémonique* >> of the surname. This function has got a double value, an anaphoric one – that refers to the character's past – and a *"cataphorique"* one – that announces the horizon of their future. To call oneself a Rougon or a Macquart, or to have in one's veins the blood of these two lineages, is like falling under the blow of a persistent inheritance and, implicitly, to become the victim of a catastrophic destiny[471].

Claude's brother, the one called Jacques[472], has got an ambiguous sexuality in **La Bête Humaine** where his head buzzes with the most curious confusion with

---

[468] The case of Claude Lantier seems to contradict the opinion of Maarten Van Buuren, in **Les Rougon-Macquart d'Émile Zola. De la Métaphore au Mythe**, who considers that only the geniuses are struck by the crack or the neurosis, op. cit. p. 191. Indeed, if one must accept that Pascal and Octave are geniuses, it is hard to admit that Claude Lantier and Lazare Chanteau are also geniuses, as Van Buuren asserts. In addition, Maxime and Renée - among many others - are also cracked without having the slightest genius whatsoever in them.

[469] Philippe Hamon : **Le Personnel du Roman. Le Système des Personnages dans Les Rougon-Macquart de Zola**, op. cit. p. 204.

[470] David Baguley : **Zola et les Genres**. op. cit. p. 88.

[471] Philippe Hamon, in the above book, pp. 108-111.

[472] Geoff Woolen, Nelly Wilson, Chantal Morel and Pauline McLynn believe that if Zola, who had planned this role of a serial killer for Étienne Lantier, finally decided to give it to Jacques towards the end of the draft of the novel, it is precisely because of the case of *Jack the Ripper*, an English ripper, who had murdered many women in Whitechapel in the fall of 1888. Zola is believed to have followed this case closely in **The Manchester Guardian**, see **Zola, La Bête Humaine: texte et explication**, Geoff Woollen (éd.), op. cit. pp. 68-100 ; pp. 123-135 et pp. 76-81.

unknown origins. The strongest expression of that confusion is that he is perceived as the avenger of all males, the fella invested with an equally incredible mission: that of avenging the ancient and original betrayal. That is why he suffers a special kind of thirst: he longs for bleeding a young woman[473]. The murderous madness that strikes him fades away for a moment only when he slaughters Séverine, his beloved mistress. Then his thirst comes back after a while. Yet Jacques has a conscience; he often cries in despair because he is aware of his inability to emancipate himself from that madness that starts with terribly violent headaches. But what can he do against an evil transmitted to him by his great-grandmother and his grandfather, Antoine Macquart, who himself transmitted it to his daughter, Gervaise, Jacques' mother[474]? This poisoned inheritance is inevitably shared by his brothers, Claude and Étienne - the hero of Germinal - and by his half-sister, Nana. As the saying goes, it runs in the family. It is for example that heritage that motivates Étienne's desire to kill his rival - Chaval - in the Voreux: << *Étienne, à ce moment, devint fou. Ses yeux se noyèrent d'une vapeur rouge, sa gorge s'était congestionnée d'un flot de sang. Le besoin de tuer le prenait, irrésistible, un besoin physique, l'excitation sanguine d'une muqueuse qui détermine un violent accès de toux. Cela monta, éclata en dehors de sa volonté, sous la poussée de la lésion héréditaire [...]. Toutes ses luttes lui revenaient à la mémoire, cet inutile combat contre le poison qui dormait dans ses muscles, l'alcool lentement accumulé de sa race* >>[475]. As Roger Ripoll attests, violence is the true original fault that caracterises the whole of human history[476].

It must be pointed out that the hereditary illness that the family has been dragging for nearly a century and which irrigates the veins of each of the individuals who compose it, functions as the unifying thread that unites them and shows them belonging to the same rotten << race >>. This thread also leads them to the supreme sanction, like the strings of the Parques in Greek mythology. Apart from these cases studied specifically, other characters are victims of disruptions in the corpus, their << *folie* >>, however, remains more

---

[473] Claude Seassau notes that : << *Le mythe de la bête humaine, fondé sur la première tromperie de la femme du temps des cavernes, revient comme un leitmotiv dans le roman; dans l'imaginaire zolien, l'homme des cavernes a été trahi par la femme qui l'a trompé avec un autre, aussi doit-il venger sa virilité offensée, en possédant à nouveau la femme, dans toute sa brutalité de mâle, jusqu'à l'éventrer, la détruire, pour qu'elle lui appartienne à jamais. [...]. Cela explique pourquoi Jacques tue Séverine; conformément à son ancêtre il doit tuer celle qu'il aime, pour l'arracher définitivement aux autres* >>, in **Émile Zola, Le Réalisme Symbolique**, op. cit. p. 258.

[474] Émile Zola writes about the ravages of the hereditary defect in Jacques Lantier's mind: << *La famille n'était point d'aplomb, beaucoup avaient la fêlure. Lui, à certaines heures, la sentait bien, cette fêlure héréditaire ; non pas qu'il fût d'une santé mauvaise, car l'appréhension et la honte de ses crises l'avaient seules maigri autrefois ; mais c'étaient, dans son être, de subites pertes d'équilibre, comme des cassures, des trous par lesquels son moi lui échappait, au milieu d'une sorte de grande fumée qui déformait tout. Il ne s'appartenait plus, il obéissait à ses muscles, à la bête enragée* >>, in **R. M. V**, op. cit. p. 1043.

[475] Émile Zola: **R. M. III**, op. cit. 1571.

[476] Roger Ripoll: **Réalité et Mythe chez Zola**, op. cit. p. 112.

contextual and sporadic. The characters that fall into this category are Buteau, Cabuche, Renée, Nana, Roubaud, Georges and Hilarion. Children with debauched and/or crazy parents may be subjected to other sanctions, such as imbecility.

2.5. The characters lacking intelligence

The most unprecedented and probably the most original sanction that awaits the offspring of the debauched character is the idiocy or the lack of intelligence that strikes them in **Les Rougon-Macquart**. From **La Fortune des Rougon**, the narrator insists on this fate, starting with Pierre Rougon, the eldest child of the grandmother. Then comes Pierre's son, Eugène Rougon, the customerless solicitor. Pierre's nephew, Silvère Mouret, is particularly silly despite the apparent sympathy the narrator feels for him. The situation is hardly better for Claude Lantier, the perfectly silly and talentless painter who is never visited by the god of the arts. The same goes for his son, Jacques. When it comes to the female agents, Estelle Muffat and especially Tatan Néné are the living symbols of feminine idiocy in **Nana**.

Pierre Rougon, from the outset, is presented as << *le plus taré* >> of all the sons of Plassans[477]. His son, Eugène, does not only inherit his broad face but also his pale head that lacks genius. As a result, both are opportunistic and envious calculators. But the sexual agent that is the most devoid of intelligence in **Les Rougon-Macquart**, is without a doubt, Silvère Mouret, about whom the narrator asserts: << *Il se mit à fréquenter l'école de dessin où il se lia avec un jeune échappé du collège qui lui prêta son ancien traité de géométrie. Et il s'enfonça dans l'étude, sans guide, passant des semaines entières à se creuser la tête pour comprendre les choses les plus simples du monde. Il devint ainsi un de ces ouvriers savants qui savent à peine signer leur nom et qui parlent de l'algèbre comme d'une personne de leur connaissance. Rien ne détraque autant un esprit qu'une pareille instruction, faite à bâtons rompus, ne reposant sur aucune base solide* >>[478].

The consequences of this autodidactic were catastrophic for the young man because his knowledge was so incomplete and so << *mal digérées, qu'il ne réussit jamais à (les) classer nettement dans sa tête* >>[479]. Despite his courage similar to that of Sisyphus - his mythical counterpart - Silvère achieved no concrete results as he was never visited by Prometheus. As it has been mentioned before, heredity is the transcendental force that refuses to bow down to any exemption or redemption. It is a visceral tare anchored in the depths of the personality of the subject, for heredity is not a mask that can be removed when you feel like it.

---

[477] Émile Zola: **R. M. I**, op. cit. p. 243.
[478] **Ibidem**, p.138
[479] **Ibidem**, p. 137.

In **L'Œuvre**, the idiot par excellence is named Jacques, whose father recognises, with bitterness: << *-Non, ma parole! il devient idiot ... Vois-moi sa tête, s'il n'a pas l'air idiot. C'est désespérant* >>[480]. How could it be otherwise when he, the father, sank << *au fond de la folie héroïque de l'art* >>[481], << *cette faillite du genie* >>[482] ? The idiocy of the little Jacques, however, does not come only from his heavy heredity, but rather mainly from his brutal separation with the countryside where he was born. The rotten environment[483] of Paris had a significant impact on his physical and mental development. In Paris, in fact, where his parents settled down in the run-up to his fourth birthday, misery strikes hard Jacques' family. The father then became angry and brutal towards his offspring. The son is beaten and reprimanded each time he moves while he is being painted. His mother, the poor Christine, who is a passionate lover but an equally poor mother, joins the father in exacerbating the child's martyrdom[484]. Such an austere education rendered the lad taciturn, introverted, with the perpetual fear of making a reprehensible mistake. In such a miserable environment, Jacques is led to so much cretinism. In Zola's world, in fact, man is subjected to a double fatality that governs his entire life: that of heredity on the one hand and that of the environment on the other hand.

Nevertheless, with the same initial hereditary handicaps, two children from the same parents develop very differently when Zola places them in different environments. That is why Maxime becomes a vicious and a debauched young man in the Parisian rotten environment[485] while Clotilde flourishes both in her physical and in her mental health in the Plassans countryside. The milieu proves fatal for the former – Maxime became ataxic and died at the young age of thirty-three - whereas a reverse and a positive fatality corrects Clotilde's hereditary deficiencies to make her the ideal woman and the mother of the unknown child, who is cleansed of the ancestral crack. The panacea that cures Clotilde is called by a name: the Souleiade, that country property that is a symbol of the great

---

[480] Émile Zola: **R. M. I**, op. cit. p. 217.
[481] **Ibidem**, p. 257
[482] **Ibidem**, p. 257.
[483] Maarten Van Buuren recognises that in Zola's works, the environment has a double edge with its social and natural conditions, see **Les Rougon-Macquart d'Émile Zola. De la Métaphore au Mythe**, op. cit. p. 274.
[484] Chantal Bertrand- Jennings puts her in the category of women who make the misfortune of their children - with Mrs. Josserand, Marthe Mouret, La Grande, Gervaise and Mrs. Duveyrier - in **L'Éros et la Femme chez Zola**, op. cit. p. 97. Long before that, literary criticism considered Christine as a woman belonging to the class of *femmes fatales*, despicable nymphomaniacs, and precisely in the subgroup of the skinny and withered women as opposed to the curvy and appetising women, p. 61.
[485] The city of Paris is clearly identified as an accomplice when it comes to committing debauchery and incest in **R. M. I** of Émile Zola, op. cit. p. 458.

nature where the scientific truth of Dr. Pascal has replaced the fever[486] of the flesh and the profit-making machine that shakes Paris to its core.

Moreover, the character of Tatan Néné suffers from such a sad idiocy that the girl is constantly labelled a << *dindonnette* >> in **Nana**. Her only name sounds like a non-articulate language, the language of a child learning to speak. Even though she is an adult, she stagnates at the infantile stage with regard to her mental and intellectual faculties' development. It is unfortunate to note that the novel offers no idea of her parentage and that lack of background information prevents the reader from appreciating if any share of her idiocy rests on her ancestors' shoulders given Zola's theory of heredity.

All the sanctions studied so far are heralding an apocalypse that will soon strike Zola's characters and, hence, the entire imperial society. The author had indeed stated that his characters << *racontent le Second Empire à travers leurs drames individuels* >>[487] in the general preface of July 1st, 1871.

2.6. The early and untimely death

We have just seen that in **Les Rougon-Macquart**, sexual debauchery and perversion lead to disastrous and inevitable consequences. For Zola, the question is simple: early sexuality and dissipation inevitably lead to an early and an untimely death. As evidence, in **La Fortune des Rougon**, Miette dies at fourteen and her boyfriend, Silvère, at seventeen[488]. As for Renée, she passes away at thirty years old[489] in **La Curée** and her incestuous lover, Maxime, bows out at thirty-three. His son, Charles, died at the age of fifteen in **Le Docteur Pascal**. Nana does not cross the threshold of nineteen years of age in the novel that bears her name[490], while her son, Louiset, was old enough to die towards his fifth year. Palmyra dies at the age of thirty, struck by a sunburn in **La Terre**. Her brother and incestuous lover, Hilarion, is killed, aged twenty-four. Jacques Lantier died on his eighth birthday in **L'Œuvre**. His father, Claude, followed suit

---

[486] For Maarten Van Buuren, << *Dans les* **Rougon-Macquart***, la fièvre résulte d'un excès de sensations et Zola désigne les développements sociaux sous le Second Empire comme la source principale de cette surexcitation* >>, see **Les Rougon-Macquart d'Émile Zola. De la Métaphore au Mythe**, op. cit. p. 196.

[487] Émile Zola: **R. M. I**, op. cit. p. 3.

[488] According to Chantal Bertrand-Jennings, << *Ce sont particulièrement les couples d'enfants, d'adolescents ou de jeunes vierges qui sont chargés de signifier le sacrifice de l'amour au dieu de la chasteté* >>, in **L'Éros et la Femme chez Zola**, op. cit. p. 31.

Roger Ripoll qualifies the deaths of those two young men as a *plénitude suprême*, in **Réalité et Mythe chez Zola**, op. cit. p. 474.

[489] For Roger Ripoll, to assimilate Renée (and Nana) to Venus already means the murder of others and of themselves since << *Vénus est une puissance destructrice, le triomphe de Nana correspond à la ruine et à la mort des hommes qui l'entourent, des forces mauvaises s'incarnent dans les figures des dieux. [...] Les images des dieux portent en elles l'énergie primitive d'une sexualité dévorante* >>, in **Réalité et Mythe chez Zola**, op. cit. p. 82.

[490] **Ibidem**, p. 82.

in his mid-thirties. In the same novel, it is obvious that the Dubuche children will not endure the fresh air and the sun for a long time, although their death is not announced anywhere. In **La Bête Humaine**, it is Flore who commits suicide at twenty-one. Then Séverine is slaughtered by her lover, Jacques Lantier, when she is around twenty-eight years old. Her killer is also killed by his rival, Pecqueux, when he is about thirty years old. Louise, raped by Président Grandmorin, dies at sixteen. Angélique also dies at twenty, a few minutes after her marriage[491], in **Le Rêve**. To that list of fatalities, one must add the fetuses which were never lucky enough to be born. They seem to have paid the highest possible price for the rapes suffered by their mothers, Renée and Nana (her second pregnancy). Those two pregnancies both ended in miscarriages.

In the margins of those sexual agents who die early, there is another class of agents who, without necessarily dying young, are still killed for their sexual vice. They are essentially Vandeuvres in **Nana**, Hourdequin and Françoise in **La Terre**, Claude Lantier in **L'Oeuvre** and finally Président Grandmorin in **La Bête Humaine**. It would, however, be prudent to split those sexual agents into two classes: first, the class of agents murdered for sexual motives, and secondly, that of suicidal subjects as a result of a sexual frustration.

Hilarion belongs to the first class. He is a rapist killed by his grandmother, La Grande in **La Terre**. In the same novel, Françoise is killed accidentally by her sister Lise, who had just helped her husband, Buteau, rape her in the fields. Hourdequin was later killed by Tron, his valet and love rival who set up a deadly trap for him. All those facts make **La Terre** the black novel of the French peasantry. By the game of symmetries of which Zola alone held the secret, **La Bête Humaine** is the black novel of the railways. Indeed, there are several villainous crimes in it, like that of Roubaud who slaughters his rival, Président Grandmorin. Then Jacques Lantier slaughters his mistress, Séverine, who is at the centre of so many crimes of passion. As a real catalyst, she is targeted by her unsuspected rival, Flore, the virgin in love with Jacques. Flore provoked the death of twenty innocent victims by derailing the train only because she wanted to kill her love rival, Séverine[492]. At the end of the novel, if death hangs over the heads of hundreds of soldiers, maybe even thousands of them, it is because a crazy train is launched at a brisk pace for reasons of jealousy. In that case, it was Philomène's fault since her two lovers, Jacques and Pecqueux, were at each

---

[491] In **Réalité et Mythe chez Zola**, op. cit., Roger Ripoll presents the death of Angélique as a sign of grandeur and purity, for the myth demands death, op. cit. p. 110.

[492] Jacques Noiray affirms that the woman and the machine maintain relationships of exclusion, opposition and substitution and that << *Cet antagonisme profond, source de terreur ou de haine, impose peu à peu l'idée d'une vengeance nécessaire de la femme contre la machine usurpatrice. Quand Flore cherche à se venger de Jacques, c'est d'abord contre la Lison que son geste est dirigé, et ce geste ne tue que la machine* >>, in **Le Romancier et la Machine, I, L'Univers de Zola**, op. cit. p. 413.

other's throats[493], demanding blood either by killing the other or being killed by him. That quarrel of rivalry turned into a mass slaughter that remains unresolved[494]. And it's because of all those horrors that Seassau claims that **La Bête Humaine** is the novel of extreme violence related to sexuality[495], just like **L'Assommoir, Germinal, La Terre** and like **La Débâcle**. For him indeed, those titles constitute the most violent novels of the **Rougon-Macquart** series and rightly so[496].

The second class is made up of suicidal people including Vandeuvres, Georges Hugon, Claude Lantier, Flore and François Mouret. The first and last ones come together to the extent that they immolate themselves by fire. I will return later on to the symbolic power of fire in the corpus. In addition, Claude hangs himself while Flore throws herself in front of the train. Those deaths are all atrocious and the rare violence that characterises them is in line with the apocalypse announced above. They also symbolise the ruthless supreme sanction that their creator has in store for them to clearly show his disapproval of their lust and dissipation. The Zolian narrator is, from this point of view at least, a moralist in my eyes. He is a moralist who tries to prove that immorality is a capital crime punishable by death[497]. His impassibility before the fate of those characters sentenced to the death penalty - or even forever damned - is obvious. Like an implacable executioner, he strikes them pitilessly and wipes them off the surface of the earth they so polluted in his eyes.

The rule is simple to understand: to live too fast is to burn the candle at both ends; it wastes one's energy and irremediably leads to death in **Les Rougon-Macquart**. This novelistic series offers indeed an entropic vision of society. In total, one can admit with David Baguley that : << *At the heart of naturalist vision, then, there is a poetics of disintegration, dissipation, death, with its endless repertory of wasted lives, of destructive forces, of spent energies, of crumbling moral and social structures, with its promiscuity, humiliations, degradation, its decomposing bodies, its invasive materialism, its scenes of mania, excess, destruction, the hovels and brothels, the ''assommoirs'' and the*

---

[493] Claude Seassau shows that jealousy leads to extreme violence and that, as a consequence, jealous characters are indeed ferocious beasts, in **Émile Zola, Le Réalisme Symbolique**, op. cit. p. 257.

[494] Jacques Noiray can see in Zola's works a war between man and the machine, the latter being an instrument of death and being responsible for a cataclysmic end of civilisation in **Le Romancier et la Machine, I, L'Univers de Zola**, op. cit. p.425 et p. 448.

[495] Claude Seassau : **Émile Zola, Le Réalisme Symbolique**, op. cit. p. 257.

[496] Seassau notices that: << *La violence est partout, dans les relations humaines, dans la sexualité et dans les affrontements où elle atteint une intensité telle qu'elle rejoint les rites de violence les plus primitifs. La violence est au cœur des romans de Zola, elle exprime les conflits les plus banals comme les plus aigus, tout s'organise autour d'elle* >>, **ibidem**, p. 187.

[497] In **L'Éros et la Femme chez Zola**, Chantal Bertrand-Jennings assumes that one cannot climax without punishment in Zola's novels where evil is always punished, sooner or later. She sees the moralising lexicon as evidence of that assertion as such choice of vocabulary associates sexual intercourse with evil, fault, sin, shame, crime and even stain, op. cit. pp. 13-14.

"abattoirs", the hospitals and the cemeteries, the mud and the blood, the rain and the pain, along with all the "theriomorphic", "nyctomorphic" and "catamorphic" images >>[498].

Yet, the fatality that strikes Zola's characters is an endogenous inevitability because they pay a heavy price for the faults they have committed. Such a fatality has nothing to do with that which strikes, for example, the Racinian heroes that are victims of the revanchist spirit of the gods, those heartless exogenous powers. For example, Iphigenia did not do anything to deserve to be sacrificed to the gods so that the winds would be favourable to the ships of Agamemnon's allies, but her heavy destiny compelled her to carry out that fatal duty. On the contrary, the Nanas and the Renées are sanctioned not under the influence of a divine fatum but only because of their own dissipation.

We have already seen that the being of the character was first of all all about their sexuality. Let us now add to that reaity the fact that the characters' doing and their becoming are also led by and towards their sexuality.

This is the place to reiterate our hypothesis of the probable presence of some specific neurotic-type sexual elements related to Zola's own biography, elements that may have betrayed his unconscious in order to free himself by means of his novelistic creative work. This study amounts to a review of the metalinguistic and the poetic functions of the **Rougon-Macquart**'s novelistic discourse. The next chapter is devoted to the study of such functions and it should make it possible to better understand that question of great psychoanalytic interest.

---

[498] David Baguley: **Naturalist Fiction. The Entropic Vision**, op. cit. p. 222.

CHAPTER III: THE METALINGUISTIC AND THE POETIC FUNCTIONS IN THE ROUGON-MACQUART OR THE PREVISIBILITY OF THE FATALITY OF SEXUALITY

Roman Jakobson[499] and the linguists distinguish six functions of language devolving respectively into the six entities of the diagram of communication. Thus, to the sender, it is attributed the expressive function and to the addressee or the receiver, the conative function is attributed. At the contact level, we attribute the phatic function while the poetic function should be attributed to the message itself. Finally, to the referent corresponds the referential function and to the code, we attribute the metalinguistic function. Among these cardinal functions, I will only be interested in the poetic and the metalinguistic functions. Indeed, the study of those two functions should make it possible to discover any networks of metaphors, any haunting mythical figures and any repetitive dramatic situations that are necessary in the fundamental operation of the superposition of the texts of a given author in the psychoanalytic method.

I will then combine those themes with Zola's dreams in the realm of sexuality in order to discover his personal myth. Such operation is the second step of the aforementioned method. The third step will try to unmask the author's unconscious and the fourth[500] and final step will endeavour to compare Zola's biography with the personal myth discovered in the second step, for verification purposes. Admittedly, this chapter only concerns the first two stages in the psychoanalytic method since the last two stages will appear in parts III and IV of this book.

I. THE METALINGUISTIC FUNCTION OR THE MYTHS AND THEIR "*SIGNIFIÉ*" IN THE LOGIC OF SEXUALITY

To understand **Les Rougon-Macquart**, one must understand the code chosen by their narrator and mythology is part and parcel of that code. Like the other codes, the myth requires a kind of initiation before the receiver of the message thus coded can fully grasp it. It is the metalinguistic function which imposes on the receiver many references outside the immediate message. It calls upon a previous culture that one must master before grasping completely the current message dished out by the sender or the transmitter. It is, in short, an intertextual phenomenon. I will identify and classify the myths that Zola recovers and translates in a certain way in the corpus. I will not approach this study in the sense of Roger Ripoll, that is, by showing the close relationship between myth and reality in the Zolian novel, much less like Van Buuren who showed how Zola is progressing from metaphor to myth to the detriment of the realism and the naturalism he so loudly claimed throughout his writing career.

---

[499] Roman Jakobson : **Essais de Linguistique Générale**, Paris, Éditions de Minuit, 1966, p. 17.
[500] For more information on those steps in the psychoanalysis method, please refer to the introduction.

My ambition, on the contrary, is to show that Zola's myths and metaphors all converge towards a characterisation of the inevitability of sexuality. Indeed, if the metaphor is a privileged means to expressing sexuality, the reference to an ancient myth introduces a notion of certain inevitability.

1. The identification and the classification of the myths

The myths will be divided into two categories: the Christian myths and then the pagan myths[501]. By Christian myths, I mean myths whose origin is biblical while pagan myths are those of any other origin.

1.1. The Christian myths

In the corpus, the Christian myths are related to the Original Fault in the Garden of Eden and then to the question of the Devil and death. Of course, those religious episodes will appear in **Les Rougon-Macquart** in a metaphorical form that does not go without the belief in the existence of hell, which is the final dwelling place of the damned under the gaze of a dismayed God, but a God that is implacable in his revenge on the ungodly sinners. The first Christian myth of interest is that of the Garden of Eden and the original fault of which Adam and Eve, the first two human beings on earth, were the perpetrators.

1. 1. 1. The Garden of Eden and the Original Sin.

If no space is explicitly designated by the transparent name of *"Garden of Eden"*, it does not prevent the reader from considering certain spaces in the corpus as its replicas, either descriptively or functionally. The myth of the Garden of Eden is indeed present both in **La Curée**, parodically embodied[502] by the greenhouse of the Hotel Saccard, and again in **La Faute de l'Abbé Mouret** with the Paradou. The former squeezes and smothers Renée who ate the fruit of the forbidden tree[503] within. The latter, the Paradou, is less morbid than the first space but it still remains the space where the new Adam - Father Mouret - and the new Eve - Albine - like their biblical ancestors, experiment lust before engaging into sexual intercourse leading to shame and, ultimatey, to exile. Certain spaces in Zola's works are indeed sinful places for dissolution and shame. Such places are all reminiscent of the Second Empire era, a rotten regime that is so dissipated that it is doomed forever. Is it necessary to insist again on the sweetness of paradise that rings in the name Paradou? Unlike all the other spaces identified as the Garden of Eden in a rather equivocal or a totally figurative way, this space

---

[501] Dans **Réalité et Mythe chez Zola**, Roger Ripoll prefers the equivalent terminology of Greco-Latin and Judeo-Christian origin, op. cit. p. 60.
[502] **Ibidem,** Ripoll also believes that the myths that Zola updates in his novels are intended either to parody the original myths, or to restore their power, p. 60.
[503] It can be read in Maarten Van Buuren's book that the greenhouse is a << *paradis perverti* >>, << *une mère pervertie* >>, in opposition to the << *Bonne mère* >> that nature is, see **Les Rougon-Macquart d'Émile Zola. De la Métaphore au Mythe**, op. cit. p. 142 et p. 143.

is truly a paradisiacal space with its lush flora that acts like an aphrodisiac. <<*Le Paradou*>> is an exciting sexual agent indeed and as such, it arouses Albine and the priest, Serge Mouret, healthily[504] however, in he eyes of Zola. The analogy is sometimes striking between the novelistic text of **La Faute de l'Abbé Mouret** and the biblical text in the book of **Genesis.**

Everything begins during Serge Mouret's recovery from sickness in the Paradou when Albine, like Eve, goes in search of the tree that was duly and formally << *défendu* >> and << *où l'on meurt* >>. Like Adam, Serge is the force that tries to oppose her by repeating : << *Tu sais que c'est défend* >>[505], before adding: << *Qu'est-ce que tu cherches donc là? cria-t-il. Tu sais bien que c'est défendu* >>[506]. But, because he is nothing but the new Adam, Serge cannot resist the temptation when it comes from his beloved Eve: << *Mais nous ne mourrons pas, continua-t-elle* (Albine) [...]. *C'est un arbre de vie, un arbre sous lequel nous serons plus forts, plus sains, plus parfaits* >>[507].

Having consented to help find Albine's tree of life, Serge, in an internal monologue, cannot help but sense an imminent misfortune, a bad omen that will crush both of them soon enough. On the spot, he first gives up God, then the Virgin Mary whom he used to adore on his knees[508]. Afterwards, he deifies Albine by declaring : << *[...] je le sais bien à cette heure, tu es ma maîtresse, ma souveraine, celle que je dois adorer à genoux* >>[509]. Albine's victory over the Virgin Mary is the victory of life over death, that of procreative sexuality over abstinence and also the victory of nature over religious dogma. The love affair between Albine and Mouret is not a fault in Zola's eyes, especially because Albine

---

[504] Jean-François Tonard gives the greenhouse an actantial role, and rightly so, in **Thématique et Symbolique de l'Espace Clos dans le Cycle des Rougon-Macquart d'Émile Zola**, Frankfurt, Berlin, Bern, New York, Paris, Wien, Peter Lang, collection Publications Universitaires Européennes, 1994, p. 37.

Philippe Hamon adds, in **Le Personnel du Roman. Le Système des Personnages dans Les Rougon-Macquart d'Émile Zola**, that the Paradou is a destinator, op. cit. p. 230.

Roger Ripoll does not say the opposite when he relies on sheet 10294 of the manuscript of **La Faute de l'Abbé Mouret**, where Zola clearly writes that << *C'est la nature qui joue le rôle du Satan de la Bible ; c'est elle qui tente Serge et Blanche* [qui deviendra finalement Albine] *et qui les couche sous l'arbre du mal par une matinée splendide*>>, in **Réalité et Mythe chez Zola**, op. cit. p. 114.

[505] Émile Zola: **R. M. I**, op. cit. p.1359.

[506] **Ibidem**, p. 1367.

[507] **Ibidem**, p. 1402.

[508] Roger Ripoll, in the above work, considers that the Virgin Mary, for Serge Mouret, is the woman to be loved, so his devotion to Mary is the expression of his repressed desires, which will resurface in the form of his love for Albine, whom he takes for Marie, p. 108.

Maarten Van Buuren agrees that Mary's veneration prefigures Serge's love for Albine, see **Les Rougon-Macquart d'Émile Zola. De la Métaphore au Mythe**, op. cit. p. 173.

[509] Émile Zola: **R. M. I**, op. cit. p. 1406.

This passage makes Roger Ripoll write that Serge starts confusing Albine and Marie from that moment on, granting the former the neurotic love he had for the latter, a love he had hitherto repressed in his unconscious, see **Réalité et Mythe chez Zola**, op. cit. p. 108.

conceives that day. Everything converges towards that goal : both plants, animals and minerals convey towards that reproductive act that brings about new life: <<*C'était le jardin qui avait voulu la faute. Maintenant, il était le tentateur dont toutes les voix enseignaient l'amour [...].*

Les prairies élevaient une voix profonde, faite des soupirs des millions d'herbes que le soleil baisait, large plainte d'une foule innombrable en rut, qu'attendrissaient les caresses fraîches des rivières, les nudités des eaux courantes, au bord desquelles les saules rêvaient tout haut de désir [...].

Les bêtes du jardin, à leur tour, leur criaient de s'aimer [...].

La fatalité de la génération les entourait. Ils cédèrent aux exigences du jardin. Ce fut l'arbre qui confia à l'oreille d'Albine ce que les mères murmurent aux épousées, le soir des noces.

Albine se livra. Serge la posséda [...].

Le parc applaudissait formidablement>>[510].

The analogy between the two texts goes further when, a few moments after their sin of the flesh, Albine and Serge hear a voice coming to them, that of the terrible Brother Archangias, this parody of the Archangel Gabriel. Like Adam and Eve, the sexual heroes are so ashamed of their actions that Albine declares: << *Cachons-nous, cachons-nous, répétait-elle d'un ton suppliant* >>[511]. Like her predecessor in the Christian myth, Eve, Albine then covers herself with a necklace of leaves and gives one to Serge, saying : << *Ne vois-tu pas que nous sommes nus?* >>[512].

Frère Archangias then confirms their nakedness by throwing this at them: << *Je vous vois, je sais que vous êtes nus [...]. C'est une abomination* >>[513], before warning priest Mouret about the snake while expelling the two love birds from the 'Garden of Eden'[514] : << *Ne voyez-vous pas la queue du serpent se tordre parmi les mèches de ses cheveux ? [...]. Lâchez-la, ne la touchez plus, car elle est le commencement de l'enfer [...]. Au nom de Dieu, sortez de ce jardin* >>[515]. The whole episode is a transparent rewriting of **Genesis** chapter 3 in the **Bible**. However, despite the fact that the fiction is fully mirroring the Holy Scripture here, for Zola, Albine and Priest Mouret are not at fault. The only fault committed here, it seems, is indeed that of Brother Archangias, the homewrecker who expells them from the Garden of Eden while Albine had just conceived there. She is therefore the one that obeys God's commandment to reproduce the human species by being fruitful and to fill the earth[516]. Archangias is therefore the herald of a God of Death and Punishment. He embodies Satan

---

[510] Émile Zola: **R. M. I**, op. cit. pp. 1407-1409.
[511] **Ibidem**, p. 1412.
[512] **Ibidem,** p. 1412.
[513] **Ibidem**, p. 1417.
[514] Roger Ripoll sees in this his highly symbolic role as the God of anger in charge of expelling the lovers from the Paradou, in **Réalité et Mythe chez Zola**, op. cit. p. 95.
[515] Émile Zola: **R. M. I**. op. cit. p. 1417.
[516] **Genesis 1.28, The Bible**, op. cit.

himself in Zola's view for he is the driving force behind Albine's abandonment by her lover and the father of her unborn baby. Brother Archangias is also the angel of death for his actions led to Albine's suicide and to her baby's death in the womb.

In the same category, one can point out <<*l'aire Saint-Mîttre*>> in **La Fortune des Rougon** and <<*le bois de Boulogne*>> in **La Curée** as spaces with biblical tone. <<*L'aire Saint-Mîttre*>> is an abandoned graveyard where a multitude of plants grow with various fruits that nobody dares to eat in Plassans. It is that equivocal space that serves as a meeting place for the two young lovers, Miette and Silvère, and it is in there that they swear to love each other forever, even though they do not taste the forbidden fruit. The chastity of their love saves them from damnation, it seems. They die innocent, both killed only by the soldiers of Napoleon III.

Unlike the previous space, << *le bois de Boulogne* >> incites to debauchery. The Paris socialites go in there at dusk hoping to meet people, and if necessary, to seduce someone. It is precisely in there that Renée vaguely formulates, for the first time ever, the vow to commit incest which is designated periphrastically by << *une autre jouissance plus âcre* >>. Indeed, the wood sharpens the curiosity of the woman and incites her to commit the fault. For David Baguley indeed: << *Cette Belle* [Renée] *aux cheveux "fauve pâle", infidèle à la promesse de la chanson de sa jeunesse - "Nous n'irons plus au bois" - s'est aventurée dans le Bois, dans le lieu symbolique des contes de fées, lieu de l'aventure, des dangers, de la perte des valeurs acceptées et de la perte de la sécurité de la vie familiale* >>[517].

So, the very evening of her *"fatal"* revelation in chapter I, Renée entered the greenhouse, that winter garden with its exotic flora and, stifled with jealousy - Maxime was smiling at his fiancée, Louise de Mareuil - she bites a leaf of the Tanghin tree. That's when she realises that she is in love with her husband's son, and that << *cette autre jouissance rare* >> she hoped for, was in fact an apex that is called by one name: incest. On the other hand, that mouthful in a poisoned leaf by Renée is nothing less than a symmetry of Eve eating the forbidden fruit in the Garden of Eden. One can remember that in retaliation, the descendants of Adam and Eve were condemned to live by the sweat of their face, to give birth in pain and, ultimately, to die[518]. In **La Curée**, the tanghin flavour represents the fault and the origin of Renée's curse. Her eyes were then open to evil, that is to say the truth about her incestuous attraction to Maxime. Since the curse is a fatality, she could no longer resist incest; and death, implicitly, was part and parcel of her narrative programme from there on. According to Baguley, this episode digs the distance between Renée and Blanche Neige since the latter spits the apple while the former swallows it. That is why,

---

[517] David Baguley: **Zola et les Genres**, chapter III : *La Curée* : La Bête et la Belle, op. cit. p. 36.
[518] **The Holy Bible**, *Genesis,* chapter 3, verse 19, op. cit. pp. 3-4.

unlike Blanche Neige, << *Elle [Renée] figure la Belle qui se transforme en Bête* >>[519].

Moreover, the two lovers have enjoyed their wildest nights of love in the greenhouse as if they were returning to the place of the Original Fault, like a criminal who would return to their crime scene. This return must be seen as an admission of guilt on the one hand. On the other hand, the lovers show no remorse whatsoever and therefore there is absolutely no hope for forgiveness for them. The narrator, emulating God, overwhelms them with the harshest punishments to avenge the divine commandments[520] that they have broken. This is the moment to look into how the novelistic hypertext translates that phase of punishment that sanctions the fault.

1.1.2. The punishment or the penalty for disobedience to God

Albine and Mouret are de facto expelled from the Paradou by Brother Archangias. Elsewhere, Nana and Renée, like << *serpents* >> - metaphor + myth - are the root cause for human misfortune, for it was the serpent that misled Eve in the Garden of Eden. Symmetrically, those two ladies were misleading figures that subdued influential men during the Second Empire and brought them down to Hades. The whole imperial society was brought down to its knees and vanished precisely because it could not resist the temptation of the flesh. However, the divine punishment also stipulated in addition that the woman would give birth in pain while the man would eat bread by the sweat of his face.

In a certain way, the novelistic story in **Les Rougon-Macquart** corroborates this last religious narrative to the extent that the Rougons are fat because they are active and hardworking while the Macquart, who are drunk and lazy, die of hunger. In addition, the miscarriages of Renée, then of Nana, are perceived as painful trials and tribulations. In the particular case of Serge and Albine, the woman dies shortly after her lover abandons her in favour of priesthood. Albine, only sixteen years old, dies[521] indeed while she is about three months[522] pregnant. It is not risky to argue that this anticipated death prevents her from going through the pangs of child birth. Serge followed them a few years later. He passes away because of phthisis in **Le Docteur Pascal**[523], around the age of thirty-three[524].

---

[519] David Baguley: **Zola et les Genres**, op. cit. p. 38.
[520] This is also the opinion of Chantal Bertrand-Jennings in **L'Éros et la Femme chez Zola**, op. cit. p. 13.
[521] For Roger Ripoll, in **Réalité et Mythe chez Zola**, the mythical dimension of Albine makes her death inevitable, op. cit. p. 109.
[522] Émile Zola: **R. M. I**, op. cit. p. 1516.
[523] Émile Zola: **R. M. V**, op. cit. p. 1215.
[524] For Maarten Van Buuren, the mortifications that Serge imposes on himself are a threat to his own life, in **Les Rougon-Macquart d'Émile Zola. De la Métaphore au Mythe**, op. cit. p. 146.

There is, in the light of these findings, that Zola's Romanesque text attains the status of a realistic text insofar as the hypertext shows a certain fidelity towards the hypotext from which it has borrowed storylines. That fidelity only reinforces the referential illusion in the reader's mind[525] even if this realism comes around at the stiff price of a compromised naturalism: the myth is essentially all about unnatural events that put into motion the most unnatural protagonists[526]. It must be remembered that literary naturalism is more of an aspiration than a reality since if words can more or less describe nature, they cannot represent it as it is. Naturalism, in this respect, is more about an imitation of nature than its reproduction; it is more an attempt to replicate nature than a finished product representing it. Nevertheless, we cannot forget that myths function as a sort of crystallisation of human psychology. Indeed, the myth appears as the base of each people's cultural reality and identity. For that reason, separating myths from the so-called realistic novel can only be done at the high price of a very restrictive conception of the very notion of realism[527].

1.1.3. The damnation of the sexual subject

From the outset, let us lift an equivocation: the damnation that awaits the sexual subject in Zola's works is not imputable to God, still less to a god. It is a punishment inflicted on them by other characters - especially the priests and servants of God - who present themselves as heralds of God, even as his emulators. In various titles of the cycle, they proffer explicit threats against the debauched subjects-operators that they present as candidates for << *l'enfer* >>, term that recurs cyclically in the four novels that are: **Pot-Bouille, La Conquête de Plassans, La Terre** and **La Faute de l'Abbé Mouret**. Yet what is paradoxical is that priests too have unorthodox attitudes in the corpus.

This is how Father Mauduit - /is he cursed/? - encourages debauchery by making himself an accomplice to the multiform adulteries that abound in **Pot-Bouille**. Father Mouret - /was he dying/? - despite his vow of chastity, fell into the sin of the flesh with Albine first, then once back in the church, he let his lover die with his unborn baby. Yet it is written: << *Tu ne tueras point* >>[528]. Frère Archangias takes this command quite wrongly by opting for the massacre of everyone that belonged to the weaker gender in **La Faute de l'Abbé Mouret** where Father Caffin had also tasted the pleasures of the flesh. Does Brother Archangias not

---

[525] Roger Ripoll thinks that Zola did indeed take into account the relationship between beliefs and popular imagination in **Réalité et Mythe chez Zola**, op. cit. p. 32. In Volume II of the same work, the author insists on the complementarity between myth and realism in Zola's novels, to the point that nothing should be privileged between them, nor should we oppose them to each other, p. 924.

[526] **Ibidem**, Ripoll recalls how Zola viewed mythology as a superfluous ornament that had to be discarded because it was so far away from reality, p. 29.

[527] We will return to this question in the 2. The relevance of these myths and again in the fourth part.

[528] **La Sainte Bible**: *Exode*, chapter XX, verse 13, op. cit. p. 76.

say this about women: << *Elles ont le diable dans le corps. Elles puent le diable, elles le puent aux jambes, aux bras, au ventre, partout [...]. C'est ce qui ensorcelle les imbéciles* >>[529]. For him, therefore, there is no doubt that women are personalised demons and active agents of damnation that must be cast out.

Father Faujas - /faux/ + /goujat/? - is a usurper of space, that of the Mouret family. He then acts on the weak spirit of Marthe in **La Conquête de Plassans**. As for the abbot Godard - /God/[530] + /ard/, either a pejorative or a negative god - if one remembers Philippe Hamon's analysis of names ending in the negative syllable -ard[531] -, he is not better aligned since he is the minister of a God of wrath, a revengeful and a resentful God in **La Terre**. Does he not personally send to hell who he wants ? In the absence of the good God himself, the zealous person that characterises himself as the spokesman for the Almighty God in **Les Rougon-Macquart** is truly Frère Archangias, the self-proclaimed: << *gendarme de Dieu* >>[532]. Indeed, like any good gendarme, he has set for himself the duty to enforce the divine laws on earth by monitoring the Artauds to detect impiety within their community and to punish them personally. His mantra is the following maxim: << *Dieu n'a pas de miséricorde pour les impies. Il les brûle. Tenez-vous-en à cela* >>[533]. What seems to motivate the anger of Brother Archangias is to see that the Artauds are not Christians according to his definition. Talking to Father Mouret, he simply compared them to mere dogs: << *Mais les Artaud se conduisent en bêtes, voyez-vous ! Ils sont comme leurs chiens qui n'assistent pas à la messe, qui se moquent des commandements de Dieu et de l'Église. Ils forniqueraient avec leurs pièces de terre, tant ils les aiment !* >>[534].

In front of a village so little inclined to abide by the laws of God, Archangias makes a relentless judgment and without appeal: << *Il faudra le feu du ciel, comme à Gomorrhe, pour nettoyer ça* >>[535]. Furthermore, Brother Archangias also portrays himself as the spokesman of God. When he finds out about the fault of the flesh committed by the priest Mouret - his superior according to the Church - he gives him the following message: << *Écoutez, monsieur le curé, votre faute a fait de moi votre supérieur, Dieu vous dit par ma bouche que l'enfer n'a*

---

[529] Émile Zola: **R. M. I**, op. cit. p. 1278.
[530] I assume that Zola certainly knew the English word "God".
[531] Philippe Hamon: **Le Personnel du Roman. Le Système des Personnages dans Les Rougon-Macquart d'Émile Zola**, op. cit. p. 115.
[532] Émile Zola: **R. M. I**, op. cit. p. 1440.
[533] **Ibidem,** p. 1238.
[534] **Ibidem,** p. 1237.
[535] **Ibidem,** p. 1237.
About the Zolian vision of Christianity, Roger Ripoll writes : << *Il faut noter toutefois dès maintenant que pour lui, il ne semble exister que deux visions, difficilement conciliables, du christianisme : d'une part la banalité et la douceur écœurante de l'imagerie édifiante, d'autre part la vue très sombre d'un Dieu impitoyable, d'un enfer de cauchemar, d'une rreligion ennemie de la vie* >>, in **Réalité et Mythe chez Zola**, op. cit. pp. 92-93. Fire and blood would thus be the images and symbols of the divine vengeance, p. 94.

pas de tourments assez effroyables pour les prêtres enfoncés dans la chair >>[536].
That threat from Archangias plunges us into the dogma of hell.

1.1. 4. The devil, death and hell

As it has been shown, some sexual subjects are known agents of the devil, like Renée, Nana, Jacques Lantier and Flore, considering their devilish behaviours in the field of sexuality. One can confidently assert this since they want to satisfy a compelling sexual urge or because they are libidinally frustrated. Taking into account what characterises sex in the **Rougon-Macquart** series, it is fair to say that it is a vector of life and death[537]. In fact, individual and collective deaths are chained to convey the devil's followers to their final dwelling place: hell. It is in this sense that Nana must be understood when she declares: << *J'ai peur de mourir... J'ai peur de mourir...* >>[538], and that she confesses her despair in an internal monologue that goes like this: << *[...] c'était réglé d'avance, toutes les femmes qui n'étaient pas mariées et qui voyaient des hommes, allaient en enfer* >>[539].

Naturally, the fear of hell in her is related to the giant flames that are said to devour the damned[540] therein. The abbot Godard affirms it in any case in **La terre**. Brother Archangias abounds in this way by constantly threatening the sexually active subjects of the fire of hell. Yet this threat that not lead the sexual subject to repent nor to return to God. On the contrary, the fears of hell invariably lead to a deeper descent into the sin of the flesh. In all, only three agents repent in **Les Rougon-Macquart**. Only two of them succeed in getting rid of their sin and thus escaping hell. First, it is the Abbé Mouret who devotes himself to his ministry after his fault and Count Muffat, who goes back to worship his lord as soon as he loses everything: his mistress Nana, his wealth, his wife Sabine, his daughter, his dignity as a chamberlain and as a man. Unfortunately, the same cannot be said about Palmyre, in **La Terre,** as she prefers to assume her own share of sin and that of her brother and lover, Hilarion. She asks for the clemency of her God for the latter, on the grounds that he is somewhat retarded, therefore irresponsible since he cannot distinguish evil from good. All the degradations - diseases, animalisation, reification, mythification, social collapse, ruin and atrocious death - which inevitably lead to the sexual agents

---

[536] Émile Zola **R. M. I.** op. cit. p.1508.
[537] Claude Seassau stresses is **Émile Zola, Le Réalisme Symbolique**, op. cit. that in Zola's works, sexual pleasure is both infernal and diabolical. That is why it is a vector of death (p.215). That seems to be so true, but only for the majority of cases. The affairs of Pascal and Clotilde Rougon, then of Serge Mouret and Albine though, eloquently refute Seasseau's statement. Sexual act is perceived in their cases as a purely salvatory, a healing process and a renewal of human race. Sexual pleasure for Pascal is clearly qualified as a << *festin royal* >>.
[538] Émile Zola: **R. M. II**, op. cit. p. 1411.
[539] **Ibidem**, p. 1410.
[540] Roger Ripoll opposes in **Réalité et Mythe chez Zola**, the myths of virginity - inspired by Mary - to those of punishment - inspired by God – the formers made of sweetness and the latters made of fire and blood, op. cit. pp. 93-94.

to death constitute the entropic dimension of the romantic naturalism. But we must not lose sight of the fact that Zola is first and foremost a naturalist novelist. The question that is of interest at this time is this: what is the relationship between religious myths and nature in Zola's works ?

1.1. 5. The opposition between Christian myths and nature

From the foregoing, it can be argued that Christian myths are opposed to nature in Zola's works[541]. Nature indeed allows the reproduction of species in the image of Noah to whom God commanded to go out in the world and to populate the earth:

<< *Alors Dieu parla à Noé, en disant :*
Sors de l'arche, toi et ta femme, tes fils et les femmes de tes fils avec toi.
Fais sortir avec toi les animaux de toute chair qui sont avec toi, tant les oiseaux que le bétail et tous les reptiles qui rampent sur la terre, qu'ils soient féconds et [se] multiplient sur la terre >>[542].

The vow of chastity of priests is thus defeated in reading this divine prescription of the biblical hypotext. It is a wish disavowed by the narrator especially after the << *faute* >> of the abbé Mouret. Let us reiterate that his fault was not that of the flesh - because his sexual relationship with Albine was described by the narrator as beneficial, beneficial and natural. In fact, his fault lies not so much in the violation of his vow of chastity, but rather in the abandonment of the fruit of his blood. That fault is all the more serious because it leads to a double manslaughter. Father Mouret refused life to choose death, he swapped nature with priesthood and culture for metaphysics.

The opposition between Christian myths and nature is constantly highlighted in **La Faute de l'Abbé Mouret.** This novel breaks all the Catholic beliefs as it has been so eloquently argued by F.W.J. Hemmings, in a communication about Zola and the written religion: << *D'autre part, l'instinct sexuel, la poussée génésique sont naturels, en ce sens que la nature en a besoin pour perpétuer l'espèce. Ainsi le célibat, que sa règle [de l'église] impose, est un état anti-naturel* >>[543]. Going in the same direction, Zola chose science over Catholicism in 1886, in an article in **Le Figaro** : << *On dit : la religion est éternelle ; mais, certes, la science est éternelle aussi et plus encore. Puis, tout le malentendu vient de ce qu'on confond le mot religion et celui de catholicisme. Je veux bien que la religion, le sentiment religieux soit éternel ; je le crois. Mais, il ne s'ensuit pas*

---

[541] In **Réalité et Mythe chez Zola**, op. cit., Roger Ripoll writes of a religion enemy of life, p. 93.
Jean Borie also believes that the church represents a threat, a depth, a burial and a tomb, in **Zola et les Mythes, ou de la Nausée au Salut**, op. cit. pp-216-219.
Hemmings also saw Catholicism as a religion of death in Zola's works, in **Zola et la Religion**, an article published in **Europe: Zola**, no. 468-469, op. cit. p. 132.
[542] **La Sainte Bible**, *Genèse*, chapter VIII, verses 15 à 17, op. cit. p. 8.
[543] F.W.J. Hemmings: *Zola et la Religion*, in **Europe : Zola**, April-Mai 1968, op. cit. p. 131.

que le catholicisme soit éternel, car le catholicisme n'est qu'une forme religieuse qui n'a pas toujours existé, que d'autres formes religieuses ont précédée, et que d'autres formes religieuses peuvent suivre >>[544]. Taking his argument much further, Zola predicted that Catholicism would soon disappear in favour of science as soon as education became common among the people.:
<< *Pour moi, le catholicisme est condamné à disparaître devant la science, parce qu'elle a déjà ruiné ses dogmes et qu'elle les ruinera de plus en plus. Or, le catholicisme sans ses dogmes n'est plus le catholicisme ; il devient autre chose. C'est une plaisanterie de dire que la science est une chose et la religion une autre, celle-là influencera fatalement celle-ci. Dans un peuple instruit où l'idée du paradis et de l'enfer est ruinée, qui ne croit plus aux récompenses et aux châtiments futurs, tout le catholicisme croule ; il ne reste rien de la forme religieuse dont le siège est à Rome >>*[545].

Zola's skepticism about Catholicism and its dogmas thus transcends the **Rougon-Macquart** in general, and more particularly, the novel devoted to that religious form. It is first the cassock that is accused of effeminating priests like Mouret: << *À cette heure, il (Mouret) ne semblait plus avoir de chair, [...] toute sa virilité se séchait dans cette robe de femme qui le laissait sans sexe >>*[546], and moreover : << *Il se sentait féminisé, rapproché de l'ange, lavé de son sexe, de son odeur d'homme >>*[547]. This metamorphosis of the sexual subject due to Catholicism is a blemish in Zola's thought and it can be corrected from the moment the character concerned returns to the state of nature. For Serge, it would be about regaining his masculinity. He achieves this especially when his uncle, Dr. Pascal, the naturalist and the geneticist, transplanted him in a different environment, that of the Paradou. This change of space is very important since it removes the subject from a dogmatic and a mystical environment - the church - to put him back into the Nature. It is in this replica of the Garden of Eden that he heals by having sex with Albine. Serge Mouret is reborn to life from that very moment: << *Serge venait, dans la possession d'Albine, de trouver enfin son sexe d'homme, l'énergie de ses muscles, le courage de son cœur, la santé dernière qui avait jusque-là manqué à sa longue adolescence. Maintenant, il se sentait complet. Il avait des sens plus nets, une intelligence plus large. C'était comme si, tout d'un coup, il se fût réveillé lion, avec la royauté de la plaine, la vue du ciel libre >>*[548].

However, this newly acquired intelligence by the sexual subject did not go without consequences, among others the collapse of his faith in the Virgin Mary, in Jesus and in God: << *Sa faute avait tué la virginité de Marie. Alors, d'un effort suprême, il chassait la femme de la religion, il se réfugiait en Jésus, dont*

---

[544] Gérard Gengembre citing Zola in his "*Dossier*", in **Le Docteur Pascal**, Paris, Pocket Classiques, 1995, p. 395.
[545] **Ibidem**, p. 396.
[546] Émile Zola: **R. M. I**, op. cit. p. 1465.
[547] **Ibidem**, p. 1306.
[548] **Ibidem**, p. 1410.

la douceur l'inquiétait même parfois. Il lui fallait un Dieu jaloux, un Dieu implacable, le Dieu de la Bible, environné de tonnerres, ne se montrant que pour châtier le monde épouvanté >>[549]. To complete this loop, Serge finally denies God before yielding to the imperious need to join his beautiful mistress in the Paradou: << *Il n'y a rien, rien, rien, dit-il. Dieu n'existe pas* >>[550]. It therefore appears that the mystical subject who wants to regain their sensuality is obliged to reject religion beforehand, as stated by Chantal Bertrand-Jennings: << *S'affranchir de l'Église, c'est accepter la sexualité et, partant, la femme* >>[551].

There are times when the Zolian narrator gives the impression of sharing Serge's newfound atheism. Indeed, symbols confirm this acquaintance between their points of view on the question of faith. Among these symbols, we can mention the fact that Brother Archangias has got << *la voix d'un mort* >>[552], according to la Teuse. Désirée Mouret had already underlined the ugliness of this *"spokesman"* of God, and above all, Serge Mouret chose to span the large body of "God's gendarme" which barred him the entrance of the Paradou[553]. To all these symbols one can add the fact that Jeanbernat, the unbeliever and the *"damned"* according to Brother Archangias, manages to cut his right ear[554] off, promising to cut his left ear next time. This amputation perpetrated by a notorious atheist on a minister of God is a setback for the Supreme Being, just like the hurricane devastating the church where Father Mouret is ministering. The lamentable state in which the building is left rings the knell of faith in the priest's heart. It should be noted that this hurricane comes at a time when Serge is in the grip of an internal struggle; the struggle whose object was: must he return to the Paradou and live happily with Albine or must he keep his ministry and condemn himself to live unhappy? Albine had begged him to come back to her, to live happily together in the Paradou, but he was hiding behind the idea of sin, punishment and the hereafter. With Hemmings, we can argue that Albine's call is a call of nature, a call to fertility and life, while Serge argues for abstinence and death[555].

The devastation of the church symbolizes indeed the dazzling victory of nature on the church[556] and the religion it represents, because everything that could have kept the abbot there is destroyed: << *Un dernier souffle de l'ouragan qui s'était rué sur l'église, en balaya la poussière, la chaire et le confessionnal en*

---

[549] Émile Zola: **R. M. I**, op. cit. p. 1480.
[550] **Ibidem**, p. 1486.
[551] Chantal Bertrand-Jennings: **L'Éros et la Femme chez Zola**, op. cit. p. 87.
[552] Émile Zola: **R. M. I**, op. cit. p. 1437.
[553] **Ibidem,** p. 1496.
[554] **Ibidem,** p. 1526.
[555] F.W.J. Hemmings : *Zola et la religion*, in **Europe: Zola**, op. cit. p. 132.
[556] Émile Zola writes: << *L'Église catholique, voilà l'ennemie dont nous devons d'abord débarrasser la route [...]. Jamais nous ne ferons un pas en avant si nous ne commençons pas par abattre l'Église, la corruptrice, l'empoisonneuse, l'assassine* >>, in **Vérité** in **Œuvres Complètes**, volume XIV, Henri Mitterand (éd.), Édition du Cercle du Livre Précieux, op. cit. p. 463.

poudre, les images saintes lacérées, les vases sacrés fondus, tous ces décombres que piquait avidement la bande des moineaux, autrefois logée sur les tuiles. Le grand Christ, arraché de la croix, resté pendu un moment à une des chevelures de femme flottantes, fut emporté, roulé, perdu, dans la nuit noire, au fond de laquelle il tomba avec un retentissement. L'arbre de vie venait de crever le ciel. Et il dépassait les étoiles >>[557].

One can add to all the above clues the Abbé's own speech at the time of Rosalie's marriage with the Grand Fortuné, a speech that contradicts the celibacy of the Catholic priests. Speaking to the husband, he declared: << *Mon cher frère, [...] c'est Dieu qui vous accorde aujourd'hui une compagne ; car il n'a pas voulu que l'homme vécut solitaire* >>[558]. Amazingly enough, the priest went on to launch a scathing attack on any eventual abandonment of the wife by their husband in the name of God, the very sin he would commit soon: << *Et que vous soyez damné, si vous la délaissiez jamais ! Ce serait le plus lâche abandon que Dieu eût à punir. Dès qu'elle s'est donnée, elle est vôtre, pour toujours* >>[559].

The contradiction between the priest's speech and his conduct can be read as the denunciation of the hypocrisy of the Catholic Church, or at least the Catholic authorities. The death of Albine and her unborn baby is therefore a villainous crime which the abbot should answer before his God. The gravity of the crime is suggested by an incident that occurred during the burial of the girl. **La Terre** gave way under Serge's feet when he approached Albine's grave and he nearly fell in it[560]. This incident, which occurs in the very last pages of the narrative, appears as a symbolic death sentence handed down to the culprit and his unnatural religion. As Roger Ripoll pointed out, in Zola's novels, there are biblical myths that associate sexuality with the original sin[561].

In general, the opposition between Christian myths and nature lies in the fact that the former advocate abstinence - which is close to impotence - while nature advocates fertility because she is a nurturing mother that is eager for an abundant offspring. Nothing better embodies this nature in **Les Rougon-Macquart** than the Paradou - where the child of the abbot Mouret and Albine was conceived -; the character of the earth in **La Terre**, and finally, Valqueyras - where the family of Jean Macquart multiplies tremendously in **Le Docteur Pascal**. Ripoll has already shown that Zola received a Catholic education at the pension Notre-Dame under the direction of Isoard, a former seminarian whose teaching has left an echo on his sensitivity. Nonetheless, he went on to have a reductive vision of the Catholic religion that he would reduce to a simplistic opposition between heaven and hell[562].

---

[557] Émile Zola: **R. M. I**, op. cit. p. 1490.
[558] **Ibidem** p. 1424.
[559] **Ibidem**, p. 1424.
[560] **Ibidem**, p. 1524
[561] Roger Ripoll : **Réalité et Mythe chez Zola**, op. cit. p. 101.
[562] **Bidem**, pp. 98-99 and p. 106.

After the religious myths, I must question the pagan myths that also abound in the Zola's works.

1.1. The pagan myths

Although they are more abundant than the Christian myths in the corpus, the pagan myths are mainly borrowed from the Greco-Roman mythology. However, it must be recognised that this common source is not the guarantee of an a priori homogeneity. Greek mythology is indeed a very large network of myths as numerous as it is diverse, and so are the Roman myths.

1.1.1. The Roman myths

This paragraph will be peculiar in the sense that it will classify narrative elements of legendary or historical essence in the category of the Roman myths. Although they are not specifically of mythical essence, their current significance in the Zolian novel, which is magnified by hypertrophy, brings them closer to the myth rather than pure history or legend. This will mainly be about *Messaline* associated with Renée, and *César, Lucullus* and *Brutus* associated with Pierre Rougon.

The historical Roman hypotext tells us that *Messaline* was a Roman Empress and the wife of Claude. Famous for her legendary debauchery, she had even engaged into prostitution. The narrator associates this figure with Renée so as to reinforce the scope of her dissipation. Indeed, she shared her body between father and son. On top of that incest, Renée did not deprive herself of her five other lovers, for she lived only for sex and luxury[563], no matter how she got them. On such account, *Messaline* is therefore a negative and an immoral figure in which the image of Renée is reflected as in a mirror.

César and *Brutus* are political and warlike figures that are not to be classified a priori in the logic of sexuality. The former was an emeritus conqueror who remained the most famous in the history of all the Roman conquests and quite rightly so. He truly left his fingerprints on the Roman Empire and his influence on politics in general is unquestionable to this today. The second is a legendary traitor who was the assassin of Caesar in the Senate of Rome on March 15th, 44 BC. If the conspiracy against Caesar included several senators, Brutus was the one who gave him the *coup de grace*. Pierre Rougon is associated with these two legendary figures for purely parodic reasons, the dwarf seeing himself in the

---

[563] Maarten Van Buuren writes: << *La société sous le Second Empire se développe de manière explosive. D'importantes transformations changent le monde industriel, financier et urbain. Dans l'esprit de Zola ces changements sont intimement liés à la déchéance morale : les vices sont le produit du luxe qui est à son tour le produit des changements sociaux* >>, in **Les Rougon-Macquart d'Émile Zola. De la Métaphore au Mythe**, op. cit. p. 259.

shoes of the giant, the derisory claiming to be heroic. For the narrator, it is necessary to insist not only on his treachery, but also on the overflow of appetites characterising the Rougon-Macquart family in general, and particularly the Rougon branch to which he belongs[564]. The maternal crack is thus transformed into an imperious drive of power and glory in the son, Peter. By chance, although he is << *taré* >>, the latter attains quite unexpected dignities - though he acquired them in very dark and opaque conditions, including his association with the figure of Brutus. That is why, in the euphoria of his triumph of a parvenu, the narrator uses Pierre caricaturally as the figure of those illustrious Roman ancestors. It is in this same sense that one must take his assimilation with *Lucullus*, the Roman general (106-56 BC) who led a life whose luxury and refinement have remained proverbial. Note that the riches of the latter were acquired during victorious military campaigns. All in all, in Pierre Rougon's case, it is always an aspiration and not a reality, a semblance rather than a being[565]. It is less a question here of a legendary hero than that of a hereditary figure whose appetites veil the reality of his littleness. Indeed, the attributions that have just been made allow us to understand how far ambition can go in an individual from the line of Adélaïde Fouque. Pierre Rougon certainly does not wrong Émile Zola when he wrote his preface of July 1st, 1871, describing his anaphora characters' thirst for enjoyment. The excessive appetite of Pierre Rougon for power makes him take the municipal offices for << *un temple dont il devenait le dieu* >>[566]. Also, he does not shy away from the abominable: << *sacrifier sa famille sur l'autel de la patrie* >>[567]. The human sacrifice[568], moreover, that of an immediate relative - his half-brother Antoine Macquart - is a huge crime worthy of Brutus. In the corpus, that initial human sacrifice paves the way for success for the upstart that is Pierre Rougon. He did indeed symbolically sacrifice Silvère in **La Fortune des Rougon**. Similarly, Aristide sacrificed Angèle, his wife in **La Curée** and, finally, Octave Mouret sacrificed Madame Hedouin in **Au Bonheur des Dames**. In all, the Rougons and the Macquarts are a family of wolves that are able to sell and eat each others up[569], to the great despair of their mother.

---

[564] The Rougons are upstarts according to Maarten Van Buuren, **ibidem**, p. 13.

[565] In **Les Rougon-Macquart d'Émile Zola. De la Métaphore au Mythe**, op. cit, Van Buuren places this opposition within the scope of the metaphor of drama, p. 177.

Roger Ripoll speaks of parody, that is to say, a rather theatrical and caricatural representation, in **Réalité et Mythe chez Zola**, op. cit. p. 60. On this point, also refer to chapter 1 in the Part II.

[566] Émile Zola: **R. M. I**, op. cit. p. 229.

[567] **Ibidem**, p. 228.

[568] One can associate this with paganism of which Roger Ripoll has written about in **Réalité et Mythe Chez Zola** op. cit. p. 76.

On the theme of sacrifice, also refer to **Zola's Crowds** by Naomi Schor, op. cit. pp. 21-24.

[569] For Maarten Van Buuren, in **Les Rougon-Macquart d'Émile Zola. De la Métaphore au Mythe**, predators are profiteers, op. cit. p. 267.

Claude Seassau sees in the devoration, the cardinal image of violence; violence linked especially to sexuality or jealousy, see **Émile Zola, le Réalisme Symbolique**, op. cit. p. 203. This

1.2. 2. The Greek myths

With regard to the theme of sexuality, the Greek myths are the most recurrent and the most significant in the corpus. As evidence, one finds << *la Nymphe Écho et le beau Narcisse* >> in **La Curée** and in **Nana**; << *Phèdre et Hippolyte* >> find their way through **La Curée**; << *Vénus (Aphrodite)* >> dominates **La Curée** and **Nana** with her stunning beauty and her full might when << *Diane (Athéna)* >>, << *Jupiter (Zeus)* >> and << *Mars* >> besiege **Nana**. Again, in **Nana**[570], it is << *Athéna* >> who confronts << *Héphaïstos* >> or << *Vulcain* >>; the same one that is also found in **La Terre** and **La Curée**. << *Les Bacchantes* >> have got a representation in **La Fortune des Rougon** where there is a << *temple* >> and << *d'un dieu* >> to whom one offers a human << *sacrifice* >> on an << *autel* >>. **La Curée** suggests that << *les incestes divins* >> are fuelled by the riches and the impudent luxury of << *Plutus* >>. At the same time, the << *sphinx* >> is rampant in such an environment and finally, **La Bête Humaine** is the novel where clashes constantly erupt << *Éros* >> and << *Thanatos* >>, without them being named.

In this long enumeration of Greek myths, it is necessary to distinguish the occurrences where an agent is identified directly with a god and those where the identification is done in a more suggestive way, in particular with the technique of the mise en abyme.

The chapter of direct identifications opens on Miette who << *ressemblait à une Bacchante antique* >>[571]. The Bacchante is a priestess or a follower of Bacchus, the god of intoxicating power and vine. She is associated with drunkenness and debauchery. For her part, Miette intoxicates Silvère Mouret and incites him to commit debauchery despite their young age.

Renée Rougon dit Saccard is thus perceived by Maxime: << *Le jeune homme, couché sur le dos, aperçut, au-dessus des épaules de cette adorable bête amoureuse qui le regardait, le sphinx de marbre*[572], *dont la lune éclairait les cuisses luisantes*[573]. *Renée avait la pose et le sourire du monstre à tête de femme, et, dans ses jupons dénoués, elle semblait la sœur blanche du dieu noir*>>[574]. As such, she is a hybrid monster with her female bust surmounting a winged lion and she is incestuous. The sphinx is associated with the fulfillment

---

is how one must understand in the expression "*manger un homme*", "*wanting to kill him by all means*", jealousy being at the origin of the desire to kill, p. 198.

[570] Roger Ripoll points out, in the above book, that ancient myths are present in great numbers in **La Curée** and in **Nana**, op. cit. p. 60.

[571] Émile Zola: **R. M. I**, op. cit p. 17.

[572] Zola was inspired, about the myths at least, by the arts of his time, including sculpture, according to Roger Ripoll, in **Réalité et Mythe chez Zola**, op. cit. p. 64.

[573] Roger Ripoll believes that what characterises the myth in Zola's novels is the nakedness and the brutality of desire, **ibidem**. p. 80.

[574] Émile Zola: **R. M. I**, op. cit. p. 485.

of the oedipal incest. Although she is beautiful, Renée harbours a lot of aggressiveness and she is voracious in the field of incest. Like a cat, she snatches Maxime who is no more than a defeated and a submissive prey in her claws.

Narcissism is part of Maxime and Renée's character, just like Nana. In Nana, it reaches its climax: << *Un des plaisirs de Nana était de se déshabiller en face de son armoire à glace, où elle se voyait en pied [...]. C'était une passion de son corps, un ravissement de sa peau et de la ligne souple de sa taille*[575]*, qui la tenait sérieuse, attentive, absorbée dans un amour d'elle-même* >>[576]. No need to repeat the ultra-homoerotic tone of this passage. Like Narcissus, their mythical counterpart, these agents are characterised by their physical beauty that carries the seeds of the fatum that will soon hit them. Imbued with their "person", outrageously courted, they are called to reify themselves as Narcissus - in the prime of life - according to what I have shown in the paragraph devoted to the study of the sanction of the character.

Finally, this first category ends with << *les incestes divins* >> mentioned in Chapter 1 of **La Curée**. The reason for referring to these ancient episodes is to suggest and foresee the incestuous relationship which will link Renée to Maxime in chapter IV. It is also known that the Greek gods, headed by Zeus, were known for their multilateral and multifaceted debauches to the point where they showed complete disregard to the bonds of kinship or to the sacred bonds of marriage.

That divine incest was aimed at denouncing in advance the immoral sexual practices of the imperial high society that would be revealed in the novel. The aesthetic choice of the commitment was made by Zola from the preface of the first edition of **La Curée** : << *L'artiste en moi se refusait à faire de l'ombre sur cet éclat de la vie à outrance qui a illumine tout le règne [de Napoléon III] d'un jour suspect d'un mauvais lieu* >>. At the same time, the author did not hesitate to brand the coup d'État on December 2nd 1851 as the << *viol brutal de la France* >>[577]. Sexuality is therefore both anaphoric and cataphoric in the corpus. It is also the unifying theme of the **Rougon-Macquart** series, both narratively and semiotically.

Moreover, the myths mis en abyme have an evident narrative interest since the first narrative is repeated inside itself by means of a second narrative that overlaps it. The mise en abyme thus presents itself in the aspect of a redundancy reinforcing the significance of the first narrative in which it is inserted. Therefore, there is a transparent reflection that claims to be a guarantee of authenticity. Yet, that authenticity is only a referential illusion.

---

[575] Roger Ripoll states that classic mythology is related to the obsessive theme of nudity in Zola's works, in **Réalité et Mythe chez Zola**, op. cit. p. 81.
[576] Émile Zola: **R. M. II**, op. cit. p. .1269.
[577] **Ibidem**. p. 1582.

There is a mise en abyme in Chapter V of **La Curée** when Renée and Maxime attend the performance of **Phèdre** by Racine, in Italian. Then, in chapter VI, the same agents play the leading roles in **La Nymphe Écho et le Beau Narcisse**, a play directed by the prefect Hupel de la Noue[578]. As I have shown elsewhere, Hupel de la Noue is an << *auteur aux créations ridicules, car ses tableaux contiennent un contraste grinçant, les personnages qui jouent dans sa pièce sont minables (Maxime, Renée, Adeline d'Espanet, etc.) et son théâtre devient celui du cotillon (bal travesti) à peine la représentation terminée – le vulgaire se substituant au mythique* >>[579].

As for **Phèdre**, it should be noted that this tragedy is played on stage after the incest had been committed. If the guilty couple had not blamed themselves for any wrongdoing before, they finally end up shuddering at the end of the play as if remorseful. It is for that reason that they leave the theater in a state of bewilderment. Henceforth the voice of the conscience is heard in them, thanks in particular to this reflexive mirror which has revealed to them the truth about themselves. However, "the new Phaedrus" is not the victim of the retaliation from the gods, far from it. On her weighs the fatality of the social and the historical environment[580]. Suffices to mention here the excessive life that characterises the Empire from Zola's point of view. For example, Renée's dubious education among the ladies of the Visitation[581], not to mention the extravagant luxury in which she lives at Saccard's hotel are evidence of how corrupt were those social and historic environments. Her marriage did not bring her a home[582] either because no family link seems to bind Aristide, Maxime and Renée together as a family unit. On the contrary, they live like college students in the same dormitory, each one of them settling their own life as they see fit.

Although Renée is endowed with conscience - which explains her remorse - she cannot help but do evil as shown by Anthony Zielonka : << *Renée est consciente du mal qu'elle fait en aimant son beau-fils et en menant une vie de dissipation, mais elle ne peut pas changer son comportement. Elle cherche et accepte les vices, les perversions et les excès. Étant donné les principes théoriques de Zola, elle ne peut éviter sa destinée. Le sort de cette nouvelle Phèdre ne dépend pas*

---

[578] As Roger Ripoll puts it in **Réalité et Mythe chez Zola**, Hupel de la Noue is the "*poète ridicule*", p. 79.

Anne Belgrand adds that there is an << *opposition entre le ridicule de la création dirigée par le préfet et l'ambition artistique de Zola lui-même* >>, in Le Jeu des Oppositions dans **La Curée**, article published in **La Curée de Zola << ou la vie à outrance >>**, op. cit. p. 27.

[579] Famahan Samaké: **Procès du Second Empire dans La Curée d'Émile Zola**, op. cit. p. 43.

[580] Maarten Van Buuren: **Les Rougon-Macquart d'Émile Zola. De la Métaphore au Mythe**, op. cit. p. 145

[581] The same point of view is found in Naomi Schor's **Zola's Crowds**, op. cit. p. 94.

[582] Jean Borie, assuming that the opening of a family home in Zola's novels is diabolical, asserts that the hotel Saccard, which is open to the gallop of the whole Saccard clan, becomes the home of an off-the-wall family, see **Zola et les Mythes, ou de la Nausée au Salut**, op. cit. p. 139 et p. 144.

des décisions des dieux mais des faits qui déterminent le milieu dans lequel elle vit et des événements qui sont inscrits dans son passé >>[583].

In the play **Les Amours du Beau Narcisse et de la Nymphe Écho**, written and directed by the prefect poet Hupel de la Noue, the two heroes play their own roles. The relationship is then very direct between their roles in the first narrative and that they play in the second narrative. "Fiction and reality" overlap and occur at the same time because Renée[584] and Maxime reach the peak of their love story at this precise time in the course of the diegesis in chapter VI. The only significant opposition between the two stories is that the mythical story is that of a rejected love whereas the Zolian romantic story is that of a loving relationship fully enjoyed and satisfied. On the other hand, the tragedy strikes both lovers. Indeed, as much as Echo was consumed with pain and regret, so did Renée burn herself like a candle in the wind when she is abandoned by Maxime. He did not survive his mistress for a long time either.

1. 2. 2. 1. The myths of unfulfilled sexuality

In La Curée, two myths of unsatisfied sexuality come together. This is firstly the myth of Phèdre[585] and Hippolyte. Hippolyte's refusal of Phèdre's advances had led to tragic consequences: the atrocious death of the young man due to the sea monster, then the suicide of the young woman. Adapted to the naturalistic novel, this myth reinforces the predictability of the becoming and the sanction of the sexual agents assimilated metaphorically to those two mythical figures. Their love is certainly that of a full-blown affair in the novel - thus departing from the Racinian hypotext - but it is doomed to failure from the outset, and the punishment that awaits them will be death. This also applies to Narcisse and Écho mentioned in the paragraph above.

The intrusion of these myths into the naturalistic novel is nevertheless a sign of intensifying the predictability of the novelistic text since it suggests the reification of the two damned characters. The fatality that hangs over their heads like a sword of Damocles is more or less clearly defined from the moment they are assimilated to those mythical heroes. Yet, if the new Hippolyte fulfills the lust of the new Phèdre, it will not change much the fate that will be theirs. The intertextual character on this episode of **La Curée** and its implications have already been beautifully grasped by Philippe Hamon, who recognises one of the five processes << *accentuant la prévisibilité du texte réaliste* >>, which are : <<

---

[583] Anthony Zielonka: *Renée et le Problème du Mal* in **La Curée de Zola <<ou la vie à outrance>>**, op. cit. p. 163.

[584] Maarten Van Buuren had ranked Renée in the category of fire-loving women - alongside Nana, Philomène, and Aunt Dide - who therefore light men up in **Les Rougon-Macquart d'Émile Zola. De la Métaphore au Mythe**, op. cit. p. 255.

[585] Roger Ripoll admits, in **Réalité et Mythe chez Zola**, that the myth of Phaedrus has an ironic value in **La Curée**, since Saccard is rather an anti-Theseus and Renée an anti-Phaedrus, op. cit. p. 73.

la référence à certaines histoires connues (déjà écrites dans l'extra-texte global de la culture) fonctionne comme une restriction du champ de la liberté des personnages, comme une prédétermination de leur destin. Ainsi la référence à **Phèdre** *dans* **La Curée** *>>*[586].

Nana, who is also a narcissistic character - with tendencies to engage in long autoerotic scenes in front of her large mirrors - will suffer a fate identical to that of her role model. Narcissism is indeed a sexual inversion, and therefore a sexual aberration punishable by death in **Les Rougon-Macquart.**

1. 2. 2. 2. The myths of flourished and triumphant sexuality

These are mainly the myths of Venus[587] in **La Curée** and in **Nana** - once again - and Amour in **Nana** alone. Renée and Nana are constantly metaphorically associated with Venus - the goddess of love also referred to as Love - because they are extremely pretty and they subjugate and ravage entire battalions of men. Their sexuality will be triumphant in the corpus even though not all sexuality which is consumed is recommendable[588]. The chapter devoted to the study of the characters has extensively explained this aspect.

1. 2. 2. 3 The myths of vicious sexuality

These are the myths whose heroes practice sexual vices such as adultery and incest. In this case, one can count Diane, Vénus, Mars and Vulcain in **Nana** when it comes to commiting adultery. Then there are Phèdre and Hippolyte in **La Curée** with regard to incest.

In the first case, the beautiful Diane catches her husband, Mars, while he was seducing Vénus, the goddess of love and Vulcain's wife for the latter is the god of the cuckolds. This scene played in the theatre from the opening chapter of **Nana**, with Nana in the role of Vénus, works to perfection as the ultimate transparent exhibition scene. Zola seems to suggest that this novel will be the theatre of frequent and multilateral adulteries. Indeed, that first chapter of **Nana** draws the curtains on a world of debauchery and, with David Baguley, we can say that: << *Cette scène d'ouverture, qui se joue dans la salle du théâtre des Variétés, est extraordinairement programmatique* >>[589].

---

[586] Philippe Hamon : *Pour un Statut Sémiologique du Personnage* in **Poétique du Récit**, op. cit. p. 163.

[587] Roger Ripoll associates Venus with the destructive power, ruin and death, in **Réalité et Mythe chez Zola**, op. cit. p. 82.

[588] Maarten Van Buuren thinks that fire-loving women, like Nana, put men and society on fire, see **Les Rougon-Macquart d'Émile Zola. De la Métaphore au Mythe**, op. cit. p. 262.

[589] David Baguley: **Zola et les Genres**, VI. Nana, Roman Baroque, op. cit. p. 66. Baguley goes even further by making this point: << *Nana ne fait pas seulement son chemin dans le monde du théâtre, elle transforme le monde en théâtre* >>, p. 66.

As for the myth of incest – be it virtual or real - Phèdre and Hippolyte are its heroes. However, its transposition into the naturalistic novel with Renée and Maxime in the leading roles makes it realistic because the second narrative – the mythical narrative - justifies the first - the romantic narrative. Is not naturalism also a realism[590]?

1. 2. 2. 4 The myths of the perverted sexuality

The vice is not very far from the perversion and the short step is quickly crossed by Renée, when she becomes a Sphinx by means of metaphor, the monster with a woman's head. As a sphinx[591], she will be defeated by Maxime, the new Oedipus, who abandons her in the last chapter of the novel to marry Louise de Mareuil.

The destiny of Maxime in parallel to that of Nana because both are narcissistic. Nevertheless, because narcissism involves a sexual subject that falls in love with themselves as a sexual object, it is an inversion close to homosexuality or better, to what Freud called *l'autoérotique*. This fact implies that the two agents will be effeminate for one, and phallic for the other, in order to find within themselves their ideal sexual partner.

Yet, one thing is to identify sexual myths and another is to capture their relevance in the naturalistic narrative.

1. The relevance of these myths

The myth is originally a sacred narrative, an old story that is rooted in the collective consciousness. It therefore benefits from an a priori of truth for having imposed itself through the ages[592]. Therefore, its presence in a modern text can be seen as a process of sacralisation and intensification.

1.1. The sacralisation of the 'chimeric'

To make a novel, until the seventeenth Century, was, pejoratively, to write chimeras. However, Honoré de Balzac rehabilitated the genre with what is now

---

Roger Ripoll points out that in the representation of **La Blonde Vénus**, <<*Vénus, parfaitement confondue avec Nana, s'impose dans toute sa puissance*>>, in **Réalité et Mythe chez Zola**, op. cit. p. 80.

[590] Remember that for Roger Ripoll, the myth is not opposed to realism, and besides, the myth would be one of the means to build the novelistic reality, in **Réalité et Mythe chez Zola**, op. cit. volume II, op. cit. p. 924 et p. 926.

[591] Jean Chevalier and Alain Gheerbrandt indicate that the symbolic value of the sphinx is the perverted femininity and debauchery in **Dictionnaire des Symboles**, Paris, Laffont, 1982, p. 15 and p. 906.

[592] Roger Ripoll: **Réalité et Mythe chez Zola**, op. cit. p. 32.

known as romantic realism. Semantically, realistic is opposed to chimerical, and this opposition took on an even larger dimension with Zola who pushed realism to naturalism. Summarising the adventure of the novelistic genre, Zola wrote: << *Nous voilà loin du roman tel que l'entendaient nos pères, une œuvre de pure imagination, dont le but se bornait à charmer et à distraire les lecteurs. Dans les anciennes rhétoriques, le roman était placé tout au bout, entre la fable et les poésies légères. Les hommes sérieux le dédaignaient, l'abandonnaient aux femmes, comme une récréation frivole et compromettante. Cette opinion persiste encore en province et dans certains milieux académiques. La vérité est que les chefs-d'œuvre du roman contemporain en disent beaucoup plus long sur l'homme et sur la nature, que de graves ouvrages de philosophie, d'histoire et de critique. L'outil moderne est là* >>[593]. But as naturalist as his novel is, it is nonetheless true that myth abounds in it. Why, then, did the myth, a fabulous story par excellence, come to settle comfortably in the novel, a work of fiction that is supposed to be plausible, even realistic and naturalistic? Obviously, there is a sort of implicit contradiction between myth and naturalism; the latter having the pretension of borrowing everything from nature. That is why Jean Borie writes : << *C'est un lieu commun de soutenir que l'œuvre de Zola ne remplit guère le projet élaboré dans* **Le Roman Expérimental** >>[594]. Let us stress that in Zola's works, the characters are not directly derived from the religious myth though, nor the pagan myths either.

By their being and their doing, or even their becoming, the Zolian characters are simply the modern reflection of mythical heroes[595]. This Zolian process - the insertion of the myth into the naturalist narrative, becomes simply a guarantee of readability of the novelistic text: the novel takes on the appearance of the sacred and positions itself as superior to the profane text it was supposed to be. Zola goes so far as to create new myths like that of **Nana**'s golden fly[596]. I will call this sacralisation by the myth, the metalinguistic function in **Les Rougon-Macquart** (in the sense that this concept has in Roman Jakobson's theory). To consecrate what is of "chimeric" essence supposes its intensification.

1.1. The process of discursive and narrative intensification.

The entrenchment of the myth, a sacred and a serious narrative in the novel, the "chimeric" and profane narrative, is undeniably a factor of narrative

---

[593] Émile Zola: *Le Naturalisme au Théâtre,* first published in St. Petersburg magazine **Le Messager de l'Europe** in January 1879, and later on in **Le Naturalisme au Théâtre** in **Le Roman Expérimental**, in **Œuvres Complètes**, under the direction of Henri Mitterand, volume 9 : **Nana 1880**, presentation, notices, chronology and bibliography by Chantal Pierre-Gnassounou, op. cit. p. 378.
[594] Jean Borie: **Zola et les Mythes, ou de la Nausée au Salut**, op. cit. p. 9.
[595] Roger Ripoll talks about the << *renouvellement des mythes* >>, in **Réalité et Mythe chez Zola**, op. cit. p. 65.
[596] Ripoll says that since the Draft of the novel, Nana had been assimilated to the Devil, while during the actual writing of the novel, she has gradually become evil Goddess, **ibidem**, p. 76.

intensification[597] in itself. The two narratives fit together to repeat themselves inside the novel, what was already said outside of it, namely, the original myth anchored in the collective consciousness. There is therefore a strong accent of predictability of the hypertextual fiction[598]. In addition, the hypotextual mythical narrative seems to bring a credit of realism, a guarantee of trustworthiness to the novel, as if the narrator no longer invented a new story, but that he was rewriting an old story that is globally accepted by the collective consciousness as a universal cultural heritage: << *Aussi, ce qui paraît être une déformation, au premier abord, constitue-t-il un moyen essentiel pour accéder à la lisibilité du réel, et du texte qui devient ainsi plus transparent. En d'autres termes les archétypes glissés dans le texte, permettent de réaliser, à leur lumière, une lecture plus profonde et plus satisfaisante de celui-ci. Images, symboles, mythes, glissés dans l'écriture sont autant de signes qui* << *parlent* >> *à l'homme* >>[599].

Discursively, the redundancy of the same myths from one novel to another - like the myth of Venus in **La Curée** and **Nana**, or the myth of the original fault in **La Faute de l'Abbé Mouret** and in **La Curée** - is an incessant return to oneself or on the same one. The narrator seems to have the intention of influencing his narrataries by means of repetition. By this pedagogical means, he tries to convince them of the realism of his story. Roland Barthes had summed up all the characters of the myth in one word: wealth. For him: << *le mythe est trop riche, et ce qu'il a en trop, c'est précisément sa motivation* >>[600]. It can be argued that the myths, whether pagan or religious, enrich the naturalistic fiction by expanding its field of significance, to borrow the word from Greimas.

As Roger Ripoll has shown, the myth does not only have a superior aesthetic value in Zola's novels[601], but also a parodic and an ironic value[602]. For example, there are dwarves roaming free in his fiction works that have the vanity to put on the boots of the gods. It should be kept in mind that in the Zolian novel, there are obvious annoying signs of an apocalypse that would sweep away the corrupt

---

[597] Claude Seassau writes: << *Le mythe n'est donc pas une fioriture ou un embellissement gratuits ; il s'agit d'une modalité de narration, utilisée à des fins d'expressivité, et pour faire jaillir le sens, l'amplifier et le rendre prégnant* >>, in **Émile Zola, Le Réalisme Symbolique**, op. cit. p. 428.
[598] L. Jenny: << *Hors de l'intertextualité, l'œuvre littéraire serait tout simplement imperceptible, au même titre que la parole d'une langue encore inconnue. De fait, on ne saisit le sens et la structure d'une œuvre littéraire que dans son rapport à des archétypes, eux-mêmes abstraits de longues séries de textes dont ils sont en quelque sorte l'invariant [...]. Vis-à-vis des modèles archétypiques, l'œuvre littéraire entre toujours dans un rapport de réalisation, de transformation ou de transgression* >>, in *La Stratégie de la Forme* published in **Poétique**, no. 27, Paris, 1976, p. 257.
[599] Claude Seassau: **Émile Zola, Le Réalisme Symbolique**, op. cit. pp. 429-430.
[600] Roland Barthes (editor): **Essais Critiques**, Paris, Seuil, 1964, p. 234.
[601] Roger Ripoll: **Réalité et Mythe chez Zola**, op. cit. p. 66.
[602] Ripoll sees mockery indeed in the assimilation of Rose Mignon to the goddess Diana in **La Curée**: it is the <<*mythe burlesque d'une décomposition sociale*>>, **ibidem**, p. 175. Moreover, Nana being perceived as Venus would have a parodic and a satirical value since it would degrade the gods while meaning the corruption of the imperial society, pp. 74-75.

world of the Second Empire[603] like a hurricane does to a costal city. These signs are of several orders but at this stage of my investigation, they are essentially related to the treatment of the notion of the character. In addition, the myth brings to the Zolian novel a guarantee of universality and eternity[604], a certain grandeur and prestige, while placing the reader on the vision that Zola had of the world[605], that is to say, a colourful world that is dominated sexual violence.

It has been shown above that the characters of the corpus undergo various processes of metamorphosis - reification, animalisation and mythification - and this contributes to the creation of a cluster of convergent phenomena in the sense that the finality of the process is death, pure and simple. In a communication about **La Curée**, Jean de Palacio believed that mythology, and more precisely the mythological referential overload - Jocaste, Phèdre, Nymphe Écho, Sphinx, etc.-, kills off Renée's character : << *Dans* **La Curée**, *la prépondérance de la mythologie et l'emprise du vêtement sont une mise à mort plus efficace que l'imprévisible méningite sous laquelle le romancier l'accable comme en passant, et comme pour rétablir* in extremis *les droits de la physiologie* >>[606]. This judgment can be easily applied to Nana, another follower of fashion just like Renée. In the light of all the above, one must consider that Zola is the Ovid of the modern times, the creator of new myths. The extent of the mythical rhetoric in **Les Rougon-Macquart** recalls the famous **Metamorphoses**[607] by Ovid. Zola resurrects indeed many ancient myths inspired by ancient poets - including Sophocles, Ovid, Aeschylus and Euripides - as well as from the **Bible**[608]. He then updates them in line with the modern context of the nineteenth Century giving them sometimes new connotations.

When Zola recovers ancient myths, he has the merit of not deliver them in their primitive form. On the contrary, the author of the **Rougon-Macquart** series adapts them, he reinvents them so to speak[609], according to his literary objectives which are naturalistic and aesthetic. The result gives another story but it retains its originality[610] and its authenticity. Is it necessary to recall that

---

[603] Roger Ripoll: **Réalité et Mythe chez Zola**, op. cit, p. 75.
[604] **Ibidem**, p. 71.
[605] **Ibidem**, pp. 77-80. For Zola's vision of the world, also refer to Claude Seassau's **Émile Zola, Le Réalisme Symbolique**, op. cit. p. 428.
[606] Jean de Palacio : **La Curée** : *Histoire naturelle et sociale ou agglomérat de mythes ?* in **La Curée de Zola << ou la vie à outrance >>**, op. cit. pp. 175-176.
[607] On the Homeric and the Ovidian origin of certain Zolian myths, refer to Roger Ripoll's **Réalité et Mythe chez Zola**, op. cit. p. 63.
[608] In **Émile Zola, Le Réalisme Symbolique**, Claude Seassau recognises that the intertextual richness of Zola's works is largely due to the concomitant use of Hellenic and Biblical myths, op. cit. p. 326.
[609] **Ibidem**, Seassau asserts that Zola << *modifie* >> the intertexts that he recovers, p. 326.
Roger Ripoll does not say anything less when he writes about the << *puissance de création à partir des mythes empruntés* >> by Zola, in **Réalité et Mythe chez Zola**, op. cit. p. 111.
[610] For Ripoll, if the myth in Zola's works assumes the roles of decoration, parody, criticism and expression of the author's worldview, its peculiarity is pagan eroticism, **ibidem**, p. 80.

such a narrative technique is a manifestation of intertextuality that considers that every literary creation is dependent on a loan[611]?. Each author is therefore in a certain way, a borrower and an imitator, without ceasing to be more or less deeply original, provided they have talent[612]. And without question, Zola had massive talent to spare.

This study of the myths in the Zolian novel proves that one cannot fully study them outside of a global study of the fictional characters - like Roger Ripoll did - at the risk of presenting incomplete results. It also proves that any study of the system of Zolian characters which that does not take into account the mythical dimension of the text - like Philippe Hamon did - would be just as incomplete. Indeed, it happens that in Zola's novels, the myths are sexually motivated, like the characters. On another level, studying the Zolian myths and symbols without setting them in their natural space, the inevitability of sexuality - like Maarten van Buuren and Claude Seassau have done - would taste like an unfinished business. There are indeed no characters on the one hand, and myths on the other in Zola's works. These two narrative components are nested one inside the other in order to overbid the meaning of the story. Although the modern character appears to be the victim of both a scientific fatality - by the game of genetic transmissions - and of a fatality due to the environment - dominated by social and economic progress -, they have nothing to envy their ancient counterparts which were mercilessly struck by the gods. In Zola's fictional world, the naturalist character is at first the victim of their sexuality and that of their procreators, then they are also the victim of the decadent milieu of the Second Empire. They get hit hard by the novelist, their creator who casts them out and sends them down to Hades in an excess of anger worthy of Zeus.

Moreover, the enrichment of the Zolian novel also comes from the proliferation of the figures of rhetoric. This particularly poetic character is undoubtedly one of the manifestations of the author's personal genius.

II. THE POETIC FUNCTION OR THE FIGURES OF RHETORIC SERVING THE THEME OF SEXUALITY

According to Roman Jakobson[613], the poetic function is defined in relation to the emphasis on the beauty of language by projecting the paradigmatic axis – the

---

[611] Julia Kristeva highlights that : << *Tout texte se construit comme une mosaïque de citations, tout texte est une absorption et une transformation d'un autre texte* >>, in **Séméiotikè : Recherches pour une Sémanalyse**, Paris, Seuil, 1969, p. 29.

[612] Roger Ripoll, in volume II of **Réalité et Mythe chez Zola**, insists on the fact that << *Zola méritait d'être traité comme un écrivain à part entière* >>, mainly because of << *La création mythique* >>, which he demonstrates in his novelistic writing, op. cit. p. 922.

Claude Seassau endorses this analysis by treating Zola as a << *créateur artiste* >>, in **Émile Zola, Le Réalisme Symbolique** op. cit. p. 427.

[613] Roman Jakobson: **Essais de Linguistique Générale**, Paris, Minuit, 1966, p. 60.

axis of selection - on the syntagmatic axis – the axis of combination. The figures of rhetoric contribute to a large extent to this poetic function.

As far as the figures of speech are concerned, we distinguish << *fonctions* >> from << *indices* >> in the Barthian sense, meaning in the sense that the << *Fonctions et Indices recouvrent donc une autre distinction classique : les Fonctions impliquent des relata métonymiques, les Indices des relata métaphoriques, les unes correspondant à une fonctionnalité du faire, les autres à une fonctionnalité de l'être* >>[614].

In the following section, I will investigate metaphors and comparisons in the context of indices, then metonymies and synecdoches within the framework of the functions as long as they carry a certain interest in the field of sexuality.

1. The functions

For Roman Jakobson, metaphor is opposed to metonymy in that the former refers to relations of similarity, and the latter to relations of contiguity[615]. The metonymic relata that are the functions imply not only the metonymy as such, but also the synecdoche.

1.1 The metonymy

Metonymy often refers to the container to express the content as is the case in the descriptions. Metonymy is the figure par excellence, the figure probably the most used by realist novelists in general and by naturalists[616] writers in particular. Besides, for Roman Jakobson : << *La primauté du procédé métaphorique dans les écoles romantiques et symbolistes a été maintes fois soulignée mais on n'a pas encore suffisamment compris que c'est la prédominance de la métonymie qui gouverne et définit effectivement le courant littéraire qu'on appelle ''réaliste'', qui appartient à une période intermédiaire entre le déclin du romantisme et la naissance du symbolisme et qui s'oppose à l'un comme à l'autre. Suivant la voie des relations de contiguïté, l'auteur réaliste opère des digressions métonymiques de l'intrigue à l'atmosphère et des personnages au cadre spatio-temporel* >>[617].

---

[614] Roland Barthes: *Introduction à l'Analyse Structurale des Récits* in **Communications, 8**, op. cit. p. 15.
[615] Roman Jakobson: << *Le développement d'un discours peut se faire le long de deux lignes sémantiques différentes : un thème (topic) en amène un autre soit par similarité soit par contiguïté. Le mieux serait sans doute de parler de procès métaphorique dans le premier cas et de procès métonymique dans le second* >>, in **Essais de Linguistique Générale**, op. cit. p. 6.
[616] Maarten Van Buuren disputes this assertion because, according to him, and in accordance here with L. Frappier-Mazur, << *la métonymie n'est pas plus fréquente dans le discours réaliste, ni plus caractéristique que la métaphore* >>, see **Les Rougon-Macquart d'Émile Zola. De la Métaphore au Mythe**, op. cit. p. 273.
[617] Roman Jakobson: **Essais de Linguistique Générale**, op. cit. p.62-63.

When one is interested, for example, in a space like Nana's bedroom, or Renée's, or at the Saccard Hotel's greenhouse, it is easy to see how much space can reflect the character that occupies it. The space overdetermines its occupant, it requalifies it or deepens its psychological study[618]. From this point of view, Nana's residence is presented as follows: << *Dans son hôtel, il y avait comme un éclat de forge. Ses continuels désirs y flambaient, un petit souffle de ses lèvres changeait l'or en une cendre fine que le vent balayait à chaque heure. Jamais on n'avait vu pareille rage de dépense. L'hôtel semblait bâti sur un gouffre, les hommes avec leurs biens, leurs corps, jusqu'à leurs noms, s'y engloutissaient, sans laisser la trace d'un peu de poussière* >>[619].

The reader realises from the analysis of this excerpt, that the house is as debauched as its anthropomorphous occupant, and as devastating as it is, to the point where one wonders if it is the space that brings about such behaviour on the character's part, or if, on the contrary, the latter shapes the space in their own image.

Such ambiguity disappears, however, when the anthropomorphous sexual subject chooses to create their entire space, as when Nana plans to make a bed worthy of her status as the Venus of prostitution.: << *Nana rêvait un lit comme il n'en existait pas, un trône, un autel, où Paris viendrait adorer sa nudité souveraine. Il serait tout en or et en argent repoussés, pareil à un grand bijou, des roses d'or jetés sur un treillis d'argent ; au chevet, une bande d'Amours, parmi les fleurs, se penchaient avec des rires, guettant les voluptés dans l'ombre des rideaux. Elle s'était adressée à Labordette qui lui avait amené deux orfèvres, on s'occupait déjà des dessins* >>[620]. Such a description reveals all the psychology of the anthropomorphous sexual agent, namely, their status as a prostitute that aspires to multiply its clientele, their penchant for jewelry and fortune, their admiration for their own nudity – which is a narcissistic phenomenon - and their resemblance to the sovereign goddess of love. Space is in this sense the doublet of the character that dwells in it.

The greenhouse works in the same way in **La Curée** and if Renée prefers to consume incest with Maxime therein - rather than in any other logically more appropriate space - it is for several reasons. First, the greenhouse contains an oval basin containing a weird liquid that recalls the maternal egg at the beginning of the gestation. This basin prefigures the quasi-maternal bond that binds the two sexual subjects and reinforces the notion of incest between them. Then, the greenhouse that is overheated in winter, attracts Renée[621] who is constantly chilly. She constantly needs Maxime's human warmth in addition to the artificial

---

[618] This gives unquestionable credit to the position of Roman Jakobson expressed in the preceding quotation.
[619] Émile Zola: **R. M. II**, op. cit. pp. 1432-1433.
[620] **Ibidem**, p. 1434.
[621] Renée is introduced as a << *fleur de serre* >>, in **R. M. I.** d'Émile Zola, op. cit. p. 497.

heat of her favourite space. Finally, she feels in control of herself and of Maxime in that greenhouse since the latter perceives her in there as a true sphinx and lets himself be manipulated by her. Renée is the phallic mistress full of initiatives in the greenhouse. She is completely in charge when the lovers are in that space which therefore appears to gather a condensed meaning. It is in there that Renée is branded a cold woman, a phallic woman, an infernal[622], a mythical, a monstrous, a nymphomaniac, an enigmatic and dangerous character.

In short, description is the privileged place for the metonymy that resolutely puts itself at the service of the narrative. Thus, description is no longer perceived as a dead time in the narrative, but as an accelerator of the speed of the diegesis[623]. The description thus reaches a higher narratological status in the modern novel than what was offered by the literature of the time before the Century of Zola[624]. The novelist did write in 1880 : << *Nous estimons que l'homme ne peut être séparé de son milieu, qu'il est complété par son vêtement, par sa maison, par sa ville, par sa province ; et, dès lors, nous ne noterons pas un seul phénomène de son cerveau ou de son cœur, sans en chercher les causes ou le contrecoup dans le milieu. De là ce qu'on appelle nos éternelles descriptions. [...]. Je définirai donc la description : un état du milieu qui détermine et complète l'homme* >>[625]. Jean-François Tonard was well aware of this aspect when recognising that description used to occupy a secondary place in the seventeenth Century literature while it occupies a preponderant place in that of the eighteenth and nineteenth Centuries[626]. As far as Zola is concerned, he readily admits in this author, a << *débauche descriptive* >>[627] thanks to which << *Zola a donné naissance à une spatialité littéraire active* >>[628]. Based exclusively on the description of the closed space, the critic argues, and rightly so, that it becomes a dynamic element in Zola's work by occupying the foreground of the character and reaching the rank of protagonist by the

---

[622] Émile Zola : **R. M. I**, the greenhouse is a << *mer de feu* >> where Renée and Maxime are thrown into << *en plein enfer dantesque* >>, op. cit. p. 357 et p. 488.

[623] Roland Barthes writes about **Nana**: << *le récit s'accélère, les mois de la fin sont comme les minutes du commencement ; la dégradation est emportée dans un mouvement progressif, qui rend d'une façon hallucinante son caractère implacable* >>, in La Mangeuse d'Hommes published in **Guide du Livre**, XX, Paris, Seuil, 1955, p. 227.

David Baguley does not say anything different when he postulates that: << *The naturalist novel in general, not just* **La Bête Humaine**, *tends to go off the rails, as the novelist pushes his heroines and heroes beyond the rational order* >>, in **Naturalist Fiction. The Entropic Vision**, op. cit. p. 212.

[624] David Baguley recalls that in Zola's theoretical writings, the words *nature, naturalisme* and *description* have become interchangeable at one time, including that in the drafting of his **Roman Expérimental** in 1880, **ibidem**, p. 184,

[625] Émile Zola: *De la description* in **Le Roman Expérimental** (1880), in **Œuvres Complètes**, under the direction of Henri Mitterand, volume 9 : **Nana 1880**, op. cit. p. 425.

[626] Jean-François Tonard: **Thématique et Symbolique de l'Espace Clos dans le Cycle des Rougon-Macquart d'Émile Zola**, op. cit. pp. 1-5.

[627] **Ibidem**, p. 4.

[628] **Ibidem**, p. 2.

game[629] of metaphoric figures. He writes: << *La personnification des lieux clos, acquise par la surenchère descriptive, fait qu'ils participent autant que les hommes à la marche du récit* >>[630]. The description, needless to say - in addition to the metonymy - can be done in a synecdochic form.

1.2. The synecdoche

Generally speaking, there is a synecdoche whenever a speaker - a narrator in this case - designates a sexual agent by the mere designation of any part of their body, or by an object belonging to them. The narrator then presents themselves as a cameraman that zooms in on the characteristic parts of the character in question: << *L'auteur réaliste opère des digressions métonymiques de l'intrigue à l'atmosphère et des personnages au cadre spatio-temporel. Il est friand de détails synecdochiques* >>[631], writes Roman Jakobson.

This is why in **La Curée**, Renée is constantly designated by her superb << *épaules* >> seen through the unveiling of her cleavage. Her << *gorge* >> is held in the same esteem because it enjoys a special attention from the narrator and the Emperor, including the crowd at the ball held at the imperial court. The same goes for her omnipresent and omnipotent << *cuisses* >> in the novel. Naturally, these three bodily parts suggest the beautiful young woman she is, and they also reinforce her referentiality to the blonde Venus.

In **Nana**, Nana enjoys a similar treatment with a particular emphasis on << *ses jambes plantureuses* >> and on << *sa peau laiteuse* >>. In the same way, how not recall what Genette calls *paralipse* - la Cognette whose << *fesses ont beaucoup plus travaillé que les mains* >>[632] ? All these synecdochic designations reveal sexual characteristics, including physical beauty, prostitution and debauchery leading to easy social ascension.

If one refers to the characters of the figures according to Lamy, it is obvious that the Zolian narrator is << *un homme passionné (qui) aime à se répéter, comme l'homme en colère aime à porter plusieurs coups* >>[633]. According to these characteristics, the omnipresence of sex in **Les Rougon-Macquart** would be << *l'hypotypose* >> or << *la présence obstinée de l'objet aimé* >>[634]. Thus, the minute descriptions of the characters would constitute a << *distribution* (which) *dénombre les parties de l'objet de sa passion* >>[635]. Distribution therefore amounts to a synecdoche. Undoubtedly, one of the most beautiful examples of

---

[629] Jean-François Tonard : **Thématique et Symbolique de l'Espace Clos dans le Cycle des Rougon-Macquart d'Émile Zola**, op. cit. p. 5.
[630] **Ibidem**, p. 4.
[631] Roman Jakobson: **Essai de Linguistique Générale**, op. cit. p. 63.
[632] Émile Zola: **R. M. IV**, op. cit. p. 610.
[633] Gérard Genette citing Lamy in **Figures 1**, Paris, Seuil, 1966, p. 217.
[634] **Ibidem**, p. 218.
[635] **Ibidem**, p. 218.

hypotyping is offered by Serge Mouret when he addresses his sweetheart - Albine - not knowing which part of her body seems to be the most desirable. According to the narrator : << *il répétait : - Ton visage est à moi, tes yeux, ta bouche, tes joues [...]. Tes bras sont à moi, depuis tes ongles, jusqu'à tes épaules [...] tes pieds sont à moi, tes genoux sont à moi, toute ta personne est à moi* >>[636]. This crumbling of the body parts of Albine shows that the sexual subject-operator, Serge, has a hard time making a choice among the different body parts indicated as he likes them all as much as the others. He is so passionate about Albine that he sublimates each component of her body; each of them being perceived as a treasure in itself. The desired sexual-object is, from the perspective of the subjugated sexual-subject, an inexhaustible gold mine.

Let us end this paragraph with the mirror that implies narcissism. It is part of the synecdoche because it reflects the image of its user or owner. About the aspect of reflection, Gérard Genette writes : << *En lui-même, le reflet est un terme équivoque : le reflet est un double, c'est-à-dire un autre et un même* >>[637]. The mirror allows, for example, Maxime, Renée and Nana, to always see each other again and to arrange to be or remain sexual objects pleasant to see and to covet. It is therefore the primordial instrument of the sexual subject who, while remaining themselves, would like to become another from the judgment of their double. The mirror is perceived as an instrument of improvement for the sexual subject who possesses it whereas the narrator perceives it as an equivocal instrument and an instrument of death. Beyond the metonymic relata that accentuate the knowledge of the character's work, the metaphorical relata do the same for their being.

2. The indices

The study of the indices will include metaphors themselves, comparisons and sexually connoted periphrases.

2.1. The metaphors

The census of the figures os speech cannot be exhaustive without a review of the metaphors or the whole exercise would be a waste of time[638]. But it must be remembered that most of the metaphors in the corpus designating anthropomorphic characters have already been studied in the second part of this study, in Chapter II.

---

[636] Émile Zola: **R. M. I**, op. cit. p. 1406.
[637] Gérard Genette : **Figures 1**, op. cit. p. 21.
[638] Many critics have sometimes devoted voluminous books to the study of the networks of metaphors in the corpus, however, without having exhausted the theme. I can mention among them, Claude Seassau and his **Émile Zola, le Réalisme Symbolique** ; Jacques Noiray's **Le Roman et la Machine, I : L'Univers de Zola** ; Maarten Van Buuren's **Les Rougon-Macquart d'Émile Zola. De la Métaphore au Mythe** ; Michel Serres and his **Feux et Signaux de Brume, Zola**, to mention only but a few of them.

The most recurrent metaphors in the corpus[639] on the isotopic axis of animality are: the snake, the beast, the goat, the brute, the rabid beast, the predator, the wolf, the pig, the dog, the bitch, the cat, the female cat, the monster, the vermin, the horse, the lamb, the she-devil, the goat, the vulture, the fly, the rooster. It should be noted that this lexical field is that of debauchery of animal type, the diabolical and the monstrous, even the infernal type as it has been shown above. Each of the metaphors is used in different novels of the corpus and in a redundant way. This redundancy is certainly a sign of obsession, but also proof that Zola had a specific vision of the world: a world dominated by lust and violence inherent to sexuality.

When it comes to metaphors, Van Buuren distinguishes, for example, the metaphors related to animals from the metaphors related to plants; these being positive while those ones negative[640]. For the metaphors related to animals, he also distinguishes three different axes: the metaphors of hunting - opposing hunters to their prey -, the metaphors of domestication - which oppose the rulers to the submissive people - and finally that of the human beast - that is neurotic and unbalanced in nature. Finally, the critic insists on the textile vocabulary designating parts of the female body[641]. In another register, Noiray sees in the metaphor of the machine, the image of death[642] and of the cataclysmic end[643]. Indeed, for him, the technology represents the forces of evil so much so that the women that are assimilated to broken sexual machines are barren[644]. He goes on to argue that the deep hostility between the woman and the machine comes from the fact that they are rivals who oppose, exclude and substitute for each other[645]. In summary, with Zola, we are dealing with a narrator obsessed by sex and whose passion transpires in the iterative, the synecdochic and the metaphorical phenomena.

2.2. The comparisons

---

[639] Maarten Van Buuren notes that the metaphors are very abundant in Zola's novels and he is surprised that this characteristic is absent from the theoretical writings of Zola. Moreover, he goes so far as to recognise that the stylistic problems are carefully avoided in Zola's theory, **Les Rougon-Macquart d'Émile Zola. De la Métaphore au Mythe**, op. cit. pp. 14-15.

Let us recall that Jean Kaempfer had very clearly emphasised, in **D'Un Naturalisme Pervers**, Zola's hesitations with regard to style and form and his embarrassment leading him to somewhat skip this question instead of developing it, op. cit. p. 157.

[640] Maarten Van Buuren in the above book, p. 40.

[641] **Ibidem**, Maarten Van Buuren writes: << *Un groupe nombreux de métaphores réciproques concerne la description des charmes féminins en termes d'étoffes, une* << *peau de satin* >>, *des épaules* << *d'un luisant de soie* >>, *un menton comme* << *du velours rose* >>. *Inversement, les étoffes d'**Au Bonheur des Dames** évoquent des nudités de femmes* >>, p. 280.

[642] Jacques Noiray: **Le Roman et la Machine, I : L'Univers de Zola**, op. cit. p. 304.

[643] **Ibidem**, vegetal p. 448.

[644] Jacques Noiray: **Le Roman et la Machine, I : L'Univers de Zola**, op. cit. p. 404.

[645] Maarten Van Buuren, in **Les Rougon-Macquart d'Émile Zola. De la Métaphore au Mythe**, op. cit. p. 413.

They are not fundamentally different from metaphors in that they associate anthropomorphic sexual subjects with mythical animals, plants, or heroes, usually by means of a comparison term like *"such"* or *"as well as"*. The animals, the mythical heroes and the plants are then the *comparants* and the *comparés* are the anthropomorphic characters. Roughly speaking, they are the same animals that I mentioned in the metaphor section with the same sexual semantics as it was shown in the second part, chapter II. Let us end this paragraph by a brief study of the sexually connoted periphrases.

2.3. The periphrases

They are immediately significant as they make explicit the sexual agents they designate. So, in **La Terre**, we read that La Cognette is : << *une câtin* >>, << *une femme vengeresse* >>, << *un ancien petit torchon* >>, while her lover, Tron, is << *une grande brute* >>, << *cet impudent* >>, << *un insolent* >>. Moreover, she's << *une bête carnassière* >>. It goes without saying that she is - with regard to this minimal list of periphrases - without morality. La Cognette is a woman of low morals and she is dangerous a priori. She is obviously devoid of intelligence. The pair Tron-La Cognette constitutes a wholly bestial couple focused solely on sex, so to speak. La Cognette recalls Adèle[646] in **Pot-Bouille**, that << *bête sale et gauche* >>, << *un torchon* >>. The notion of dump cloth extends into **Nana** when Nana[647] herself is seen as << *une dévoreuse d'hommes* >>, << *la mouche d'or envolée de l'ordure des faubourgs, apportant le ferment des pourritures sociales, [qui] avait empoisonné ces hommes, rien qu'à se poser sur eux* >>[648]. The notion of dump cloth - which constitutes a true isotopy - presupposes a cheap sexuality which is away from moral precepts, hence the need for cleaning, literally and figuratively. If such cleansing begins with the relentless disappearance of Nana, it ends however in **La Débâcle** with the big sweep that cleanses France of Napoleon III's regime.

As for the notion of the vengeful woman, it also appears in the periphrases designating Nana and continues with those that designate La Belle Normande in **Le Ventre de Paris**. The latter is seen as a dump cloth which constitutes a true isotopy. The latter is seen as << *une femme dangereuse* >>, << *une femme vengeresse* >>, as well as Clorinde[649] in **Son Excellence Eugène Rougon**. The

---

[646] Claude Seassau has shown in **Émile Zola, Le Réalisme Symbolique**, that the name may be used in the Zolian novel ironically, or for the purpose of deceiving the reader. That is how the name Adèle is supposed to work, for it means << *noble* >>, op. cit. p. 36.
[647] Chantal Bertrand-Jennings brings together Nana, La Cognette, Christine, Renée, Gasparine and others in the category of despicable nymphomaniacs, in **L'Éros et la Femme chez Zola**, op. cit. p. 61.
[648] Émile Zola: **R. M. II**, op. cit. p. 1470.
[649] Maarten Van Buuren clearly established the metaphorical cannibalism in the Clorinde-Eugène Rougon relationship in **Les Rougon-Macquart d'Émile Zola. De la Métaphore au Mythe**, op. cit. p. 171.

situation is not much better when it come to Victor Rougon[650], the son of Saccard who is labelled << *un enfant mûri trop vite* >> with << *les appétits exaspérés de sa race, une hâte, une violence à jouir* >>[651]. All these references show how sex can be an instrument of destruction and revenge. This is why the Zolian narrator seems to advise that one must be wary of it, which the anthropomorphic characters of the corpus cannot do. Moreover, they will be struck by the heavy sanctions studied above. Only Clotilde and Pascal enjoy the sympathy of the narrator in their assimilation to the young Sunamite, Abisaïg, and the old King David. Pascal's old age is seen as an all-white beauty[652], and the youth of Clotilde, like a feast, a delicious meal. For all these reasons, they give birth to the child that is free from the hereditary crack[653].

In considering all those stylistic elements, it is necessary to draw the following lesson: by the use of the rhetorical means, the narrator intensifies the dramatic, the tragic, the comical, the vicious and the coprolalic aspects of sexuality[654] of his paper beings. In such a particular context, how can one envisage the discovery of the personal myth of the **Rougon-Macquart** author?

III. DISCOVERING THE PERSONAL MYTH OF THE AUTHOR

This stage is the third of the four moments that make up the psychocritical method[655]. One can now make the following hypothesis: Zola is undoubtedly a sex obsessed writer. He seems to be obsessed with sexual impotence, obsessed with the vision of the woman that he considers an abyss, like a devious being preparing a relentless revenge against the male gender. He is also obsessed with the phobia of early death and of infertility. These postulates are based on the remarks that have been given throughout the work of superimposing the texts of the corpus in the preceding sections.

---

[650] Victor is no more than a << *boue humaine* >>, according to the expression of Jean Borie, in **Zola et les Mythes, ou de la Nausée au Salut**, op. cit. p. 160.

[651] Émile Zola: **R. M. V**, op. cit. p. 157.

[652] Maarten Van Buuren shows that Pascal is both a << *messie* >>, the << *bon Dieu* >>, and at the same time a << *divine bonté* >> and a << *martyr* >>, in **Les Rougon-Macquart d'Émile Zola. De la Métaphore au Mythe**, op. cit. p. 158.

[653] Chantal Bertrand-Jennings believes that Clotilde's son is << *le messie* >>, essentially because his dad, Pascal, is << *le rédempteur* >>, in **L'Éros et la Femme chez Zola**, op. cit. p. 114 et p. 109.

[654] Edmond and Jules de Goncourt wrote: << *Rien n'est moins poétique que la nature et que les choses naturelles : c'est l'homme qui leur a trouvé une poésie. La naissance, la vie, la mort, ces trois accidents de l'être, symbolisés par l'homme, sont des opérations chimiques et cyniques. L'homme pisse l'enfant et la femme le chie. La mort est une décomposition* >>, 4 February 1861, **Journal. Mémoires de la Vie Littéraire**, volume I, Robert Ricatte (éd.), Paris, Fasquelle-Flammarion, 1956, p. 78.

[655] See the Introduction to read about the different steps of this method.

Indeed, looking back at his determination to write about - even to dwell on - the theme of sexuality[656] in all his romantic works, Zola looks like a sex obsessed[657] writer. The designations of his characters and the descriptions are ingenious pretexts to rehearse the sexual tendencies of the anthropomorphic characters concerned. In this same way, the figures of rhetoric come to insist on the theme in question as if it were a great river in which all the literary confluences came to throw themselves.

Zola seems haunted by sexual impotence[658] and by women just like some of his male characters such as Eugène Rougon, Florent and Brother Archangias respectively in **Son Excellence Eugène Rougon**, in **Le Ventre de Paris** and in **La Faute de l'Abbé Mouret**. For him as for them, the woman is nothing less than a gulf, an abyss whose depth is simply immeasurable. Why then would one throw themselves into such a terrifying and an unfathomable deph ? Answering that question by an absolute negation, neither Archangias nor Florent will experience women. There is no doubt though that this rather unusual behaviour of man vis-à-vis the woman is a token of psychosis and of neurosis whose origins are as confused as distant. The idea of the dangerous and vengeful woman continues to carve out its way through **Germinal** where the miners' wives collectively emasculate the merchant, Maigrat[659], in retaliation for the sexual assaults they had to suffer at his hands before obtaining flour and other necessities[660]. They went on to exhibit << *la virilité morte* >> of the victim as an << *abominable trophée* >>[661].   There is indeed a phobia of castration in Zola's works, an obsession that leads him to be wary of priests, for those men are symbolically castrated by the dogma of celibacy.

He is also haunted by barrenness that he seems to exorcise by evoking the terms of fertilisation, fertility, germination, thrust, etc. In this same context, miscarriages – true *nausea* - of Renée, then of Nana, suggest that these

---

[656] David Baguley believes in **Naturalist Fiction. The Entropic Vision**, that if adultery is an eminently literary theme, it is preponderant among the naturalist writers, op. cit. p. 207.

[657] Roger Ripoll writes: <<*L'association du mal et de la sexualité traduit bien plus les hantises de Zola que les conceptions qu'il entendait mettre en œuvre dans son roman*>>, in **Réalité et Mythe chez Zola**, op. cit. p. 115.

[658] Jean Borie writes about the novelist Sandoz in **L'Œuvre** (whose proximity to Zola himself is well established) that: <<*Castration et exclusion sont le prix d'un <<bonheur>> qui ressemble fort à une régression infantile à l'ombre d'une épouse trop maternelle*>>, in **Zola et les Mythes, ou de la Nausée au Salut**, op. cit. p. 23.

[659] Naomi Schor believes that women in Zola's novels are fundamentally more violent than men: <<*Nowhere does Zola exhibit more openly his espousal of the myth that women are innately more violent than men. The final paroxysm of this subhuman, specifically female brand of violence is, of course, the castration of Maigrat*>>, in **Zola's Crowds**, op. cit. p. 104.

[660] Claude Seassau reminds us of this: <<*Les femmes, en suivant la Brûlé, semblent conscientes d'accomplir un rite ; elles ont émasculé celui qui se comportait comme un <<chat>>, eu égard à sa lubricité et à la façon dont il les contraignait à subir ses violences sexuelles en échange de nourriture*>>, in **Émile Zola, le Réalisme Symbolique**, op. cit. pp. 255-256.

[661] Émile Zola: **R. M. III**, op. cit. p. 1453.

unsuccessful maternities are also a form of barrenness since Renée no longer procreates and that Nana, having lost her Louiset later on, dies without leaving any offspring to perpetuate her name and her memory. They certainly did not lack lovers[662]. *In extenso*, it can be argued that Zola himself was haunted by the prospect of not having a child that could perpetuate his name on this earth.

One must also take into account the early sexuality that causes an early death in the **Rougon-Macquart**. To support this statement, let us recall here only the passing of Louiset in **Nana**, that of Jacques, son of Claude Lantier in **L'Œuvre**, and finally the little one of La Rosalie in **La Faute de l'Abbé Mouret**. In dealing with the issue of the character's punishment, the paragraph on the early and untimely deaths, a longer list of sexual agents and/or their offspring that died far too early was provided. This impressive list shows that Zola has the obsession with this type of fatality linked to the lubricity of minors[663].

So basically, this study of agents has found that although they are sexually manipulated, they remain competent. In fact, one can say that all the destiny of the characters is governed by their sexuality, which belies the assertion of Philippe Hamon that stresses that the characters' sexuality in Zola's works is subordinated to their territorialisation[664]. They abuse above all their competence and it follows that their sexual performance is all about vice and perversion. It is because of these vices and perversions that their sanctions is heavy and implacable. Also, the metalinguistic and the poetic functions are resolutely at the service of the fatality that strikes the characters. These functions also make it possible to discover the myth of the author Zola[665] : his obsession with women, his obsession with sterility and castration, his haunting by the idea of early death. The poetic function, for example, in the Zolian novel, resolutely falls within the framework of the inevitability of sexuality. This reinforces my initial assertion that sexuality, for the Zolian naturalistic view

---

[662] They are some << *machines sexuelles détraquées* >> and they are, therefore, deprived of children, according to Jacques Noiray, in **Le Romancier et la Machine, I : L'Univers de Zola**, op. cit. p. 404.

In the same way, Chantal Bertrand-Jennings admits in **L'Éros et la Femme chez Zola**, that many bad women are deprived of children in Zola's fiction works, op. cit. p. 97.

[663] Colette Becker: << *Dans **Thérèse Raquin**, par exemple, roman dans lequel Zola réaffirme constamment son projet scientifique, l'étude physiologique du << cas >> médical disparaît derrière la mythologie et les hantises personnelles de l'écrivain : peur de la Femme, peur de la fêlure, des forces incontrôlées et incontrôlables qui détraquent l'homme et le conduisent à la folie, hantise de l'émiettement physique et moral, de l'engrenage et de la mort, difficile acceptation de la vie trop << bourgeoise >> menée entre sa femme et sa mère, que trahit, entre autres, une étonnante obsession du chiffre 3, etc.* >>, article *Zola*, published in **Dictionnaire des Littératures de Langue Française**, op. cit. p. 2693.

[664] Philippe Hamon: **Le Personnel du Roman. Le Système des Personnages dans Les Rougon-Macquart**, op. cit. p. 205.

[665] The author's personal myth is to be found in the haunting of a small number of characters, as Maarten Van Buuren recalls in **Les Rougon-Macquart d'Émile Zola. De la Métaphore au Mythe**, op. cit. p. 46.

point, is an extremely unifying theme. That is why the networks of metaphors, of comparisons, of periphrases, of myths and of the symbols that refer to the characters all fall within the framework of this inevitability of sexuality, the very essence of naturalism. The unifying character of the theme will be revealed more clearly through the study of the spatio-temporal component for the literary characters are born, they develop and they reproduce themselves, then they die in a given space and at a given time. They are likely to be influenced by their space and time, both in a positive and in a negative way, but never in a neutral manner.

PART III: THE RELEVANCE OF THE SPATIO-TEMPORAL COMBINATORICS IN RELATION TO THE FATALITY OF SEXUALITY

The narrative is a succession of fictitious events occurring at a given time and in a given space. That is why it is really essential to question the secrets of this couple known as *chronotope* – to borrow a word coined by Mikhail Bakhtin - if one ambitions to go beyond the first level of reading. The literal nature of a text resides for the most part in the treatment reserved to these two instances. When he questioned the usefulness of these two fictitious entities in the literary work, Aragon came to the conclusion that they ultimately answer a need for coherence, therefore of legibility of the story: << *L'espace et le temps figuratifs renvoient non aux structures de l'univers physique, mais à celles de l'imaginaire. Les liens entre les éléments se mesurent en terme non d'exactitude, mais de cohérence* >>[666].

As far as I am concerned, I intend to first study the entity of time in **Les Rougon-Macquart**, with all that it implies – the external times and the internal time, the verbal time and the temporal symbolism. I shall then focus on the entity of space - its configuration and its possible influences on the anthropomorphic characters. This should make it possible to understand to what extent the study of space and time is crucial in the global apprehension of the literary character, for the character is not a free electron that can be apprehended independently, and beyond its environment. The literary character does evolve in a story that takes place over a given period that is limited. One could even argue that in **Les Rougon-Macquart**, the character is constrained to a sexuality that is programmed and to which an alloted time has been granted.

CHAPTER I: THE TIME IN THE ROUGON-MACQUART: THE PROGRAMMED AND TIMED OUT SEXUALITY

Time has an abstract character since it belongs to the realm of referential illusion. In this regard, Roland Barthes writes that << *le* << *vrai* >> *temps est une illusion référentielle* >>[667]. The temporal universe is all the more important since it is in relation to it that one can grasp the evolution of the narrative. Time thus appears to be the main support, the thread of the succession of events. In any case, it is in this sense that Valéry writes: << *La croyance au temps comme agent et fil conducteur est fondée sur le mécanisme de la mémoire et sur celui du discours combiné* >>[668].

As far as this study is concerned, I will study on the one hand the external times - which are paratextual in nature - and, on the other hand, the internal times - which are rather intratextual or immanent in nature. It is rather curious that the critical works on the entity of time in the Zolian novel are so rare, unlike the works devoted to that of space, or the myths, the metaphors and the characters

---

[666] Louis Aragon: **Je n'ai jamais appris à écrire ou les incipits**, Genève, Skira, 1969, p. 78.
[667] Roland Barthes: *Introduction à l'Analyse Structurale des Récits* in **Communications, 8**, op. cit. p.18.
[668] Paul Valéry: **Tel Quel**, volume II, Paris, Gallimard, 1960, p. 348.

to which the critics of Zola have afforded great interest and effort. However, Zola's treatment of time is no less important than that of the space for example. That is why I believe that this imbalance in the interest of criticism must be dealt with and calibrated in fairness. This chapter is a first step - as far as I am concerned - towards a critique that would take into account all the essential components of Zola's novels.

In the understanding of the structuralists, when one evokes the temporality of a literary text, one thinks primarily of the so-called external times, then the internal ones. This means that the story is at least twice temporal. To begin with, I will expand on the external times that are not immanent to the story.

I. THE EXTERNAL TIMES

The external times will be studied according to Goldenstein's classification which defines external time as being << *l'époque à laquelle vit, ou a vécu, le romancier d'une part, celui du lecteur de l'autre (sans oublier la période historique au cours de laquelle est censée se dérouler l'action)* >>[669].

1.1. The author's time

1.1.1. The time Zola lived: 1840-1902

From 1840 to 1902, Zola lived sixty-two years of poverty first. He went on to embrace several careers to ensure his daily bread: once a clerk, then a polemic journalist, then political and literary journalist, an amateur painter in his spare time, etc. He later became a prolific and a talented novelist. His era was marked by the July Monarchy of Louis-Philippe 1st - from 1840 to 1848, with regard to Zola precisely -, then by an aborted Republic - from 1848 to 2nd December 1851. He was especially marked by his strong execration of Napoléon III's regime known as the Second Empire. In Zola's understanding, this monarch was nothing but a usurper of power and a violator of the constitution. Other regimes, such as the Commune and the Third Republic, succeeded the Second Empire without much change in the life of Zola[670]. Still, the era of the production of the works also belongs the time of the author.

1.1.1.1. The era of the production of the Rougon-Macquart (1870-1893)[671]

This romantic cycle aimed to paint the imperial society in all its components, or almost. But since the Second Empire crumbled on September 2nd, 1870 and the publication of **La Fortune des Rougon** was effective in bookstores on October

---

[669] Lucien Goldenstein: **Pour Lire le Roman**, Bruxelles, De Boeck-Duculot, 1989, p. 101.
[670] For more information on this period of Zola's life, refer to Colette Becker's book: **Les Apprentissages de Zola**, Paris, PUF, 1993.
[671] For this period of the life of the author, refer to the first volume of Henri Mitterand's biographical trilogy: **Zola, I. Sous le Regard d'Olympia**, Paris, Fayard, 1999.

14th 1871, and finally, given the fact that **Le Docteur Pascal** was published in July 1893, one can only point out that the time of the novelistic writing is posterior to the historical period it depicts. This anachronism is due to the fact that the narration usually comes after the events, except for the radio or television journalist who can do a simultaneous narration or a live broadcast. Following the author's time, it is necessary to question that of the story told.

1.1. The historical time or the era of the fiction

This represents the duration of the action and it provides a figurative support for the narrative situations and the characters. The **Rougon-Macquart** are the the painting of a purely fictional world which started during the week of resistance to the coup – the so-called << *semaine sanglante* >>, from the 7th to the 14th December 1851. It ended historically with the massacres of La Commune in Paris, followed by the anarchist tendencies that unfolded after the fall of Napoléon III, between September 1870 and 1871. This urban guerilla is narrated in **La Débâcle**. However, the time of the nuclear fiction - I will call that way the time of the story told in the novels of the corpus - will be enriched by abundant discursive anachronisms in the **Rougon-Macquart**. Those anachronisms are essentially analepses and prolepses that continually stretch the roots of the story in a past or in a future relatively far away from the historical limits intended: << *Dans la mise en place de cet univers symbolique et mythique, le temps de l'écriture l'emporte souvent sur celui de l'Histoire, et la parole de l'écrivain sur celle du narrateur. Les anachronismes, tout à fait volontaires, se multiplient, le temps se resserre* >>[672]. Thus, in **La Fortune des Rougon**, from the first chapter, the narrator depicts Silvère and Miette, just as they are preparing to follow the insurgents, the day after December 2nd, 1851.

In chapter two, however, the narrator takes his narrataries back to the eighteenth Century to tell the stories of Rougon and Macquart, starting with the birth of Adélaïde Fouque, in 1768. He tells the story of her marriage, the birth of her children and her grandchildren, including Silvère. So, while the real story of the novel is squeezed in more or less in just one week[673], the analepsis of chapter two makes it possible to ttime travel through nearly a Century. In reality, the march of the insurgents in Plassans – historically Aix-en Provence in the Var region - which lasted a week, was crushed by the gendarmerie in a blood bath. The roots of the immediate story are thus deeply immersed in an older story with more elucidated outlines. That story ends with the execution of Silvère[674] in the last chapter of the novel.

---

[672] Colette Becker : *Zola* in **Dictionnaire des Littératures de Langue Française**, op. cit. p. 2694.
[673] In **Structure et Unité dans Les Rougon-Macquart d'Émile Zola (la Poétique du Cycle)**, Neide de Faria believes that short stories are indeed those of a crisis, op. cit. p. 205.
[674] **Ibidem**, Neide de Faria then speaks of the circular time of the eternal return, and the mythical time in Zola's works, p. 210.

However, this anachronism inside the text of fiction is not far from recalling that of the reader's time.

1.1. The reader's time

The reader's time is the biggest anachronistic phenomenon in literature since a reader can discover Ovid or Aeschylus in 2003 or in 2023, thousands of years after the disappearance of these ancient authors. In my case, without necessarily falling into a millennial anachronism, I was not spared an anachronism whose amplitude is more than a Century. Indeed, I read Zola more than a Century and twenty years after the publication of his novels.

Why, then, would a reader of today be interested in naturalism, a literary school that is more than outdated ? It seems obvious that Zola's literature, though apparently outdated and old-fashioned, continues to touch the hearts of its readers, not only because it teaches about the era of the Second Empire, but also because it is original. The academician Jean Rostand was certainly right in 1968 when he called Zola << *un grand et inépuisable écrivain* >>. He exalted << *l'éminence, et la permanence, d'une œuvre qui, comme disait Mallarmé, a doté la littérature de quelque chose d'absolument nouveau en faisant de la vérité* << *une forme populaire de la beauté* >>>>[675].

This brief look at the external times leads straight to the more meaningful internal times for those who want to reach the elixir in the analysis of a literary work.

II. THE INTERNAL TIMES

The internal times are notably the time of the enunciation, the verbal tenses and the temporal symbolism.

2.1. The time of the narrative enunciation

As a general rule, one can agree with Christian Metz for whom << *le récit est une séquence deux fois temporelle : il y a le temps de la chose racontée, et le temps du récit (temps du signifié vs temps du signifiant)* >>[676]. The narrator has a great deal of freedom in that they are not obliged to start narrating their story from the beginning. It is not required to make a chronological narration either. So, having the authority to start their story at any point, including starting at the end, the narrator sometimes imposes on the *diégésis* a more or less fanciful order, which they choose for their *mimésis*. This is when the problem of order arises.

---

[675] Jean Rostand: *L'œuvre de Zola et la pensée scientifique*, **Europe : Zola,** op. cit. p. 360.
[676] Christian Metz: **Essais sur la Signification au Cinéma**, Paris, Klincksieck, 1969, p. 27.

2.1.1. The order in zola's Les Rougon-Macquart

It does not exist a zero degree in the corpus - and it seems improbable to find it elsewhere - where the story perfectly coincides whith history on the temporal axis. On the other hand, many anachronisms are found in **Les Rougon-Macquart**. These discursive anachronies are called prolepses - a process of anticipating the story over the historical event - and analepsis - a process of story-telling after the facts, or flashback. Prolepses or beginnings of the story *in medias res* are one of the favourite *topoi* of Zola[677].

This is how in **Nana**, from the first chapter, Nana is a popular actress and later on, the narrator reveals her difficult beginnings[678]. In **L'Œuvre**, Claude Lantier is already an established painter living in Paris since the outset of the novel before the reader is informed much later on of his past. **La Curée** does not innovate in this area because in the incipit, the narrator focuses the attention of the reader on the incestuous desire of Renée for Maxime, before we know how they became related[679] to each other.

It can be argued that almost not a single novel in the **Rougon-Macquart** series escapes the rule of the analepsis at the incipit. Could one draw up a conclusion from that there is a narrative monotony in Zola's works ? Or was it an essential characteristic trait of his personal genius ? The answer can be positive to those two questions because at first glance, the incessant use of the same technique in different novels could easily lead to a tiresome monotony. Nevertheless, one must see beyond that because Zola seems to draw his originality from that particular technique which, aesthetically, opens the novel on the *topos* that will give birth to the main drama. To understand the acuteness of this drama - which will form the core of the plot and will reach its peak in the middle of the story - backtrackings or analepses will be necessary to recall the characters'[680] past and access their consciousness and their unconscious. In addition, one can notice that the range of Zola's anachronies is variable from one novel to another, from one chapter to another within the same novel, and the amplitude of their scope is also likely to vary. For example, in chapter 1 of **La Bête Humaine** three years of marriage are layed out on a page and a third, a complete analogy recalls the romance of Roubaud with Séverine, leading up to their wedding and their marital

---

[677] David Baguley: **Zola et les Genres**, chapter IV : *Histoire et mythe dans **Son Excellence Eugène Rougon***, op. cit. p. 43.

[678] Neide de Faria on the question of analepsis, in **Structure et Unité dans Les Rougon-Macquart de Zola (la poétique du cycle)**, op. cit. p. 187.

See also Sarah Capitanio who did the same on **La Bête Humaine**, in *La Bête Humaine: intertextualité et intratextualité*, **Zola, La Bête Humaine : texte et explication**, Geoff Woollen (éd.), op. cit. p. 112.

[679] In the above work, Neide de Faria asserts that the analepsis and the free indirect speech slow down the Zolian narrative, op. cit. p. 217.

[680] This must be related to the long-lived novels that narrate a whole life, according to Neida de Faria, in **Structure et Unité dans Les Rougon-Macquart de Zola (la poétique du cycle)**, op. cit. p. 187.

life, a condensed summary of their love story that begins like this: << *Et ce petit objet avait suffi, toute l'histoire de son mariage se déroulait. Déjà trois ans bientôt* >>[681].

In **La Curée**, on the other hand, in Chapter II, we have a large amplitude analepsis because on sixty-seven pages, the narrator tells the story of Aristide and his wife, Angèle's arrival in Paris. He recounts the difficult beginnings of the couple three or four years later - after December 2nd, 1851 to 1854 - and then Aristide's marriage with Renée following the death of Angèle. The alternation analepsis-prolepsis is above all a process that tends to suspend the time and to slow down the pace of the story. Yves Chevrel clearly perceived this aspect when he pointed out that: << *Comme il a déjà été noté, le temps reçoit un traitement particulier dans La Curée, il semble se figer, se suspendre ; les procédés narratifs y contribuent largement : le début du chapitre IV reprend la narration au point où l'avait laissé le chapitre I, et à la fin de ce même chapitre IV, Zola interrompt la narration au moment où Renée embrasse Maxime pour placer une description de l'appartement : ce baiser annonce le vrai départ de leur liaison, et semble ainsi indéfiniment prolongé* >>[682].

If we compare these two analeptic amplitudes, three years on less than two pages in **La Bête Humaine** and three or four years for sixty-seven pages in **La Curée**, there is a blatant inequality in their respective treatments. The latter is very large while the former is narrowed. Where the amplitude is great, the narrator insists on the anachronism because it has a dramatic or a capital effect on the rest of the story that will unfold. The smaller amplitude on the contrary is given to trivial details, the minor incidents, or even the brief reminders that it is good to have in mind[683].

The variation of the amplitude therefore poses the problem of the speed of the narrative.

2.1.2. The duration

Gérard Genette has already warned everyone on this point writing that: << *nul ne peut mesurer la durée d'un récit* >>, because << *contrairement à ce qui se passe au cinéma, ou même en musique, rien ne permet ici de fixer une vitesse normale* >>[684]. Nevertheless, it is agreed to make an effort to calculate the speed of the story according to the following formula: TR/TH. It should be remembered that TR represents the time of the narrative - which is noted in

---

[681] Émile Zola: **R. M. IV**, op. cit. p.1000.
[682] Yves Chevrel: **La Curée** : *un roman d'étrange éducation ?* in **La Curée de Zola << ou la vie à outrance >>**, op. cit. p. 70.
[683] Maarten Van Buuren thinks that the discursive anachronisms are all the more numerous since 18 years were far too insufficient to tell the story of four generations of the Rougon-Macquart family in **Les Rougon-Macquart d'Émile Zola. De la Métaphore au Mythe**, op. cit. p. 14.
[684] Gérard Genette: **Figures III**, op. cit. p. 119.

terms of pages - and that TH represents the time of the story - which is noted in terms of days.

Comparing the two examples above gives 1095 days of history occurring in three years and told only on a page and a half, or 1095/1.5 = 750 in one case, while in the other, substantially the same duration of three years, or 1095 days of history are recounted on 67 pages, which can be arithmetically posed as follows: 1095/67 = 16.34. This means that in **La Bête Humaine**, the narrator devotes only one and a half pages to the proleptic narration of three years of events - each year is then told on half a page. This means that life in the home of Roubaud and Séverine was certainly lull, uneventful and it was all business as usual. The high speed that marks this story[685] proves that there was almost nothing to report in their quiet existence back then. On the other hand, in **La Curée**, only a little more than sixteen days of story are told on each proleptic page as if to insist on the suffering endured by the couple Aristide-Angèle in those first three years of their life in Paris. The details then make the story swell because the narrator seems to have a lot to say about their adventures during that difficult beginning. It is a question of painting in detail the exasperation of the husband in front of Angèle's refusal to die quickly because her death would allow him to marry Renée Béraud Du Châtel as he was very much interested in her sizeable dowry to the highest point.

Notwithstanding, the high speed is not the prerogative of **La Bête Humaine** since in this same novel, just a few hours of Roubaud's jealousy are rendered on thirty-three pages, 1/33 = 0.03. This extremely slow speed emphasises in great detail the grave maceration of Roubaud's furious and angry jealousy, a jealousy described in its slightest manifestations, almost minute after minute, to better show its impact on the character. Beside these speeds that can be calculated, it is necessary to point out the presence of what Genette calls *achronie*, that is to say << *une anachronie privée de toute relation temporelle, et que nous devons donc considérer comme un événement sans date et sans âge* >>[686].

For example, one can read in **L'Œuvre** about Claude Lantier: << *Il avait raté son existence* >>[687]. This retrospective does not specify anything at all, neither on the timeline nor on the speed of the story. It gives itself as an affirmation to take it or to leave it. From then on, Claude cannot catch up anymore with his peers because his failure is final without appeal.

The ellipse is always related to the duration. Let us note that the ellipse can be *déterminée, indéterminée, explicite* or *qualifiée* in the theory of Genette. Thus, in **Pot-Bouille**, there is an ellipse with Octave Mouret, << *dès le lendemain* [...]

---

[685] See David Baguley on the acceleration of Zola's narrative, in **Naturalist Fiction. The Entropic Vision**, op. cit. p. 212.
[686] Gérard Genette in **Figures III**, op. cit. p. 119.
[687] Émile Zola: **R. M. IV**, op. cit. p. 246.

>>[688], conducted his inquiries to discover the habits of the desired woman, Madame Valerie. Furthermore, another ellipse which is indeterminate, shows that: << *pendant des semaines le projet de mariage entre Octave et madame Hédouin semblait être au point mort tant les deux fiancés évitaient d'en parler* >>[689]. A good example of a qualified ellipse is found in **Nana** though, where the Marquis de Chouard cumulates << *soixante ans de débauche* >>[690].

It should be noted that the essentially descriptive breaks mark not an acceleration of the story, much less a slowdown, but rather a momentary suspension of the storyline in question. They are so numerous in the corpus that it is useless to study them here since I shall return to them in the fourth part.

Finally, *la scène* - or part dialogue – matches, so to speak, TR and TH. Indeed, there is a *scène* when the characters exchange directly between them while the narrator fades away as much as possible. The *scène* has the advantage of putting the responsibility for the speech squarely on the shoulders of the person who speaks, thus exonerating that of the main narrator. That is the case in **La Terre** where Mr. and Mrs. Charles disclose in veiled words the adultery of their son-in-law who works as a pimp in the city: << *- Enfin, il monte lui-même avec celle du 5, une grosse [...].*
-Qu'est-ce que tu dis-là ?
-Oh ! J'en suis sûre, je les ai vus >>[691].

Unlike the narrative or historical utterances where the narrator *"speaks"*, the discourse supposes a speaker and a listener. The two instances, the " I " and the *"you"* thus designated, inform each other and inform the reader thanks to the narrator, the accidental listener in his hidden god position. The narrator then transcribes, gives away the confidences he overheard. This narrative technique allows them to claim their neutrality instead of their responsibility in the narrative act exercised by their characters.

To close this paragraph, it must be recalled that the Zolian narratives are generally of a short duration ranging from one week in **La Fortune des Rougon** to a few years in **La Curée**. The **Rougon-Macquart** recount the story of a family in a hurry to live, better still, to enjoy outrageously the pleasures of the flesh. This is probably why the narrator is also eager to tell their story at a fast pace[692]

---

[688] Émile Zola: **R. M. III**, op. cit. p. 59.
[689] **Ibidem**, p. 341.
[690] Émile Zola: **R. M. II**, op. cit. p. 1463.
[691] Émile Zola: **R. M. IV**, op. cit. p. 600.
[692] For David Baguley, the rhythm in **Nana** - but also in the other novels of the cycle – is indeed << *un rythme furieux, frénétique, frémissant* >>, in **Zola et les Genres**, op. cit. p. 66.
Note that Colette Becker shares this opinion when she believes that << *Le spectacle impérial sera, comme tout spectacle, et parce qu'il n'est rien d'autre qu'un spectacle, éphémère* >>, in *Illusion et Réalité : la métaphore du théâtre dans* **La Curée**, article published in **La Curée de Zola << ou la vie à outrance >>**, op. cit. p. 127.

for the characters are in a mad rush to enjoy their lives. As David Baguley writes, the Zolian time is characterised by its constant erosion for it is a problematic time[693].

This is the place to study another element of the time of the narrative enunciation.

2.1.3. The frequency

The frequency is simply a phenomenon of repetition in the story. Genette distinguishes four types of frequencies that are: << *Raconter une fois ce qui s'est passé une fois (1R/1H) = récit singulatif ; raconter n fois ce qui s'est passé n fois (nR/nH) = récit anaphorique mais singulatif ; raconter n fois ce qui s'est passé une fois (nR/1H) = récit répétitif ; raconter une seule fois (ou plutôt en une seule fois) ce qui s'est passé n fois (1R/nH) = récit itératif* >>[694]. I will only provide a single illustration of each of the cases indicated above. With regard to the singular narrative or 1R/1H, one can refer to the adultery of Claude Lantier: << *même il découcha une nuit* >>[695]. He was then in the arms of Irma, the demimondaine. The singular narrative is evidence that what happened is not in the habit of the character, but rather a conjunctural event which took place in exceptional circumstances.

Regarding the case of the anaphoric but singular narrative - or nR/nH - one can mention the numerous incestuous occurrences of Renée and Maxime in **La Curée**. Many times over, that has been narrated in the novel, just as the frivolity of Nana is narrated almost on ninety different pages - out of a total of four hundred and eight pages - or once in every four and a half pages. The anaphoric but singular narrative seems to reflect as faithfully as possible what a character does day by day, without bothering to tire the reader. The narrator seems to be convinced of the need for this continuous narration of the same episode several times over. It is a form of insistence that aims to characterise a given protagonist by his favourite deed, which does account for their true being better than their speech, or indeed the speech of others about them.

Regarding the repetitive narrative, nR/1H, I can take as an example the multiple appearances of the natural son of Aristide Rougon, Victor, in **L'Argent**. The boy is the end result of a brutal rape that occurred once but all his appearances constantly remind the reader of his painful conception. The repetitive narrative thus functions like a mischievous narrative that constantly repeats the same thing in a veiled way without seeming to repeat what has already been said.

---

[693] David Baguley: **Naturalist Fiction. The Entropic Vision**, op. cit. p. 222.
[694] Gérard Genette: **Figures III**, op. cit. pp.146-147:
[695] Émile Zola: **R. M. IV**, op. cit. p. 249.

There is also a case of iterative narrative - or 1R/nH – in **La Terre**, which states that : << *Cette nuit-là, comme presque toutes les nuits, Hourdequin était venu retrouver Jacqueline dans sa chambre* >>[696]. This habit, which has become commonplace, does not seem to require a narration each time it is renewed. That is why the narrator avoids rehashing it to make sure he does not annoy his narrataries. The repetitive narrative is therefore an economic narrative which summarises several narrative situations in a few words. It must be noted that in total, the singular narrative is reserved for the uncommon events that are borderline banal. On the other hand, the repetitive narrative testifies to the consequences, or, if one prefers, the multiple and unfortunate consequences of a previous event. Lastly, the anaphoric narrative stipulates the overabundance of a phenomenon, for example the phenomenon of outrageous debauchery in **Nana** which is narrated with a frequency that defies all competition. Finally, the iterative narrative tends to minimise subsequent occurrences of an event as unimportant since the former would be valuable to others. It thus results in a unique account of what is commonly happening.

The mode is, however, associated with the question of frequency of the narrative.

2.1.4. The mode

The question of mode will be addressed in its three aspects namely the distance, the perspective and the voice.

2.1.4.1. The distance

Since Plato, it has been agreed to distinguish two narrative modes which are the *mimésis* – or the imitation – and a *diégésis* - or pure fiction. For Genette, << *la mimésis se définissant par un maximum d'informations et un minimum d'informateur* >>[697], is ideally suited to the passages of dialogue where the narrator hides behind the referential illusion to make the characters assume the conduct of certain remarks. This is characteristic of literature in Genette's understanding.

In **La Terre**, for example, whenever incest between Hilarion and Palmyra is mentioned, it will be in the form of direct speech, that is, during a dialogue between two or more characters, one knowing and another wanting to know what is going on between the two incestuous protagonists. So, everything happens as if the first narrator did not know, as if the reader learned the odious information at the same time as the main narrator.

---

[696] Émile Zola: **R. M. IV**, op. cit. p. 439.
[697] Gérard Genette : **Figures III**, op. cit. p. 187.

On the contrary, as part of the pure narrative, the narrator assumes responsibility for their own speech and allows the reader to grasp what is happening in the "skull" of the character through very rich descriptions that are detailed and pictorial like those offered in abundance in **Les Rougon-Macquart**. The narrator makes use of the free indirect speech as a novelist anxious to penetrate all the psychology of their characters. Of course, this is not done without running the risk of becoming a hidden god knowing everything about the character, including their dreams that are not yet actualised. By knowing more about their << *êtres de papier* >> that they do know about themselves, the novelist jeopardises their credit of neutrality and truthfulness. This poses the problem of the point of view in the story.

2.1.4.2. The perspective or the point of view

Goldenstein defines the concept of perspective as follows: << *On appelle vision ou point de vue, la perspective narrative adoptée pour présenter les faits rapportés dans le récit. En effet, si le romancier est toujours présent derrière les lignes que nous lisons, il peut choisir la façon de se manifester, ou de feindre de disparaître, dans son ouvrage* >>[698]. Thus, there are roughly three different points of view: the narrative with the *focalisation zéro* – according to the word of Genette - where there is a *gnarus*[699] narrator, or what Stanzel calls an *auktoriale Erzählsituation*. That is, in simpler terms, an omniscient narrator[700]. Moreover, the narrator can be one of the characters of their story and deliver it under a perspective known as *focalisation interne* or an *Ich Erzählsituation* according to Stanzel, in which case the narrator knows as much as any of the characters. The third possibility is to narrate a story with the *focalisation externe* or the *personale Erzählsituation* in Stanzel's theory, where the narrator knows less than the character[701].

In **Les Rougon-Macquart**, the narrator is almost always omniscient, except when arises the need to announce certain sexual ignominies. Then, pretending not to know anything about it, the narrator lets an educated person come along to inform another character who does not know the facts. The reader is thus unduly informed, as was the case when announcing the pederasty of Baptiste in **La Curée**. It is Céleste, Renée's maid, who was in charge of this mission in the very last chapter of the novel. Benefiting from a narrative power by delegation, she comes to announce to her mistress: << *Il paraît que ces vilaines choses se*

---

[698] Lucien Goldenstein : **Pour Lire le Roman**, op. cit. p. 29.
[699] Stanzel quoted by Jean-Pierre Faye : **Théorie du Récit**, Paris, UGE 10/18, 1978, p. 51,
[700] Tzvetan Todorov: << *Le narrateur en sait davantage que son personnage. Il ne se soucie pas de nous expliquer comment il a acquis cette connaissance. Il voit à travers les murs de la maison aussi bien qu'à travers le crâne de son héros. Ses personnages n'ont pas de secrets pour lui* >>, voir Les Catégories du Récit Littéraire in **Communications, 8**, op. cit. p. 147.
[701] Tzvetan Todorov: << *Le narrateur en sait moins que n'importe lequel des personnages. Il peut décrire uniquement ce que l'on voit, entend, etc. mais n'a accès à aucune conscience* >>, **ibidem**, p. 148.

passaient dans les écuries >>⁷⁰², where the grooms suffered the indecent assaults of the maître d'Hôtel whose chastity and irreproachable morality had, however, been the object of constant homage from the principal narrator throughout the novel.

In a recent study on **La Bête Humaine**, Sarah Capitanio opposed the use of the omniscient narrator - *gnarus* - to that of the ignorant one, who uses second narrators that are none other but witnesses. She recalled that the stories of the rape of Louisette by Grandmorin and his incestuous relationship with Séverine are known about only from the perspective of second narrators[703]. Obviously, this technique makes it possible to release the first narrator's responsibility for the second narrative that has been inserted into his own. In the case where this meta-narrative is claimed by the rumour - as when the rumour runs rife in Rognes stating that Buteau sleeps with the two Mouche sisters in **La Terre** -, the first narrator feels no embarrassment when the facts later deny that information. Moreover, when the fact turns out to be well-founded, the narrator does not fear either to pass for a prank that builds mountains of immorality since they seem to say: <<*Tenez, ce n'est pas moi qui raconte ou qui invente cela, c'est plutôt untel qui a raconté cela en tels termes. Je me contente de vous informer de ce qui se raconte dans telle localité et à tel sujet. Je ne suis qu'un rapporteur qu'il ne faut pas blâmer* >>.

However, the mode has one last component which is called the voice.

2.1.4.3. The voice

In the narrative or fiction, there are often different narrative voices. The main voice is assumed by the main narrator who thus assumes responsibility for the global enunciation. The perception that we have of the characters, their deeds and their becoming, is communicated by the narrator as well as mentioned so well by Todorov who writes: << *En lisant une œuvre de fiction, nous n'avons pas une perception directe des événements qu'elle décrit. En même temps que ces événements, nous percevons, bien que d'une manière différente, la perception qu'en a celui qui les raconte* >>[704].

Now it happens that the narrator has a considerable lead over his possible narrataries and even with regard to his narrative. As a result, the naturalist narrator adopts a position of an arch-narrator - if one dares to coin such a word - knowing everything: the past, the present and the future of the characters, even their dreams that they easily apprehend. It was that way that the narrator read the dreams of Angelique whose reveries had no secret for them in **Le Rêve**. Never designated by an "I", or an "it", still less by any proper name, the main

---

[702] Émile Zola: **R. M. I**, op. cit. p. 591.
[703] Sarah Capitanio: **La Bête Humaine** : *Intertextualité et intratextualité*, in **Zola, La Bête Humaine : texte et explication**, Geoff Woollen (éd.), op. cit, p. 111.
[704] Tzvetan Todorov : *Les Catégories du Récit Littéraire*, in **Communications, 8**, op. cit. p. 147.

narrator in Zola's novels appears to be absent from the diegesis. In their capacity as a *heterodiegetic* narrator – who tells the story of someone else – and as an *extradiegetic* narrator – since they are physically absent from the story they tell – they deliver the story with as much detail as possible thanks to their position as a hidden god.

This position of the Zolian narrator seems to have been influenced by Flaubert's point of view on the question. In a letter to Miss Leroyer De Chantepie, dated February 19th, 1857, Flaubert wrote that: << *L'artiste doit être dans sa création, invisible et tout-puissant ; qu'on le sente partout mais qu'on ne le voie pas* >>[705].

However, in **Les Rougon-Macquart**, there are narrative relays in the dialogues where, as noted above, some characters are granted the narrative power by delegation in order to report sexual ignominies. Was it to escape the diatribe of those who accused him of immorality, or was it a deliberate aesthetic choice on Zola's part? It is plausible that those two reasons together guided his choice when writing his novels. Even the scatological details are also narrated exclusively by some of his fictional characters instead of the main narrator.

In addition, it must be noted that in **Les Rougon-Macquart**, a particular type of second narrator appears such as a Hupel de la Noue in **La Curée**, the author of **Les Amours du Beau Narcisse et de la Nymphe Écho**, a tragic play inspired by the Greek mythology. This second narrator, as a writer and a director, plays Maxime and Renée in a figurative and fictional way. Those actors then play the real drama they had been living secretly thus far: the incest. It is then that the mise en abyme – which is presented as a metanarrative embedded in the novel – comes to confirm the incestuous narrative, to authenticate it, to reflect it exactly as in a mirror. The Zolian narrator, according to Genette, has a *fonction idéologique* – as for the main narrator – and a *fonction testimoniale* – as for the second narrator, like Hupel de la Noue. The ideological function assumes that the main narrator carries an ideology, a creed more or less clearly displayed and Zola, for example, was an ideologue of the germination of a better world that would grow on the manure of the corrupt world of the imperial society[706]. Many of the explicits in his novels make that clear in the corpus. The testimonial function, on the other hand, is of a weaker nature since it puts the second narrator in the position of a simple witness whose story brings a guarantee of

---

[705] Gustave Flaubert: **Correspondance**, Paris, Édition du Centenaire, Librairie de France, 1993, p. 27.
[706] Famahan Samaké: << *Zola en voulait à l'Empire et ses personnages l'aidèrent à sonner le glas de ce régime qui lui répugnait. On peut en déduire que son projet était moins scientifique que politique, puisque son œuvre mène davantage une lutte politique (pour l'avènement de la république) qu'elle ne prouve scientifiquement que l'hérédité seule explique tous les malheurs qui frappent sa << famille-cobaye* >>>>, in **Fondements, Caractéristiques et Fatalité de la Sexualité dans Les Rougon-Macquart d'Émile Zola**, D.E.A., Abidjan, Université de Cocody, 1996, p. 13.

authenticity to the first narrative on which he depends. But that does not prevent there being a fundamental opposition between those two narrators in the corpus as stipulated by Anne Belgrand for whom there is an : << *opposition entre le ridicule de la création dirigée par le préfet et l'ambition artistique de Zola lui-même* >>[707].

Overall, one should be interested in the *incipits* and the *explicits* of Zola's novels. Goldenstein had insisted on the capital importance, for the narratologist, of the incipit and the explicit in a narrative. In the specific case of Zola, one can read for example at the end of **Germinal** : << *Des hommes poussaient, une armée noire, vengeresse, qui germait lentement dans les sillons, grandissant pour les récoltes des siècles futurs, et dont la germination allait faire bientôt éclater la terre* >>[708], whereas the incipit was taking place in << *la plaine rase* >>[709]. Here, incipit and explicit are diametrically opposed[710], for the former is marked by a sort of sterility, and the latter by an immense hope of fertility and fecundity.

The incipit of **Pot-Bouille** directs the reader to the << *Rue Neuve Saint-Augustin* >>[711] while the explicit throws: << *C'est cochon et compagnie !* >>[712], as if to insist one last time on the physical and the moral decadence of the bourgeoisie behind the appearance of luxury and irreproachable morality[713].

In **La Bête Humaine,** the explicit is all about a crazy train steaming at full speed without a driver to guide it, or to stop it[714]. This apocalyptic vision ends with a machine << *chargée de cette chair à canon, de ces soldats déjà hébétés de fatigue, et ivres, qui chantaient* >>[715], unaware that they were heading to the slaughterhouse in Sedan, if they ever made it that far. Therefore, this particular explicit works as a premonition of what would be known as **La Débâcle**, the novel devoted to war itself. But it also suggests Zola's opinion of the powerful and previously untamed machine, man's own creation that could become the

---

[707] Anne Belgrand: *Le Jeu des Oppositions dans* **La Curée,** in **La Curée de Zola << ou la vie à outrance >>**, op. cit. p. 27.
[708] Émile Zola: **R. M. III**, op. cit. p. 1591.
[709] **Ibidem**, p. 1133.
[710] Anne Belgrand believes that the internal structure of Zola's novels rests on the interplay of oppositions: << *On retrouve ce même phénomène en examinant des unités plus petites : opposition entre les différents romans du cycle des* **Rougon-Macquart**, *opposition, dans chaque roman, entre les différentes séquences, ou parfois d'un paragraphe à l'autre* >>, voir *Le Jeu des Oppositions dans* **La Curée** in **La Curée de Zola << ou la vie à outrance >>**, op. cit. p. 23.
[711] Émile Zola: **R. M. III**, op. cit. p. 3.
[712] **Ibidem**, p. 386.
[713] For Jean Borie, in **Zola et les Mythes, ou de la Nausée au Salut**, the bourgeois are simply, and nothing more than << *les tartufes des* **Rougon-Macquart** >>, op. cit. p. 142.
[714] Émile Zola: **R. M. IV**, op. cit. p. 997.
[715] **Ibidem**, p. 1331.

instrument of the apocalypse of our age[716], for it could obliterate our way of life.

At the incipit of **La Débâcle**, one can read : << *À deux kilomètres de Mulhouse, vers le Rhin, au milieu de la pleine fertile, le camp était dressé* >>[717], while the explicit paints a very gloomy picture of France in that it announces << *[...] la grande et rude besogne de toute une France à refaire*>>[718]. These explanations clearly show that the narrator is out of touch with the world he describes, a world of monstrous debauchery that must disappear in order to allow the emergence of a better one that would be more chaste, a more moral world. But rebuilding is a difficult task, and strong arms and strong hearts are needed to carry it out. The Zolian narrator is biased for sure as he carries an ideology. Indeed, he takes a stand against the world of the Second Empire and for the emergence of a new society that he wants just, moral and fertile. As for the second narrators, they have a testimonial function in the sense that they are used either as witnesses of the events that they utter, or simply as witnesses of the main narrator.

There are also real or virtual narrates to consider. Let us remind the reader that each time there is a dialogue, the transmitter becomes the narrator and the receiver is their designated narratee. But who is the narratee of the main narrator? This question seems very difficult to solve in **Les Rougon-Macquart** because just as the referential illusion wrongly associates the narrator with the author, it also confuses the virtual reader with the narratee. Now the truth of the matter is that the narratee is to be found in the novel, just as the narrator is an intratextual figure and not outside the text. If in Balzac's works the narrator is present and speaks fluently to their readers – they thus have a clutch function – in direct style, the situation is different in Zola's works. Indeed, the Zolian narrator is more veiled, as if absent, in the manner of the Flaubertian narrator. The narratee of the main narrator in the corpus is therefore of an extradiegetic and heterodiegetic nature, that is to say that they are not only outside the diegesis, but in addition to that, they tell the history of others. The narrataries of the second narrators are most often intradiegetic and heterodiegetic in nature. Indeed, they are inside the novels – sometimes they are the secondary characters like the villagers of Rognes in **La Terre** – and are told stories about others. Thus, Buteau, as a second narrator, addresses his narrataries, who are Father Fouan, La Grande, Delhomme, Mr. and Mrs. Charles, Élodie and Jean Macquart, claiming that he sleeps regularly with Lise and Françoise and therefore, the latter cannot marry Jean Macquart[719].

---

[716] For Jacques Noiray, in **Le Romancier et la Machine, I : L'Univers de Zola**, op. cit., the machine is linked to a mythology of catastrophe (p. 508) in the sense that the technique and the forces of death are linked (p. 424); the machine being an instrument of death, or better still, the instrument of the cataclysmic end of civilisation (p. 480).
[717] Émile Zola: **R. M. V**, op. cit. p. 401.
[718] **Ibidem**, p. 912.
[719] Émile Zola: **R. M. IV**, op. cit. p. 604.

In a literary work, however, studying the temporal component would have a taste of incompleteness if one does not study the verbal tenses of the enunciation.

2.2. The verbal tenses of the enunciation in Zola's fiction works

According to Harald Weinrich, there are << *les temps commentatifs (présent de l'indicatif, passé composé, futur) et les temps narratifs (passé simple, imparfait, plus - que - parfait, conditionnel)* >>[720]. Jean-Michel Adam has enriched this distinction between verbal tenses by adding the features [+ description]; [- narrative]; [- agent] for the imperfect, and [- description]; [+ story]; [+ agent] for the past simple also called the *aoriste*[721]. I will endeavour to study briefly each of the main tenses mentioned in the corpus in order to evaluate their particular meaning in the perspective of the inevitability related to sexuality.

2.2.1. The present tense

It is the tense of the speech par excellence and it is used when two characters exchange words directly between them. For example, in **Germinal**, when La Brûlé narrates the emasculation of Maigrat, she launches: << *Faut le couper comme un matou!* >>[722]. Similarly, when Séverine talks about Cabuche's manic love for her, she says: << *Et puis, il me* **vole** *tout, des affaires à moi, des gants, jusqu'à des mouchoirs qui* **disparaissent***, qu'il* **emporte** *là-bas dans sa caverne, comme des trésors* >>[723].

This last quote is not only grammatically rich - with the multiple use of the present tense - but also psychoanalytically. It shows indeed that Cabuche is a sexual neurotic character who remained at the infantile stage. He then satisfies his libido in a scopic and a fetishistic way, that is to say by playing the voyeurs and by collecting all the small apparently insignificant objects that belonged to the desired sexual object. Yet his love for Séverine remains repressed and sublimated in his unconscious. The olfactory pleasure that the handkerchiefs of Séverine give him contributes to this neurosis or sexual immaturity. At the grammatical level, the present translates here a set of actions occurring in the usual way, as well in past, in the present and in the future. Apart from this unusual use, the present of the indicative translates in principle the moment of actuality in which one speaks, when the act of speech perfectly coincides with

---

[720] Harald Weinrich : **Le Temps du Récit**, Paris, Seuil, 1979, p. 115.
[721] Jean-Pierre Adam : *Langue et Texte : Imparfait/Passé Simple* in **Pratiques, no. 10**, Paris, Seuil, 1976, pp. 48-49
[722] Émile Zola: **R. M. III**, op. cit. p. 1452.
[723] Émile Zola: **R. M. IV**, op. cit. pp. 1284-1285.

the realisation of the *procès*[724] the characters are talking about, process expressed by the verb conjugated in the present tense.

The present indicating an ongoing process at the time of speech is often used in **La Faute de l'Abbé Mouret,** like when Serge Mouret and Albine declare their mutual love:
    <<-*Je t'aime, Albine.*
    -*Serge, je t'aime*>>[725]. It is clear that here the two sexual subjects love each other at the moment when they make their declarations to one another, making perfectly coincide the dialogue and the feeling of mutual love.

There is another use of the present of the indicative, the one which translates a permanent process, one which is often used in proverbs, or to express an idea or an eternal truth. It is therefore the privileged verbal tense for anyone who wants to make a maxim like Duveyrier for whom: << *On ne **guérit** pas de la débauche, on la **coupe** dans sa racine* >>[726].

The present tense can also express a progressive process with inchoative aspect. There are several occurrences of that in **Nana**, like when Satin speaks of her partner. The change in the character of this lesbian partner is narrated into these terms: << *Elle **devient** ridicule de jalousie. L'autre soir, elle m'a battue* >>[727]. Here the present tense indicates that Madame Robert's character was neither jealous nor violent in the past, and that these character traits are new, and will no doubt continue to worsen in the future.

The present tense may also reflect a possible or a hypothetical process. It then expresses the present or the future condition or eventuality. It is also found in **Nana** with Clarisse who declares: << *Moi, vous savez, quand les gamins **donnent** dans les vieilles, ça me **dégoûte*** >>[728]. There is eventuality here because the disgust in this act12ress, is circumstantial since it is linked to the condition to witness from the start a love affair between a male youth and an old age lady.

Finally, the present tense may have a near future value and express an imminent process that is not yet realised at the moment when one speaks. Suffices it to mention a single example in **La Fortune des Rougon** with Miette when she tells

---

[724] I will use this term of *"procès"* following the structuralist and the generativist grammarians, who use it instead of the word *"action"* used in traditional grammar. It is obvious that (all) the verbs of the French language do not express only *actions*. The term *"procès"* has the advantage of rendering all the nuances that a verb can express: *action, state, feeling, doubt, supposition, existence, becoming, wish* and many others. For further information on the concept of *"procès"*, refer to the **Grand Larousse de la Langue Française, VII, S-Z**, Paris, Librairie Larousse, 1976, pp. 5989-97. It's me who emphasise the conjugated verbs in this section.
[725] Émile Zola: **R. M. I**, op. cit. p. 1409.
[726] Émile Zola: **R. M. III**, op. cit. p. 380.
[727] Émile Zola: **R. M. II**, op. cit. p. 1319.
[728] **Ibidem**, p. 1179.

her friend, Silvère: << *Tu vas croire que je suis une enfant* >>[729]. Temporarily, the process of believing belongs to the future, but grammatically speaking, it is part of the present, the verbal tense of the semi-auxiliary *to go*. Miette, as a sexual object, would like to convince the sexual subject, Silvère, that from now on she is a woman ready for love.

Although it is the tense of the actuality, the present of the indicative can express, under certain modalising circumstances, narrative situations whose temporal value is quite different from the actuality. But ultimately, the present tense is not the main tense used to tell a story.

2.2.2. The past simple

The past simple - or the aorist - is the time of the narrative par excellence. It can render both a singular, an iterative and a repetitive narrative sequence. The essential value of the aorist is the singularity and the punctuality of the facts it translates. Anna Bondarenco calls << *événementiel* >>[730] any process rendered in the simple past, and that she opposes to the << *stéréotypé* >>[731], which is any process given to the imperfect - whose tendency is rather habitual and repetitive. To illustrate the first value of the aorist, let us keep Claude Lantier's adultery already mentioned: << *même une nuit, il découcha* >>[732].

Let us also take one example of an iterative narrative rendered in the past simple in **La Curée** << *Maxime revint chaque nuit* >>[733] to fill Renée with his favours. Writing of Jacques and Séverine in **La Bête Humaine**, the narrator argues that Roubaud caught his wife with her lover in the marital bed and that: << *Dès ce jour, Séverine et Jacques eurent liberté entière. Ils en usèrent sans se soucier davantage de Roubaud* >>[734].

These singular and iterative narratives show that the aorist perfectly fits all kinds of narrative situations and is therefore the privileged and the unavoidable tense of the process of narration. It makes it possible to skip unnecessary and repetitive details of any event that has occurred. Moreover, the past simple is used mainly to express a completed process at a given moment in the past, a process without any more links with the present of the enunciation and whose characteristic is punctuality. It is the tense of the distant past processes that have the trait [- durative] and [+ punctual]. In this sense, the jobs of the past simple with the traits [+ iterative] and [+ repetitive] have contextual variants in

---

[729] Émile Zola: **R. M. I**, op. cit. p. 165.
[730] Anna Bondarenco: *Le stéréotypé et l'événementiel dans* **Germinal** *d'Émile Zola*, texte inédit, international colloquium at the University of Cambridge, **New Approaches to Zola**, 16-17 April 2002, p. 1.
[731] **Ibidem**, p. 1
[732] Émile Zola: **R. M. IV**, op. cit. p. 246.
[733] Émile Zola: **R. M. I**, op. cit. p. 483.
[734] Émile Zola: **R. M. IV**, op. cit. p. 1224.

Les Rougon-Macquart since the author then leaves the usual register in which the aorist plays out to adapt it to any narrative situations to which the imperfect tense normally suits better.

In this logic, the past simple is used with the distinctive feature [+ durative] in **Nana** where one can read: << *Ce **fut** l'époque de son existence où Nana **éclaira** Paris d'un redoublement de splendeur. Elle **grandit** encore à l'horizon du vice, elle **domina** la ville de l'insolence affichée de son luxe, de son mépris de l'argent, qui lui faisait fondre publiquement les fortunes* >>[735].

All of these performances by the sexual subject-operator, Nana, have an obvious [+ durative] character since they indicate the period when the young demimondaine woman reaches her prime; the heyday that she enjoyed for more or less long time in the past.

Nevertheless, the importance of the past simple must not make the reader lose sight of that of the imperfect and its composite form, other significant tenses that are found in the narrative.

2.2.3. The imperfect and the pluperfect.

The imperfect is the verbal tense used to express the background scenery. It serves mainly to support the description and it is almost at the same level as the pluperfect. Only this last one can serve more in the free indirect speech which is the word of the character uttered by the "mouth" of the narrator. The two tenses are also very often combined in **Les Rougon-Macquart** like for example in **La Débâcle** where one can read: << *On **avait mangé** quarante mille chevaux, on en **était arrivé** à payer très cher les chiens, les chats et les rats. Depuis que le blé **manquait**, le pain fait de riz et d'avoine, **était** un pain noir, visqueux, d'une digestion difficile. La mortalité **avait triplé**, les théâtres **étaient transformés** en ambulance* >>[736].

It is necessary here to notice, from this quote, that the imperfect expresses rather the immobility of the process, a state [+ durative] and [+ stable], while the pluperfect takes forward the unfolding process with an accomplished aspect - [+ accomplished]; [+ progressive] - as in **L'Assommoir** where << *Nana **était débauchée** par une autre ouvrière, ce petit chameau de Léonie* >>[737]. The debauchery of Nana is indeed a *fait accompli*, a process completely wrapped up at the moment of the enunciation. On the other hand, the lack of wheat during the war of September 1870 works as the background picture with the aspects [+ stable] and [+ durative]. It was in this context that the people had eaten horses,

---

[735] Émile Zola: **R. M. II**, op. cit. p. 1432.
[736] Émile Zola: **R. M. V**, op. cit. pp. 865-866.
[737] Émile Zola: **R. M. II**, op. cit. p. 724.

rats, dogs and cats and that the mortality rate became high. These latest processes suggest a progression in the food shortage and the dire health crisis.

When used alone, the imperfect also reflects a perceived past process in its course of completion. It has two specificities of use that are the commentary and the description: it becomes a commentative tense when, following a process expressed in the past simple or in the present perfect, it comments on a later process by adding details to it. For example, in **Nan**a, one can read the jealousy of Muffat after he was made cuckolded by the kid Georges Hugon. The verbs conjugated in the imperfect then describe Muffat's disillusionment and disbelief - which lasted in the past - while his exigency and decline were brief and punctual.

The imperfect can equally well express the description of a setting in a general context in which other processes rendered in the past simple or present perfect. Thus, narrating the madness of destruction that seizes Nana – a madness considered as a backdrop - the narrator uses the imperfect tense and reserves the past simple for the narration of Philippe Hugon's reaction as a witness of the incident: <<*Le comte **se laissa** fléchir. Il **exigea** seulement le renvoi de Georges. Mais toute illusion **était morte**, il ne **croyait** plus à la fidélité jurée*>>[738]. The verbs conjugated in the imperfect tense describe Muffat's disillusionment and disbelief which lasted in the past, while his exigency and his sagging were brief.

Similarly, the imperfect tense can equally well express the description of a setting in a general context in which other processes expressed in the past simple or in the present perfect. The madness of destruction that seizes Nana (considered as the scenery) is described by the narrator using the imperfect tense while the past simple is used for the narration of Philippe Hugon's reaction to to the scene he witnessed: << *C'**était** une gaieté nerveuse, elle **avait** le rire bête et méchant d'un enfant que la destruction amuse. Philippe **fut pris** d'une courte révolte ; la malheureuse **ignorait** quelles angoisses lui **coûtait** ce bibelot. Quand elle le **vit** bouleversé, elle **tâcha** de se retenir* >>[739].

There is no doubt, in light of this scene, that the imperfect verbs express the particular context in which the upheaval and the revolt of the lover – Philippe - are located. The two reactions - the revolt of Philip and Nana's attempt to calm him down - because they are abrupt and sudden, are expressed in the past simple tense because of their punctuality in a past. Also, they were completed processes at the moment the narrator recounted the incident because the narration succeeds the event. On the other hand, the cheerfulness, the ignorance of Nana, and the mischief which Philip gave himself to acquire the trinket, have been

---

[738] Émile Zola: **R. M. V**, op. cit. p.1432.
[739] **Ibidem**, p. 1435.

relatively prolonged in the past, whence their enunciation in the imperfect tense.

The imperfect tense, however, remains a tense capable of expressing a past process with different aspects. For example, the narrator uses it instead of the past simple with an aspect [- durative] and [+ punctual] to express the birth of Jacques Lantier, the second child of Gervaise Macquart: << Il n'**arrivait** que le second >>[740]. It is certain that this << *arrive* >> does not last long in the past, nor does it repeat itself; it intervenes only once in the past and in the space of a few minutes or even a few hours at most.

The imperfect tense expressing an iterative event also finds its place in **Les Rougon-Macquart** and its use has the advantage of expressing in one go what has happened several times over, thus saving the annoying repetitions that could have the inconvenience of annoying the narratee(s). To illustrate this point, one could refer to the following passage about Christine and Jacques Lantier : << *Et toujours et partout, ils **se possédaient**, avec le besoin inassouvi de se posséder encore* >>[741].

Naturally, the richness of the use of the verbal tenses continues with the pluperfect which not only advances the narrative, but also presents a past process that was accomplished before another process transcribed in the imperfect or in the past simple tense. The fundamental value of the pluperfect is indeed the expression of anteriority in the past: << *Et, à cette heure qu'il [Jean Macquart] avait Françoise, depuis deux ans qu'ils **étaient mariés**, pouvait-il se dire vraiment heureux ? S'il l'aimait toujours, lui, il **avait** bien **deviné** qu'elle ne l'aimait pas, qu'elle ne l'aimerait jamais, comme il aurait désiré l'être, à pleins bras, à pleine bouche [...]. Mais ce n'était point ça, il la sentait loin, froide, occupée d'une autre idée, au lit, quand il la tenait* >>[742]. So, Jean got married and later on guessed his wife's disenchantment. He came to terms with the idea that his wife would never be in love with him after all. These later porcesses are thus rendered to the imperfect tense contrary to the previous ones stated in the pluperfect.

To this fundamental value expressing anteriority, the expression of contingency is added when the past of the conditional is replaced by the pluperfect, especially in a segmented sentence. For example, the violence of Roubaud following his jealousy, is thus rendered by the narrator: << *Il redevenait la brute inconsciente de sa force, il l'*[Séverine] ***avait broyée**, dans un élan de fureur aveugle* >>[743]. The crushing of Séverine is therefore not a cyclical fact, but rather an accidental occurrence since Roubaud is usually not a violent man. That sudden violence erupted in him only under the condition of extreme jealousy. In

---

[740] Émile Zola: **R. M. IV**, op. cit. p. 1043.
[741] **Ibidem**, p. 148.
[742] **Ibidem**, p. 737.
[743] **Ibidem**, p. 1001.

a word, the narrator seems to say that a husband, without being really violent, could become a beast if his wife cheated on him.

Furthermore, the pluperfect tense can also be used with a hypothetical value: << *Cette femme, puisqu'il ne l'**avait** pas **tuée** tout de suite, il ne la tuerait pas maintenant* >>[744]. The killing of Séverine was therefore not a possibility to be dismissed in the jealous sexual subject's perspective. However, Roubaud dismisses that eventuality for the simple reason that he has not been able to fulfill the first condition of that enterprise: to kill her immediately, spontaneously, upon finding out about her affair. But having dismissed the possibility of killing Séverine just after learning of her treason, Roubaud foresees instead the killing of his wife's lover, Président Grandmorin. And this time, he fulfills the condition of the immediacy of the action when he sets up a honey trap for his love rival in order to eliminate him in the express train of six thirty[745].

All these examples of the pluperfect can be used to corroborate what I said earlier, namely, that it is the tense of the free indirect speech par excellence. This form of expression allows the narrator to penetrate into the inner life of the character to translate all their thoughts, their aspirations, their emotional state of mind and their conscious and even their unconscious motivations. As David Baguley has already shown, the free indirect speech allows the narrator to interpret the origins of Jacques Lantier's destructive instinct[746]. It is therefore the time of the violation par excellence; the violation of the character's private life, the violation of their aspirations, their dreams and motivations. It is also the time of indiscretion and divination because the narrator, posing as a fortune teller, acquires suddenly and without any explanation whatsoever, the competence required to know everything about their paper being. Then, they establishe the performance to reveal everything to their narrataries since the narrator remains the indiscreet instance in the process of the narration. Another important verbal tense is the future of the past or the conditional, which is an unavoidable tense in the corpus.

2.2.4. The conditional mode

The conditional is the mode of the unreal and the hypothesis. Commonly called future of the past, it reports a past process that is in the future compared to another process also expressed in the past. Then, more often than not, it expresses a wish, a hypothesis, contrary to the other process that expresses a certainty and which is a process that is rendered in the imperfect tense, or in the present perfect, or even in the past simple tense. For example, when the prosecutor Denizet brings in the victim's sister during his investigation into the passionate murder of Président Grandmorin, the latter declares, speaking of

---

[744] Émile Zola: **R. M. IV**, op. cit. p. 1018.
[745] **Ibidem**, p. 1021.
[746] David Baguley: **Naturalist Fiction. The Entropic Vision**, op. cit. p. 208.

Cabuche, the main suspect: << *Il était réellement fou de rage, il répétait dans tous les cabarets que, si le président lui tombait sous la main, il le **saignerait** comme un cochon...* >>[747]. The process of bleeding Président Grandmorin – the second process –, although perceived in the past, is a future and a virtual process compared to the fact that he falls under the hands of Cabuche – first process –; the second process is hypothetical to the extent that its realisation depends on that prior or first process. In the same sense, Cabuche uses a conditional past to say: << *Ah ! Nom de Dieu, le cochon ! J'**aurais dû** courir le saigner tout de suite !* >>[748].

To consider everything, ene must recognise that the conditional is the mode of the unreal, the hypothesis, the deep aspirations and the testimony of the sexual subjtect's frustrations and failures, as in the case of Cabuche. The tense closest to the conditional is the future of the indicative.

2.2.5. The simple future of the indicative

The future is the tense of the future and the virtual in the sense that it accounts for a process that has not yet been actualised at the moment when one speaks. The realisation of the process expressed in the future is therefore held only for probable. This fundamental value clearly opposes it to the present. Thus, aware of his failing genius, the painter Claude Lantier aspires, in the future, to be visited by the Muse: << *Je vais m'y mettre, répéta Claude, et il* [le travail] *me **tuera**, et il **tuera** ma femme, mon enfant, toute la barque, mais ce **sera** un chef-d'œuvre, nom de Dieu !* >>[749].

The future thus employed here expresses a fierce determination to the point of constituting no longer an unreal process in the present, but more of a reality or a certainty in the future. There is the impression that the process of killing his family is already accomplished in the future, just as if one were in sheer premonition. Claude appears a little like a diviner when he utters these words because the future proves him right, at least partially with the death of his son Jacques first, followed by his suicide and finally, the agony of his widow, Christine, at the Laribousière hospital. The annihilation of his entire family has only one cause: his stubborn work as a talentless painter. Even if he clearly felt the power of that mortal enemy, Claude could not escape it for one does not escape their destiny: destiny is an inescapable fatality. Claude's merit is that he stoically expects this series of tragedies that ultimately strike his family without complaining about his thankless task of painting. It is as if, notwithstanding his programmed and certain defeat, achieving a masterpiece would be his final and

---

[747] Émile Zola: **R. M. IV**, op. cit. p. 1092.
[748] **Ibidem,** p. 1100.
[749] **Ibidem,** p. 265.

eternal victory[750] over the fatality of idiocy that strikes him, and thus his victory over death itself. Is it not argued that great artists never die since they leave to mankind masterpieces that immortalise them?

Verbal tenses, with what has been covered this far, are part and parcels of the dialectic of the significance in a literary work. But one must go beyond the verbal tenses to examine some symbols related to the wider temporality component.

3. The temporal symbolism in the Rougon-Macquart.

3.1. The night or the time of the convergent sexuality

The night helps conceal the actions of the sexual agents through the opaque veil it offers them. It is the privileged time for incestuous relationships, homosexuality, adultery, large-scale debauchery, prostitution and passionate murder. Incest is for example found in **La Curée** where each night Maxime and his mother-in-law, Renée, engage in this ignominy: << *la nuit ardente qu'ils y* [in the greenhouse] *passèrent fut suivie de plusieurs autres* >>[751]. In the same way, it is always during the night that Nana offers her favours successively to Count Muffat, to his father-in-law, the Marquis de Chouard, and to his son-in-law, Daguenet, in the novel that bears her name. This is also the case for Hilarion and his sister Palmyre in **La Terre**. That dark list goes on with Victor Saccard who, at only fifteen years old, is already sleeping with his foster mother - Eulalie - and whom he dares to call << *ma femme* >> in **L'Argent**.

Moreover, in **La Curée**, homosexuality is happened impudently only at night with Baptiste entering the stables under the cover of darkness to satisfy his libido to the detriment of the grooms. The lesbianism of Satin and Nana also reaches alarming proportions at night at the expense of the male suiters who line up hoping for a chance to entice one of them. Similarly, in **Pot-Bouille**, adulterers abound with Duveyrier and Mouret, among others In **L'Assommoir**, Gervaise Coupeau born Macquart and her lover, Lantier, consume adultery at night. In **La Terre**, it is Jesus Christ and La Bécu - his best friend's woman - who share happy moments at night. This also applies to the other titles of the **Rougon-Macquart**, for even Clotilde loses her virginity to her uncle, Pascal, during the night in **Le Docteur Pascal**.

As for the outrageous debauchery, it happens only at night too. Let us stress from the outset that the night is also the time for murder. It is during the night that paedophiles like Grandmorin, Eulalie and Baron Gouraud, respectively in **La Bête Humaine**, in **L'Argent** and in **La Curée** create havoc among local

---

[750] Let us recall that for Neide de Faria, victory for Claude Lantier consists in painting the Woman, in **Structure et Unité dans Les Rougon-Macquart d'Émile Zola (la Poétique du Cycle)**, op. cit. p. 72.
[751] Émile Zola: **R. M. I**, op. cit. p. 486.

communities. Luxury prostitutes like Rose Mignon and Countess Muffat in **Nana** also get involved in debauchery at night. The debauchery of the Emperor himself - in **La Curée**, and especially in **Son Excellence Eugène Rougon** - happens at night. The same goes for the prostitution of the demimondaine women: Blanche Muller, Mme Michelin, Laure d'Aurigny and Sylvia in **La Curée** and of Nana in **Nana**.

The night is finally the time for crimes of passion as it was the case above. For example, it is during the night that Président Grandmorin is assassinated by his love rival, Roubaud. Pecqueux's jealousy towards Jacques Lantier - which will cause the atrocious death of the two protagonists - and the virtual crash of the crazy train, both also take place during the night. In total, it is during the night that all the masks fall off and that the characters are shown in their true dimension which is total perversion. The murders of Hourdequin by his rival, Tron, in **La Terre**, that of Séverine by his lover, Jacques Lantier, in **La Bête Humaine**, the suicide of Georges Hugon and Vandeuvres - both lovers disappointed by Nana - or that of Claude Lantier in **L'Œuvre**, are happening again and again, only at night. All these voluntary murders and suicides have this in common: they proceed from the same logic, that of killing oneself or killing for an unsatisfied love, or for fear of being dispossessed of one's sexual value-object. In general, it is clear that the night has a bad connotation in the novels of Zola. It is the best time to conceal the sexual deprivations that society would not tolerate if they happened in daytime.

Nonetheless, darkness can take on a more mystical or downright metaphysical dimension in Zola's works: << *Car Zola n'emploie pas la couleur noire en vue d'effets seulement esthétiques. L'usage qu'il en fait a une signification plus profonde, qui est métaphysique. Il suffit pour s'en convaincre de considérer le caractère spécifique de sa vision des ténèbres [...]. Les ténèbres sont donc pour Zola, dans leur opacité liquide, un élément menaçant qui submerge et qui tue. Mais si elles sont douées de ce pouvoir maléfique, c'est aussi que la nuit représente le moment où se dérègle l'ordre du monde, où s'affrontent les forces primitives, provisoirement libérées* >>[752]. According to Neide de Faria, the opposition between light and darkness << *délaye les frontières du réel, permettant alors l'apparition d'êtres* << *mythiques* >>, *ou suscitant l'irruption d'un monde fantastique* >>[753].

In another sense, there are normal couples who share relative happiness at night that I will call *convergent love*. However, it must be noted that this convergence of happiness is also a convergence towards misfortune[754]. Indeed, they always

---

[752] Jacques Noiray: **Le Romancier et la Machine, I : L'Univers de Zola**, op. cit. p. 303.
[753] Neide de Faria: **Structure et Unité dans Les Rougon-Macquart d'Émile Zola (la Poétique du Cycle)**, op. cit. p. 267.
[754] Jean Borie writes: << *La nuit est mère, la nuit est féconde, et toute la terre aussi* >>, in **Zola et les Mythes ou de la Nausée au Salut**, op. cit. p. 167. It seems to me, however, that this fertility is rather a bearer of misfortune, of cataclysm, and consequently, a fertility in reverse.

end up being struck by the supreme sanction which is death, or madness for the lucky ones. This is explained by the fact that, apart from their convergent love, each element of the couple pursues a divergent love affair in the form of nocturnal performances in the field of debauchery. In all, the night can be understood as the abyss, the unfathomable, in a word, a diabolical and an infernal time. The darkness of the night is also the symbol of death, or of mourning. To engage in a certain nocturnal dissipation is to turn oneself into a consenting victim of Satan, to head for suicide or for collective murder. Such a society - here the Second Empire - is predestined for Gomorrah and Sodom's fate[755] : utter disappearance. With David Baguley, one can say that darkness takes precedence over the character in the naturalistic novel[756].

This is the place to approach daytime as the corollary of the night.

3.2. The day or the time of the divergent sexuality

A first, a temporal opposition takes place between day and night in the sense that the second corresponds to convergent sexuality where the former consecrates a divergent sexuality. In **Les Rougon-Macquart**, the day is indeed the time of crises: rapes, fierce jealousy and passionate murders. Sometimes, it marks a timeout in the race to debauchery which I will call sexual inactivity.

In **Les Rougon-Macquart**, five rapes take place. In **La Curée**, Renée is pregnant as a result of the rape she suffered in the countryside. Françoise Mouche is twice the victim of rape in **La Terre**, first by Jean Macquart, her future husband, and then by Buteau, her brother-in-law. These two rapes take place in the fields. To these three rapes, one must add that of Victor Saccard on the young nurse, Alice de Beauvilliers, in **L'Argent**. So, there is almost a tragi-comic coincidence that makes Victor, the product of a rape become a brutal rapist in his turn. His father, Aristide, had tumbled a young lady on the stairs of their building in Paris to father him indeed.

There is an example of angry jealousy in **La Bête Humaine** where Flore is secretly in love with Jacques Lantier ten becomes so jealous of Séverine, the lover adored by her desired sexual value-object, that she derails a train[757] for the sole purpose of killing the latter! Jealousy and murder are indeed intimately linked in **Les Rougon-Macquart**, one justifying the other. The narrator, by means of the free indirect speech, enters into the consciousness of the murderer and depicts it in the following terms: << *Mais lorsqu'elle* [Flore] *reconnut Séverine, ses yeux s'agrandirent démesurément, une ombre d'affreuse souffrance noircit son visage pâle. Et quoi ? Elle vivait, cette femme, lorsque lui certainement était mort ! Dans cette douleur aiguë de son amour assassiné, ce coup de couteau*

---

[755] Roger Ripoll highlighted the assimilation of the city of Paris to the doomed biblical cities, refer to **Réalité et Mythe chez Zola**, op. cit. p. 101.
[756] David Baguley: **Naturalist Fiction. The Entropic Vision**, op. cit. p. 202.
[757] Émile Zol : **R. M. IV**, op. cit. p. 1260.

qu'elle s'était donné en plein cœur, elle eut la brusque conscience de l'abomination de son crime. Elle avait fait ça, elle l'[Jacques] avait tué, elle avait tué tout ce monde ! Un grand cri déchira sa gorge, elle tordait ses bras, elle courait follement >>[758].

In light of this passage, the reader realises that the light of day does not guarantee security for the Zolian character. It is neither the time of happiness, nor that of the fullness of love. On the contrary, the day can be the time of the supreme and fatal sanction which is at the end of the harmful and negative sexual performances accomplished at night. It is as if the light of day had the divine authority to sweep away the rotten Rougon-Macquart race.

The day can also be a moment for sexual inactivity for the vast majority of sexually marked characters. Two eloquent examples will suffice to show it. Among the female characters that abound in **Les Rougon-Macquart**, there are two that stand out from all others because of their excessive lubricity. They are Renée and Nana, both of whom are cloistered at home by day only to better satisfy their greedy sexuality when the night falls. Like some vampires that cannot sustain the light of day, they rush into their apartments as in a coffin inside which darkness protects them. They thus get spared the punishment of daylight so that they can be ready for more nocturnal sexual performances.

Beyond the opposition day versus night, let us look at colours which, without having a direct relationship with the time, can only be appreciated under the natural light of the sun, or the artificial light of the lamps and the gas spouts.

3.3. The symbolism of colours (vivid vs. dark)

The male characters in the corpus do not have the colour fever unlike their female counterparts. This is not curious at first because women have a predisposition for colours, especially the bright colours of yellow, gold, silver and red. But these precious stones and bright colours do not have a positive effect if one believes Jean-François Tonard who writes this about the decoration of Nana's bedroom: << *La décoration est extravagante, la débauche des couleurs et des métaux précieux peut aller jusqu'à provoquer chez le lecteur, étonné par la description de cet autel dédié à l'amour, la nausée, voire l'overdose* >>[759]. Renée and Nana are indeed the two prototypes of the colourful character, and this is hardly surprising, because here are two characters loving silver and pink - colour and lovers' flower. Silver symbolises easy money since they are expensive lovers and downright prostitutes. They love jewelry, the adornment of the woman that aspires to please. In the midst of these bright colours, they live, they blossom like flowers, their metaphor, but they also fade away far too early

---

[758] Émile Zola : **R. M. IV**, op. cit. p. 1262.
[759] Jean-François Tonard: **Thématique et Symbolique de l'Espace Clos dans le Cycle des Rougon-Macquart d'Émile Zola**, op. cit. p. 203.

likewise. Renée, for example, dies at thirty years of age while Nana passes away at barely nineteen. Axel Preiss recalls that gold, silver and sapphire are the colours of Suzanne Haffner, Adeline d'Espanet and Mme de Leuwerens, all ladies of questionable morality. They are lesbians - for the first two - and they belong to the upper middle class or the aristocracy[760]. He also believes that the opposition between green and red/pink has a sensual value: << *Ainsi Renée, bleue et or lorsqu'elle est en représentation, se voit mêlée de vert et surtout de rouge lorsqu'on la prend en tant que Phèdre solaire et amoureuse* >>[761]. The feminine nature of Maxime is thus betrayed by the pink and red colours that he wears under the advice of the Marquise d'Espanet[762].

Another important element is Zola's mirrors that are close to daylight and their ability to reflect images. They actually perform a duplication of the character according to the original. The result is a split of the character who can then self-observe[763], weigh up their sedative capacity and assess the damage done to their body, if there is any. It is symptomatic to note that the two sexual agents just mentioned above are also fans of the mirror: Renée and Nana spend long hours in front of the mirror in their respective apartments. Using the large mirrors, they carefully wear makeup to please men. But the mirror suggests narcissism, which is far from being positive in itself. Their affinity with that mythical hero presupposes their future reification, to respect the symmetry of representations. According to Jean de Palacio, Renée is doomed because of the combination of mythology and clothing: << *Dans* **La Curée**, *la prépondérance de la mythologie et l'emprise du vêtement sont une mise à mort de la femme plus efficace que l'imprévisible méningite sous laquelle le romancier l'accable comme en passant, et comme pour rétablir* in extremis *les droits de la physiologie* >>[764].

One can oppose on the same axis the continuous times and the discontinuous times.

3. 4. The opposition between continuous times/discontinuous times

In the theme of sexuality, I conceive continuous times as moments in which the love affair is uninterrupted and by discontinuous times, I mean the moments of interruption of this connection. With regard to the first case, let us refer, as an example, in **La Bête Humaine**, to the eight months during which Jacques and Séverine loved each other tenderly to the point of conspiring to physically

---

[760] Axel Preiss: *Les Couleurs de La Curée* in **La Curée de Zola << ou la vie à outrance >>**, op. cit. p. 149.
[761] **Ibidem**, p. 151.
[762] **Ibidem**, p. 153.
[763] Philippe Hamon, in **Le Personnel du Roman. Le Système des Personnages dans Les Rougon-Macquart d'Émile Zola**, op. cit. pp. 152-153, writes of an "*auto-portrait*" of the character because of the use of a mirror.
[764] Jean de Palacio: **La Curée** : *Histoire sociale ou agglomérat de mythes ?* in **La Curée de Zola << ou la vie à outrance >>**, op. cit. pp. 175-176.

eliminate the husband, Roubaud, whom they perceived as an obstacle to their happiness. The same pattern is found in **La Curée** - for the eight or nine months of the incestuous affair between Renée and Maxime. The continuous times have the trait [+ durative] and are moments of happiness and fullness for the sexual agent in Zola's **Les Rougon-Macquart**.

However, generally speaking, things do not always happen that way, since discontinuous times take over very quickly and overrun continuous times. The consequence of this state of affairs is that happiness remains limited and circumscribed in Zola's fiction works. Thus, Renée broke up with M. de Saffré, M. de Mussy, the chargé d'Affaires at the Embassy of the United States and with all of her other lovers as soon as she fell in love with Maxime. The most telling example is that of the unknown Georges, whom she slept with only twice. The time of happiness, in the perspective of rejected lovers, is discontinuous, fleeting, unlike the time of suffering due to the loss of the sexual value-object which is prolonged indefinitely. For example, Renée never returns to any of her jilted lovers once she dumps them. In **Nana**, the eponymous heroine also dumps ler lovers at a vertiginous speed: Fauchery, Daguenet, Steiner, Philippe and Georges Hugon and the Marquis de Chouard are all mercilessly thrown out of her heart.

It should simply be noted that these discontinuities in romantic relationships lead to unfortunate consequences. Thus, the young George commits suicide when he realises his mistress' unfaithful. He could simply not forsee a future for himself without Nana. This means that the discontinuous time is the mortal enemy of the anthropomorphic sexual agent in Zola's universe. For example, the coachman Tron, in **La Terre**, for identical motives, murders his love rival and boss, Hourdequin, and then burns the farm down thus endangering the lives of dozens of innocent characters. François Mouret himself, frustrated at having been robbed of his wife and home by Father Faujas, returns to set it ablaze[765] in **La Conquête de Plassans**. Sexual and moral frustration brought about by the abandonment of the beloved sexual object can lead the sexual subject to the most eccentric follies[766]. In **Le Docteur Pascal**, Pascal is completely happy for months until his separation from Clotilde, who leaves their Plassans home to take care of her brother, Maxime, paralysed in Paris. He does not survive that separation for more than a month: the discontinuous time is equivalent to the sexual subject's death sentence.

Let us take a look now at the seasons which I will oppose on the hot-cold axis.

---

[765] This is the << *feu destructeur* >> in the terminology of Maarten Van Buuren in **Les Rougon-Macquart d'Émile Zola. De la Métaphore au Mythe**, op. cit. p. 254.
[766] The act of the sexually frustrated arsonist approaches the infernal fire about which Roger Ripoll writes: << *Feu des vengeances divines, feu de l'enfer ; le démon apparaît aux côtés du Dieu impitoyable* >>, in **Réalité et Mythe chez Zola**, op. cit. p. 94.

3.5. The seasons and the sexual ambivalence.

In each of the novels of the **Rougon-Macquart** cycle, it turns out that the cold season - winter - is associated with excessive debauchery. Winter indeed leads to an orgy of alarming proportions. Does not coldness command that people warm up? In any case, love sometimes follows the evolution of the seasons as it is the case in **La Faute de l'Abbé Mouret**. In this respect, Maarten Van Buuren notes that: << *La vie des protagonistes est liée au déroulement des saisons, elle suit un cycle végétal. Serge et Albine <<s'épanouissent>> au printemps ; en automne, Serge quitte le Paradou et Albine meurt. Mais la nature végétale d'Albine enlève à sa mort son aspect tragique. Si elle meurt, c'est pour mieux renaître au printemps suivant [...]* >>[767]. In **La Terre**[768], Palmyre justifies her incest with her younger brother, Hilarion, by the freezing condition in their common hut during the winter. She argues that their space is unbearable to live in otherwise. The winter also sees the culmination of the incestuous relationship between Renée and Maxime as they rush to the greenhouse. The winter garden is where a suffocating heat allows them to have sex and triumph over the inhibitory coldness freezing the outside world.

In the end, the cold weather requires the search for sources of heat. That is why Maxime and Renée spend a few days by the seaside to enjoy the sun in winter. But fire is the main source of heat in **Les Rougon-Macquart**. Fire is indeed the favourite haven of Nana and Renée who are always cold. They literally burn themselves continually at the fireplace like the damned self punishing ahead of the last judgment.

Can fire therefore be considered as a purifying tool? No doubt, especially in the perspective of the arsonists in **La Débâcle** who are sparking gigantic flames from all over Paris, a city overwhelmed by an all-out insurrection. The pyromaniacs for reasons of jealousy that are Tron and Mouret, also perceive it in that perspective. It seems obvious that in **Les Rougon-Macquart** fire is the vectorial force that ravages a cursed and corrupt space. It reminds the reader of the infernal flames of the lake of fire. It thus purifies a world in agony[769] which must give way to another, with a better morality, with more justice and more chastity.

Finally, note that the time is not globally in conjunction with the character in the Romanesque world of the **Rougon-Macquart**. Even though it often seems to enter in conjunction with the anthropomorphic character, it is always fleeting. Time brings them only ephemeral happiness followed by a more prolonged misfortune which is characterised by a terrible heartbreak. The character is thus inevitably sanctioned psychically and/or physically by an oppressive time.

---

[767] Maarten Van Buuren: **Les Rougon-Macquart d'Émile Zola, De la Métaphore au Mythe**, op. cit. p. 146.
[768] Émile Zola: **R. M. IV**, op. cit. p.484.
[769] Jacques Noiray wrote that this is a << *feu vengeur et purificateur* >> in **Le Romancier et la Machine, I : L'Univers de Zola**, op. cit. p. 419.

Temporality is, from that point of view, a component that must be taken into account in any study of the fatality and the sexuality in Zola's works. It is indeed a short time, a narrow time scope, a timed out and a fleeting time; a time that exerts a strong pressure on the sexual characters, forcing them to enjoy themselves in a short space of time. But it is also a time threatening to execute them thereafter. It is clear to me that there is a clear temporalisation of the Zolian character at the same time as their territorialisation[770] as Philippe Hamon had found. The naturalistic characters are in a rush as their time is running out fast. And because their time is so short, they run around trying hard to enjoy their lives to the fullest extent. They try their hands at every single sexual pleasure and aberration available on earth. They seek the ultimate climax here and now, no matter how much it would cost them. In any case, it seems very paradoxical that Zola's critics have so far afforded so little interest to the study of the temporal component in **Les Rougon-Macquart** as if it were less interesting than the countless studies devoted to the myths, the metaphors, the notion of reality, the characters and to the notion of space in the corpus.

Notwithstanding, this inevitability of temporal component will be combined with that of the spatial component.

---

[770] Philippe Hamon: **Le Personnel du Roman. Le Système des Personnages dans Les Rougon-Macquart d'Émile Zola**, op. cit. p. 205.

CHAPTER II: THE SPACE IN THE ROUGON-MACQUART: THE FRAGMENTED BUT THE DELIMITED SEXUALITY

Many studies have already shown the importance of the space in a fictional work. Let us just remember here with Roland Bourneuf that: << *le personnage est indissociable de l'univers fictif auquel il appartient* >>[771]. Philippe Hamon, who worked a lot on the character at Zola, talks about << *la territorialisation du personage* >> and points out that the space builds the character as much as the character builds their space too[772]. There is therefore an intimacy, even an undeniable interaction between the character and their space so that no study of the narrative can claim to be exhaustive while obscuring one of these two instances. Through the play of description pushed to hypertrophy since Balzac, one also knows that the space is not only invested by the character as a simple support to their realisation, but that the space does reflect and characterise the character that dwells in it, either by metaphor or by metonymy. Some evidence has been given in Chapter III of Part Two. This present chapter will help appreciate the configuration of the space in **Les Rougon-Macquart** as long as the space is the << *foyer de pulsion ou de repulsion* >>[773]. It will also point out its influences on the anthropomorphic character.

I. THE SPATIAL CONFIGURATION AND THE MUTATION OF THE SEXUAL AGENT

Philippe Hamon has already shown that the description of the space constitutes << *un reportrait du personnage, un doublet du personnage* >> and that the space could be an << *actant collectif ou un personnage à part entire* >>[774]. But the enhancement of the status of the space in the narrative rising to the rank of a full character, passes by the implementation of a precise rhetorical means: << *Sur le plan stylistique, on peut remarquer également que la description est le lieu privilégié de la métaphore [...]. D'une part, on peut remarquer que ces métaphores sont anthropomorphiques, c'est-à-dire qu'elles corroborent et accentuent le centrage du récit sur le personnage* >>[775]. In a rather methodical approach, I will study the open spaces in their relationship with the characters that venture in there or who live therein as opposed to the closed spaces. Then I will contrast the open spaces with the closed-open spaces including the stairs inside the buildings. Then, I will direct my investigation towards the opposition deep spaces/surface spaces because the space, in Zola's works, is always <<

---

[771] Roland Bourneuf: **L'Univers du Roman**, Paris, PUF, 1985, p. 150.
[772] Philippe Hamon: **Le Personnel du Roman. Le Système des Personnages dans Les Rougon-Macquart d'Émile Zola**, op. cit. pp. 205-222.
[773] **Ibidem**, p. 217.
[774] Philippe Hamon: *Pour un statut sémiologique du personnage* in **Poétique du Récit**, Paris, Seuil, 1977, p. 162.
[775] **Ibidem**, p. 163.

ellipsoidal >>[776]. It is indeed organised on the basis of opposition. Finally, I will look at how the space can become the *doublet du personnage*[777] in the corpus.

1. The open spaces or the unprotected sexuality

Open spaces are those in which lust, debauchery, sexual violence and death usually take place. For illustrate the lust related to open spaces, I will be satisfied with the following examples: Longchamp in **Nana,** the Bois de Boulogne in **La Curée**, the. Paradou in **La Faute de l'Abbé Mouret** and the wheat fields in **La Terre**. All those spaces have this in common: they seem to be inhabited by a demon of temptation for they are all spaces that push the anthropomorphic characters to engage into debauchery. In Longchamp, Nana is the star. More than the horse races, it is she who creates sensation and temptation. Renée is symmetrically the great attraction at the Bois de Boulogne. This is where these gentlemen see her and lust after her[778]. Her individual power of seduction combined with the temptation of the woods excite social walkers. The woods excite precisely the desire for incest in Renée right from the first chapter of **La Curée**. Renée << *ne reconnaissait plus le Bois* >>, she rather perceived it as a sacred and a mythical space: << *Cette nature si artistiquement mondaine, et dont la grande nuit frissonnante faisait un bois sacré, une de ces clairières idéales au fond desquelles les anciens dieux cachaient leurs incestes divins* >>[779]. Of course, it must immediately be pointed out that this perception is predictive and premonitory as this will open Renée's eyes to her incestuous inclination. The woods - or nature - thus appears like a destinator that infuses incestuous lust into Renée just like the gods who did the same to Phaedrus. In naturalistic tragedy though, nature replaces the gods but their end results are exactly the same.

The Paradou has the same function of destinator when it incites the abbot Mouret[780] to commit Adam's Original sin with his new Eve named Albine. It is undoubtedly the most powerful lustful space in the entire romantic cycle that

---

[776] Philippe Hamon: **Le Personnel du Roman. Le Système des Personnages dans Les Rougon-Macquart d'Émile Zola**, op. cit. p. 225.

[777] Philippe Hamon: *Pour un statut sémiologique du personnage* in **Poétique du Récit**, Paris, Seuil, 1977, p. 162.

[778] Maarten Van Buuren, in **Les Rougon-Macquart d'Émile Zola. De la Métaphore au Mythe**, reckons that one goes to the Bois de Boulogne to watch others and be seen by them, op. cit. p. 179.

[779] Émile Zola: **R. M. I**, op. cit. p. 326.

[780] For Philippe Hamon, in **Le Personnel du Roman. Le Système des Personnages dans Les Rougon-Macquart d'Émile Zola**, the Paradou is one of the anthropomorphised places that are like characters and act as senders, op. cit. p. 230.

Jean-François Tonard deduces from that the << *rôle central* >> of the Paradou and the greenhouse in matters related to sexuality and debauchery in **Thématique de la Symbolique de l'Espace Clos dans le Cycle des Rougon-Macquart d'Émile Zola**, op. cit. p. 37.

For Roger Ripoll, if the Paradou holds the role of a sender, it is that of the << *Diable* >>, in **Réalité et Mythe chez Zola**, op. cit. p. 114.

make up the corpus of this study: << *La forêt soufflait la passion géante des chênes, les chants d'orgue des hautes futaies, une musique solennelle, menant le mariage des frênes, [...] tandis que les buissons, les jeunes taillis étaient plus d'une polissonnerie adorable, d'un vacarme d'amants se poursuivant. Et, dans cet accouplement du parc entier, les étreintes les plus fortes s'entendaient au loin, sur les roches, là où la chaleur faisait éclater les pierres gonflées de passion* >>[781]. When nature is itself so amorous and debauched, and when one lives in there like Albine and Serge, undoubtedly anyone that bets on them to remain chaste[782] have lost in advance. The most significant element in the Paradou is the tree named on purpose, << *l'arbre de vie* >> which presents itself both as a tutelary figure and, to borrow the word of Hemmings, << *un phallus* >>[783], precisely because of its great debauch of sap that is reminiscent of human ejaculation. But the Paradou is not indefinitely heavenly, for as Maarten Van Buuren has shown, it becomes a vicious and even a hostile vegetation after the fault of the flesh has been committed; the lianas then becoming snakes among other animal metaphors[784].

The vast fields of wheat act almost identically on the characters of **La Terre**, though in a much more equivocal way since they incite more specifically to rape. This is where Jean Macquart rapes Françoise and takes her virginity with brutality. Much later on, Buteau rapes her in the same fields while she is heavily pregnant. Wheat fields are therefore the space for sexual morbidity if one refers to these two brutal rapes, especially the second one during which the unfortunate victim is disembowelled, thus losing her baby as well as her own life.

Another open space encourages Silvère and Miette to break the ice of their reciprocal virginity in **La Fortune des Rougon**. In the middle of the countryside, in the woods where they were resting before continuing their march of insurgents against the coup d'État of December 2nd (1851), they have sexual intercourse before being shot down by the gendarmes' firing squad. This campaign of Plassans then works as a space of premonition that incites to sin precisely in anticipation of the imminent death of the young lovers. I have already argued above that early sexuality leads to early death in the **Rougon-Macquart**. The open space thus represents the theatre of denial of all moral barriers, the theatre of total freedom and of moral license in the domain of sexuality. One

---

[781] Émile Zola: **R. M. I**, op. cit. p. 1408.
[782] Philippe Hamon asserts, in **Le Personnel du Roman. Le Système des Personnages dans Les Rougon-Macquart d'Émile Zola** that Nature traces for the two young people an implacable itinerary leading them straight to the fault, op. cit. p. 231.
[783] F.W.J. Hemmings: *Zola et la religion* in **Europe : Zola**, op. cit. p. 134.
    In the same sense, Maarten Van Buuren says that the tree of life is the powerful symbol of the Great Mother, refer to **Les Rougon-Macquart d'Émile Zola. De la Métaphore au Mythe**, op. cit. p. 141.
[784] **Ibidem**, pp. 141-142.

can even formulate incestuous desires therein and commit passionate and collective murders in them like Flore did in **La Bête Humaine**.

If lust means a lack to be filled, debauchery properly fills that gap. This is how to read the frivolous La Trouille in **La Terre**, who always has someone << *sur le ventre* >>[785] in the brushwood[786].

Violence related to the satisfaction of the libido bears the respective names of sadism and masochism depending on whether the sexual subject gets pleasure in inflicting pain on their sexual value-object - in order to double their own enjoyment and climax - or that the sexual subject demands that such pain be inflicted upon them as a catalyst for their climax. The massacre perpetrated by Flore[787] in **La Bête Humaine** as well as Jean's rape of Françoise in **La Terre** are manifestations of their sadism.

On the other hand, though, the rape of Françoise by Buteau[788] is a sado-masochism in that by brutally raping her, the male satisfies his libido by sadism to the detriment of his victim who, paradoxically, approves this suffering by pressing hard her abuser and by shouting loud with joy and excitement when she climaxes for the very first time in her entire life. Françoise enjoys sex in pain, a phenomenon called masochism by psychoanalysts. Renée's rape in the countryside is also a sado-masochism. In total, the open space is nothing less than a space of punishment and death. It is the space of emptiness, of nothingness, or rather of annihilation, like the space of the cemetery Saint-Mîttre in **La Fortune des Rougon**, which is at the same time inciting to love and leading to death[789] : << *Et ils* [Miette and Silvère] *n'emportèrent de l'ancien cimetière qu'une mélancolie attendrie, que le pressentiment vague d'une vie courte ; une voix leur disait qu'ils s'en iraient, avec leurs tendresses vierges, avant les noces, le jour où ils voudraient se donner l'un à l'autre. Sans doute ce fut là, sur la pierre tombale, au milieu des ossements cachés sous les herbes grasses, qu'ils respirèrent leur amour de la mort, cet âpre désir de se coucher ensemble dans la terre* [...] >>[790]. The attraction of the open spaces on the characters is very negatively charged because it carries the premonition of death. Death is indeed closely linked to the satisfaction of the libido. The open

---

[785] Émile Zola: **R. M. I**, op. cit. p. 552.
[786] In **Les Rougon-Macquart d'Émile Zola. De la Métaphore au Mythe**, Maarten van Buuren believes that Pascal and Clotilde also obey the constraints of the environment since it is Nature that drives them to love, op. cit. p. 281.
[787] Jacques Noiray suggests in **Le Romancier et la Machine, I: L'Univers de Zola**, op. cit., that the suicide of Flore - following these massacres - is a rape and that her death is a loss of virginity, the only sexual act she has ever known, p. 423.
[788] **Ibidem**, Noiray says the conclusion of rape is nothing but death, p. 423.
[789] Chantal Bertrand-Jennings: **L'Éros et la Femme chez Zola**, op. cit. p. 14.
See also Philippe Hamon: **Le Personnel du Roman. Le Système des Personnages dans Les Rougon-Macquart d'Émile Zola**, op. cit. pp. 252-257.
[790] Émile Zola: **R. M. I**, op. cit. pp. 208-209.

space seduces the anthropomorphic agents and kill them afterwards[791]. While being aware of what will happen to them if they commit the sin of the flesh, the young lovers will not be able to refrain from it as if, like a magnet, death exerts an ostensible pull on them, an attraction which is nothing but fate.

Another particular open space is of much concern in the corpus in that it offers a symbolism like no other. That space is the land or the earth that had been perceived above as a character. Nevertheless, it does not cease to be etymologically and fictitiously an open, wide and polysemic space in Zola's work. In the novel that bears its name, the earth presents itself cumulatively as the foster mother of the peasants and as their incestuous lover. The particular kind of sexual relationship that unites Mother Earth to her lover-sons is therefore an incestuous relationship by metaphor[792]. In terms of mythology, the matings of Gaia - the earth - and Ouranos - the sky[793] - did produce the giants.

In the corpus, however, Gaia only produces dwarves which she exhausts quickly and then eats up greedily. There is therefore incest, infanticide and cannibalism in this particular relationship. It is the Oedipus complex that seems to explain the pseudo-sexual and pseudo-incestuous relationship between Mother Earth and her children, the peasants. According to Baguley, **La Terre** << *est aussi le roman de la toute-puissance maternelle, celle surtout de la Terre-Mère, avec son inépuisable fécondité, qui plie tous (ou peu s'en faut) à son autorité* >>[794]. Baguley insists on its destabilising character and its incitement to discord and revolt. He argues that it was Gaia's fault if Cronos revolted against Ouranos, and if Zeus then rebelled against Cronos[795]. The earth appears roughly like a nymphomaniac lover, an insatiable[796] female that is always ploughed, always fertilised and always breeding. So, she is assailed by many lovers, the most popular of whom are the most virile ones. It is this fact which explains the passage of the earth-mistress from the arms of father Fouan - when he became less vigorous - to those of the virile Buteau[797]. She likes lovers with a lost of stamina.

---

[791] For Chantal Bertrand-Jennings, in **L'Éros et la Femme chez Zola**, these children are sacrificed to the god of chastity, op. cit. p. 31.

[792] In **Les Rougon-Macquart d'Émile Zola. De la Métaphore au Mythe**, Maarten Van Buuren is of the opinion that in the framework of hierogamy - the myth of heaven-earth marriage - the relationship between earth and men is incestuous: << *La terre est une mère. Elle met au monde l'homme qui, devenu adulte, devient son amant* >>, op. cit. p. 266.

[793] This is the hierogamy mentioned by Maarten Van Buuren in the above work, op. cit. p. 265.

[794] David Baguley: **Zola et les Genres**, chapter IX : *le réalisme grotesque et mythique de La Terre*, op. cit. p. 99.

[795] **Ibidem**, p. 100.

[796] **Ibidem**, David Baguley indicates that the land that gives life and then death is inexhaustible and insatiable, p. 100.

[797] **Ibidem**, David Baguley asserts that indeed << *le culte païen de la fécondité domine ce roman* >>, p. 95.

I can also mention the earth's pimping and prostitution in the sense that it throws itself to the first comer, provided they be manly and virile enough. In addition to that, it pushes the anthropomorphic characters to engage in widespread debauchery as it has already been mentioned above.

At the antipodes of the open spaces, there are some enclosed spaces that have the capacity to hide the sexual agents and to cover their misconducts.

1.2. The confined spaces or the intense and the protected sexuality

The confined or closed spaces are the most abundant in the corpus and are the scenes of several sexual situations. Jean-François Tonard believes that they are the << *reflets d'état d'âme des personnages* >>[798] who are under their influence. They are also spaces of intimacy, tenderness, incest, homosexuality, sexual inversions, in a short, of immorality and death. All these negative connotations make claustration an eminently propitious factor for the celebration of orgies. An enclosed space, like the interior of horse drawn carriage, symbolises the promiscuity and laxity of morals both in **La Curée** and in **Nana**. It incites the characters who travel in it to engage into incest by reinforcing the intimacy between them. They are respectively Maxime and Renée on the one hand, and Nana and Georges Hugon on the other.

Similarly, the greenhouse of the hotel Saccard and Renée's cabinet are restricted and closed spaces where incest and adultery take place throughout **La Curée**. The greenhouse is a hotbed of scandal[799] : moral scandal of incest; erotic scandal since Renée is the man and Maxime is the woman in there; geographical scandal with its exotic and living flora that is opposed to the still life of the Parc Monceau; generic scandal also since mythology therein substitutes for naturalism with the various metamorphoses of Renée. In total, the greenhouse is inseparable from the character of Renée for it is << *la grotte de Vénus* >>[800], according to Philippe Berthier. Alain Rochecouste, on his part, associates the greenhouse to hell and right so : << *Les images thermiques de la serre surchauffée qui s'opposent de façon frappante au froid sibérien à l'extérieur évoquent l'enfer surtout par la référence directe à une* << *flamme si lourde* >>>>[801]. It is not by chance that the novelist sets the most horrible scenes in that artificial space, the true symbol of a fake progress: << *Si Zola situe les scènes les plus dépravées de son roman dans une serre, c'est pour exprimer la crainte que les développements industriels et sociaux extrêmement rapides sous*

---

[798] Jean-François Tonard: **Thématique et Symbolique de l'Espace Clos dans le Cycle des Rougon-Macquart d'Émile Zola**, op. cit. p. 5.
[799] For more on this, refer to, Philippe Hamon: **Le Personnel du Roman. Le Système des Personnages dans Les Rougon-Macquart d'Émile Zola**, op. cit. p. 223.
[800] Philippe Berthier: *Hôtel Saccard : état des lieux* in **La Curée de Zola << ou la vie à outrance >>**, op. cit. p. 110.
[801] Alain Rochecouste: *Isotopie catamorphe*, **Ibidem**, pp. 44-45.

le Second Empire amènent en vérité ce qu'on appelait à son époque << un progrès à rebours >>>>[802].

Talking about the metamorphoses that Renée undergoes in the greenhouse, they can only be appreciated thanks to the contrast resulting from the confrontation of shadow versus light as Neide de Faria revealed its importance: << *l'excès de lumière, ou sa négation, l'ombre, ou surtout l'opposition entre foyer lumineux et ténèbres, introduit le clair-obscur, délaye les frontières du réel, permettent alors l'apparition d'êtres << mythiques >>, ou suscitant l'irruption d'un monde fantastique*> >[803]. Very fair assessment since it is the pale light of the moon that allows Maxime to see the monstrous side of Renée: << *Le jeune homme, couché sur le dos, aperçut, au-dessus des épaules de cette adorable bête amoureuse qui le regardait, le sphinx de marbre, dont la lune éclairait les cuisses luisantes. Renée avait la pose et le sourire du monstre à tête de femme, et, dans ses jupons dénoués, elle semblait la sœur blanche de ce dieu noir* >>[804]. In keeping with the symbolic value of the sphinx, Renée embodies the perverted female sexuality, the debauchery and the perverse domination[805]. With regard to this narrative episode, one can agree with Jean-François Tonard who remarks that the enclosed and suffocating spaces lead to pleasure, to ecstasy even, and to lubricity in women and dizziness in men[806].

Similarly, the shed where the coal is stored at the train station in **La Bête Humaine** is at the same time a closed and a reduced space where Jacques and Séverine enjoy their adulterous love. It is not different from the Paradou either. Although it is vast, the Paradou has a hybrid status of an open space in appearance, while being a closed space with its impressive walls. Each wall constitues a hard border, and in this case, it marks the frontier between nature – the Paradou – and culture – the village of Artaud. It is also a hard border

---

[802] Maarten van Buuren: *La Curée, roman du feu*, in **La Curée de Zola << ou la vie à outrance >>**, op. cit., p. 159.

[803] Neide de Faria: **Structure et Unité dans Les Rougon-Macquart de Zola (la poétique du cycle)**, op. cit. p. 267.

[804] Émile Zola: **R. M. I**. op. cit. p. 485.

[805] Chevalier et Gheerbrant: **Dictionnaire des Symboles**, op. cit. p. 215 et p. 906.

[806] Jean-François Tonard: **Thématique et Symbolique de l'Espace Clos dans le Cycle des Rougon-Macquart d'Émile Zola**, op. cit. p. 204.

Philippe Hamon believes that Renée's presence in the greenhouse marks her passage from honesty to fault, in **Le Personnel du Roman. Le Système des Personnages dans Les Rougon-Macquart d'Émile Zola** op. cit. p. 223.

Maarten Van Buuren abounds in the same direction in **Les Rougon-Macquart d'Émile Zola. De la Métaphore au Mythe**, op. cit., when he writes that the greenhouse pushes Renée to incest, p. 281, especially as the outgrowth of plants goes hand in hand with the growth of her incestuous love for Maxime, p. 142.

between Edenic happiness[807] and earthly suffering. This wall[808] which is seemingly impassable, has yet its Achilles heel: a hole large enough to allow an anthropomorphic character to enter it or to leave it. This hole is both an opening and a danger that threatens the sexual character who finds themselves entrenched in the garden. Indeed, it is this opening that allows Brother Archangias to enter the garden and to expel Father Mouret[809] from it. It is therefore the opening that allows the other to violate the premises for the gaze of the other landing on the sexual subject is a breach of secrecy and a judgment. Therefore, it is a judgment pronounced on the sexual immoral character that was hiding in it. The openness of the garden is also an invitation to the sexual subject to open their eyes and to examine external social realities. In any case, this is the effect it makes on Serge when he sees the village and especially his church through it. He then seems to wake up from a bad dream and becomes aware once again of his priesthood and the fault he has committed.

The barn where La Cognette is constantly << *culbuter* >> at all times by her many lovers in **La Terre** only adds further evidence to what has already been pointed out, namely that closed spaces are really those where sexuality is protected from the gaze of others and where it is fully practiced. The intimacy does not go without tenderness and one can notice that all the spaces mentioned in this paragraph are those where the tenderness between the lovers is tenfold. One can simply add to those close spaces Renée's apartments, those of Nana and the Croix-de-Maufras in **La Bête Humaine,** the space where Séverine is the most tender towards Jacques.

The peculiarity of the hovels, the closets and the rooms of the ladies is that these are the spaces for adultery, for incest and for paedophilia. To this end, let us recall the hovel of Palmyre and Hilarion in **La Terre**, or that of the mother Eulalie in **L'Argent** which are both spaces for incest.

One cannot, however, by means of a paralipse, forget about or leave aside the cabinets and the rooms of Renée and Nana which are spaces for incest and excessive adultery. Séverine's room and that of Pecqueux in **La Bête Humaine** can be interpreted in the same way. With Van Buuren, I can say that women

---

[807] Maarten Van Buuren: **Les Rougon-Macquart d'Émile Zola. De la Métaphore au Mythe**, notes that the Paradou is a paradise garden before the sin of the flesh is committed in it, op. cit. p. 141.

[808] For Jean Borie, the wall is the reverie and it remains a strategic place, refer to **Zola et les Mythes, ou de la Nausée au Salut**, p. 130.

For Philippe Hamon, the wall is first of all a frontier. Thus, the wall that separates the Rougon home from that of Macquart in **La Fortune des Rougon**, marks a legal difference (legitimate/illegitimate); an economic difference (rich/poor); an ethnological difference (sedentary/vagabond); a sexual difference (woman/man) and a culinary difference (market gardener/poacher), in **Le Personnel du Roman. Le Système des Personnages dans Les Rougon-Macquart d'Émile Zola**, op. cit. pp. 211-212.

[809] Archangias is the expelling god according to Roger Ripoll's word in **Réalité et Mythe chez Zola**, op. cit. p. 95.

reflect their rooms[810] for the bedroom of the female sexual agent is generally obscure and is an invitation to sleep[811] over. While recognising that the woman's room is similar to their body, Jean Borie distinguishes good rooms from cursed rooms, these being constantly closed, those open to nature through the windows[812].

The confined space is often linked to sexual morbidity which Freud calls sexual inversions. Cabuche falls in that category because he happens to transfer his lust for his sexual object toward anything she has ever possessed or touched. He collects them as memorabilia which he treasures. That makes him a neurotic subject in Freud's therory. A similar neurosis strikes Jacques who loves La Lison, his locomotive, just like a mistress. At the same time, he is scared to touch the real woman until he meets Séverine. The closed space of the locomotive has a cathartic influence on him in that it allows him to suppress the urge to kill his sexual object. Jacques Noiray had insisted on the erotic relationship between Jacques and his beloved machine like a woman of flesh[813]. Their conjugal bond which includes Pecqueux, he argues, is closer to the three-way household uniting Zola to Alexandrine and Jeanne Rozerot[814]. Noiray goes on to point out that the Lison became a shrewish woman like Mrs Zola[815] at some point in that crowded marriage. Why not put the neurotic and the pathological << *cas* >> of Jacques in line with that of Roubaud, his love rival and friend?

Roubaud gets so addicted to gambling that he abandons his attractive wife after the murder committed on his love rival, Président Grandmorin. After the crime, all his libido suddenly vanishes and is then transferred to his newfound gambling activity. Philippe Hamon argues in this regard that << *l'activité ludique* >> leads to << *l'inexistence de l'activité sexuelle*>>[816] just like it was the case for Mrs. Faujas and François Mouret in **La Conquête de Plassans**. That was also the case for Archangias and la Teuse in **La Faute de l'Abbé Mouret**. The Roubaud home becomes the space of a broken household, the space where the husband disappears from to make room for his wife's lover. And he disappears all the more cheerfully as he loses larger amounts of money to gambling. François Mouret also fades away before the Faujas clan because of his repeated losses in the card game in front of Madame Faujas. Archangias is another example of a losing player in front of La Teuse. These losses through games and gambling are therefore never about mere games because they foreshadow a complete failure

---

[810] Maarten Van Buuren also states that some strong men also assimilate to their rooms, as is the case of the abbot Faujas, see **Les Rougon-Macquart d'Émile Zola. De la Métaphore au Mythe**, op. cit. p. 278.
[811] **Ibidem**, p. 78.
[812] Jean Borie : **Zola et les Mythes, ou de la Nausée au Salut**, op. cit. pp. 193-201.
[813] Jacques Noiray : **Le Romancier et la Machine, I : L'Univers de Zola**, op. cit. pp. 405-407.
[814] **Ibidem,** p. 410.
[815] **Ibidem**, p. 408.
[816] Philippe Hamon: **Le Personnel du Roman. Le Système des Personnages dans Les Rougon-Macquart d'Émile Zola**, op. cit. p. 204.

in the life of the male character defeated by a female character. Moreover, any man that gets accustomed to losing that way also loses their interest in sexual activities. All their libido vanishes before being transferred toward their addiction to gambling. It is fair to argue that gambling ultimnately is a libido killer in the eyes of Zola.

The studio of the painter Claude Lantier is a closed space that becomes the space of a conjugal drama: a neglected wife, a painting activity adored by the artist who ends up losing his mind and committing suicide in front of his work. Hamon also considers that if the intellectual activity does not suppress sexual activity, it << *réduit* >> and renders it << *méfiante* >>[817]. This is how to understand the reduced sexuality of Dr. Pascal until the edge of his sixties. One can deduce from all the examples quoted here that the character with a morbid sexuality is a kind of psychopath, a maniac who inevitably falls into lucid or furious madness. In addition, homosexuality also occurs in enclosed spaces. Thus, the pederast Baptiste gets involved in this mania in the stables, an enclosed space in **La Curée**, while in **Nana**, the lesbians Satin and Nana, engage in lesbianism in Nana's room. The so-called << *les deux inséparables* >> Adeline d'Espanet and Suzanne Haffner, are always lying down << *amoureusement* >> side by side in a cab, another enclosed space.

The opposition between closed spaces and open spaces thus studied shows that there is no real opposition between them: the same sexual inversions occur in both. In all cases, the character is debauched, suffers and dies to the point that it can be argued that the opposition between those two types of spaces is only a feigned one. What if the space is a closed-open one?

2.3. The closed-open spaces or the morbid sexuality

By this apparently ambiguous term, I mean the semi-open or the semi-closed spaces that are the stairs in buildings. They are closed because they are included in a larger set but they remain open at the same time insofar as they allow the circulation of co-tenants in both directions - ascending and descending. In **Les Rougon-Macquart**, the staircase is the space for rape and for spreading the most ignominious rumours - which also amounts to violating the privacy of others. Thus, in **La Curée**, Aristide Rougon dit Saccard rapes a neighbour on the stairs of their common building and the result of that rape is none other than Victor Rougon, the bandit. The latter is evidence that the fruit conceived in violence becomes violent and full of vices. He becomes an individual thirstier for enjoyment than his rapist parent. The staircase also allows, according to Jean-François Tonard, the downwards movement and foreshadows the decadence[818]

---

[817] Philippe Hamon: **Le Personnel du Roman. Le Système des Personnages dans Les Rougon-Macquart d'Émile Zola**, op. cit., p. 204.
[818] Jean-François Tonard: **Thématique et Symbolique de l'Espace Clos dans le Cycle des Rougon-Macquart d'Émile Zola**, op. cit. pp. 217-218. Admittedly, it is necessary to take this

of the characters living on the upper floors that are descending the steps on a daily basis.

The staircase in **Pot-Bouille** is above all the ideal space where incongruous confidences are let out. When the maids gather in there, the latest versions of the adulteries happening behind closed doors are delivered with disconcerting impudence. Jean Borie argues in this regard that :<< [...] *les bonnes sont les hérauts infernaux du corps* >>[819] because of the physical and the verbal dirt that they pour onto the staircase. With its spiral configuration, the staircase represents the spiral of rape and of the disclosure of secrets that derives from espionage[820]. The semi-opening of the staircase allows the characters to communicate with the outside world and it also allows the discovery of secrets hidden in the various apartments from the outside world by means of peddling news. Indeed, the maids, once informed by each other, return home and do not keep for themselves their bosses' secrets. Let us schematise this with A.J. Greimas[821] :

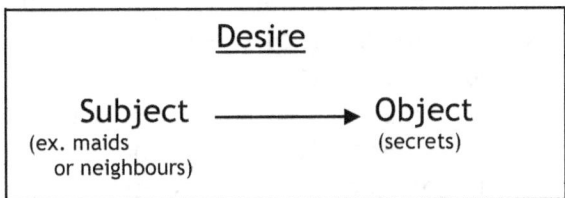

This greimasian diagram applied to the corpus shows that the characters' desire in a building is to collect confidences about their neighbours in order to disclose the debauchery that they wanted to keep secret. Naturally, any *gnarus* character will share their information with any other *ignare* character. After the closed spaces, the open spaces and the closed-open spaces, it is necessary to question the depths or abysses in opposition to the surface spaces.

3.4. The couple deep spaces/surface spaces: the descent into hell?

The deep space - or the abyss - is characterised by the unknown, the unfathomable which is frightening. It would be surprising to find in **Les Rougon-Macquart** a deep space positively connotated. If one takes for example the well in which Tron draws his love rival, Hourdequin, in **La Terre**, it is clear that that

---

decadence with caution because, otherwise, it will be necessary to concede an elevation each time that they go back up to their flats.

[819] Jean Borie : **Zola et les Mythes, ou de la Nausée au Salut**, op. cit. p. 29.

[820] Philippe Hamon insists largely on the importance of *"la quête d'information"* in Zola's novels, quest that manifests itself through *l'espionnage, le soupçon, le pressentiment et le blackmail,* in **Le Personnel du Roman. Le Système des Personnages dans Les Rougon-Macquart d'Émile Zola**, op. cit. pp. 286-293.

[821] Algirdas Julien Greimas quoted by Gilles Gritti, in his article *"Un Récit de Presse"* published in **Communications, 8**, op. cit. p. 101.

space is a trap, a snare, a space for atrocious and vicious death. It recalls the Voreux in **Germinal** which is seen by the narrator as a monster that swallows the miners. The Voreux is also the scene of Chaval's murder at the hands of his love rival, Étienne Lantier. Those spaces are both macabre, for Hourdequin breaks his neck in Tron's well. That senseless murder was crafted by Tron who wished to rob him of La Cognette, their common love interest. Next, Étienne has sexual intercourse with Catherine Maheu on the verge of death[822] inside the Voreux just after killing Chaval, the girl's lover. Their sexual relationship is curious in that they confess their mutual love only then and that Catherine dies shortly after satisfying her libido. Moreover, it must be considered that the depth, which cannot be measured by the naked eye, and the darkness which is at the bottom of the wells, are all elements announcing death. The characters that venture into such spaces ultimately lose their lives[823]. The examples of such deaths are not lacking in the corpus.

As early as in **La Fortune des Rougon**, the adjoining well which serves as a meeting place for Silvère and Miette, functioned as the space announcing their tragic and early end. To consider everything, it is necessary to point out that they used to communicate thanks to the reflection of their images in the water of the bottom of it. This show, although romantic in their eyes, bears some mythological hints with the episode of Narcissus. However, like the tragic hero in the Greek mythology, Miette and Silvère will suffer a tragic death in the prime of their lives. The unfathomable, like nothingness, hardly forgives. It is neither simply a place of sanction and any sexual performance realised there, inevitably leads to the death of the performing character. They thus become agent of their own disappearance. For Sylvie Collot, the well << *est l'un des lieux les plus riches de l'univers de Zola* >>, and most importantly, she warns: << *n'oublions pas qu'en hébreu, le même mot désigne le puits et l'épouse* >>[824]. Singularly, the adjoining well << *joue le rôle, dans* **La Fortune des Rougon**, *de lieu de communication primitif* >>[825].

Overall, the well is not far from the tunnel since their physical resemblance is combined with their symbolic equivalence. For Jean-François Tonard, << *le cauchemar du tunnel* >> justifies << *la passion dévastatrice de Jacques Lantier* >> and of Flore[826]. To sum it up, << *la mort s'engouffre dans le tunnel* >>[827],

---

[822] Émile Zola: **R. M. III**, op. cit. p. 1579.
[823] Dans **Émile Zola, Le Réalisme Symbolique**, Claude Seassau believes that the Voreux << *instaure le rite barbare* >> of devouring, op. cit. p. 202.
Maarten Van Buuren goes in the same direction as he sees the Voreux as a << *monstre chthonien goulu* >> and as a << *glouton* >>, refer to **Les Rougon-Macquart d'Émile Zola. De la Métaphore au Mythe**, op. cit. p. 32 et p. 35.
[824] Sylvie Collot: **Les Lieux du Désir. Topologie Amoureuse de Zola**, Paris, Hachette, 1992, p. 139.
[825] **Ibidem**, p. 139.
[826] Jean-François Tonard: **Thématique et Symbolique de l'Espace Clos dans le Cycle des Rougon-Macquart d'Émile Zola**, op. cit. p. 253.
[827] **Ibidem**, op. cit. p. 254.

since it is in the tunnel that Grandmorin is slaughtered and that Flore commits suicide. The tunnel represents, in Tonard's view, the space of madness, crime and death[828]. The tunnel and the well have this in common: they are the allegory of the female sex. In the imagination of Zola, the latter is to be feared as much as the former. Zola feared the female sex which he perceived as an unfathomable abyss, a scary chasm.

On the other hand, the surface space is essentially a solid ground that has already been studied above and it would be superfluous to return to it here. In total, any space is the doublet of the character that dwells in it. A room will have a large bed decorated with bright colours - pink, yellow, for example - when the character who lives in there is a woman focused on debauchery and easy money that only prostitution provides.

Nonetheless, the study of the space thus presented would be incomplete if one does not take into account the situation of conflict that breaks out between the character and their space in the Zolian novel.

II. THE CONFLICTUAL SITUATION BETWEEN THE SEXUAL AGENT AND THEIR SPACE

It is not always that the character enters in conjunction with their space. On the contrary, they very often enter into disjunction with them, inevitably and tragically.

1. <u>The space and the aggression of the sexual agent</u>

The character in disjunction with their space enters into an open conflict with it. The space acts first on the character and leads them to achieve some sexual performances in disregard of all social norms as it has been shown for the wheat fields, the greenhouse and the hovels. The spatial eroticism is a real aggression that infuses the desire for sexual aberrations into the mind of the anthropomorphic character. But everything starts from lust that creates a need, a lack to fill. Wanting to eliminate an initial lack by filling it is to seek to improve an uncomfortable situation. And according to Claude Bremond's *la logique des possibles narratifs*[829], any improvement process initiated goes hand in hand with their possible degradation. Once the improvement is achieved though, the degradation is no longer accomplished but it remains at the stage of virtual abortion.

For example, Henri Dauvergne undertakes in **La Bête Humaine** the conquest of Séverine Roubaud. A priori, he enjoys a possible improvement since the young

---

[828] Jean-François Tonard: **Thématique et Symbolique de l'Espace Clos dans le Cycle des Rougon-Macquart d'Émile Zola**, op. cit. p. 254.
[829] Claude Bremond: *"La Logique des Possibles Narratifs"* in **Communications, 8 : Analyse Structurale des Récits**, op. cit. p. 68.

woman might agree to be with him and to satisfy his libido. He triggers on the basis of that hope a process of improvement as soon as he begins the operation of seduction. But a possible improvement has its reverse which is a possible degradation since the young woman might as well refuse to give in to the seducer. Finally, she refuses to give in, thus completing the degradation that was only virtual at some point in time. At the time of the assessment, the improvement hoped for by Dauvergne is not obtained with its final failure. Let us schematise this episode as follows:

Diagram n°.1:

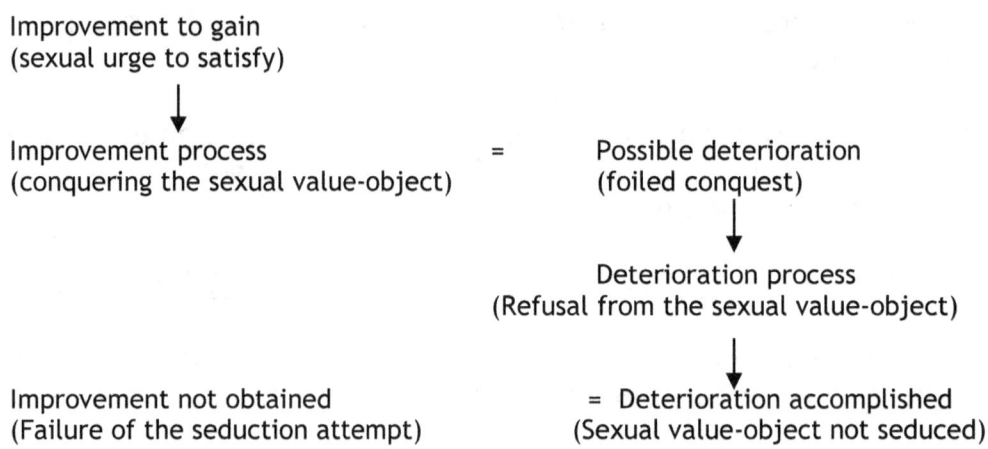

This first diagram shows that all the attempts of seduction and conquest of the sexual value-object do not result in a great success. Such a diagram would be appropriate to represent canonically the attempts of seduction exerted by Henri Dauvergne on Séverine, or that of Cabuche on the same woman, or that of Flore on Jacques Lantier, only in **La Bête Humaine**.

Such a narrative statement occurs in Le **Docteur Pascal** when Dr. Ramond falls in love with Clotilde. He then starts a process of seduction with great hope at first, since nothing seems to block his way. Uncle Pascal seems to be in favour of the marriage; the grandmother, Félicité, is even eager to hasten the engagement, etc. However, this hope is ruined when Clotilde, against all odds, decides to answer his request in the negative way, only to end up in the arms of her own uncle and foster parent. What these sexual subjects have in common, is that their improvements to be obtained have all ended in accomplished degradations.

The failure in the conquest of the sexual value-object is always very badly received, and that leads very often to atrocious massacres as it was the case with Flore in **La Bête Humaine**. In contrast to the first diagram, let us establish a second one on the axis of seduction as follows:

Diagram n°. 2:

Improvement to obtain
(Sexual value-object to conquer)
↓
Improvement Process   =   Possible Degradation
(Process of seduction started)   (refusal of the sexual value-object)
                                                              ↓
                                                              Degradation process
                                                              (hesitation of the sexual value-object)
                                                              ↓
Improvement obtained   =   Degradation not completed
(sexual value-object conquered)   (acceptance of the sexual value-object)

This second diagram applies to all the sexual relationships that take place in the corpus. For example, Jacques Lantier covets and conquers Séverine, getting the improvement he wanted to achieve. His example is like those of the triumphant seducers of M. de Mussy, M. de Saffré, Maxime, and many others who triumph over Renée. It also applies to Count Muffat, Georges and Philippe Hugon, the Marquis de Chouard, Daguenet, Fauchery, Steiner and the many other lovers of Nana[830]. Note that this second diagram applies to the majority of the characters in the corpus[831], which explains why debauchery is at the centre of all the narratives[832] in **Les Rougon-Macquart**.

It happens, however, that this canonical diagram is more or less complex from the moment it poses a preliminary obstacle which must necessarily be discarded before enjoying the sexual object-value. An example of such can be found in **La Terre** with the coachman, Tron, who sets up a trap to eliminate his rival, Hourdequin, in order to keep for himself alone, La Cognette, their common mistress. Eventually, he succeeds only partially because if the rival is killed, the sexual value-object refuses to belong to him. That puts Tron in the same situation as Flore, who massacred innocent victims in **La Bête Humaine** in order to eliminate Séverine, the main obstacle to her union with Jacques Lantier. She is the only one who fails miserably in her macabre business.

---

[830] For Philippe Hamon, in **Le Personnel du Roman. Le Système des Personnages dans Les Rougon-Macquart d'Émile Zola**, the woman << *donne* >> and << *se donne* >>, op. cit. p. 192.
[831] **Ibidem**, p. 201, Hamon mentions a << *guerre des sexes* >> in **Les Rougon-Macquart**. This is not without consequence since, obviously, heterosexuality is abounding in the corpus where male and female characters covet each other tirelessly even if conflicts arise very often between them - mainly due to jealousy - but not because of any atavistic antagonism between the genders. The notion of the war of the sexes is, in my eyes, simply an exaggerated claim.
[832] Roger Ripoll reckons that the theme of nudity is haunting in the corpus, in **Réalité et Mythe chez Zola**, , op. cit. p. 81.

It is in this ultimate perspective that Bremond establishes the following diagram[833] that I will illustrate with the help of what relates to sexuality.

Diagram n°. 3:

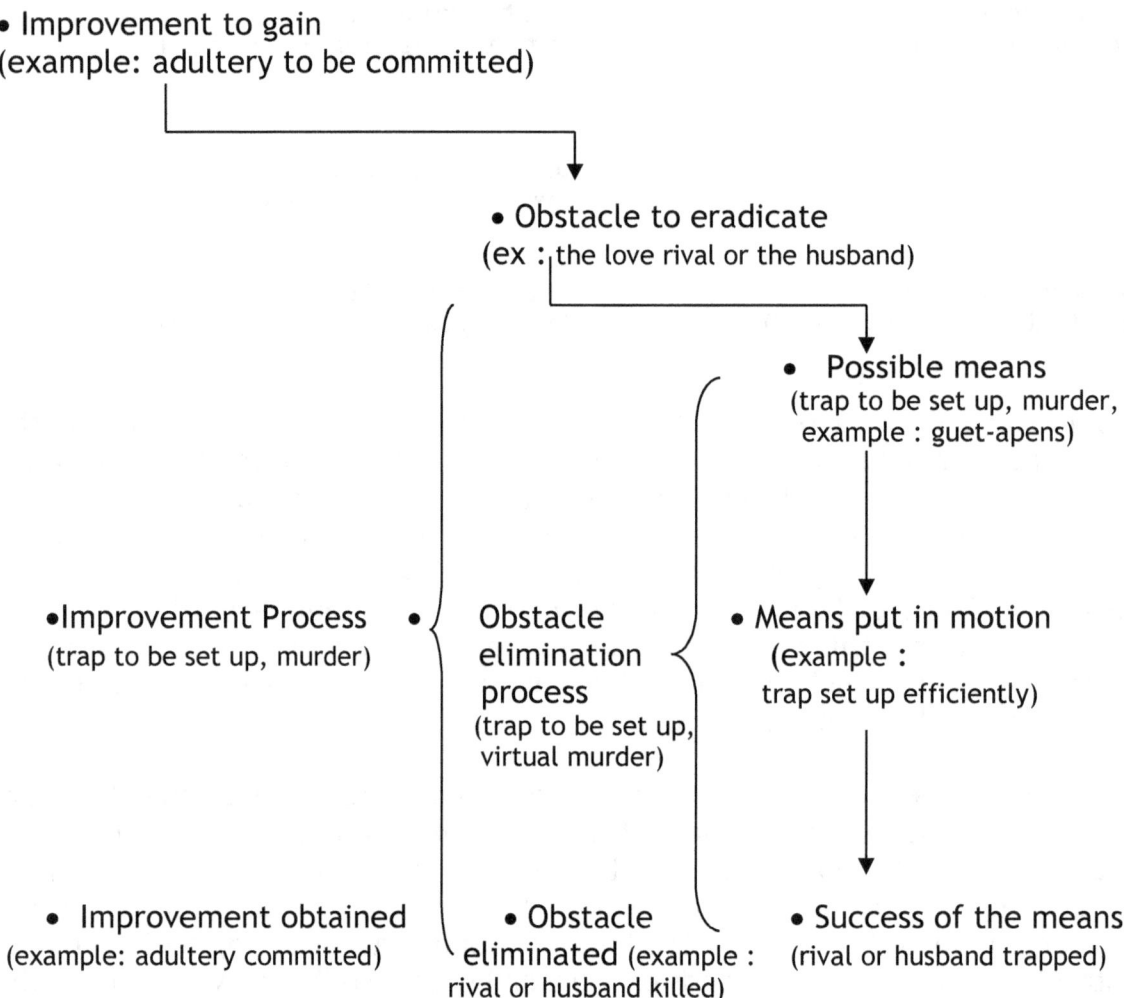

On the other hand, Roubaud executes this scheme perfectly in the six-thirty express train by slaughtering Président Grandmorin. He then intially keeps for himself only his sexual value-object, his wife Séverine, but only for some time. The assassination was carried out in a small car - inside the train - which was supposed to protect the privacy of Grandmorin as a first-class passenger. Later on, Jacques and Séverine jointly plan the execution of that narrative structure by planning the murder of the husband, Roubaud, in order to live together freely. The trap set up would have managed to catch its victim since Roubaud actually

---

[833] Claude Bremond: *"La Logique des Possibles Narratifs"* in **Communications, 8**, op. cit. p. 69.

travels to the Croix-de-Maufras[834] where his executioners were waiting to slaughter him. He gets a reprieve though only when Jacques, caught by his madness to slaughter a female, fails to resist the temptation to kill right away: he rather slaughters Séverine[835] and flees the scene before Roubaud's arrival. Jacques thus obtains an inverted success to the extent that he eliminates his sexual value-object instead of the obstacle to its acquisition. No doubt the space of the Croix-de-Maufras has acted with all its weight in this deviation of Jacques' objectives. This house is the space of debauchery and paedophilia because the president Grandmorin used to abuse Séverine in there, his goddaughter and the future wife of Roubaud, since his young age[836]. It is the space for paedophilia, for incest too - since Grandmorin was her foster dad. But it is also the space for adultery. In all, the Croix-de-Maufras is a lugubrious space which is very negatively charged[837]. While it was intended to be the space for the elimination of an obstacle in order to unite two lovers forever, it is transformed into the space of forever separation, inciting Jacques to turn away from his initial objectives.

In all, **Les Rougon-Macquart** depict a world of exacerbated depravity and of perdition; a world where everything converges to a triumphant and sometimes morbid sexuality. Obnubilated by their sexual appetite, the Zolian characters do not shrink from anything atrocious when the sexual urge is compelling. Thus, they do not retreat before incest - literally as well as figuratively - neither in front of paedophilia nor before homosexuality – sodomy and lesbianism -, still less before mass murder. Sex is their tool of recreation and not only the means for procreation. It goes without saying that the hotbeds of conflicts that sometimes appear between them are essentially motivated by jealousy[838]. What should one remember from all these remarks?

First, that the spatial eroticism is a source of sexual perversion. Secondly, that the anthropomorphic character is influenced by their space just as they are influenced by the temporal component. They are unable to change the spatio-temporal element into good, or to improve them. The space-time component presents works as an active accomplice and a destinator in the process of sexual depravity which pushes the Zolian characters to their death. There is a conflict

---

[834] Claude Seassau shows that the Croix-de-Maufras means << *qui fait mal* >>, in **Émile Zola, Le Réalisme Symbolique**, op. cit. p. 35.
[835] Jacques Noiray, in **Le Romancier et la Machine, I : L'Univers de Zola**, op. cit. p. 411, asserts that it is rather the fault of the Lison if Jacques kills Séverine.
[836] Maarten van Buuren writes that: << *Grandmorin, le président de la Cour de Rennes, abuse de son pouvoir de parrain et tuteur (sa << paternité >>) pour séduire Séverine (sa << fille >>)* >>, in **Les Rougon-Macquart d'Émile Zola. De la Métaphore au Mythe**, op. cit. p. 184.
[837] According to Jean-François Tonard, in **Thématique et Symbolique de l'Espace Clos dans le Cycle des Rougon-Macquart d'Émile Zola**, op. cit. p. 253, it is not by chance that the tunnel separates the Croix-de-Maufras and the house of Misard when one remembers the negative connotation of the tunnel. It is thus the hyphen between two spaces of abject crimes.
[838] Claude Seassau shows that jealousy is at the origin of the desire to kill in **Émile Zola, Le Réalisme Symbolique**, op. cit. p. 198.

between the character and their space to the point where it is legitimate to ask who benefits from the confrontation between the two of them. And who ultimately comes out on top in that conflict?

2.1. The defeat of the sexual agent

Unable to enter in conjunction with their space and to transform it into a moral and a chaste space, the anthropomorphic character suffers a resounding defeat as is the case in **La Terre** where, despite the relentlessness of the peasants on the earth, despite the energetic efforts, the earth remains immense and always reinvigorated. All the while, the characters sink into debauchery; they fade away and die. The vanity of their multiple efforts to subdue their rebellious space can be read on every page of the novels. The full power of the space through its eroticism allows it to manipulate the anthropomorphic character. The latter is then led to perform a never improving and degrading sexual performance[839].

In **Les Rougon-Macquart**, the *paratopiques* and the *utopiques* spaces melt in the same mould: the characters acquire their competence and realise their performances in one and the same space[840]. That is a clear sign of cohesion in Zola's novelistic construction. It is also evidence enough that the anthropomorphous agent totally depends on their space which forms and uses them at will.

For example, in Chapter I of **La Curée**, it is in the greenhouse that Renée realises that she is definitely in love with Maxime. It is there that she becomes jealous of Louise de Mareuil, the young man's future bride. Having acquired her incestuous skills in the greenhouse, she goes back soon in there to accomplish her sexual performance using the greenhouse as an erotic space, her favourite space to fully enjoy the incest in the arms of Maxime by the << *nuits froides de l'hiver* >>. In an identical logic, the omnipotence of the space is reflected in the severe punishment it inflicts on the character. The anthropomorphic character is resigned to being a mere sacrificial victim of their space. They stoically undergoe their sanction in their favourite space much like Claude Lantier who commits suicide in his painting studio.

---

[839] Jean-François Tonard believes that the character is therefore under the influence of the << *dynamisme inquiétant de la nature qui, métamorphosée, devient un monstre vivant* >>, refer to **Thématique et Symbolique de l'Espace Clos dans le Cycle des Rougon-Macquart d'Émile Zola**, op. cit. p. 69.

Maarten Van Buuren goes on to say that man is determined by their environment, or milieu, as far as the naturalist writers are concerned, and that the city of Paris, for example, is complicit in the debauchery of the characters, in **Les Rougon-Macquart d'Émile Zola. De la Métaphore au Mythe**, op. cit. pp. 276-277.

[840] If Neide de Faria is right to say that time is circular in **Les Rougon-Macquart**, one can also affirm that the Zolian space is also circular since the character acquires their competence in a given space, and then returns to accomplish their sexual performance therein, in **Structure et Unité dans Les Rougon-Macquart d'Émile Zola (la poétique du cycle)**, op. cit. p. 210,.

Symmetrically, Miette and Silvère meet every night in a disused cemetery and they always sit on the same gravestone whose epitaph reads << *Ci-gîst Marie* >>. Mary being Miette's real name, one realises the premonitory value of that stone. They young lovers appear then as some resigned victims, therefore, and they die in the prime of their lives: Miette dies in the countryside and Silvère, precisely in the cemetery. This law of the return on oneself in **La Fortune des Rougon** reflects the action on itself, it returns the character to their space of predilection to sanction there right there. It also shows how much << *Le personnage est indissociable de l'univers fictif auquel il appartient* >>[841].

To these examples, let us add that of Jacques and Séverine which is the Croix-de-Maufras. That is the space of a fiduciary contract concluded between the two sexual agents. Indeed, the woman convinces her lover to murder her husband in order to keep her for himself as a reward. Jacques accepts that contract and they both prepare an ingenious plan to fulfil it. They choose the murder weapon together: a knife. The house only becomes the space of a broken contract - or rather a poorly filled one when Jacques slays the wrong target, shedding his mistress' blood instead. In the same order of ideas, let us mention the suicide of Georges Hugon who returns to kill himself at Nana's place, in the very apartment where he had come to see her for the first time with a bouquet of flowers that already symbolised his funeral wreath. Similarly, François Mouret had returned home to immolate himself in the huge fire that burnt down his building, the space of his wife's betrayal in **La Conquête de Plassans.**

Such sanctions were undoubtedly predictable because when the anthropomorphic mortals attack the immortals – the time and the space - except for a miracle, the outcome cannot be favourable to them. The defeat of the former is all programmed in advance like that of humans before the Greek gods. Who can conquer the god Chronos and keep the benefits of their triumph forever? Who can defeat the goddess Gaia and enjoy their victory indefinitely? The inevitability of sexuality is also and above all a fatality of their space and a fatality of the time they live in as well as the inevitability of the disappearance of the corrupt society[842] of the Second Empire that is doomed from the outset.

2.1. The revenge of the sexual agent on their space or the emergence of pyromaniacs

---

[841] Roland Bourneuf : **L'Univers du Roman**, op. cit. p. 150.
[842] Émile Zola writes: << *Remarquez que notre théorie des milieux et le rôle que nous donnons en physiologie aux questions de l'hérédité, remplacent strictement la fatalité antique. Les dieux autrefois voulaient les crimes ; mais les dieux n'étaient autre chose que le milieu et les influences héréditaires* >>, article about the play by Darwitz, **Le Puits des Quatre Chemins**, published in **Le Voltaire** of 20th April 1880 and then in Zola's **Œuvres Complètes**, XII, Henri Mitterand (éd.), op. cit. p. 239.

The only revenge the character can take on their space seems to be outright destruction by fire. It is thus that Tron, conceiving the space of the farm as hostile to the fulfillment of his love, sets it on fire in **La Terre**. Mouret had also set fire to his home in **La Conquête de Plassans** as a sign of revenge. As for Vandeuvres, indirectly ruined by Nana, after having played and lost all his fortune in a horse race -, he burns his stables and burns himself down with everything else.

Pyromania is the admission of the impotence of the anthropomorphic character in flagrant disjunction with their space from which they are ejected[843]. The space where there is no hope of achieving the least sexual performance does not deserve to exist in Zola's fiction. As a result, the frustrated sexual agent harbours nihilistic ambitions: they want to raze everything to the ground, leave nothing standing once they have lost their sexual value-object. The arsonist character does not have any qualms when they start a criminal fire[844] for it does not matter to them whether they endanger the lives of innocent people or not. The sexually frustrated figure seems to treat their space like those ancient plague-infested cities, which were set ablaze at night to raze them to the ground in order to purify them and to protect other cities from the great evil[845]. The similarity is great indeed between the treatment of those ancient cities and that of the world of the **Rougon-Macquart** since the sexual subjects in the corpus exercise their pyromania only during the night. The repetition of those incendiary impulses still brings to light another personal myth of Zola.

2.1. Highlighting another personal myth of the author and its psychoanalytic interpretation.

I already postulated that Zola was a sex addict[846] who was haunted by women[847], by the aborted maternities and by early death due to fatal genetic transmissions.

---

[843] For Naomi Schor, << *the (spatial) superiority of women* >> is a fact, that's why Nana and Satin expel Muffat from the Nana's mansion just as Marthe expels François Mouret from their family home, in **La Conquête de Plassans**. Refer to **Zola's Crowds**, op. cit. p. 98,

[844] Claude Seassau writes : << *La destruction nihiliste a un aspect mystique, seuls le sang et le feu peuvent nettoyer la terre comme dans les rites purificateurs* >>, in **Émile Zola, Le Réalisme Symbolique**, op. cit. p. 251.

This kind of fire is the most destructive in the terminology of Maarten Van Buuren, in **Les Rougon-Macquart d'Émile Zola. De la Métaphore au Mythe**, op. cit. p. 255.

[845] About this rapprochement between Paris and the cities of Sodom and Gomorrah, see Roger Ripoll, in **Réalité et Mythe chez Zola**, op. cit. p. 101.

[846] Roger Ripoll writes: << *L'association de la sexualité et du mal traduit bien plus les hantises de Zola que les conceptions qu'il entendait mettre en œuvre dans son roman* >>, in **Réalité et Mythe chez Zola**, op. cit. p. 115. I think that these fires have a double purpose for they are both punitive and purifying.

[847] Let us remember that for Maarten van Buuren, the personal myth of the author (or his unconscious personality) is revealed through the obsession of a small number of characters, see **Les Rougon-Macquart d'Émile Zola. De la Métaphore au Mythe**, op. cit. p. 46.

Now Philippe Hamon has just shown that Florent is haunted by the woman killed on the barricades while Souvarine is haunted by the woman hung during the Moscow revolution.

It can also be argued that his obsession extended to the general idea of death and nothingness given the impressive number of deaths recorded in his works[848] and the nihilistic tendencies of some of his characters such as the arsonists like Souvarine, **Germinal**'s Russian. Does he not sabotage the coal mine in order to destroy the Montsou workers' world?[849]

Moving on to the third step in the psychoanalytic method, namely the interpretation of the personal myth of the author, based on all of the above, it seems that literature gives Zola the opportunity to express his own unconscious fantasies by disseminating its relevant clues through his works[850]. My postulate is therefore the following: Zola exorcises his own demons that he is afraid to face in the contingent reality and it is for that reason that his artistic works are presented as a catharsis for the neurotic artist he was[851].

However, it is imperative to verify such an assertion by confronting it with Zola's biography as it should be in the fourth and final phase of the psychoanalytic method. It may be remembered from Zola's biography that until the age of fifty, this man was deprived of children despite a quarter of a century of life together with his wife, Gabrielle-Alexandrine Meley. Highly disturbed by this sterility that struck their home, Zola ended up having an affair with Jeanne Rozerot, his wife's maid[852]. It is from that adulterous union that his only two children - Denise in

---

Jacques Lantier is haunted by the living woman whereas Serge Mouret is haunted by the Virgin Mary and Claude Lantier by the Woman – the virtual and the artistic version of the female boby - see **Le Personnel du Roman. Le Système des Personnages dans Les Rougon-Macquart d'Émile Zola**, op. cit. 252. The obsession of this small group of characters undoubtedly betrays the obsession of Zola himself.

[848] Naomi Schor stressed that: << *The specter of the dead woman haunts* **The Rougon-Macquart** >>, in **Zola's Crowds**, op. cit., p. 21.

[849] Claude Seassau writes in **Émile Zola, Le Réalisme Symbolique**, op. cit.: << *La violence la plus aiguë est celle du nihiliste Souvarine voulant totalement anéantir la création par un déluge* >>, p. 251.

Jean Borie believes that the catastrophes (fire, flood, epidemic and invasion) are of a prodigious wealth in the works of Zola. Thus, the destruction of the Voreux is significant when one remembers that it represents a father - since it possesses a penis - and a mother – for having a wide and deep vagina. As a phallic woman therefore, it represents a castrating threat that could justify its sabotage, see **Zola et les Mythes, ou de la Nausée au Salut**, op. cit. pp. 108-110.

[850] For Colette Becker, << *Le roman devient, pour Zola, un exorcisme contre l'angoisse de la mort, les obsessions anciennes ravivées par la maladie, les deuils, la hantise de la page à écrire, de l'œuvre à achever* >>, in her article Zola, in **Dictionnaire des Littératures de Langue Française**, op. cit. p. 2694. Well before that, Becker mentionned that << *les hantises personnelles de l'écrivain : peur de la Femme, peur de la fêlure, des forces incontrôlées et incontrôlables qui détraquent l'homme et le conduisent à la folie, hantise de l'émiettement physique et moral, de l'engrenage et de la mort [...]* >>, p. 2693.

[851] << *Les lectures contemporaines, usant des ressources de la psychanalyse ou de l'analyse thématique, commencent à dévoiler la richesse de cette œuvre où peut se lire le combat que mène un homme pour arriver à vivre - l'affrontement courageux de ses fantasmes, une exigence de clarté, un tâtonnement vers une guérison* >>, **ibidem**, op. cit. p. 2693.

[852] Jacques Noiray puts this triumvirate which includes Jacques, Pecqueux and Lison, in relation with the home, in **Le Romancier et la Machine, I : L'Univers de Zola**, op. cit. p. 410. He adds

1889 and Jacques in 1891 - were born. Only then did Zola finally become really happy[853]. It is extremely interesting to note the double coincidence which led Zola to name his two children exactly after his heroine, Denise, of **Au Bonheur des Dames**, published in 1883, six years before the birth of his daughter, and Jacques, the namesake of Jacques Lantier, hero of **La Bête Humaine** published in 1890, a year before the birth of his son. In **L'Œuvre**, published in 1886, Claude Lantier's son was also named Jacques. One can assume that these were Zola's favourite first names that he attributed to the characters he could create instead of children of flesh he could not procreate. So, he did not hesitate to name his children after these paper beings as soon as a reverse in fortune allowed him to do so for real. It seems obvious that these are not a mere coincidence since the man Zola had given the names of the heroes born of his creative mind to the children born of his blood.

On the other hand, it must be noted that in **Pot-Bouille** - published in 1882 – the maids are harassed by their bosses. Did Zola, in turn, harass his maid, Jeanne Rozerot, just like the bourgeois in **Pot-Bouille**? If it is risky to answer this question in the affirmative, it is safe to say without fear that he committed at least adultery like them. His position as the boss was undoubtedly a factor likely to influence the young woman working at his home. It should be noted that his adultery is posterior to that of his literary characters as if the unconscious dream slipped incognito into the works preceded the reality. The property of the premonitory dream is recognised in this mark of anteriority on its satisfaction in reality. This dream once realised, Zola was filled with joy when the actual births of his children took place. To measure the impact of those happy events on the life of the author, let us refer to these remarks of the emeritus critic, Professor Henri Mitterand, who has worked hard on him and who writes: << *Il [Zola] mincit, découvre à cinquante ans les joies de la paternité, retrouve l'énergie fougueuse de sa jeunesse* >>[854].

Moreover, his young admirers of a moment, disappointed by **La Terre**, published in 1887, published against him a pamphlet known as the *Manifesto of the Five*. While browsing the pages of this document, the reader gets revealing clues about Zola's life: his shyness in front of women, his belated knowledge of the woman and his kidney disease that is supposed to have made him fear a possible impotence. For the five reactionaries to naturalism: << *Jeune, il [Zola] fut très timide, et la femme, qu'il n'a point connue à l'âge où l'on doit la connaître, le hante d'une vision évidemment fausse. Puis le trouble d'équilibre qui résulte de sa maladie rénale contribue sans doute à l'inquiéter outre mesure de*

---

that the love affair between the Lison and Jacques is very similar to Zola's marriage with Gabrielle-Alexandrine, the Lison becoming shrewish at a given moment, just like Madame Zola, before becoming a soothing mistress (p. 408), like Jeanne Rozerot.

[853] **Ibidem**, Jacques Noiray thinks that the birth of Zola's children motivates his positivism towards the end of the **Rougon-Macquart**, op. cit. p. 506.

[854] Henri Mitterand: *Notes* in **L'Argent** by Émile Zola, Paris, Gallimard. 1980, p. 511.

certaines fonctions, le pousse à grossir leur importance >>⁸⁵⁵, and before that they claim: << *Alors, tandis que certains attribuaient la chose à une maladie des bas organes de l'écrivain, à des manies de moine solitaire, les autres y voulaient voir le développement inconscient d'une boulimie de vente [,...] (le) romancier percevant que le gros de son succès d'éditions dépendait de ce que* << *les imbéciles achètent* **Les Rougon-Macquart**, *enchaînés, non pas tant par leur qualité littéraire, que par la réputation de pornographie que la vox populi y a attachée* >>⁸⁵⁶.

Despite the exaggeration of these diatribes, the fact of the kidney disease⁸⁵⁷ is proven because other biographers of Zola have confirmed it. So, I think that some of the Zolian obsessions in his fictional world find their sources in the life of the author. Even the fear of death seems closely linked to the sudden passing of his father when Zola was only seven years old. It is also true that the man was a natalist, a populist and as such, an anti-Malthusian intellectual who paid tribute to the Jews in **L'Argent** - and almost identically in **Le Docteur Pascal**⁸⁵⁸ - by writing : << *C'était toute cette poussée libre d'un peuple fort et vivace, dont l'œuvre devait conquérir le monde, ces hommes à la virilité jamais éteinte, ces femmes toujours fécondes, cette continuité entêtée et pullulante de la race* >>⁸⁵⁹, before emphasising << *la lignée nombreuse qui fait la force et qu'on défend* >>⁸⁶⁰.

Another personal myth of the author might be highlighted here. In that, fearing sexual impotency, he wanted to have a large number of offsprings to perpetuate his name through it. As for his sexual obsession, it must find its origin in the education received from his single mother in the absence of his late father, althrough the grandparents were long present at their side. The phenomenon of the perspiration of one's unconscious repressions in their works of art has been described by the psychoanalyst Sigmund Freud in these terms: << *L'artiste, comme le névrosé, s'est retiré d'une réalité insatisfaisante dans ce monde de l'imagination mais à la différence du névrosé, il savait comment retrouver le terrain solide de la réalité. Ses œuvres, comme les rêves, sont la satisfaction imaginaire de ses souhaits inconscients* >>⁸⁶¹. This sufficiently transparent passage could apply to Zola in light of the study just made here.

---

⁸⁵⁵ Marcel Girard reproduces entirely the **Manifeste des Cinq** signed by Rosny, Bonnetain, Descaves, Margueritte and Guiches, article published for the first time in **Le Figaro** on the 18th August 1887, in his *Archives de l'œuvre* in **La Terre** by Émile Zola, Paris, Garnier-Flammarion, 1973, p. 499. We can also read it in Émile Zola: **R. M. IV**, op. cit. p. 1526.

⁸⁵⁶ **Ibidem**, p. 500.

⁸⁵⁷ Henri Mitterrand, building on Edmond de Goncourt, confirms this in his *Étude* in the **R. M. III**, op. cit. p. 1606.

⁸⁵⁸ These same lines are read word for word in **Le Docteur Pascal** by Émile Zola, **R. M. V**, op. cit. p. 1079.

⁸⁵⁹ Émile Zola: **R. M. V**, op. cit. p. 1079.

⁸⁶⁰ **Ibidem**, p. 94.

⁸⁶¹ Sigmund Freud: **Trois Essais sur la Théorie de la Sexualité**, op. cit. p. 148.

Once again, this study shows that naturalism is a saga centered on sexuality, which is the mythical and the unifying theme of the whole story told in its masterpiece, **Les Rougon-Macquart.** From the notion of the character to that of space, including the myths, the metaphors and the chronotope, everything evolves around the theme of sexuality. Together, these concepts converge towards the vision of a world dominated by sex, i.e. by the reproductive process and the instinct of violence that underlies sexuality. It also lays bare the vision of a world fatally doomed to utter destruction. Also, the bet that consists in studying only one part of this naturalistic edifice could be misleading since it would fail to show the whole scope of the building. If sexuality is its cornerstone, the foundation is fatality while the different rooms are indisputably about the characters, the myths, the poetic function, the time and space in which the characters live.

Once the characters and the spatio-temporal universe to which they belong have been apprehended, it would not be superfluous to look into the question of sexuality in its fruitfulness through the works of Émile Zola. One can wonder in this precise context what are the novelties - at the artistic level - that this theme brings, especially in the renewal of fiction writing. This question once resolved, will allow the discovery of another aspect of the man Zola.

PART IV: THE FERTILITY OF THE THEMATICS OF SEXUALITY IN THE ROUGON-MACQUART

As noted above, before Zola, the theme of sexuality was not commonplace in French literature. I do not argue here that he was the first to dare introduce it in literature for authors like Baudelaire, Molière, Racine and especially the Marquis de Sade had made a case of it, to a certain extent, according to their own temperament. But I assume that Zola was assuredly the one that tackled sexuality head on. He did so very openly with all the dirt attached to it[862]. He was an innovator when he approached the problem from the specific point of view of the reproduction and the transmission of hereditary traits within a family. His originality also lies in the fact that he no longer spoke only of the beauty of the woman nor of the strength of the feelings of a sexual subject for a given sexual object. He excelled in the painting of their sexual relationship, in painting all the sexual perversions that can be found in society. Of course, one can always argue that the Marquis de Sade was a forerunner in that field, but one must consider that he was radically opposed to Zola not only because of his ideas, which had nothing to do with science, but especially because of his raw and filthy language[863]. His accounts of sexual libertinage were so off the wall with his absurd incests; his accounts of men having sex with animal and giving birth to monsters, etc. Sade told stories whose outcomes were scientifically and genetically impossible. That opposes him categorically to Émile Zola.

Naturally, as a pioneer, Zola faced a huge challenge due to the novelty of the thematics of sexuality: renewing the novel writing both at the vocabulary level and at the level of the syntactic and the narrative structures.

CHAPTER 1: SEXUALITY AND THE RENEWAL OF THE FICTION WRITING TECHNIQUES

It must be said that the theme of sexuality as treated in **Les Rougon-Macquart**, even in the literary stream that is naturalism in general, has led to a renewal of the fiction writing. I will try here to briefly summarise four major characteristics of this renewal of writing due to naturalism.

---

[862] One remembers the famous conception of the Goncourt when they said that the father pees the child while the mother shits it, in their **Journal. Mémoires de la Vie Littéraire**, volume I, op. cit. p. 78. They saw sex as a "dirty" thing in itself, and it is certainly not Zola who has attached dirt to it after all.

[863] For example, **La Philosophie dans le Boudoir** (1795) by Sade is a lesson of cruel libertinage given to a very young girl by two adult men, while in 1785, **Les 120 Journées de Sodome ou L'École du Libertinage**, already denied the existence of God, the goodness of Nature and praised everything in Nature as inherently natural, including debauchery, rape and sadistic murder, etc. In 1797, **Justine ou les Malheurs de la Vertu** banished virtue that would always be punished, while the **Histoire de Juliette** generously rewarded vice. Everywhere, the Marquis de Sade used a totally crude language unlike the language used by Zola, which is a language made of half-words, allusions and metaphors. In Sade's works, for example, men mate with animals to generate monsters with which they also sleep. Scientifically, this is certainly impossible, even absurd, since their chromosomes are so different that they could never, under any circumstances, procreate.

I. THE ALLUSION AND THE SAYINGS WITHOUT HAVING TO SPELL THINGS OUT

The allusion is understood as an insinuation, an understatement as much as the sayings without having to spell things out, that one employs without being sufficiently explicit for who has a little ability of understanding, while remaining implicit, thus comprehensible and grasping, for whoever has intelligence. Luckily, the treatment of the theme of sexuality in Zola's novels is not done in a crude way. The narrator avoids all vulgarities and does not express anything sexual without taking gloves at times. He uses the sayings without having to spell things out that have the advantage of expressing the raw reality by way of euphemisms and allusions. Therefore, it may seem paradoxical that Zola was accused of making putrid literature while in his novels the description of the sexual act itself does not exist anywhere. And what's more, when he describes the atmosphere, he uses this technique of expression to only suggest things, and never to say them. The intelligence of the reader alone allows them to grasp it completely.

So, when Renée gives in to Maxime for the very first time in **La Curée**, incest is mentioned in some two innocuous sentences: << *Et tout fut dit. Quand ils se retrouvèrent côte à côte, assis sur le divan, il balbutia, au milieu de leur malaise mutuel : - Bah ! Ça devait arriver un jour!* >>[864]. One has the clear impression that, in order not to offend his narrataries, the Zolian narrator spares them certain raw words, even certain scenes that would be too obscene for some readers. This naturally answers a need for decency on his part.

That is why even the lesbianism of Suzanne Haffner and Adeline d'Espanet is never clearly written about. It remains confined in this equivocal formula: << *Les inséparables, comme on les nommait d'un air fin* >>[865]. In the same work, Baptiste's pederasty was never rendered in the right and accurate word. It is Céleste who denounced his << *vilenies* >>[866] towards the end of the novel when she received by delegation, the power of enunciation. It also answers a concern for chastity on the part of the first narrator rather than showing their ignorance. The Zolan narrator usually shows indeed the greatest lexical precision, whether it be in slang or scholar language. This hiding of the narrator behind the rumour or behind any knowing character, is one of the innovations that Zola has brought to the romantic genre according to Halina Suwala[867]. With her, one can agree that the responsibility for the speech is thus shared between the narrator and the whole neighbourhood that conveys the rumour[868].

---

[864] Émile Zola: **R. M. I**, op. cit. pp. 456-457.
[865] **Ibidem**, p. 323.
[866] **Ibidem**, p. 591.
[867] Halina Suwala : *À propos de quelques techniques narratives du naturalisme*, **Autour de Zola et du Naturalisme**, Paris, Honoré Champion Éditeur, 1993, p. 204.
[868] According to Claude Seassau, gossip introduces a << *facteur de pittoresque et de couleur locale* >> in the realistic novel, and at the same time they show the deeply epic character of Zola's

The situation is hardly different when it comes to presenting the Charles' profession in **La Terre** where modesty also prevails over franckness. On purpose, the establishment of those brothel promoters is referred to as an << *épicerie* >> both by the Charles themselves and by the narrator so that their little girl, Élodie, raised in the convent, knows nothing about the money-making scheme of her parents and grandparents. In this logic, when at the end of the novel, heredity not betraying itself, the girl learns the truth about the job of her parents, fatally, she demands to take over from them. Everything is said in a way that has no crudity. Indeed, while the Charles strove to veil the bitter and confusing truth, Élodie lashes out: << *Je sais* >>[869]. And, to justify her firm desire to take over from her parents, she adds: << *On ne peut pas lâcher ça, c'est trop bon, ça rapporte trop ... Est-ce que ça doit sortir de la famille?* >>[870]. The double question of heredity and correctness in the language was thus resolved simultaneously in that confession by Élodie.

As mentioned above, it is striking to see that some self-righteous minds back in the time of Zola had conspired against him and accused him of sinking into << *l'immondice* >>. The accusations were all the more outrageous if one refers to the painting of the dishonourable sexual habits of Baron Gouraud for example in **La Curée** or that of Président Grandmorin in **La Bête Humaine**. The narrator was happy to use the simple words of "*honte*", of "*cochonneries*" or "*histoires qui couraient*" on their behalf, so as not to give away the sordid details of the infamy which those respectable gentlemen engaged into.

Ultimately, on this point, it should be remembered that if what the characters did was dirty and filthy, one must, however, avoid stepping over the frontiers of literature by systematically grabbing the author by the collar and start accusing him of all evils and of using sordid words where obviously, there is a clear effort of chastity on his part. I find that there were many errors of appreciation in the case of Zola[871], including coming from those who were considered to be the brightest minds at the time, such as Anatole France. The referential illusion associated with literature, which wrongly associates the fictional character with the living person, has also wrongly associated the narrator with the novelist for far too long. In extenso, some have thought that the novelist was behind each of the characters who live in their fictional narrative. A false image of Zola as the rider of a vulgar pig, had been made, like the caricature published in a Berlin newspaper[872] the day after the publication of **La Terre**.

---

works with their association with the blowing, the wind and the deadly storm, in **Émile Zola, Le Réalisme Symbolique**, op. cit. p. 188 et p. 190.

[869] Émile Zola: **R. M. IV**, op. cit. p. 787.
[870] **Ibidem**, p. 78
[871] This is also the opinion of Claude Seassau, in **Émile Zola, Le Réalisme Symbolique**, op. cit. p. 7.
[872] Marcel Girard: "*Préface*" in **La Terre** by Émile Zola, op. cit. p. 9.

In fact, Zola denounced since January 1st 1877 - in the preface of **L'Assommoir** -, << *les jugements tout faits, grotesques et odieux* >>[873]. The controversial author himself went on to sketch his own portrait that he would like us to believe was the true version of him. He stated in substance: << *Si l'on savait combien le buveur de sang, le romancier féroce, est un digne bourgeois, un homme d'étude et d'art, vivant sagement dans son coin, et dont l'unique ambition est de laisser une œuvre aussi large et aussi vivante qu'il pourra !* >>[874]. This denial of the accusations of being a novelist obsessed with garbage and horror speaks for itself!

Another characteristic of the treatment of the thematics of sexuality in Zola's **Les Rougon-Macquart** is the mise en abyme or the repetition of a narrative sequence inside another similar story.

II. THE MISE EN ABYME OR THE REPETITION

The mise en abyme is defined as the << *récit dans le récit, film dans le film, peinture représentée dans une peinture* >>, an << *œuvre montrée à l'intérieur d'une autre qui en parle, lorsque les deux systèmes signifiants sont identiques* >>[875]. This definition is quite close to mine because I mean by mise en abyme, any dramatic sequence or narrative inserted in the general narrative of the corpus when the two narratives reflect each other as if in a mirror. This mini fictional or dramatic story is then supposed to be written by an author other than Émilo Zola, while keeping a rather close link with the macro Zolian narrative. In other words, the mise en abyme works as a reflexive mirror where the first narrative comes to reflect itself, to repeat itself in the meta-narrative or second narrative, which has become embedded in it. In **Les Rougon-Macquart**, let us focus only on three very explicit mises en abyme in **La Curée** first, then in **Nana**.

La Curée offers two beautiful mises en abyme, the first of which relates to the myth of Oedipus. It is Maxime and Renée who go to the theatre and discover that the play on stage is **Phèdre** by Racine. If they come out of the theatre looking upset and disturbed, it is because they found themselves in Hippolyte for one, and in Phèdre for the other[876]. This mise en abyme had a premonitory value, the fictional text suggesting itself within itself, predicting the outcome of the

---

[873] Émile Zola: **R. M. II**, op. cit. p. 3748.
[874] **Ibidem**, p. 374.
[875] **Le Nouveau Petit Robert 1**, op. cit. p. 5.
[876] David Baguley presents Renée as an << *anti-Phèdre* >>, a Phaedra revised and corrected in a social context where tragedy can only subsist in the degraded form of the joke, in his article **La Curée** : La Bête et la Belle in **La Curée de Zola << ou la vie à outrance >>**, op. cit. p. 142.

In **Réalité et Mythe chez Zola**, Roger Ripoll believes that the fundamental difference between the female heroe in Zola's works and their Racinian counterpart lies in the fact that they are subjected to a physiological analysis, while the latter is subjected to the myths; the influence of heredity and of their environment on the former is replaced by that of the ancient fatality influencing the latter, op. cit. p. 78.

tragedy unfolding before the readers' eyes, so to speak. Philippe Hamon reckons this predictability of the fictional text as one of the criteria for recognising the realistic text whose proximity to the naturalistic text is well known. The genealogical tree and the criterion of genetic transmission contribute to this predictability of the naturalistic text in particular, and of the realistic text in general, as Hamon admits in his brilliant article *Un Discours Contraint* published in **Littérature et Réalité**[877].

The second mise en abyme covers five pages and concerns the tragedy entitled **Les Amours du Beau Narcisse et de la Nymphe Écho**, written and directed by the prefect-poet Hupel de la Noue. As if by chance, it is still Maxime and Renée who play these transparent roles. Fiction and reality meet in this way and merge to mutually repeat each other. They then vastly increase the dramatic and even the tragic intensity of their situation. If the inner audience that make up the Saccard clan do not suspect anything at that stage, the readers and spectators from outside know that Renée and Maxime live an incestuous idyll when they mime their dissatisfied love on stage. Therefore, the readers are struck by the repetition of the same storyline in different forms in the Zolian naturalist text.

Let us stop for a moment to note that the first two mises en abyme are devoted to episodes drawn from Greek mythology and that they are particularly tragic. This presupposes a tragic end awaiting the sex agents involved. The mise en abyme is to be read as a condensed signifier whose meaning must be sought in the area of strengthening the realism of the Zolian text and its predictability on the one hand, and, on the other hand, the degree of dramatisation of the narrative episodes in question[878].

The third interesting mise en abyme is the one found in **Nana** where, in the very first chapter, the heroine Nana plays her own role in the theatre, in a play titled **La Blonde Vénus**. Like her counterpart, she is blonde, beautiful and busty, a true goddess of Love, all-powerful and devastating[879]. To parallel all those physical attributes, she is as unfaithful as her referent. The narrator sets the scene from the outset in the thematic frame in which the fiction will unfold in terms of seduction and debauchery. One is thus prepared to receive all that the narrative programme inspired by the myth supposes in advance[880]. Those

---

[877] Philippe Hamon: *Un Discours Contraint* in **Littérature et Réalité**, Paris, Seuil, 1982, pp. 124-142.

[878] This predictability of the text is done naturally at the expense of the restriction of the character's field of freedom. Indeed, the character becomes a prisoner of a predetermined narrative programme and therefore of a destiny fixed in advance, as Philippe Hamon shows in his article *Pour un Statut Sémiologique du Personnage,* in **Poétique du Récit**, op. cit. p. 163.

[879] In **Réalité et Mythe chez Zola**, Roger Ripoll admits that it confers a mythical grandeur to Nana, a greatness which does not go without an extreme belittlement when Venus decomposes, op. cit. p. 77 et p. 75.

[880] See David Baguley and his **Zola et les Genres**, VI : *Nana, Roman Baroque*, op. cit. p. 66 and the article *Pour un Statut Sémiologique du Personnage,* by Philippe Hamon, mentionned above, op. cit. p. 163.

expectations will not be disappointed because this narrative programme will be fully executed to the end. Nana seduces men at will; her victims get slaughtered; she is outrageously attractive to the point where the great Gustave Flaubert[881] did not hesitate to assert that Nana turns into a myth without ceasing to be real. In fact, the fictional character played the mythical heroine so much so that she transformed herself into a new myth, or into a mythical heroine of literature at large. The mythical grandeur of Nana is undoubtedly measured on the scale of her impact on contemporary society: << [...] *la société est à la fois un immense théâtre, dévoué au spectacle du corps de Nana, un immense bordel s'adonnant à toutes sortes de promiscuités, un immense temple consacré à la religion de la sexualité de Nana* >>[882].

In total, David Baguley writes about the *malédiction du genre*[883] in Zola's novels in that they combine the natural with the cultural, the concrete with the abstract, the historical with the universal. So, a novel like **Germinal** becomes a potpourri of genres in an attractive acrostic:

>*Grotesque*
>*Epique*
>*Romanesque*
>*Mythique*
>*Idyllique*
>*Naturaliste*
>*Allégorique*
>*Lyrique*[884]

III. THE OPULENCE OF THE DISCURSIVE ANACHRONISMS

I have already addressed the issue of the discursive anachronisms in the chapter devoted to the study of the temporal compenent but it is necessary to insist here on their opulence in the Zolian novel. When one takes a novel such as **La Fortune des Rougon**, from the very first pages, the reader meets the idealistic young lovers, Silvère and Miette, on the eve of their death. The story begins practically at its very end. On the other hand, the narrator is forced to go back to chapter two to introduce Silvère's family, from the great-grandfather to his uncles, to Aunt Dide, his grandmother. This flashback thus spans almost a whopping Century while chapter three goes right back into the historic[885] present events.

---

[881] Roger Ripoll recalls what Gustave Flaubert said in his *Introduction* à **Nana** by Émile Zola, Paris, Garnier-Flammarion, 1968, p. 24
[882] David Baguley: **Zola et les Genres** : I : *La Malédiction du Genre*, op. cit. p. 67.
[883] **Ibidem**, pp. 4-9.
[884] **Ibidem**, Chapter VII : *Ge(n)rminal*, op. cit. p. 81.
[885] Maarten Van Buuren justifies the opulence of the discursive anachronisms in the corpus by the fact that 18 years of Napoléon III's reign were obviously way too insufficient to tell the story of four generations of the Rougon-Macquart family, in **Les Rougon-Macquart d'Émile Zola. De la**

To a lesser degree, I can mention chapter one of **La Curée** where Renée and Maxime go to the Bois de Boulogne, then to the ball organised by Aristide Saccard. This first chapter ends with Renée discovering her shameful love for Maxime. That sequence happens at the end of 1861 or in the beginning of the year 1862. But chapter two suspends the action there to maintain the suspense by means of a retrospective which retraces the ten previous years. Chapter Three takes that flashback much further and it is necessary to wait until chapter four to discover Renée's incestuous feelings. All those two chapters of discursive anachronisms come together in one point, namely, to insist on the culminating point of play: the incest[886]. In journalistic slang, one would speak of the ''attack'' and at the theatre, of knot or crux. It is common knowledge that Zola tried his hands at writing plays without much success before focussing on writing novels and that he was also a journalist for most of his life, with far greater success though.

It is undoubtedly the accomplished journalist in him that attacked his plots right from the exhibition chapter, or the playwright in him who exposed the crux of the matter right from the beginning. Later on, of course, he would have to go back to the particular circumstances in which the drama is set and unfolds and unravels. This technique has the advantage of inciting the interest of the reader and keeping them glued to the story. It also allows the reader to better understand the main drama through this semblance of erudition of the narrator who, suddenly, knows everything about the past of their characters, their mind and their psyche, even their entire lineage. The technique of discursive anachronisms also makes it possible to intimately link the phatic and the metalinguistic functions. It baits the readers and keeps them on edge by forcing them to refer to very old mythical episodes that are indispensable supports to the fictional narrative they are about to read[887]. Anothther characteristic of the naturalist novel, and not the least, is the preponderance of details as Zola meant when he wrote with lyricism to his friend, Henry Céard: << *J'ai l'hypertrophie du détail vrai, le saut dans les étoiles sur le tremplin de l'observation exacte* >>[888].

IV. THE HYPERTROPHY OF TRUE DETAIL

Métaphore au Mythe, op. cit. p. 14. Discursive anachronisms were therefore essential to Zola, especially for reasons of verisimilitude and realism.

[886] Claude Seassau writes that the organisation of Zola's novels shows his strong will to give them << *structure signifiante* >>, in **Émile Zola, Le Réalisme Symbolique**, op. cit. p. 317.

[887] **Ibidem**, Seassau reckons that Zola's writing is certainly an << *écriture surmodalisée* >>, which does not go without its paradox since the most distorting mirror that is the myth serves to make the romanesque text more readable, more transparent, op. cit. p. 318 and pp. 428-429.

[888] Émile Zola: **Correspondances, tome V : 1884-1886**, Édition Bakker, Becker, H. Mitterand, D. Morgan, A. Pagès, Presses de l'université de Montréal, édition du CNRS, 1985, p. 249.

One of Zola's reproaches to Stendhal was that he had missed a great opportunity and undermined a large romantic scene in **Le Rouge et Le Noir**. Stendhal had merely conjured up in a few banal phrases the hands of Julien Sorel and Mme de Renal touching each other, with tacit complicity[889]. For Zola, such a scene, in a naturalistic novel, would have had another colour and tone: << *Donnez l'épisode à un écrivain pour qui les milieux existent, et dans la défaite de cette femme, il fera entrer la nuit, avec ses odeurs, avec ses voix, avec ses voluptés molles. Et cet écrivain sera dans la vérité, son tableau sera plus complet* >>[890].

What is important to the naturalistic novelist is not so much the narration of the facts, but especially the necessity to insist on the background, the outlines and the details pushed to hypertrophy. The true detail is about nothing at all at face value; it is this useless usefulness that embellishes the fiction; that salt that enhances the literary sauce i.e. the events, without which everything becomes bland. Zola was an emeritus descriptor, a quality that no one dared to deny him until now. Certainly, some could say that his details added to the horror of his literature, which Zola does not dispute a priori: << *Sans doute, il peut y avoir abus, dans la description surtout ; la virtuosité emporte souvent les rhétoriciens ; on lutte avec les peintres, pour montrer la souplesse et l'éclat de sa phrase. Mais cet abus n'empêche pas que l'indication nette et précise des milieux et de l'étude de leur influence sur les personnages, ne soient des nécessités scientifiques du roman contemporain* >>[891].

The true detail is also about painting accurately the time and space in which the story unfolds. The chronotope acts indeed more or less directly on the anthropomorphic figure in all works of fiction. It is also gathers a far more important proportion as the narrative progresses. Jean-François Tonard does not hesitate to argue that with Zola, the literary space has taken on a greater significance by participating in the general march of the narrative[892]. However, the hypertrophy of the true detail is not only directed to space alone since the character also benefits from it. As Philippe Hamon writes, the major originality of the Zolian text lies in << *le système des personnages* >>[893]. Hamon believes that the Zolian protagonist is characterised by an << *hypertrophie de la*

---

[889] Émile Zola: study on *Stendhal*, published for the first time in **Le Messager de l'Europe** in Mai 1880, and then in **Les Romanciers Naturalistes** in 1881 and again in **Le Roman Naturaliste**, edited by Henri Mitterand, op. cit. p. 49.
[890] **Ibidem**, p. 49.
[891] Émile Zola: study on *Stendhal*, in **Le Messager de l'Europe,** Mai 1880, and then in **Les Romanciers Naturalistes** in 1881 and in **Le Roman Naturaliste**, edited by Henri Mitterand, op. cit. p. 48.

For Jean Kaempfer, Zola's naturalism is a << *vérité virile et brutale* >>, in **D'Un Naturalisme Pervers ; L'Esthétique de Zola**, op. cit. p. 241.
[892] Jean-François Tonard: **Thématique et Symbolique de l'Espace Clos dans le Cycle des Rougon-Macquart d'Émile Zola**, op. cit. p. 2.
[893] Philippe Hamon: **Le Personnel du Roman. Le Système des Personnages dans Les Rougon-Macquart d'Émile Zola**, op. cit. p. 313.

circulation de l'information >>. He goes on to admit that his fictional character is a << *personnage délégué* >>, and also << *un personnage motive* >>[894], unlike its Balzacian counterpart that the narrator is obliged to comment on to make them known. The huge advantage regarding the character in Zola's works seems to be his ''*lisibilité*'' according to Hamon : << *Le personnage zolien, posons-le ici tout de suite, sera un personnage lisible et délégué à la lisibilité [...]. Lieu et objet d'une lisibilité, il sera aussi sujet et opérateur de lisibilité* >>[895].

This hypertrophy of the true detail, sometimes, leads Zola to write very long sentences that contains many asyndetes. This form of expression is especially suited to the free indirect speech. In **Pot-Bouille**, free indirect speech[896] allows for example the narrator to paint, through the thought of the character of Madame Vuillaume: << *Les portes fermées, les fenêtres closes, jamais de courants d'air, qui apportent les vilaines choses de la rue* >>[897]. In **La Curée**, one can refer to the moment when incest is committed for the very first time between Maxime and Renée. The narrator writes: << *Ce fut le seul murmure de ses lèvres* [of Renée]. *Dans ce grand silence du cabinet, où le gaz flambait plus haut, elle sentit le sol trembler et entendit le fracas de l'omnibus des Batignolles qui devait tourner le coin du boulevard. Et tout fut dit* >>[898]. While the incestuous sexual act is rendered in one short sentence << *Et tout fut dit* >>,[899] the general atmosphere in the cabinet and outside that space is studied in great detail. These opulent descriptions prolong the sexual act and push its roots and tentacles deep into the surrounding environment, both near and far. This is a clear sign of the interdependence between the character and their spatio-temporal environment. Indeed, when Zola evokes the hereditary phenomena, he uses practically the same technique, like in **L'Œuvre** where he presents the Margaillan in the following way: << *le père, gros, apoplectique* >> and << *la mère, d'une maigreur de couteau* >>, all things that results in << *une fille réduite à rien, déplumée comme un oiseau malade* >> and together, << *tous les trois laids et pauvres du sang vicié de leur race, ils étaient une honte, en pleine vie de la terre, sous le grand soleil* >>[900].

---

[894] Philippe Hamon: **Le Personnel du Roman. Le Système des Personnages dans Les Rougon-Macquart d'Émile Zola**, op. cit. pp. 103-105.

[895] **Ibidem**, p. 38.

[896] Halina Suwala speaks of the narrator's deletion in the free indirect speech and the ambiguity of the resulting point of view. See *À propos de quelques techniques narratives du naturalisme* in **Autour de Zola et du Naturalisme**, op. cit. p. 207.

[897] Émile Zola: **R. M. III**, op. cit. p. 66.

[898] Émile Zola: **R. M. I**, op. cit. p. 456.

[899] Jean Kaempfer: << *le style est maintenant un effet automatique, et premier, en lui se recueille le double (et fort zolien au demeurant) déterminisme d'une hérédité et d'un milieu : Zola n'est pas exceptable des lois qui régissent ses créatures ; il apporte son style comme d'autres leur alcoolisme, - et n'y peut rien* >>, in **D'Un Naturalisme Pervers : L'Esthétique de Zola**, op. cit. 169.

[900] Émile Zola: **R. M. IV**, op. cit. p. 151.

Continuing along that path, the narrator makes the following description of Les Halles de Paris which << *apparurent comme une machine moderne, hors de toute mesure, quelque machine à vapeur, quelque chaudière destinée à la digestion d'un peuple, gigantesque ventre de métal, boulonné, rêvé, fait de bois, de verre et de fonte, d'une élégance et d'une puissance de moteur mécanique, fonctionnant là, avec la chaleur du chauffage, l'étourdissement, le branle furieux des roues* >>[901].

In summary, the hypertrophy of the true detail gives the impression that the naturalist writer is a visionary, a hallucinist who sees the supernatural beyond the natural; the chimerical and the extravagant beyond the visible reality[902]. The descriptions of the Voreux in **Germinal** or that of the hysterical crowds in that novel confirm this assessment[903]. Are there not already the premises of a limited naturalism[904]? Or can the verb claim to reproduce nature[905] with exactitude?

---

[901] Émile Zola: **R. M. I**, op. cit. p. 626.
Claude Seassau rightly asserts that Zola dismounts, shows and demonstrates things in his narration, whereas the realist writers are content to reproduce the similarities, see **Émile Zola, Le Réalisme Symbolique**, op. cit. p. 276.

[902] Claude Seassau writes: << *La prégnance du symbolique est d'autant plus puissante que Zola transfigure spontanément le réel en symboles, la réalité en images surnaturelles* >>, **ibidem**, op. cit. p. 320.
In the same vein, Jean Kaempfer notes: << *Mais alors que la poétique sur le versant de la nature prescrivait, en ce point, que le romancier s'en tînt scrupuleusement aux faits observés et disparût, gardant* << *pour lui ses émotions* >>, *la poétique du tempérament enjoint à une véritable transformation émotive du réel* >>, in **D'Un Naturalisme Pervers : L'Esthétique de Zola**, op. cit. p. 213.

[903] Jacques Noiray studies the fantastic and the surnatural appearance of the Voreux and many more machines in **Le Romancier et la Machine, I : L'Univers de Zola**, op. cit. pp. 297-298. For that reason, Zola is, therefore, supposed to put himself in the shoes of a visionary rather than in that of a naturalist.

[904] Jean Kaempfer is more categorical on that point since he admits that naturalism does not exist and that naturalist theory is a usurpation, see the book above, op. cit. pp. 162-163.
Claude Seassau is more nuanced when he notes that naturalism is an effect of reality, an illusionism and that there is indeed a hiatus between naturalist theory and practice, which would justify the difference between **Le Roman Expérimental** and the novels of Zola, in the above book, op. cit. p. 274 et p. 276.

[905] Jean Kaempfer postulates that: << *Le style marque la limite infranchissable du rêve de transparence naturaliste* >>, in the above book, p. 168.

CHAPTER II: ZOLA AND NATURALISM

In this chapter, I shall try to write Zola's autobiography on the one hand, and on the other hand, to criticise him. It is therefore a question of presenting both sides of the famous writer that he was and that he still is to this day: an author that was jeered as loudly as he was applauded. Zola was indeed the epitome of the controversial novelist as he was applauded and hailed with respect by some of his contemporaries as well as by critics of our time. However, he was also wildly vilipended and dragged through the mud by many in his time. I will therefore try to raise the ambivalence of his personality before being able to offer my own assessment of his quality as a novelist and as a literary mind.

I. THE AUTOBIOGRAPHY OF ZOLA: AN AUTHOR OBSESSED WITH SEXUALITY

This part will take a look at the natalist writer that Zola was. It will then insist on his quality as a *"forçat"* of literature to which he devoted his whole life as to a worshipped mistress[906], without respite. Finally, the theoretician of heredity will interest me to the extent that, without this element, the genesis, the writing and the publication of the **Rougon-Macquart** series would have been simply impossible. Finally, what was Zola's ideology when opposing the Second Empire so vehemently and without any concessions? And why such an obsession with human reproduction[907] in his fictional works?

1.1. The natalist? Certainly, but a socialist?

It was **Germinal**'s fault if people labelled Zola a *''socialist''*. The certain sympathy of the narrator for the miners of Montsou largely contributed to that assessment of the writer in the general opinion. People thought that because the narrator had sympathy for those starving families grappling with greedy fat cat employers, the writer himself was surely a socialist, standing shoulder to shoulder with the poor. Yet, as Madeleine Rebérioux affirms: << *Certes, pour aucun critique socialiste, Zola n'est devenu socialiste* >>[908]. Roger Ripoll espouses this thesis by saying that for Zola: << *Tout comme l'espérance religieuse, l'espérance socialiste est une illusion pathétique, et seulement une illusion* >>[909]. Maarten Van Buuren goes in that same direction in these

---

[906] Maarten Van Buuren finds that Zola and Dr. Pascal have an identical activity, one cloistered by writing and the other cloistered by science, see **Les Rougon-Macquart d'Émile Zola. De la Métaphore au Mythe**, op. cit. p. 161 et p. 158.

[907] David Baguley indicates that the themes of heredity and sexuality constitute a myth in the **Rougon-Macquart** : << *Zola, in typical fashion, mythologized this process in the* **Rougon-Macquart** *series, endowed it with an obscure mythical past conveyed across the generations in the tainted blood of his accursed fictional family* >>, in **Naturalist Fiction. The Entropic Vision**, op. cit. p. 208.

[908] Madeleine Rebérioux: *Zola et la critique littéraire française socialiste et anarchiste ; 1894-1902* in **Europe : Zola**, op. cit. p. 12.

[909] Roger Ripoll: **Réalité et Mythe chez Zola**, volume II, op. cit. p. 733.

unequivocal terms: << *L'attitude critique de Zola vis-à-vis du socialisme est suffisamment connue [...]. Les métaphores reflètent ce scepticisme ; elles comparent le socialisme naissant à la première église chrétienne, ses adhérents aux premiers chrétiens, enthousiasmés par le rêve d'un monde meilleur, animés d'une ferveur apostolique* >>[910].

Henri Guillemin also notes that Floquet had violently attacked, in November 1879, **L'Assommoir**, which he saw only as a ridiculous pamphlet against the worker class[911]. It would take six more years after that novel before Zola was really appreciated in socialist circles: << *Avec* **Germinal**, *et quelles que soient les réserves, c'est le triomphe. Clavis Hugues y décèle pour la première fois la défaite de la charité et l'appel impérieux de la justice sociale [...]. De toutes parts la presse socialiste, provinciale, étrangère, demande à Zola l'autorisation de reproduire en feuilleton le roman. Et Zola de répondre au* **Peuple** *de Bruxelles, le 15 novembre 1885 :* << *Prenez* **Germinal** *et reproduisez-le. Je ne vous demande rien, puisque votre journal est pauvre et que vous défendez les misérables* >>>>[912].

However, that honeymoon between the author and the socialist critics was short-lived, or more exactly dotted with more or less important breaks. So, << *En lisant* **Fécondité** *en feuilleton, écrit Péguy, nous* [the socialists] *avions formé* << *le secret espoir [...] que Mathieu deviendrait socialiste* >>. *Espoir déçu : Mathieu devient patron, et son fils Nicolas, colon. Zola reste* << *indifférent au salariat, comme l'Évangile de Jésus fut indifférent à l'esclavage* >>>>[913]. Moreover, there is no doubt that the left unanimously gathered at the funeral of the writer on October 5th, 1902, to pay tribute to the immense writer that he was.

Finally, one must share the caution of Paul Lidsky for whom: << *On a trop souvent classé Zola parmi les écrivains républicains avancés, sinon les socialistes [...]. Au contraire, il semble bien que le républicanisme de Zola soit avant tout* << *raisonnable et pondéré* >>, *se refusant à toute violence, à toute transformation brutale et révolutionnaire de la société. Zola manifeste constamment une profonde méfiance vis-à-vis des socialistes et de ce qu'il appelle à travers tous ses livres les* << *exaltés* >>>>[914]. To justify his skepticism about Zola's socialism, Lidsky recalls that novels like **Germinal**, **La Terre**, and **La Débâcle**, << *portent une condamnation du socialisme, à travers le portrait du mauvais ouvrier,*

---

[910] Maarten Van Buuren: **Les Rougon-Macquart d'Émile Zola. De la Métaphore au Mythe**, op. cit. p. 159.
[911] Henri Guillemin: **Présentation des Rougon-Macquart**, Paris, Gallimard, 1964, p. 139.
[912] Madeleine Rebérioux: *Zola et la critique littéraire française socialiste et anarchiste ; 1894-1902*, in **Europe : Zola**, no. 468-68, op. cit. pp. 8-9.
[913] **Ibidem**, p. 12 (the author quoted the article of Péguy titled *Les récentes œuvres de Zola* published in **Le Mouvement Socialiste** in November 1899).
[914] Paul Lidsky: **Les Écrivains contre la Commune**, Paris, François Maspero, 1982, p. 121.

socialiste par ambition ou par rancune, qui a toujours mal digéré les bouts de lecture hétéroclites qu'il a pu absorber >>[915].

It is certain in any case that Zola fought for the emergence of a fairer and a more humanistic society. That is why, deeply shocked by the scandalous riches amassed by a handful of men perfectly integrated into the system set up by Napoléon III, Zola decided to write **Les Rougon-Macquart** as the << *Histoire naturelle et sociale d'une famille sous le Second Empire* >>. The satirical value of this novelistic cycle is well established. Zola painted a striking picture of the entire contemporary French society in its diversity. So, the reader finds in it the work of market gardeners, that of the merchants and the poachers in **La Fortune des Rougon**, while the world of high finance is visited in **L'Argent** and that of luxury prostitutes is put under the spotlight in **Nana**. The world of the highest political spheres is not forgotten either because it is the subject of **Son Excellence Eugène Rougon**. The soldiers of the Franco-Prussian war and the Communards square up in **La Débâcle**, while the workers, the main victims of the industrial progress, are **Germinal**'s heroes. In **L'Assommoir**, it is rather the private sector workers such as the carpenters, the welders, the laundresses and other entrepreneurs of the informal sector such as the innkeepers that are the heroes of that first masterpiece of his. Some of Zola's contemporaries have lashed out at the dark side of that novel and especially when it comes to the written language used by the author in it. Yet, defending himself on that point, Zola wrote: << *Mon crime est d'avoir eu la curiosité littéraire de ramasser et de couler dans un moule très travaillé la langue du peuple. Ah ! la forme, là est le grand crime ! [...].*
Je ne me défends pas, d'ailleurs. Mon œuvre me défendra. C'est une œuvre de vérité, le premier roman sur le peuple, qui ne mente pas et qui ait l'odeur du peuple >>[916].

Defending himself against the accusers who claimed to see garbage in the novel, Zola protested and claimed his honesty instead, claiming he could not paint anything but reality, i.e. he could not have settled for a truncated and romanticised image of that reality. In the same preface, he had to specify: << *Est-il bien nécessaire d'expliquer ici, en quelques lignes, mes intentions d'écrivain ? J'ai voulu peindre la déchéance fatale d'une famille ouvrière, dans le milieu empesté de nos faubourgs. Il y a un relâchement des liens de la famille, les ordures de la promiscuité, l'oubli progressif des sentiments honnêtes, puis comme dénouement, la honte et la mort, c'est de la morale en action, tout simplement.* **L'Assommoir** *est à coup sûr le plus chaste de mes livres* >>[917].

---

[915] Paul Lidsky: **Les Écrivains contre la Commune**, op. cit. p. 120.
[916] Émile Zola: *Préface* of **L'Assommoir**, 1st January 1877, **R. M. II**, op. cit. pp. 373-374.
[917] **Ibidem.** p. 374.

It is a known fact that Flaubert had advised him not to expand on his intentions as a writer in his prefaces, not to reveal his secrets as a writer in them, but the polemicist in Zola could not remain silent in the face of the attacks of which he and his works were victims. It is for that reason that in the preface to the second edition of **L'Assommoir**, he strove to demonstrate the morality of his novel: to defend the poor that lived in the slums because they were deprived of any bite in the imperial cake. He also denounced the few - the greedy fat cats and the hunting dogs like Aristide Saccard - that ate up all the preys while the many spent their time in the cabarets, vainly seeking the solution to their multiple existential problems in the depths of the bottles of alcohol, like Gervaise and her husband, Coupeau, or Joséphine Gavaudan in **La Fortune des Rougon**. For Zola, no one can drown their problems in alcoholic drinks.

In a letter dated February 13th, 1877, addressed to the Director of **Le Bien Public**, Zola drew in a single sentence the conclusion to his controversial novel: << *Si l'on voulait me forcer absolument à conclure, je dirais que tout L'Assommoir peut se résumer dans cette phrase : fermez les cabarets, ouvrez des écoles* >>[918]. It cannot be denied in good faith, in the light of that declaration of intent, that the author was fighting for a society better educated and more emancipated, and consequently, a society less focused on drunkenness[919] and ignorance.

Considering that Napoléon III had broken the social fabric of France, the truth and honesty, Zola posed as the spokesman for the people in the newspapers first, from 1868, and in his novels from 1869- 70. How not see in **Germinal** his almost admiration - albeit nuanced - for someone like Étienne Lantier, a self-declared unionist, or for someone like Souvarine, the nihilist who dreams of sweeping a vicious and an unjust world in the hope that another world would blossom; a brave new world, reviewed and corrected, which would bear none of the previous faults and inequalities that marred the former? Likewise, at the explicit of **La Débâcle**, there is << *toute une France à refaire* >>[920]. Long before the explicit, the hidden god who had access to the conscience of the hero, Jean Macquart, saw well << *le grand rêve noir qu'il avait fait, cette grandiose et monstrueuse conception de la vieille société détruite, de Paris brûlé, du champ retourné et purifié, pour qu'il poussât l'idylle d'un nouvel âge d'or* >>[921].

That same hope almost always exists at the end of all his novels, especially in **Germinal**, where although the miners' strike ended in failure, it is still perceived

---

[918] Émile Zola: **Correspondance, II, 1868-mai 1877**, Édition Bakker, Becker, H. Mitterand, Presses de l'université de Montréal, Éditions du CNRS, 1980, p. 537.
[919] Claude Seassau classifies the characters of **L'Assommoir** into two distinct groups: the drunkards and the non-drunkards; the latter being the domestic or familiar animals, and the former being the wild or low animals and the raw beasts, see **Émile Zola, Le Réalisme Symbolique**, op. cit. p. 55.
[920] Émile Zola: **R. M. V**, op. cit. p. 912.
[921] **Ibidem**, p. 911.

as a seed that was sown, which will germinate because << *Des hommes poussaient, une armée noire, vengeresse, qui germait lentement dans les sillons, grandissant pour les récoltes du siècle futur, et dont la germination allait faire bientôt éclater la terre* >>[922].

Those nihilistic tendencies, however, did not prevent Zola from being a natalist. Exasperated by the infertility of his wife, he praised love, reproduction and the large family such as the Gundermann family in **L'Argent**. The Natalist in Zola swarmed, probably unconsciously, the chosen words of *"féconde"*, *"fécondité"*, *"virilité"*, *"semence"* and *"enceinte"* in his many novels. He who only experienvced four years before the end of the publication of the **Rougon-Macquart** the joy of being a father. One can probably understand his frustration due to the hazards of nature that denied him for nearly fifty years, such a simple and candid joy. For someone like him, the naturalist in chief[923], it must have been sheer torture ! Does not this, in a certain sense, excuse his infidelities to his wife, Gabrielle-Alexandrine, for the purpose of procreating, with Jeanne Rozerot, Denise and Jacques, the beings of flesh and bones[924]?

The Zolian narrator writes, not without lyricism, in **Le Docteur Pascal**, in a redundant way: << *Aucun don ne peut égaler celui de la femme jeune qui se donne, et qui donne le flot de vie, l'enfant peut-être* >>[925]. At the time he wrote that novel, between 1892 and 1893, Zola was between fifty-two and fifty-three years old. For a little over four years, he had been having an affair with Jeanne Rozerot as Gérard Gengembre asserts: << *En effet, en 1888, Zola rencontre Jeanne Rozerot, une jeune lingère qui lui donnera deux enfants et qui métamorphosera sa vie, une femme en qui s'incarne des êtres de fiction où le romancier avait fixé tel ou tel de ses fantasmes et qui devient à son tour modèle pour la fiction. Il suffit de citer la dédicace manuscrite privée écrite pour cette seconde épouse pour se convaincre du rapport intime qui existe entre la vie et le roman* >>[926]. Gengembre then refers to Henri Mitterand who reproduced this dedication in the volume V of the **Rougon-Macquart** in the Pléiade edition: << *À ma bien-aimée Jeanne, - à ma Clotilde, qui m'a donné le royal festin de sa jeunesse et qui m'a rendu mes trente ans, en me faisant le cadeau de ma Denise et de mon Jacques, les deux chers enfants pour qui j'ai écrit ce livre, afin qu'ils sachent, en le lisant un jour, combien j'ai adoré leur mère et de quelle*

---

[922] Émile Zola: **R. M. III**, op. cit. p. 1591.
[923] Jacques Noiray believes that if Zola went from the mythology of the catastrophe - due to his despair around 1880, which is reflected in the first novels of the corpus - to reach the mythology of regulation in the last novels of the cycle, this is due to the birth of his children, the source of his late positivism, in **Le Romancier et la Machine, I : L'Univers de Zola**, op. cit. pp. 506-508.
[924] Jean Kaempfer admits that the love of life is Zola's most constant obsession in **D'Un Naturalisme Pervers: L'Esthétique de Zola**, op. cit. p. 237.
[925] Émile Zola: **R. M. V**, op. cit. p. 1130.
[926] Gérard Gengembre: *"Préface"* of **Le Docteur Pascal** by Émile Zola, op. cit. p. 11.

respectueuse tendresse ils devront lui payer plus tard le bonheur dont elle m'a consolé dans mes grands chagrins >>>>[927].

This direct assimilation of Jeanne Rozerot to Clotilde Rougon is neither isolated nor fortuitous. It is part of a larger entrenchment of the fictional into the real world. Not only Dr. Pascal is Zola's spokesperson[928] in this last novel of the cycle, in the sense that he lends him his own character and his own scientific convictions, especially as regards to the theory of heredity, but in addition, he entrusts him with the elaboration and the explanation of the genealogical tree of the Rougon-Macquart[929]. Also, Pascal summarises before Clotilde, and for the readers, all the saga of the **Rougon-Macquart**. Gengembre pointed out that even << *la chaîne aux sept perles offerte par le docteur à Clotilde [...] est la réplique d'un bijou offert par Zola à Jeanne* >>[930]. Fiction thus catches up with reality.

However, analogy is not identity. If one believes Marcel Girard, << *elle* [Jeanne] *devient la maîtresse de Zola en décembre* [1888] >>[931] while Zola is almost forty-nine years old. Pascal is fifty-nine when he begins his affair with Clotilde. The fictional narrative is also clearly distinguishable from reality when the myth invades it, the biblical myth of the old King David and the young Sunamite, Abisaig, then that of Booz and Ruth[932], who come in to pardon the incestuous relationship between the uncle and the niece. Those mythical episodes absolve their sin in Zola's narrative and redeem their offspring, the unkown child that is born without the slightest trace of the hereditary crack.

Moreover, if Zola was excited in 1893 due to the birth of his two dear children, if he was so happy in the dedication to Jeanne mentioned above, it is noteworthy that that text was the complete reversal of what Zola wrote back in 1871 against the decree of the Commune that was taken in favour of all natural children throughout France. Posing as a moraliser, he wrote harshly in **Le Sémaphore de Marseille**, on the 26th May 1871: << *Ceci est du plus haut comique, et l'on croirait que ces messieurs ont semé des bâtards dans leur jeunesse, à ce point qu'ils chargent la patrie de donner une mère à leur nombreuse famille* >>[933]. It is true that at that time, Zola was not yet haunted by sterility or impotence. He was a young man back then, aged thirty-one and he was very much looking forward to fathering children of his own with his wife. It took time for him to realise that his relationship with Gabrielle-Alexandrine would remain barren for

---

[927] Henri Mitterrand quotes this handwritten dedication of the copy of **Le Docteur Pascal** offered by Zola to Jeanne Rozerot on June 20th, 1893, in the **R. M. V**, op. cit. p. 1573.
[928] Maarten van Buuren argues that Dr. Pascal is the most reliable spokesperson for Zola in the **Les Rougon-Macquart d'Émile Zola. De la Métaphore au Mythe**, op. cit. p. 25.
[929] **Ibidem**, Maarten Van Buuren emphasises the assimilation of the family tree to a holy relic, p. 159.
[930] Gérard Gengembre: "*Préface*" in **Le Docteur Pascal** by Émile Zola, op. cit. p. 11.
[931] Marcel Girard: "*Chronologie*" in **La Terre** de Zola, op. cit. p. 7.
[932] Émile Zola: **R. M. V**, op. cit. pp. 1078-1079
[933] Zola quoted by Paul Lidsky in **Les Écrivains contre la Commune**, op. cit. p. 70.

ever, and that the only alternatives available to him were to either father his own bastards or to adopt children. When old age threatened him with the prospect of dying without children that could perpetuate his name, he probably shared Pascal's dream about a child:<< *Oui, l'œuvre rêvée, la seule vraie et bonne, l'œuvre que je n'ai pu faire* >>[934]. As a writer, he probably had also blamed, like the researcher Pascal, << *Ces froides pages de manuscrits, auxquelles il avait sacrifié la femme* >>[935].

In any case, it seems normal that sexuality takes such a prominent place in Zola's work because of his ideological conception of natality. In fact, any society requires more than one individual, and for a society to survive and sustain itself, there are hardly thirty-six solutions. It is necessary for the individuals who compose it to have sexual intercourse in order to multiply themselves like the characters of the **Rougon-Macquart** did. From this basic point of view, sexuality is not a derisory and/or an ignominious paraphernalia in Zola's fiction. On the contrary, one must recognise the importance of sexuality in society and even in Nature at large.

With Zola, it is therefore a return to normal for this theme that has remained taboo for centuries, even for millennia, for pseudo-ethical[936] reasons. Too often, prude minds have stirred clearly away from all debates about sexuality as if man refused to look at this reality of our daily existence. But humanity would be better off facing it with courage, to analyse and explain it. Such an approach, however, was reserved solely to the very few scholars i.e. researchers, biologists and psychoanalysts. Well, Zola refused to align himself to this conformism and tackled the problem head on, in defiance of the jeers of his contemporaries. That is why he fully deserves the homage paid to him nowadays. Zola got to the heart of the problem of sexuality to observe its causes, to analyse its manifestations in their most austere truths and to describe its effects. In doing so, the writer wanted to lay down all his findings in the public domain so that everyone could be educated on this matter.

Although he was a moderate Republican and a loyal natalist, Zola was also an anti-communist militant.

1.2. Zola: The anti-communard

The defeat of the French armies in Sedan brought about the fall of the Second Empire and the beginning of the Third Republic, which settled in a bloodbath

---

[934] Émile Zola: **R. M. V**, op. cit. p. 1154.
[935] **Ibidem**, p. 1158.
[936] Let us remember that the Marquis de Sade spent decades in French jails because of his debauchery and that his works have long remained, if not unknown, at least poorly recognised because they were met with silence, and were sometimes printed very late.

that historians have called << *la semaine sanglante du 21 au 28 mai 1871* >>[937]. Thiers, the future president-elect and his followers - the Field Marshall de Mac-Mahon and his thirty thousand soldiers - undertook to reconquer Paris then held by a government dominated by the Socialists, known as **La Commune**. They mercilessly crushed the Communards' rebellion of twenty thousand Parisian insurgents[938]. The authors Bouillon, Sohn and Brunel mentioned the figure of about thirty thousand victims, not to mention the forty-seven thousand trials that took place up until 1875. Still according to them, magistrates, clergymen, women, old men and even children were murdered at the same time[939].

Oddly enough though, Zola applauded this collective massacre of the communards in **Le Sémaphore de Marseille** on the 8th June 1871: << *Le bain de sang qu'il* [le peuple de Paris] *vient de prendre était peut-être d'une horrible nécessité pour calmer certaines de ses fièvres. Vous le verrez maintenant grandir en sagesse et en splendeur* >>[940]. Twenty-one years later, he almost repeated word for word the same idea in **La Débâcle**: << *Mais le bain de sang était nécessaire, et de sang français, l'abominable holocauste, le sacrifice vivant, au milieu du feu purificateur [...] la nation crucifiée expiait ses fautes et allait renaître* >>[941].

For Zola, La Commune had no real political meaning. On the contrary, for him, it was designed to redeem and to avenge the shame of a clique of bandits. That was indeed the way it looked in the perspective of the hero of **La Débâcle**, Maurice Levasseur, as the narrator wrote: << *La Commune lui apparaissait comme une vengeresse des hontes endurées, comme une libératrice apportant le feu qui ampute, le feu qui purifie* >>[942]. From the beginning of the novel, the narrator had gone to great length to present Maurice Levasseur[943] as having committed << *de grandes fautes, toute une dissipation de tempérament faible et exalté, de l'argent qu'il avait jeté au jeu, aux femmes, aux sottises de Paris dévorateur, lorsqu'il y était venu terminer son droit et que sa famille s'était saignée, pour faire de lui un monsieur* >>[944].

The critic Roger Ripoll went further, in the magazine **Europe** from April to May 1968, stating that: << *[...] pour le Zola qui prépare* **Germinal**, *il n'y a pas de différence entre un communard et un criminel* >>[945]. Strikingly, Paul Lidsky sums up the situation by arguing about the three successful novels that were

---

[937] Bonin-Kerdon, Burlot, Nonjon, Nouschi and Sussel: **Histoire: Héritages Européens**, Paris, Hachette, 1981, p. 252.
[938] **Ibidem, p. 252.**
[939] Bouillon, Sohn and Brunel : **1848-1914 : Histoire**, Paris, Bordas, 1978, p. 170.
[940] Zola quoted by Paul Lidsky in **Les Écrivains contre La Commune**, op. cit. p. 52.
[941] Émile Zola: **R. M. V**, op. cit. p. 907.
[942] Émile Zola: **R. M. V**, op. cit., p. 874.
[943] Maurice represents << *la France déréglée* >>, according to the word of Maarten Van Buuren, in **Les Rougon-Macquart d'Émile Zola. De la Métaphore au Mythe**, op. cit. p. 185.
[944] Émile Zola: **R. M. V,** op. cit. p. 405.
[945] Roger Ripoll: *Zola et les Communards* in **Europe : Zola**, op. cit. p. 23.

Germinal, **La Terre** and **La Débâcle**, that : << *Tous ces livres marquent la même condamnation de la Commune, dont Zola n'a jamais compris la signification sociale* >>[946]. In fact, for Roger Ripoll, << *Zola n'a jamais été favorable à la Commune, et il ne pouvait en être autrement* >>[947]. His opposition the La Commune[948] seems to have led him to a shallow study of the Communards in **La Débâcle**, as Ripoll put it so well : << *Prisonnier d'un schéma fixé à l'avance, il [Zola] n'a pu analyser les antagonismes réels et étudier les hommes. Le roman sur les Communards, projeté dès 1872, n'a jamais été écrit* >>[949].

In any case, his opposition to La Commune did not alter his will to contribute to national reconciliation by demanding an amnesty for the Communards, from October to November 1871, in place of the heavy sentences that they were handed down to them: << *Si la punition ne doit pas être trop sévère, c'est parce que la Commune a été une folie collective. Pour Zola, les Communards sont des inconscients. Les chefs, fous inoffensifs, ont été poussés au crime par la masse qu'ils avaient déchaînée ; les combattants se sont engagés dans la lutte sans savoir pourquoi* >>.[950]

More generally, Zola has always engaged in a Herculean struggle for the establishment of a fairer society and a more prosperous one. To achieve this, he had a creed: hard work.

1.3. The workaholic or work seen like a libido

It is well known that the author of the **Rougon-Macquart** was a tireless worker. Here is a series of twenty novels of about eight thousand pages and two thousand anthropomorphic characters, published in twenty-three years - 1870-1893. On average, that works out at the rhythm of a novel every fifteen months and six days. All his biographers agree on one point: that Zola produced on average four pages of fiction per day, and this in parallel with his no less assiduous work as a journalist and essayist, a lecturer and a photographer. At the same time, he was collaborating with directors to bring his novels to the stage at various theatres. Zola was also a prolific correspondent because, according to his **Œuvres Complètes** gathered and edited under the direction of he late Professor Henri Mitterand, we owe him at least twenty thousand letters addressed to various correspondents on various subject matters. It is established that he hardly went out and spent all his time writing as he devoted up to ten hours a day to his writing activity. For this very reason, he might have rushed his famous investigative trips that lasted only a week at most before going home to work on the draft of his next novel.

---

[946] Paul Lidsky: **Les Écrivains contre La Commune**, op. cit. p. 120.
[947] Roger Ripoll: *Zola et les Communards* in **Europe : Zola**, op. cit. p. 26.
[948] Maarten Van Buuren says that for Zola, the Commune was a foolishness, see **Les Rougon-Macquart d'Émile Zola. De la Métaphore au Mythe**, op. cit. p. 185.
[949] See the above article by Roger Ripoll, p. 26.
[950] **Ibidem**, p. 22.

Thus, to prepare **Germinal** for example, Zola went to a mine in the north, in Anzin, just as he went to the Beauce region to prepare **La Terre**. He remained there for four to five days at most. He would come home right after those short trips to build up his novel and write it, having it partially published in the newspapers even before it was completed. That probably hastened him even further in his literary production. However, such an arduous and scattered work always leaves a legacy on one's body.

Logically, Zola's health progressively declined before seriously deteriorating from 1880, after the deaths of his mother and Gustave Flaubert. He had contracted a kidney disease by sitting down for very long hours. In the preparatory file of **Le Rêve**, Zola confessed his workaholic habits: << *Moi, le travail, la littérature qui a mangé ma vie, et le bouleversement, la crise, le besoin d'être aimé* >>[951]. This short quote with its beautiful metaphor focuses on the privations he had imposed himself in order to achieve his goals. And, certainly, the greatest privation consisted in renouncing all private life, in refusing to live so to speak, for the sole purpose of devoting himself entirely to a titanic work. Admittedly, the passion of work is not blameworthy in itself because, as Zola wrote in an open letter to Francisque Sarcey and published on March 1st, 1887 in *Le Bien Public*: << *la passion est encore ce qui aide le mieux à vivre* >>[952].

It is that great positive passion that made him the great architect that built the novelties' store that is in **Au Bonheur des Dames**, or the imposing Halles in **Le Ventre de Paris**. It is finally that passion which forged the admiration of some eminent authors such as Flaubert and Huysmans. The first saw in Zola a "male", while the second applauded him, referring to the colossal novelties' store in **Au Bonheur des Dames**, which he could only explain by << *la force des reins qu'il faut avoir pour bâtir un pareil edifice* >>[953].

When an artist is straining in this way for << *laisser une œuvre aussi large et aussi vivante qu'*[on] *pourra* >>[954] to posterity, and that they are reviled by a certain press or criticism, it is understandable if they feel hurt in their self-esteem. That was the case for Zola who ended up defending himself by repeatedly taking his pen to lash out: << *la banalité et la médiocrité* >>[955] of some critics who discouraged << *les tentatives Nouvelles* >>[956]. Indeed, after

---

[951] Émile Zola: **R. M. IV**, op. cit. p. 1625.
[952] Émile Zola: **Correspondance, Tome VI : 1887-mai 1890** : Édition B.H. Bakker, O. Morgan, B. Sanders, Dorothy Speirs, H. Mitterand, Presses de l'université de Montréal, Éditions du CNRS, 1987, p. 87.
[953] Henri Mitterand quoting J.-K. Huysmans : *Lettre à Zola*, March 1883, in his *Étude*, **Au Bonheur des Dames** by Zola, **R. M. III**, p. 1701.
[954] Émile Zola: *Préface* of the second edition of **L'Assommoir** in **R. M. II**, op. cit. p. 174.
[955] Émile Zola: **Correspondance, Tome VI: 1887-mai 1890** : Édition B.H. Bakker, O. Morgan, B. Sanders, Dorothy Speirs, H. Mitterand, op. cit. p. 92.
[956] **Ibidem**, p. 92.

the attacks of the critical journalist, Francisque Sarcey, who whistled the adapted play from the novel **Le Ventre de Paris**, Zola admitted that the latter had awakened in him the polemicist: << *[...] mon vieux sang de polémiste s'est échauffé* >>[957]. That admission was a striking curiosity since the naturalist author was therefore of sanguine temperament, just like his Rougons whose thirst for life, power, and enjoyment was legendary. The coincidence gets to a point where in Zola, the hard-working writer and the designer of huge money-making machines, we find a bit of Aristide Rougon dit Saccard, the speculator obsessed with making huge wealth. There is also in Zola, a little bit of Eugène Rougon, the politician longing for power. Finally, like Maxime Rougon, he aspires to be loved and adulated.

Is it necessary to recall that, for Zola, success walked hand in hand with the scandals surrounding his book publications. This is common because people read more willingly controversial books than those which have been greeted by the critics and other exegetes of literature. Zola was very much aware of this determining factor to the point of making it his creed at some point in his career. To his friend and disciple, Joris-Karl Huysmans, Zola wrote, on August 21st, 1887: << *Plus je vais, et plus j'ai soif d'impopularité et de solitude* >>[958].

Another characteristic of the indefatigable worker that he was, was his stubborn refusal to remain in the same register for he would vary his subject matters and style constantly, while remaining faithful to his original storyline: **Histoire naturelle et sociale d'une famille sous le Second Empire**. It is in this sense that after **La Terre**, in 1887, the dark novel on peasantry - by exaggeration, he wrote in the draft of the following novel: << *Je voudrais faire un roman qu'on n'attende pas de moi [...]. Je voudrais, après* **Le Rêve**, *faire un roman tout autre* >>[959], which will become **La Bête Humaine**. The variety of his ever-changing style was surprising and seductive at the same time so much so that Anatole France wrote - after **La Bête Humaine**: << *Non, non, cet homme est un poète, son génie grand et simple crée des symboles. Il fait naître des mythes nouveaux. Les Grecs avaient créé la Dryade, il a créé la Lison ; ces deux créations se valent et sont toutes des immortelles. Il est le grand lyrique de ce temps*>>[960]. That tribute coming from someone who used to be one of his greatest literary ennemies after the release of **La Terre** is a welcome vindication of Zola's talent as a novelist.

Let us end this paragraph by recalling the other romantic cycles that Zola undertook after **Les Rougon-Macquart**, which are **Les Trois Villes** - including **Paris, Lourdes** and **Rome** - and **Les Quatre Évangiles** – which were **Fécondité, Travail, Vérité** and **Justice**. The fact that Zola had even started those romantic

---

[957] Émile Zola: **Correspondance, Tome VI: 1887-mai 1890** : Édition B.H. Bakker, O. Morgan, B. Sanders, Dorothy Speirs, H. Mitterand, op. cit. p. 87.
[958] **Ibidem**, p. 172.
[959] Émile Zola : *Ébauche de l'œuvre,* **Le Rêve**, in **R. M. IV,** op. cit. p.1624.
[960] Émile Zola: **R. M. IV,** op. cit. p. 1746.

cycles after his fiftieth - or even his sixtieth birthday for the last two titles - clearly shows that he did not regard himself as a man cut out for taking a rest or laziness, but rather that he saw himself as a prisoner of literature. In addition to his novels, Zola wrote many fairy tales, plays, literary theories and critical articles, he defended the painters of the *"outdoors"* and he was passionate about photography, not to mention journalism throughout his entire life.

In any case, Émile Zola's relentless zeal on the big literary projects and the exceptional bulimia that drove him to always get caught up in titanic works are metaphorical forms of sexual impulses too. Like a sex addict[961] who tends to neglect any other non-sexual factor, the individual that is obsessed with work sees himself for a big man[962], a sort of Priapus of work that never shies away from any workload. For such a subject, the energy released during work is tantamount to sheer climax and enjoyment. In this process, each work produced is loved and cherished with an overflowing passion, like a baby conceived with one's favourite mistress. The workaholic's case is similar indeed to that of the sexually obsessed subject. Yet, let us be clear about this: this is only a simple analogy between a man obsessed with work and one obsessed with sex, and nothing else. In reality, Zola had probably no sexual obsession. At most, his literary creation, by dealing with the theme of sexuality as I have had the opportunity to investigate so far, seems to suggest that he might have had such an obsession. No particular dissipation of his is known about, except for his indiscretion with Jeanne Rozerot, his only mistress and the mother of his children. If Gérard Gengembre talked about << *seconde épouse* >>, alluding to Jeanne, that was because Zola shared his life between her and his lawful wife, Gabrielle, between 1891 and 1902. Having bought a house in the countryside for her and the children, he would spend a few days with them before he did as much with Gabrielle-Alexandrine, rue de Bruxelles. His schedule was then split into two almost equal portions between these two women until the moment of his death in 1902. In fact, on December 11th, 1898, from England,

---

[961] Roger Ripoll acknowledges in **Réalité et Mythe chez Zola**, that at least the theme of nudity is a haunting issue in Zola's novels op. cit. p. 81.

For Maarten Van Buuren, Zola simply had a depraved taste, see **Les Rougon-Macquart d'Émile Zola. De la Métaphore au Mythe**, op. cit. p. 271.

[962] Jean Kaempfer reminded us of Zola's aversion for music in general, thinking it was responsible for emasculating the people. Music, in his eyes, was only good for women, he argues. Zola is supposed to have had an aversion for femininity and sensuality. According to the critic, Zola's love for the *"virility of truth"* is supposed to have motivated his choice for the Romanesque genre, which he regarded as *"manly"* and suitable for real hardworkers, whereas poetry was regarded by him as a feminine genre, good for poets who were no more than mere *"musicians"*, see **D'Un Naturalisme Pervers : L'Esthétique de Zola**, op. cit. pp. 240-241.

Émile Zola wrote indeed that: << *J'assigne simplement à la poésie un rôle d'orchestre ; les poètes peuvent continuer à nous faire de la musique, pendant que nous* [romanciers naturalistes] *travaillerons* >> in his **Lettre à la Jeunesse (1880),** which was published again in **Le Roman Expérimental** in **Œuvres Complètes**, under the direction of Henri Mitterand, Tome 9 : **Nana 1880**, presentation, notices, chronology and bibliography by Chantal Pierre-Gnassounou, op. cit. p. 370.

Zola wrote to Jeanne to confirm his second household and to remind her of the very first time gave in to him : << *À ma bien-aimée Jeanne, mille bons baisers du fond de mon exil, en souvenir du 11 décembre 1888, et en remerciement de nos dix années d'heureux ménage, dont le lien a été pour jamais resserré par la venue de notre Denise et de notre Jacques* >>[963].

Zola also loved his works like a man loves his favourite mistress. His passion for the fruits of his creative genius and his power of work led him to defend them fiercely whenever the opportunity to do so arose. His prefaces and press articles were all put to use for this purpose. Like a mother hen, whenever he found criticism outrageous or unfounded, Zola stood up and arrogated himself the right to defend his novels. As a talented polemicist, he stepped forward to defend his literary movement – naturalism. He also did the same for some particular novels or their adaptation to the stage. Zola was a true and a fierce fighter.

Still in the dynamics of analogy, one can compare him to a jilted sexual subject. Indeed, Zola was not satisfied with a single literary genre, which would be some evidence of fidelity to a single love. On the contrary, he embraced at once the novel, the tale, the essay, literary criticism, art criticism, journalism, plays, correspondence and photography. Like Don Juan, he could not limit his ambitions for literary conquests and his love for a particular genre could not allow him to do injustice to others, for all of them had the right to charm and to seduce him. For all those reasons, sexuality was not an impromptu in **Les Rougon-Macquart** since it sums up Zola so well, allegorically. That is probably why the author became a true theorist of heredity which is a consequence of sexuality.

1. **4. The theorist of heredity**

In the **Le Salut Public** of Lyon of April 29th, 1865, Zola defined the novelist as: << *un créateur qui tente, après Dieu, la création d'une terre nouvelle [...] qui essaie de nous dire ce qu'il a vu, de nous montrer dans une synthèse le monde et ses habitants* >>[964]. Opposing the great Balzac as early as in 1868[965], at a time when he was still largely unknown, Zola defined his originality in these terms: << *Ma grande affaire est d'être purement naturaliste, purement physiologist* >>[966].

---

[963] Émile Zola : **Correspondance, IX : 1897-1899**, édition B. H. Bakker, H. Mitterand, O. Morgan, A. Pagès, Montréal/Paris, Les Presses de l'Université de Montréal/Éditions du CNRS, 1993, pp. 364-365.
[964] Émile Zola: *Article* partially reproduced by Colette Becker in her article *Zola,* published in the **Dictionnaire des Littératures de Langue Française**, op. cit. p. 2691.
[965] What makes impossible any sort of comparison between the two authors, according to Colette Becker, is that Balzac painted individual particularities, whereas Zola painted what is inside of man in general, which reproduces him again and again. In one word, Zola's literature showed his global vision of humanity at large, **ibidem**, p. 2693.
[966] Émile Zola: **R. M. V**, op. cit. p. 1737.

Zola clearly assimilated himself to a biologist, who would reconcile science and literature. He got hat enthusiasm from reading Claude Bernard and his experimental method. He was also somewhat influenced by the British scientist, Charles Darwin[967] as well French doctors Lucas and Letourneau. In fact, for Zola, was necessary to look deep into man rather than just to describe based on his outer appearance. That vision from within would require a penetration of man's psychology and physiology. The novel, in Zola's views, would no longer be a simple man of letters, but rather a true << *savant* >>. He was euphoric when he wrote: << *Je ne puis que répéter ce que j'ai dit : si nous mettons la forme, le style à part, le romancier expérimental n'est qu'un savant spécial qui emploie l'outil des autres savants, l'observation et l'analyse* >>[968].

As a medical examiner, the naturalist novelist, according to Zola, had to << *disséquer* >>[969] their characters by accessing the depths of their psychological and physiological personality. The writer should get as far as to penetrate: << *jusqu'au fond du cadavre humain* >>[970]. To achieve this, the novelist would grow his characters on different types of grounds, for example in the countryside or in the city. The novelist would observe them on those grounds and describe scientifically their behaviour in such or such environment. Finally, the character would experience various fortunes and the novelist would draw from all the data collected from that experimental phase, the conclusions that were required. If the observation were to start from some hypotheses previously formulated, the conclusions would come exclusively from the interpretation of the observations made.

The basic assumption or hypothesis is the determinism based on heredity, because for Zola, man becomes what his ancestors put in his destiny through genetic transmissions[971]. All his journey is motivated by the genes he received at his conception and if he has to pay a heavy price, he has to blame his ancestors

---

[967] Émile Zola: *Article* partially reproduced by Colette Becker in her article *Zola*, published in the **Dictionnaire des Littératures de Langue Française**, op. cit. Colette Becker writes: << *Zola se fait une conception darwinienne de la société, combat des gras contre les maigres, des fauves contre les idéalistes* >>, p. 2693.

However, as Roger Ripoll righfully revealed in **Réalité et Mythe chez Zola**, op. cit. p. 160, the direct reference to Darwin is very brief and anecdotic in **La Débâcle**, and there is no evidence to show that Zola read indeed Darwin's **De L'Origine des Espèces**, contrary to the **Traité Philosophique et Physiologique de l'Hérédité Naturelle** by Dr Prosper Lucas, which he has thoroughly read and summarised chapter by chapter, pp. 165-170.

[968] Émile Zola: **Le Roman Expérimental** in **Œuvres Complètes**, volume 9 : **Nana 1880**, op. cit. p. 346.

[969] **Ibidem**, article *Les Documents Humains*, paragraph dedicated to the novel **Les Frères Zemganno** by Edmond de Goncourt, p. 443.

[970] Émile Zola: article *Les Documents Humains*, chapter dedicated to the novel **Les Frères Zemganno** by Edmond de Goncourt, publsihed much later on in **Le Roman Expérimental** in **Œuvres Complètes**, volume 9 : **Nana 1880**, op. cit. p. 443.

[971] Roger Ripoll reckons that what characterises the works of Zola is nothing but fatality in **Réalité et Mythe chez Zola**, op. cit. p. 479.

for that. For example, the Rougons and the Macquarts all start in life with an initial handicap: the crack or the original "*tare*", which they inherited from their mother and grandmother, Adélaïde Fouque aka Tante Dide[972]. Was she "*laide*" or "*folle à délai*"?

Philippe Hamon, in any case, recognises the madness in the noun *Foulque* and notes that the hiatus A/I - in Adélaïde - redoubles and increases the madness and the crack in Tante Dide[973]. The fact remains that, from the novel of the origins, **La Fortune des Rougon,** that enigmatic character who inherited her genes from a father that died as a madman, would also and inevitably manifest signs of madness herself, be it lucid, or angry and violent. As for her offspring, each of the individuals in her bloodline had to borrow some of her madness[974]. Of course, there would be some differences in the manifestation of their madness and even in their types of madness depending on the experimentation they went through, according to the social circles in which they evolved, etc. But as a constant, there should be an intimate connection between them that would show their great unity beyond their apparent divergences. This unity would be seen as the sign of the work of their race, of the hereditary transmission that has shaped their physical and moral characters.

Yet, for the scholarly novelist, genetics is simple, rigid, even << *mathématique* >>[975]. All children from the same lineage must all, necessarily - albeit to varying degrees - bear the weight of the original "*tare*" with more or less gravity[976]. All Tante Dide's descendants had to be fiercely passionate either about politics, wealth, sexual immorality, or for more trivial things such as enjoyment, alcohol, etc. Their children had to borrow either from their father or their mother, or from both at the same time, or even from their relatives. Not only this law is valid for the anaphoric characters but it is also valid for the clutch characters that revolve around them. Since genes are inherit through the parents' sexual activity, children are at the receiving end of a bad omen, a fatality – or a *determinism*, to borrow Zola's terminology - from which there is no escape

---

[972] For Jean Borie, in **Zola et les Mythes, ou de la Nausée au Salut,** heredity itself is the biggest myth in Zola's works, op. cit. p. 69.

[973] Philippe Hamon: **Le Personnel du Roman. Le Système des Personnages dans Les Rougon-Macquart d'Émile Zola**, op. cit. p. 114 et p. 121.

[974] Let us remember that Maarten Van Buuren has sufficiently demonstrated the obsolete nature of the "*scientific*" concept that Zola borrowed from Broussais, from Auguste Comte and from Dr. Lucas, in **Les Rougon-Macquart d'Émile Zola. De la Métaphore au Mythe**, op. cit. pp. 190-191.

[975] Émile Zola: **R. M. I**, op. cit. p. 3.

[976] In **Les Rougon-Macquart d'Émile Zola. De la Métaphore au Mythe**, Van Buuren assumes that the vegetal myth of the family tree of the Rougon-Macquart has no solid basis whatsoever, op. cit. p. 140.

In **Le Romancier et la Machine, I : L'Univers de Zola**, Jacques Noiray asserts that it would be more accurate to speak of some << *légendes modernes de la machine* >>, rather than the natural and social history of the Rougon-Macquart family, or any family, especially in the case of **La Bête Humaine, Germinal** and **Travail**, op. cit. p. 299.

route. Their parents pass on to them the crack from generation to generation and there is nothing they can do to shake it. For example, Jacques Lantier's compelling drive to murder works like a rare and a compelling desire for enjoying the slaughter of a young woman, which constantly tortures him. His painful conscience can do nothing against the power of his ''ça'', to which he must obey[977]. In broad strokes, this is what genetics is all about, for Zola.

One may wonder whether the scientism of the author was founded or whether it was simply an artist's fantasy, a mystification at best.

II. THE CRITICISM OF ZOLA

Zola's detractors were as vehement as his admirers were vocal and laudatory. For the sake of a rigorous organisation, the detractors of his scientism will be distinguished from the detractors of his literary work as a collection of scatology, a bin of rubbish. I will have later on distinguish the scientific detractors then the moralists.

2.1. The rough scientism of Zola's naturalism

From the birth of the naturalistic literary movement, there was a fear of a hiatus between the literary and the biological, a divorce between scientific rigour and rigidity on the one hand and literary subjectivity on the other hand. It was shown for example through this study that Zola stuffed his fictional narrative labelled as << *scientifique* >> and << *experimental* >> with myths - old and new. His writing was strongly imaged[978], full of metaphors[979] and metonymies so much so that many critics saw in him a poet too[980]. Moreover, his very fertile imagination and his powerful ability to describe things and people - especially with regards to the hysteria of the crowds - made him also an epic author[981]. All in all, his naturalism becomes a cultural and a literary mix that loses its natural character

---

[977] Émile Zola wrote about the flight of the ''*moi*'' from Jacques Lantier in the following terms: << [...] *mais c'étaient, dans son être, de subites pertes d'équilibre, comme des cassures, des trous par lesquels son moi lui échappait, au milieu d'une sorte de grande fumée qui déformait tout Il ne s'appartenait plus, il obéissait à ses muscles, à la bête enragée* >>, in **R. M. V**, op. cit. p. 1043.

[978] Jean Kaempfer agrees that the images constitute a menace for naturalism, in **D'Un Naturalisme Pervers : L'Esthétique de Zola**, op. cit. p. 168.

[979] Similarly, in **Les Rougon-Macquart d'Émile Zola. De la Métaphore au Mythe**, Maarten Van Buuren thinks that the metaphors constitute an infringement of the rules of Zola's naturalism, op. cit. p. 29. Subsequently, the objectivity of the **Rougon-Macquart** has been damaged by the networks of metaphors, p. 272.

[980] I can confidently make such an argument, even though Zola classified himself in the category of the hardworking writers, and not in that of the musicians, meaning the category of the poets, see note 957.

[981] Jacques Noiray: **Le Romancier et la Machine, I : L'Univers de Zola**, op. cit. p. 183 et p. 508 and also Claude Seassau: **Émile Zola, Le Réalisme Symbolique**, op. cit. p. 8 et p. 15, p. 19 et p. 190, p. 215 and p. 326.

and often goes astray in the realm of the supernatural and the vision[982]. There is a fatal transgression in Zola's fiction that makes Thomas Mann say that: << *Zola transcende la doctrine simplificatrice par une imagination puissante et un souffle épique servis par une prose lyrique et un vocabulaire foisonnant ; comment méconnaître dans l'épopée de Zola, le symbolisme et le penchant au mythe, qui hausse son univers jusqu'au surnaturel ?* >>[983].

Even his former disciples, the authors of the **Manifeste des Cinq**, had also denounced what they considered Zola's ignorance in medical and scientific matters and, therefore, the falseness of the **Rougon-Macquart** : << *Puis, les moins perspicaces* [of Zola's readers] *avaient fini par s'apercevoir du ridicule de cette soi-disant* << Histoire naturelle et sociale d'une famille sous le Second Empire >>, *de la fragilité du fil héréditaire, de l'enfantillage du fameux arbre généalogique, de l'ignorance médicale et scientifique profonde du Maître* >>[984].

Although science and literature have had difficulty in smoothly blending in **Les Rougon-Macquart**, the approximate scientism[985] of Zola did not stop eminent contemporaries and later ones[986] to praise the merits of this innovative work in many respects, while others have constantly vilified the author and the work in the grossest and most excessive terms.

2.1.1. The critics of naturalism

As for the first group of such people, I can quote right away Louis Ulbach who, on January 23rd, 1868, in **Le Figaro**, attacked with a rare virulence and an outrageous sarcasm, the new literary school of which Zola drafted a definition in **Thérèse Raquin**. According to him: << *Il s'est établi depuis quelques années, une école monstrueuse de romanciers, qui prétend substituer l'éloquence du charnier à l'éloquence de la chair, qui fait appel aux monstruosités les plus chirurgicales, qui groupe les pestiférés pour nous en faire admirer les marbrures, qui s'inspire directement du choléra, son maître, et qui fait jaillir le pus de la conscience* >>[987].

---

[982] Claude Seassau: **Émile Zola, Le Réalisme Symbolique**, op. cit. p. 183 et pp. 297-298.

[983] Thomas Mann : *Zola* in **Le Robert : Dictionnaire Universel des Noms Propres**, Paris, Robert, 1989, pp. 3397 à 3398.

[984] P. Bonnetain, J.-H. Rosny, L. Descaves, P. Margueritte and G. Guiches: *Le Manifeste des Cinq* in **Le Figaro** of the 18th August 1887, and then published again in **R. M. IV** by Émile Zola, op. cit. p. 1526.

[985] For Maarten Van Buuren, in **Les Rougon-Macquart d'Émile Zola. De la Métaphore au Mythe**, Zola's scientific pretentiousness is simply not taken seriously (p. 15), because of its evidently scientific *naivety*, op. cit. p. 257.

[986] I can mention among those contemporary admirers, Gustave Flaubert and Stéphane Mallarmé, and then among the admirers of our time, scholars like Philippe Hamon, Henri Mitterand, Auguste Dezalay, Colette Becker, Robert Lethbridge, David Baguley, Chantal Bertrand-Jennings and many more.

[987] Louis Ulbach: article quoted by Carles and Desgranges in **Zola**, op. cit. p. 112.

So, for Ulbach, what shocks the most about Zola is the horror that mars his narratives. Even if his position is understandable, it is not acceptable because the discourse on morality is fundamentally the domain of moralists, of ministers of religion and other philosophers, while literature remains the domain of men of letters. Judging literary works only from the moral aspect[988] is therefore a dangerous amalgam. The risk is great indeed to get oneself involved into a false trial is the literary critic should choose to follow that path. Indeed, the purpose of the novelist is not to afford the luxury of delivering to their readers sermons and other litanies on morality and purity. If they choose such a dangerous option, production after production, they would risk irritating and alienating their readers[989]. Literature is an art which should be considered as such; its field of action being less that of immediate utility than that of beauty and sensitivity.

The wrath of moralists with regards to certain incestuous or morbid sexual relationships in **Les Rougon-Macquart** is understandable as I argued above. The perverse or aberrant sexuality found in the corpus cannot justify the sententious rejection of naturalism as a whole. This literary school is not to be drowned like a dog accused of rage. It has its strengths and its weaknesses like any other human work, and it is appropriate to accept it with them all. Unfortunately, some intellectuals have chosen the shortcut by obliterating the first and rushing to the second to try partially the leader of the naturalist novelists[990]. They were very ironical about << *la charcuterie* >>, << *l'immondice* >>, << *la scatologie* >> and << *la gauloiserie* >> in the novels of Zola[991]. An obvious example on this point is offered by Colombine who, in **Le Gil Blas** of February 6th, 1882, rebelled against the bourgeois who he accused of making Zola's success and fame. He also wondered about the alleged << *exactitude* >> of the author the day after the publication of **Pot-Bouille**. With the greatest contempt, he launched: << *Cette fois, êtes-vous contents, ô bourgeois qui avez fait le succès de M. Zola lorsqu'il dépeignait le peuple ou le monde des filles ? Croyez-vous encore à sa soi-disant exactitude ? Est-ce vrai que vous êtes un ramassis d'imbéciles, parfois monstrueux, toujours ignobles, et grotesques même dans l'ignoble ? Est-ce bien votre maison cette maison de* **Pot-Bouille** *qui ressemble à un quartier de*

---

[988] David Baguley recalls in **Naturalist Fiction. The Entropic Vision**, that an ancient definition reduced naaturalism to scandal-related topics, to the ethically and morally ugliness and to the painting of the lower classes of society, op. cit. pp. 42-43.

[989] However, for Émile Zola, the choice is quickly made: << *Un romancier qui éprouve le besoin de s'indigner contre le vice et d'applaudir à la vertu, gâte également les documents qu'il apporte, car son intervention est aussi gênante qu'inutile ; l'œuvre perd de sa force, ce n'est plus une page de marbre tirée d'un bloc de la réalité, c'est une matière travaillée, repétrie par l'émotion de l'auteur, émotion qui est sujette à tous les préjugés et à toutes les erreurs. Une œuvre vraie sera éternelle, tandis qu'une œuvre émue pourra ne chatouiller que le sentiment d'une époque* >>, Le Naturalisme au Théâtre, article published for the first time in **Le Messager de l'Europe**, a Saint-Petersburgh magazine in January 1879, and then reproduced in **Le Roman Expérimental** in **Œuvres Complètes**, volume 9 : **Nana 1880**, op. cit. pp. 378-379.

[990] According to Claude Seassau, even though Zola was heavily critised for being a minor novelist, he is nonetheless a creator, see **Émile Zola, Le Réalisme Symbolique**, op. cit. p. 7.

[991] David Baguley: **Naturalist Fiction. The Entropic Vision**, op. cit. pp. 42-43.

Bicêtre, pleine de femmes hystériques ou détraquées, avec son idiot, ses gâteux, ses crétins, ses ramollis ? >>[992].

For Zola however, the debate was elsewhere. In fact, he thought that naturalism imposed this new concept the novel, that is, to prevent the author from becoming a moraliser. Establishing the three basic criteria of the contemporary novel, he classified them as follows: to paint life exactly as it is - without a romantic make-up -, then to kill the hero - a person who was greatly increased in their ability and power - and finally, the absence and the neutrality of the narrator: << *Le romancier affecte de disparaître complètement derrière l'action qu'il raconte. Il est le metteur en scène caché du drame. Jamais il ne se montre au bout d'une phrase. On ne l'entend ni rire ni pleurer avec ses personnages, pas plus qu'il ne se permet de juger leurs actes. C'est même cet apparent désintéressement qui est le trait le plus distinctif. On chercherait en vain une conclusion, une moralité, une leçon quelconque tirée des faits. Il n'y a d'étalés, de mis en lumière, uniquement que les faits, louables ou condamnables. L'auteur n'est pas un moraliste, mais un anatomiste qui se contente de dire ce qu'il trouve dans le cadavre humain >>*[993].

Nonetheless, many critics did not understand the matters related to naturalism that way and, subsequently, Zola's condemnation increased until the publication of **La Terre**, where it reached hitherto unsuspected proportions. The situation became so unbearable that the young admirers and followers of Zola, who also claimed to be naturalist novelists, had to publicly deny him, accusing him of falling into an outrageous extremism.

2.1. 2. The extremist naturalism or the curiosity of a voyeur

The first to let go of the Master were Paul Bonnetain, Rosny, Lucien Descaves, Paul Marguerite and Gustave Guiches, known for their now infamous and regrettable **Manifesto of the Five**, published August 18th, 1887 in **Le Figaro**. For the latter, the publication of **La Terre** marked their break with Zola. They became Zola's attackers and they attacked the work and its author with some extreme verbal violence. They accused among other things the author of imposture; they challenged all his literary conceptions – the ultimate denial - and they carried out personal attacks on him. Let us quickly recall some poignant accusations from their pamphlet: << *Le Maître est descendu au fond de l'immondice [...]. Nous répudions énergiquement cette imposture de la littérature véridique, cet effort vers la gauloiserie mixte d'un cerveau en mal de succès. Nous répudions ces bonshommes de rhétorique zoliste, ces silhouettes énormes, surhumaines et biscornues, dénuées de complication, jetées brutalement en masse lourde, dans des milieux aperçus au hasard des*

---

[992] Patricia Carles and Béatrice Desgranges quoting Colombine in **Zola**, op. cit. p. 112.
[993] Émile Zola: *Flaubert, L'Écrivain,* article on Gustave Flaubert, published in **Le Messager de l'Europe** in November 1875, and then reproduced in **Documents Littéraires** (1881) and also in **Le Roman Naturaliste**, Henri Mitterand (éd.), op. cit. pp. 55-57.

portières d'express >>[994]. Although Zola had claimed a long time before: << *Pour moi, la question du talent prime tout en literature* >>[995] and not the moral criterion, he was abandoned by his peers because of the second criterion only and despite the first one he undoubtedly fully satisfied.

It is paradoxical to think that for more than twenty years, Zola's novels continued to be attacked, although he had anticipated - from the preface by **Thérèse Raquin** in 1867 - about all the criticisms that could be directed at him on the moral criterion: << *Je ne sais si mon roman est moral ou immoral; j'avoue que je ne me suis jamais inquiété de le rendre plus ou moins chaste. Ce que je sais, c'est que je n'ai jamais songé à y mettre les saletés qu'y découvrent les gens moraux ; c'est que j'en ai décrit chaque scène, même les plus fiévreuses, avec la seule curiosité du savant* >>[996].

This quote from Zola makes it possible to assert again that the work betrays the unconscious of its author - at least if Zola stated this in good faith. He slips redundantly, significant elements from his unconscious that escape his will and the control of his conscience.

Nevertheless, this statement does not seem to have reached its objectives because the novelist had to face his numerous detractors who did not cease to cry wolf until the end of the publication of the **Rougon-Macquart**. In the meantime, twenty-six years had gone by since his anticipated excuses in **Thérèse Raquin**. Taking everything into account, it is fair to say that the extremism of Zola's naturalism cost him dearly, and mainly among his literate friends, his young students, not to mention the diatribes from the journalists he endured for years. But Zola was convinced that, in the long run, he would eventually be proven right over his detractors. So, he had stated in the preface of **L'Assommoir**, << *Je ne me défends pas, d'ailleurs. Mon œuvre me défendra* >>[997].

Today it can be argued that this was a just prophecy since Zola did have the last laugh given the ever-growing interest of critics in his gigantic, diversified and rich work that he bequeathed to posterity. As Zola said: << *Le plus difficile est de faire comprendre l'originalité dans l'art. Le temps seul peut forcer les gens à rendre justice aux artistes originaux* >>[998]. Zola's literary legacy still lives on, some one hundred-twenty years after his passing.

---

[994] Émile Zola: **R.M. IV.**, op. cit. p. 1526.
[995] Émile Zola: **Documents Littéraires** and then in **Le Roman Naturaliste**, Henri Mitterand (éd.), op. cit. p. 71.
[996] Émile Zola: **Thérèse Raquin**, Paris, Fasquelle, 1983, p. 5.
[997] Émile Zola: **R. M. II**, op. cit. p. 373.
[998] Émile Zola: *Le Salon de 1875*, article published in **Le Messager de l'Europe** in June 1875 and then in **Le Roman Naturaliste**, Henri Mitterand (éd.), op. cit. p. 114.

The extremism of the Zolian narrator is very much like the curiosity of a voyeur. As such, he watches closely the sexual behaviour of his characters and listens to their conversations and he seems to enjoy that with such a pleasure, just like the shepherd Soulas does in **La Terre**. Soulas always enjoys finding himself in the spaces where he is certain to catch La Cognette in the arms of her many lovers. Like him, the Zolian narrator is an indiscreet voyeur who exposes in the public domain all the sordid details unduly observed. How can one not see then the resemblance between him and Soulas? This is a narrator taking a particular interest in contemplating and in reporting the sublime nudes of Renée in **La Curée**, or those of Nana in **Nana**, of Albine in **La Faute de l'Abbé Mouret** and of Clotilde in **Le Docteur Pascal**. Nothing escapes his gaze from << *leur chevelure d'or* >> - because they are all blonde women, as if it were a coincidence – and the << *courbes parfaits* >> of their hips, through their << *bouches délicieuses* >>, << *la fermeté et la rondeur* >> of << *leur gorge* >> and the << *satin* >> of their skin[999]. This bodily description of heroines occurs at two precise moments: first, when they are naked[1000] in front of their mirror, and then, when theyr are in the arms of their sexual partners.

But the voyeur is intrinsically a pervert. It can be argued that the Zolian narrator is also[1001] a pervert. Nevertheless, he must be distinguished from the ordinary voyeur on at least one level, that of their respective motivations. Indeed, the voyeur that I call ordinary is guided only by their will to satisfy their sexual urge by the scopic pleasure. This form of enjoyment is the result of a form of some anterior neurosis that is characterised by an inhibition of the subject-voyeur that is unable to dare go further in the satisfaction of their lust. They do not progress to the sexual act. They thus limit their conquest to the preliminary stages in the process of sexuality as if they feared not being up to the task. Certainly, the voyeurism of the Zolian narrator is epistemological as it has been shown in the chapter on the foundations of sexuality - Part I, Chapter I.

Because the scientific doctrine of naturalism was based on the theory of heredity, Zola was obliged to grant sexuality a central place in his narrative. Without sexuality, there would be absolutely no human reproduction, and hence no heredity to speak of. His perversion - if it was indeed a perversion - was justified primarily by scientific and methodological reasons. While recognising the talk about sexuality in his works, Zola defended himself, for example, from

---

[999] Refer to **Les Rougon-Macquart d'Émile Zola. De la Métaphore au Mythe** by Maarten Van Buuren for more information on the feminine charms rendered in textile related vocabulary, op. cit. p. 280.

[1000] For Roger Ripoll, nudity has got a direct rapport to the mythology in the corpus, not withstanding that it is also a haunting theme in Zola's novels, see **Réalité et Mythe chez Zola**, op. cit. pp. 80-81.

[1001] Without going any further, Jean Kaempfer assumes that Zola is indeed a real << *pervers* >>, in **D'Un Naturalisme Pervers: L'Esthétique de Zola**, op. cit. p. 193.

Refer also to the book by Maarten Van Buuren, where he reckons vaguely that Zola had "*un goût dépravé*", p. 271.

practicing what he described, not without denouncing the hypocrisy of those who berated him, but who, certainly, did these immoral things: << *On fait la chose, mais on n'en rit plus ; on en rougit et on se cache. La morale ayant été mise à dissimuler le sexe, on a déclaré le sexe infâme. Il s'est ainsi formé une bonne tenue publique, des convenances, toute une police sociale qui s'est substituée à l'idée de vertu. Cette évolution a procédé par le silence : il est des choses dont il est devenu peu à peu inconvenant de parler, voilà tout ; de telle sorte que l'homme distingué, l'honnête homme est celui qui fait ces choses sans en parler, tandis que celui qui en parle sans les faire, comme certains romanciers de ma connaissance, sont traités de gens orduriers et traînés journellement dans le ruisseau* >>[1002].

The worst was yet to come as some critics went so far as to deny Zola any talent as a novelist whatsoever.

2.1.3. Zola, the talentless novelist ?

In 1887, Anatole France was so disappointed by the publication of Zola's **La Terre** that he rejected his entire literary production: << *Son œuvre est mauvaise et il est un de ces malheureux dont on peut dire qu'il vaudrait mieux qu'ils ne fussent pas nés* >>[1003].

Without blaming the work in all its dimensions, Émile Foulget had ferociously attacked the silliness of the painting of feelings in the Zolian novel. After **Le Docteur Pascal**, acting like a merciless censor, he argued: << *M. Zola [...] n'a aucun talent pour peindre, même pour comprendre, les sentiments qui font qu'un homme aime une femme et est aimé d'elle. La vie intérieure lui est aussi fermée qu'il est possible. Dans tous ses romans, sauf (et en une faible mesure) dans* **Une Page d'Amour**, *tout ce qui est psychologique lui est absolument étranger* >>[1004].

Offended by the way Zola described how Pascal seduced Clotilde, Foulget quipped: << *[...] je crois bien qu'il n'y a que M. Zola au monde pour croire que le plus grand moyen pour séduire une vierge soit de lui raconter* **Les Rougon-Macquart** >>[1005]. He did not hesitate to show Zola in a << *mediocre* >> day that was both << *gauche* >> and << *faux* >> when it comes to writing psychological novel[1006], which he saw as Zola's Achilles heel. For Foulget, the solution did exist, however, and he proposed to indicate it to Zola, not without paternalism:

[1002] Émile Zola: **Documents Littéraires** : *De la moralité en littérature* (1882) and then in **Le Roman Naturaliste**, Henri Mitterand (éd.), op. cit. p. 111.
[1003] Marcel Girard quoting an article by Anatole France published in **Le Temps** on the 28th August 1887, in "*Les Archives de l'œuvre*" in **La Terre** by Émile Zola, op. cit. p. 501.
[1004] Gérard Gengembre quoting Émile Foulget in his *Dossier* in **Le Docteur Pascal** by Émile Zola, op. cit. p. 463.
[1005] **Ibidem**, p. 461.
[1006] **Ibidem**, p. 463.

<< Donc, maintenant que **Les Rougon-Macquart** *sont finis, plus de romans intimes, plus un seul! Si M. Zola reconnaissait, et s'il avait des amis au lieu de flatteurs, il se convaincrait de cette vérité. Elle est éclatante.* **Le Docteur Pascal** *ne fait que la confirmer douloureusement >>*[1007].

Nevertheless, Zola had an answer for all his critics, both the moralists and the apostles of talent, and he challenged them with irony: *<< En somme, on accuse tout un groupe d'écrivains de spéculer sur l'obscénité. On les hue, on ramasse la boue des ruisseaux pour la leur jeter à la face ; et non content de les salir, on tâche de les attaquer dans leur talent, en jurant que leurs livres sont tout ce qu'il y a de plus facile à faire, qu'il suffit d'y entasser des horreurs. Eh bien! essayez, ce sera drôle! >>*[1008].

Foulget and other detractors of Zola should take full responsibility for their sharp criticisms of naturalism and of Zola whom they branded a talentless writer. Let us look beyond them to see his admirers.

2.2. Tributes pouring in

They were and they are still numerous nowadays. I will only retain a few for the sake of conciseness. Writing about **L'Assommoir**, Stéphane Mallarmé noted, in a letter to Zola: *<< Voilà une bien grande œuvre ; et digne d'une époque où la vérité devient la forme populaire de la beauté! >>*[1009]. This homage reckoned that the novel had the merit of telling the truth. Therefore, Zola's approximate scientism did not mean complacent painting of society or people.

Better still, a scientist and an authoritative mind like Sigmund Freud, a doctor and a philosopher, called Zola a *<< parfait connaisseur de l'âme humaine >>*[1010]. He made such a statement given Zola's understanding and his accurate description of human behaviour in relation to the libido. Zola, in fact, offers in **Les Rougon-Macquart**, a wide range of behaviours of sexual subjects ranging from the noble sacrifice of oneself in the name of the happiness of the loved-one - as Pauline Quenu does - to the passionate murder - like the murder of Chaval by Étienne Lantier. He goes through the voyeurism of Soulas; the collection of objects that belonged to the desired sexual object, which is the case of Cabuche; he narrated the brutal rape of Françoise by Buteau; the incest between Palmyre and Hilarion; the prostitution of Nana; the pederasty of Baptiste and the paedophilia of Grandmorin, etc. This is because Zola has shown that man is first and foremost an animal with exacerbated instincts when it

---

[1007] Gérard Gengembre quoting Émile Foulget in his *Dossier* in **Le Docteur Pascal** by Émile Zola, op. cit. p. 463.
[1008] Émile Zola: *La Littérature Obscène* in **Le Roman Expérimental**, in **Œuvres Complètes**, volume 9 : **Nana 1880**, op. cit. p. 486.
[1009] Patricia Carles and Béatrice Desgranges quoting a *Lettre* by Stéphane Mallarmé to Zola, in **Zola**, op. cit. p. 113.
[1010] Sigmund Freud : **Trois Essais sur la Théorie de la Sexualité**, op. cit. p. 169.

comes down to the satisfaction of his libido. He did not agree that man was simply this being endowed with reason, and who is animated by noble feelings of love like literature had been arguing for far too long. With Zola, the lyricism of romantic poets and other novelists who joined them simply ends. He could not see himself in the shoes of writers such as Alexandre Dumas Fils and **La Dame aux Caméllias**, or Abbé Prévost and his **Manon Lescaut**. In Freud's eyes, the dark Zolian picture seemed to reflect far better the reality of things than any other pre-existing.

Maupassant also paid tribute to **Germinal** in these rave words: << *Vous avez remué là-dedans une telle masse d'humanité attendrissante et bestiale, fouillé tant de misère et de bêtise pitoyable, fait grouiller une telle foule terrible et désolante au milieu d'un décor admirable, que jamais livre assurément n'a contenu tant de vie et de mouvement, une telle somme de peuple* >>[1011]. That tribute focussed on the humanist side of Zola's literature, which people should not overlook.

From these two homages, coming from someone who had such a great knowledge of science and from someone who had such a great idea of literature, I can agree on the merit of Zola's works as a whole. Zola's merit was that he dared to reconcile these two fields of knowledge - science and literature - between which many had erected a virtually impassable wall. He reconciled them with some success to the point of reaping some satisfaction on both sides.

Indeed, Zola was not too wrong in his solitary struggle to use all the weapons available to him without exclusion. One can understand that, to achieve his ends, he had not shied away from the theme of sexuality with all its components studied above. About **La Terre**, one of the novels that dealt with the issue of sexuality with maximum perversions, Stéphane Mallarmé wrote, in a letter to Zola : << *Vous n'avez eu garde d'omettre rien de ce qui se fait bas, contre terre, l'amour divers et si épars, ou l'acte générateur : voilà qui est d'une philosophie perspicace et d'une vraie poésie* >>[1012].

It is only with talent that one can succeed the prowess to draw the beautiful and the exalted from what is basic and vile: sexuality. Zola thus joins Baudelaire who had done something a little bit similar with the prostitutes and cats in his famous sickly flowers called **Les Fleurs du Mal**. So, was Zola an immoral writer? I think the answer is a resounding ''no''. Even if by chance he were immoral, it would be necessary to qualify his immorality. What is immoral is rather what Zola describes, which he does not encourage in any way. On the contrary, he condemns it with severity.

[1011] Patricia Carles and Béatrice Desgranges quoting a *Lettre* by Guy de Maupassant to Zola, in **Zola**, op. cit. p. 113.
[1012] Marcel Girard quoting a *Lettre* by Stéphane Mallarmé to Zola, in his *Archives de l'œuvre*, in **La Terre** by Émile Zola, op. cit. p. 503.

The author gave an account of the imperial society which was immoral in his eyes, even though this bias remains very subjective. Should one then blame him if the report he comes up with shows the vicious and corrupt world he lived in? Or should the readers blame, on the contrary, the French society of that time? Deciding on the morality of the Zolian narrative and relying in particular on **La Curée**, Philippe Berthier was very adamant: << *Décidément,* **La Curée,** *roman à ne pas mettre entre toutes les mains, est d'une irréprochable moralité* >>[1013].

Somehow Zola was laughed at by many critics who derided his experimental method. Today, in fact, many new scientific discoveries make it possible to deny his understanding of heredity, which is manifested by a rigid fatality that inevitably strikes his characters. Émile Foulget is one of those irreducible slayers of the theory of heredity as presented by Zola. In the ***Courrier Littéraire*** of July 1st, 1893, referring to the character of Dr. Pascal, and beyond, to Zola himself, he wrote: << *Ses théories sur l'hérédité sont le capharnaüm le plus ténébreux qui se puisse rencontrer* >>[1014].

Nonetheless, many critics laugh at him without considering the scientific knowledge available in the time of Zola. Zola is undoubtedly wrong today in terms of scientificity, but he was probably right yesterday because his conception of genetics was consistent with the sum of knowledge available in his day. At least that is what Michel Serres has revealed: << *Je ne dis pas que la série des* **Rougon-Macquart** *munie de son texte réflexif, constitue un ensemble de résultats purement scientifiques. Je dis seulement, mais c'est énorme, que les thèses, la méthode et l'épistémologie que je découvre ici sont fidèles à ce qu'il y a de meilleur, à ce que nous jugeons le meilleur, dans les travaux dits scientifiques de ce temps* >>[1015].

That assertion, which cannot be validly disputed, shows that there would be no shame for Zola to be scientifically surpassed today because science is evolving. It is developing so rapidly that theses in genetics that were highly regarded in 1990 are sometimes wholly rejected today. The field of research works that way and it is fast moving. We must all live with that[1016]. What is inalienable though is certainly the literary value of naturalism, which remains alive to the point

---

[1013] Philippe Berthier: *Hôtel Saccard : État des lieux* in **La Curée de Zola ou << la vie à outrance >>**, op. cit. p. 117.
[1014] Gérard Gengembre quoting Émile Foulget in his " *Dossier* " in **Le Docteur Pascal** by Émile Zola, op. cit. p. 459.
[1015] Michel Serres: **Feux et Signaux de Brume: Zola**, op. cit. p. 461.
[1016] Émile Zola had understood this in an interview to the **Journal** on the 20th August 1894 when he looked back on naturalism in retrospect, with the eyes of a literary critic. He declared then: << *Oui, j'ai appliqué à la littérature les principes positivistes. Je l'ai fait avec l'enthousiasme d'une conviction récente. Je ne crois peut-être plus à ces principes aussi violemment que j'y croyais jadis. Je n'en suis pas moins sûr d'avoir eu raison à mon instant. Il y a de la vérité relative, même dans l'erreur d'une réaction. Je fus un peu sectaire. Le naturalisme, s'il doit se juger au passé, sera le premier à se reprocher d'avoir limité, fermé l'horizon* >> ; this interview was reproduced in **Le Roman Naturaliste**, Henri Mitterand (éd.), op. cit. p. 146.

where it is perhaps nowadays one of the literary movements in which the greatest number of literary critics in the world are interested, from California to France via Canada, Great Britain, Germany, Switzerland, Eastern Europe, Australia, New Zealand and Africa.

The academician Jean Rostand, in his communication titled **L'œuvre de Zola et la pensée scientifique**, insisted on the prospective nature of the Zolian enterprise, in that it probed the positive truth of tomorrow. He asserted, among other things, that great discoveries in psychoanalysis were made possible only through the prospection of Zola, Tolstoy and Dostoevsky, to whom Freud himself paid tribute[1017]. While conceding that Zola may have abused the notion of heredity and deluded himself about the scope of his work, Rostand insists that the scientific literature available to Zola was very up-to-date and he quotes **L'Hérédité naturelle** by Prosper Lucas published in 1868. That genetician, according to Rostand, << *faisait autorité à l'époque et passait pour faire la somme de tout ce qu'on savait alors sur la transmission des caractères* >>.

He also reminds us of doctors like J.-L. Brachet, Déjerine and Darwin[1018], including Darwin's theory of pangenesis, Haeckel's perigenesis, Galton's Stirps and Weismann's determinants[1019]. He then asserted that the information available to Zola was correct at the time and that certain theories developed by Pascal, in **Le Docteur Pascal** in particular, are confirmed today by molecular biology[1020]. He cited as an example the eminent French biologist, Lucien Cuénot, who was struck by Pascal's theories so much so that he wrote to Zola in 1894 to ask him what were the real-life models that helped him build this particular character[1021]. Cuénot had published in 1902 a treatise on the inheritance of pigmentation in mice and Jean Rostand questioned - without giving an answer - if Zola had influenced, or just inspired Lucien Cuénot at all. He also took the example of Mantegazza, a brilliant Italian anthropologist and the author of the **Physiologie de la Douleur** in 1880, who wrote to Zola to tell him that he was << *non seulement un des plus grands écrivains de notre siècle, mais aussi un grand physiologist* >>[1022]. This comment, from a wise man like Mantegazza, was not fortuitous in Rostand's eyes since the latter was the first scientist to suggest the

---

[1017] Jean Rostand: *L'œuvre de Zola et la pensée scientifique*, in **Europe : Zola**, n°. 468-469, op. cit. p. 363.

[1018] Émile Zola was slightly inspired by Darwin in fact, because he declared: << *Je donne aussi une importance considérable au milieu. Il faudrait aborder les théories de Darwin ; mais ceci n'est qu'une étude générale sur la méthode expérimentale appliquée au roman, et je me perdrais, si je voulais entrer dans les détails. Je dirai simplement un mot des milieux* >>, Le roman expérimental, article published in **Le Messager de l'Europe** in August 1879, and then in **Le Voltaire** on the 16th to the 20th October 1879, and again in **Le Roman Expérimental** (1880) and lastly in **Œuvres Complètes**, volume 9 : **Nana 1880**, op. cit. p. 332.

[1019] Jean Rostand : above article, p. 364.

[1020] Jean Rostand: *L'œuvre de Zola et la pensée scientifique*, in **Europe : Zola**, n°. 468-469, op. cit. p. 365.

[1021] **Ibidem**, p. 365.

[1022] **Ibidem**, p. 365.

conservation of human seeds at very low temperatures, which today allows in-vitro fertilisation. Rostand, noting that the crack in Zola's works resembles much the germplasm now proven to be invariably, and immutably, transmitted from generation to generation, praises Zola's prophetic vision that heredity has its laws just like gravity. He then stresses that science penetrated such laws later on. In fact, what Zola did not know at the time was that Johan Mendel had already laid down the essential laws[1023] of heredity.

Henri Mitterand confirmed some of those scientific sources of Zola in his preface to Zola's **Le Docteur Pascal** when he wrote: << *Il y* [in the book of Jules Déjerine] *trouve des données qu'il connaît déjà plus ou moins, sur les différentes lois de l'hérédité selon Darwin ; la loi de l'hérédité directe et immédiate, la loi de la prépondérance dans la transmission des caractères, la loi de l'hérédité en retour (qui donne à l'individu des traits de ses ancêtres), la loi de l'hérédité d'influence (par imprégnation du premier époux sur les enfants nés d'un second mariage)* >>[1024]. It would therefore be awkward, and maybe disingenuous too, to deny the scientific tone of Zola's novelistic works since he conceived them in the light of the scientific knowledge available in his time. However, no-one should pass them off as a pure physiological and/or a pure biological treatise[1025]. Zola produced what was simply a work of literature that embraced his time, an era made notorious by the widespread of scientific ideas. Zola himself was probably the first to acknowledge in 1880 that: << *Nous ne sommes ni des chimistes, ni des physiciens, ni des physiologistes ; nous sommes simplement des romanciers qui nous appuyons sur les sciences* >>[1026].

On the other hand, sexuality, despite its nasty undertone, is the engine of naturalism. In any case, this is what the critic Guy Robert seemed to confirm when he wrote in 1952: << *La vie ne se prolonge que par et dans l'ordure; tout enfantement s'accomplit dans les déchirements et les impuretés. On comprend mieux ainsi pourquoi Zola a si souvent et si crûment évoqué tout ce qui concerne l'acte de génération [...]. Mais il faut voir dans cette obsession de l'acte sexuel la manifestation d'une des forces essentielles qui animent son univers ; un seul et éternel combat s'y déroule, celui que mène la vie aux prises avec la mort. Tel est l'aspect épique des **Rougon-Macquart** [...]. Le mot Naturalisme en*

[1023] Jean Rostand: *L'œuvre de Zola et la pensée scientifique*, in **Europe : Zola**, n°. 468-469, op. cit. p. 365.
[1024] Henri Mitterand: *Préface* of **Le Docteur Pascal** by Émile Zola, Paris, Édition Folio Classique, 1991, p. 4.
[1025] Émile Zola admitted: << *Je le répète, je ne suis pas un savant, je ne suis pas un historien, je suis un romancier* >>, **Nouvelle Campagne** (1897), and then in **Le Romancier Naturaliste**, Henri Mitterand (éd.), op. cit. p. 153.
[1026] Émile Zola: **Le Roman Expérimental** (1880) and in the **Œuvres Complètes**, volume 9 : **Nana 1880**, op. cit. p. 340.

s'appliquant à Zola pourrait reprendre quelque chose de son premier sens, puisque c'est bien la Nature qui est le principe suprême >>[1027].

Finally, one must admit that Zola was a novelist who did not leave anyone indifferent, judging by the many attacks that he was subjected to and the many tributes that he received over the last Century. For that reason, one must confess his greatness even if his works had some imperfections, whether they are supposed or proven. The relentlessness interest of literary criticism in his works is undoubtedly the implicit evidence of his undeniable talent[1028]. His ever-growing audience through the centuries is another evidence of his talent and recognition.

The ultimate question which is of interest to me now is whether naturalism was Zola's own aesthetic, or whether it was a literary school or movement in its own right.

III. ZOLA, THE LONE WRITER OR THE LITERARY SCHOOL CHIEF?

This question, as curious as it may appear, is no less interesting than the others. In fact, the first thing that comes to mind when one talks about a school or a literary school is the idea of a group of writers belonging to the same era and who share the same aesthetic ideals; the same forms of expression; the production of each one of them being like one of the manifestations of their common art. Thus, the Romantics were essentially poets expressing the outpouring of their hearts where the followers of classicism found their subject matters only in the imitation of the ancients. However, when one is faced with naturalism, one immediately stumbles on the overwhelming dominance of Zola to the point where it is difficult to cite any other author that can undoubtedly be identified as a naturalist writer.

David Baguley, taking a stand on the issue, talked about << *la malédiction du genre* >>, in the sense that Zola himself was against the genres, against literary schools and all pre-established canonical forms[1029]. In fact, Baguley goes further by defining naturalism as a method rather than a genre; a formula rather than a poetics. That formula, he argued, combines the abstract i.e. the method with the concrete - the reality -. Furthermore, he saw naturalism like the general allied with the specific; the cultural with the natural; the universal with the historical[1030]. The debate would be closed if one admitted that naturalism was

---

[1027] Guy Robert: **Émile Zola, Principes et Caractères Généraux de son Œuvre**, Paris, Belles Lettres, 1952, p. 193.
[1028] In the article *Le Naturalisme,* published in **Une Campagne** (1882) and later on reproduced in **Le Romancier Naturaliste**, Henri Mitterand (éd.), Émile Zola wrote: << *Quant au romancier, en moi, il ne croit absolument qu'au talent* >>, op. cit. p. 130.
[1029] David Baguley: **Zola et les Genres**, op.cit, p. 4.
[1030] **Ibidem**, p. 5.

in fact only a writing method that tried to subjugate the novel to the rigour of the experimental method.

One may justifiably argue that the ambiguous position of Zola himself added to the confusion surrounding naturalism as a literary school: << *C'est pourquoi j'ai dit tant de fois que le naturalisme n'était pas une école, que par exemple il ne s'incarnait pas dans le génie d'un homme ni dans le coup de folie d'un groupe, comme le romantisme, qu'il consistait simplement dans l'application de la méthode expérimentale à l'étude de la nature et de l'homme. [...] Donc, dans le naturalisme, il ne saurait y avoir ni de novateurs ni de chef d'école. Il y a simplement des travailleurs plus puissants que les autres* >>[1031], he wrote in **Le Roman Expérimental**.

Yet, many critics continue to view naturalism as a literary school. Taken in this sense, it is necessary to identify the other writers of the movement that would gather behind Zola - if he was indeed the leader of such a school. The likes of Goncourt, Maupassant, Huysmans and even the authors of the famous *Manifesto of the Five*, have often been cited to support the argument of naturalism being a literary school in its own right.

3.1. Huysmans and naturalism

In her very brilliant article *Huysmans et Zola: le dialogue brisé*, first published in 1989, Halina Suwala, wondered if Zola was not the only naturalist writer after all. She hypothesized that at least the existence of several variants of naturalism should be[1032] acknowledged. For example, she noted that in Zola's definition, naturalism meant belief in human reason, the acceptance of life as such and the human condition, the return to nature - or pantheism -, and the rejection of supernatural causality, whereas for Huysmans, it meant aestheticism, the research of the "art *nouveau*" and the rejection of the Tainian theory of the medium. Suwala then referred to Huysmans' novel **À Rebours**[1033] to justify his poetics stance. In fact, Joris-Karl Huysmans had a rather different approach to Zola's. According to Couty, at the publication of Huysmans' **À Rebours** in 1884, Zola confessed that: << *le roman portait un coup terrible au naturalisme* >>, and that its author << *faisait dévier l'école* >>[1034].

[1031] Émile Zola: **Le Roman Expérimental** (1880) and in **Œuvres Complètes**, volume 9 : **Nana 1880**, op. cit. p. 343.
[1032] David Baguley admits, in **Naturalist Fiction. The Entropic Vision**, that there is no such thing as a unified body of naturalist theory and that even some naturalist writers were in fact against the views of Zola. That explains the divergent terminolgies from Goncourt, Huysmans, Maupassant and Zola for example, op. cit. p. 40.
[1033] Halina Suwala: **Autour de Zola et du Naturalisme**, article: *Huysmans et Zola : le dialogue brisé*, Paris, Honoré Champion Éditeur, 1993, p. 248.
[1034] Émile Zola quoted by Couty in his article *Naturalisme*, in **Dictionnaire des Littératures de Langue Française**, op. cit. p. 1731.

For Huysmans indeed, it was necessary to break with the dialectic of lust, which alone seemed to characterise Zola's naturalism in his eyes: << *Quoiqu'on inventât, le roman ne pouvait se résumer à ces quelques lignes : savoir pourquoi Monsieur Untel commettait ou ne commettait pas l'adultère avec Madame Une telle* >>[1035].

Moreover, in 1903, Huysmans cast Zola apart and opposed him almost all the other naturalist writers, including himself: << *Zola, qui était un beau décorateur de théâtre, s'en tirait en tirant des toiles plus ou moins précises ; il suggérait très bien l'illusion du mouvement et de la vie ; ses héros étaient dénués d'âme, régis tout simplement par des impulsions et des instincts, ce qui simplifiait le travail de l'analyse. Il remuait, accomplissait quelques actes sommaires, peuplait d'assez franches silhouettes des décors qui devenaient les personnages principaux de ses drames. Il célébrait de la sorte les halles, les magasins de nouveautés, les chemins de fer, les mines, et les êtres humains égarés dans ces milieux n'y jouaient plus que le rôle d'utilités et de figurants ; mais Zola était Zola, c'est-à-dire un artiste un peu massif, mais doué de puissants poumons et de gros poings.*

Nous autres, moins râblés et préoccupés d'un art plus subtil et plus vrai, nous devions nous demander si le naturalisme n'aboutissait pas à une impasse et si nous n'allions pas bientôt nous heurter contre le mur >>[1036].

Huysmans went so far as to brand naturalism a dead-end literature and from which he had to free itself: << *Je cherchais vaguement à m'évader d'un cul-de-sac où je suffoquais, mais je n'avais aucun plan déterminé et* **À Rebours***, qui me libéra d'une littérature sans issue, en m'aérant, est un ouvrage parfaitement inconscient, imaginé sans idées préconçues, sans intentions réservées d'avenir, sans rien du tout* >>[1037].

Beyond these motivations of aesthetic and temperamental nature, one must mention the discovery of the fervour of religious faith by Huysmans in the 1880s. From then on, he advocated another type of naturalism that he called spiritual naturalism in **Là-Bas**, which was published in 1891. This new form of naturalism was to manifest itself in the absence of preconceived ideas in the construction of the novel. In **Là-Bas**, therefore, from the first chapter, two characters are presented, one of whom, Durtal - Huysmans himself probably incarnated in that one - would like to write a novel. But then he is confronted with the difficult choice of the literary school to which his book would belong. That question of the aesthetic choice torments him for a moment and he ends up deciding to be

---

[1035] Joris-Karl Huysmans : *Préface* of the second edition of **À Rebours,** Paris, Édition Gallimard, 1977, p. 57.
[1036] **Ibidem**, p. 59.
[1037] **Ibidem**, p. 59.

a spiritualist: << *il lui suffirait peut-être d'être spiritualiste pour s'imaginer le supranaturalisme, la seule formule qui lui convent* >>[1038].

Moreover, as Suwala writes, Huysmans saw himself closer to Goncourt rather than to Zola because he was a follower of the artistic writing by the Goncourt brothers. In a correspondence to Prins, Huysmans blamed precisely the commercial success of Zola's novels as the cause of his renunciation to all forms of art in his writing. Continuing to draw up a series of oppositions between the two novelists - Zola and Huysmans, Suwala recalls the Zolian will to investigate man and society in order to discover the determinism of human phenomena, hoping that would help regulate society once the truth was discovered. On the contrary, for Huysmans, << *personne ne fait sa vie, on la subit* >>[1039].

In addition, Zola preached democracy as the right path for the future and extolled his audience as a partner in democracy in literature while for Huysmans, democracy was : << *l'adversaire le plus acharné du pauvre* >>[1040]. That is why he extolled the elitism in which one would write for a small group of the elite. Notwithstanding all these divergences, Huysmans has always proclaimed himself to be a naturalist until 1883 when, with **À Rebours**, he sharply distanced himself from the movement for good. From that date on, indeed, he displayed a blatant duplicity in his opinions of Zola and naturalism. Writing to Zola in laudatory terms about his novels, he would then write to his other friends, including Prins, criticising Zola in very harsh terms. To Prins, he wrote and lambasted Zola and his works in terms of << *la grossièreté de l'écriture* >>, << *le muflisme* >>, << *la renonciation à tout art* >>, << *la bassesse* >>, << *les idées abjectes* >>, << *le style nul* >> of the << *parvenu* >>. Meanwhile, to Zola, he would write at the same time to pay tribute to the same books, applauding their << *flamboiement* >>, the << *joli tour* >> and he would hail the author for being << *le plus prodigieux manieur de foules de toutes les littératures* >>, celebrating his << *fresque immense* >>, << *les sacrés reins* >> and << *les épaules résistantes* >> of the novelist[1041]. Suwala shows very well how the only feelings that Huysmans still had for Zola were << *haine, obsession, mépris, vomissement, méchanceté* >>[1042].

Having learned indeed the liaison of Zola with Jeanne Rozerot, he wrote to Prins : << *Vous ai-je dit qu'il [Zola] a enlevé la femme de chambre de sa femme et qu'il était père d'une fille ?* >>[1043]. Huysmans went on to make fun of the tears of joy that Zola had supposedly shed after the birth of his daughter, Jeanne.

[1038] Joris-Karl Huysmans : **Là-Bas**, Paris, 1891, Édition Maxi Poche, Classiques français, 1984, p. 23.
[1039] Halina Suwala : **Autour de Zola et du Naturalisme**, op. cit. p. 249.
[1040] **Ibidem**, p. 249.
[1041] **Ibidem**, pp. 252-254.
[1042] **Ibidem**, p. 254.
[1043] **Ibidem**, p. 254.

Another source of discord between the two men was the Jewish question, and more precisely the Dreyfus affair. Suwala demonstrates irrefutably Huysmans' violent racism and his proven and proclaimed anti-Semitism. When Zola embarked on the Dreyfusian campaign, Huysmans attacked him when he wrote to his friends and denounced his<< *folie* >> and his << *orgueil* >>[1044].

From 1896, Zola's name was completely erased from Huysmans correspondence until 1902, when he wrote again to Prins to congratulate himself for not attending Zola's funeral. That complete lack of empathy for the mortal remains of Zola was not reflected anywhere else better than in this thanks and praises that he gave Providence for having ended the earthly stay of the deceased: << *Son discrédit* [of Zola] *en France était énorme et il est mort à temps, car il eût connu, avec son train de vie, la misère. Il lui fallait avec son double ménage 100 000 francs par an. Il ne pouvait plus les gagner. La providence a donc été, en quelque sorte, très douce pour lui, en l'enlevant avant sa très prochaine et irrémédiable décadence* >>[1045].

One of the reasons for the breakdown in the two authors' relationship was the religious question. Indeed, as Hemmings pointed out in his article *Émile Zola et la religion. À propos de La Faute de l'Abbé Mouret*, Huysmans converted to Catholicism in his forties and << *il écrira à partir de **Là-Bas** toute une série de romans catholiques* >>[1046]. Zola, on the contrary, would never give up attacking Catholicism[1047].

What else can be said about the masters of Huysmans?

3.2. The Goncourt brothers and naturalism

Jules and Edmond Huot de Goncourt were the Siamese brothers of literature, writing together, jointly signing their works where they identified themselves by the pronouns ''we'' and ''us'' - especially in the prefaces. Edmond de Goncourt carried on that trend even when he alone continued to think and write for the two of them following the passing of his younger brother. They were contemporaries of Zola that had a close relationship with him.

[1044] Halina Suwala : **Autour de Zola et du Naturalisme**, op. cit. p. 257.
[1045] **Ibidem**, p. 257 - the author was referring to J.-K. Huysmans's **Lettres inédites à Arij Prins: 1885-1907**, Genève, Droz, 1977.
[1046] F.W.J. Hemmings: Zola et la religion. À propos de **La Faute de l'Abbé Mouret**, article published in **Europe**, n°. 468-469, op. cit. p. 130.
[1047] Émile Zola took offence from the fact people stole, lied and killed << *à visage découvert* >>, without being worried nor threatened with any punishement; but amazingly enough, one would be << *lapidé et hué* >, for loving in broad daylight. And he squarely blamed Catholicism for that harsh treatment: << *Il a fallu l'idée chrétienne de l'indignité du corps pour rendre le sexe honteux et mettre la perfection morale dans la chasteté. L'homme n'a plus été fait pour se reproduire, mais pour mourir* >>, in **Documents Littéraires** : *De la moralité en littérature,* and then in **Le Roman Naturaliste**, Henri Mitterand (éd.), op. cit. p. 109.

3.2.1. The Goncourts' relationship with Zola at human level

The first physical contacts between them took place in February 1865 when Zola read Balzac and Taine. Never again, did they cease to visit each other, nor to dine together as often as possible. After the early death of Jules, Edmond continued their relationship with Zola. It is nevertheless important to point out that these very close and enthusiastic relations from the beginning, were tainted with suspicion, and even animosity as time went by. In their diary, the Goncourt brothers wrote on December 14th, 1868: << *Nous avons eu à déjeuner notre admirateur et notre élève Zola* >>[1048]. Then on August 27th, 1870, two months after the passing of Jules, Edmond noted without any affection: << *Zola déjeune chez moi* >>[1049]. This evolution of their friendship towards hostility was accentuated to the point where Edmond de Goncourt wrote later, on January 25th, 1875, that his former << *élève* >> was nothing but << *un envieux* >> and << *un dominateur* >>[1050]. Nevertheless, appearances were preserved and they continued to see each other often enough. Zola, for his part, showed to the end an unshakable admiration for Edmond de Goncourt and his literature. Moreover, the latter seemed to be surprised by the praise that Zola lavished at his novels through the press.

How can one then explain the progressive animosity of the Goncourt brothers towards their pupil and friend?

3.2.2. The literary conceptions or the similarity source of conflict

Two years before **Thérèse Raquin**, Zola's first novel of naturalistic inspiration, **Germinie Lacerteux** (1865) by the Goncourt brothers was released. That novel marked the effective starting point of the so-called "*naturalistic*" adventure. For some, the novel by the Goncourt brothers was shamefully << *[de] la littérature putride* >>[1051]. For others, it was << *[du] petit roman*>>[1052]. But, accvording to Flaubert: << *Cela est atroce d'un bout à l'autre et sublime. La grande question du réalisme n'a jamais été si carrément posée* >>[1053]. In **Le Salut Public** February 25th, Zola found the book outstanding. Similarly, he paid tribute to **Madame Gervaisais** in **Le Gaulois** on March 9th, 1869. His enthusiasm for novels written by the Goncourt never faded away and that was due to several reasons.

Stylistically: << *Ils sont les romanciers artistes, les peintres du vrai pittoresque, les stylistes élégants qui s'encanaillent par amour de l'art, les instrumentistes*

[1048] Edmond and Jules Huot de Goncourt: **Journal. Mémoires de la Vie Littéraire**, Robert Ricatte (éd.), volume 2, p. 96.
[1049] **Ibidem**, volume 3, p. 154.
[1050] **Ibidem**, volume 3, p. 155.
[1051] Bellet: article "*Goncourt*", in the **Dictionnaire des Littératures de Langue Française**, tome 2, op. cit. p. 1032.
[1052] **Ibidem**, p.1032.
[1053] **Ibidem**, p.1032.

les plus remarquables dans le groupe des créateurs du roman naturaliste contemporain >>[1054], Zola wrote in a lyrical and enthusiastic style.

When it comes to the working methods, the two brothers made investigative trips before writing their novels and they gave much importance to their notes, maybe far too much. However, their ferocious realism was borderline reproduction of reality. It was for example Rose, their ex-maid that passed away in 1862, who was the almost exact model for Germinie Lacerteux in the novel of the same name.

At the thematic level, almost all their production consisted of black novels where the eponymous heroine, a hysterical and a neurotic woman, was studied "scientifically" in her epidermis, her nerves and the mystery of her psychological functioning in the face of passions[1055]. Here are some ideas that presided over the genesis of Zola's first novels, **Thérèse Raquin** (1867) and **Madeleine Férat** (1868) and even so in the **Rougon-Macquart**. Authors haunted by the omnipresent woman in their works, the Goncourt brothers never seemed to have fallen in love. Meanwhile, Zola was mocked by his critics on the pretext that he was impotent. Their common goal though consisted in winning the battle of realism and impressionism. Yet, later on, Zola seized on the degradation[1056] of the body that had become a spectacle in the Goncourts' literature, all things that fuelled Edmond's bitterness towards him.

Edmond, indeed, thought Zola had copied him since the publication of **L'Assommoir** in 1877. His bitterness from that point on went so far as to deny Zola any talent whatsoever. For him, since 1875, only Flaubert and he remained the true novelists worthy of that name. That was probably a peremptory and a boasting claim tinged with obvious bad faith. The precursor was undoubtedly saddened to be overshadowed by the ever-growing and the overwhelming fame of his young disciple who had become the spearhead of naturalism, while his new novel, **La Fille Élisa**, released that year, received a much less resounding reception and success.

In any case, one must agree that the Goncourt brothers were the true precursors of naturalism, even though they were much less famous than Zola. They were

---

[1054] Émile Zola: **Les Romanciers Naturalistes** (1881) and later on in **Le Roman Naturaliste**, Henri Mitterand (éd.), op. cit. p. 62.
[1055] In **Germinie Lacerteux,** *par MM. Edmond et Jules de Goncourt,* article publishedon the 24th February 1865 in **Le Salut Public,** and later on in **Le Roman Naturaliste,** Henri Mitterand (éd.), Émile Zola defended the Goncourt brothers in the following words: << *Un reproche fondé, qui peut être fait à* **Germinie Lacerteux***, c'est celui d'être un roman médical, un cas curieux d'hystérie. [...] Certainement leur héroïne est malade, malade de cœur et malade de corps ; ils ont tout à la fois étudié la maladie de son corps et celle de son cœur. Où est le mal, je vous prie ?* >>, op. cit. p. 16.
[1056] David Baguley mentions the poetics of dissolution in the Goncourt brothers' works, in **Naturalist Fiction. The Entropic Vision**, op. cit. p. 200. Generally speaking, Baguley remarks that naturalist novels distil human destinies in desintegrated settings, p. 201.

the first to approach literary heroes from a "scientific" perspective in that they paid a particular attention to the question of neurosis, hysteria and passions. Following in their foosteps, Zola only seized that same opportunity that would allow him to dominate the romantic creation in France for a quarter of a Century - from **Thérèse Raquin** in 1867 to **Le Docteur Pascal** in 1893. However, as he always honestly admitted, Zola admired the Goncourt brothers through thick and thin. They influenced him greatly, and they guided his aesthetic choice in the first place.

Another name that often comes up when people talk about naturalist writers is Guy de Maupassant.

3.3. Guy de Maupassant

Halina Suwala, in her communication *À propos de quelques techniques narratives du naturalisme,* at the international symposium in Catania in 1988, wrote about Maupassant, that : << *Il est convenu de le considérer comme un, voire le disciple de Flaubert, opinion dont il est d'ailleurs le premier responsable* >>[1057]. From that point of view that came from the outside, Suwala considered Maupassant as equidistant to Flaubert and Zola: << *Et l'on pourrait même risquer l'affirmation qu'il se situe à mi-chemin entre Flaubert et Zola*>>[1058]. More recently, in 1992, in her article *Maupassant et le naturalisme,* she found Maupassant << *inclassable* >> and << *indéfinissable* >> based on the analysis of the critics aimed at the author.

Indeed, Suwala pointed out that Maupassant used to be accused of practising a literature from the gutter, just like Zola. That went on up until the publication of **Mademoiselle Fifi**. However, critics gave him a place apart after **Une Vie** came out, before announcing his divorce from naturalism when he published **Miss Harriet**. And when Brunetière published his article **Les Petits Naturistes** - a formula that became famous - he included in that category Huysmans, Hennique, Daudet, Alexis and, of course, Maupassant[1059]. In short, he meant all the Medanists, i.e. all the young writers that gathered around Zola in his Médan retreat, and whose texts were published in the collection **Les Soirées de Médan.** The novel **Mont-Oriol** would have made Maupassant, in the eyes of the critics, << *un réformateur* >>, << *un dissident* >>, << *un indépendant*>>, someone who does not << *appartient à aucune école* >> ; as the book signalled << *la fin du naturalisme* >>[1060]. An argument of weight to support the thesis of the independence of Maupassant was his letter in 1876, which was sent to Camille Mendès, where he affirmed: << *Je veux n'être jamais lié à aucun parti politique [...], à aucune religion, à aucune secte, à aucune école [...], ne m'incliner devant*

[1057] Halina Suwala: **Autour de Zola et du Naturalisme**, chapter: *À propos de quelques techniques narratives du naturalisme*, op. cit. p. 208.
[1058] **Ibidem**, op. cit, p. 208.
[1059] **Ibidem**, chapter: *Maupassant et le naturalisme*, op.cit, p. 284.
[1060] **Ibidem,** p. 286.

aucun dogme, [...] et aucun principe >>. To be even more blunt, he wrote this to Paul Alexis: << *Je ne crois pas plus au naturalisme et au réalisme qu'au romantisme* >>[1061].

Maupassant was labelled by the press as a naturalist writer after the publication of **Les Soirées de Medan** in 1880. He wanted to cut short all those suppositions - which he considered as nonsense -, once his new book, **La Maison Tellier**, would come out. In a letter written in April 1880, and sent to Flaubert, he noted: << *C'est une préparation parfaite à mon volume de vers qui paraîtra mardi et qui coupera court, en ce qui me concerne, à ces bêtises d'école naturaliste qu'on répète dans les journaux. Cela est la faute du titre* **Les Soirées de Médan**, *que j'ai toujours trouvé mauvais et dangereux* >>[1062]. And after the publication of Zola's infamous **Le Roman Expérimental**, in another letter to Flaubert, he treated the essayist as no less than a << *fou* >>: << *Que dites-vous de Zola ? Moi, je le trouve absolument fou!* >>[1063].

Maupassant, if one believes Halina Suwala, was different from Zola[1064] on the fundamental concept of truth, which comes back as a leitmotif in Zola's theoretical discourse. For Maupassant, there was no such thing as a single and indisputable truth, and even there were as many truths out there as there are men on earth.

Ultimately, Maupassant never self-defined as being a naturalist author, although one can find things that he had in common with Zola, especially in terms of the impersonality of their works; the elimination of the concept of intrigue; the occultation of the composition and of the psychological analysis of the character; the absence of any conclusion and, finally, the preponderance of the description in their texts. These convergences certainly relate to points that Zola defined as naturalistic criteria.

However, the discordant points between them were so numerous that the question remains as to whether or not Maupassant belonged to the naturalist movement.

Maupassant's situation was not an isolated case though, since it was quite similar to Huysmans' position.

Unlike Zola, Maupassant entered the Yvetot seminary in 1863. Yet, he did not emerge from it more Catholic than his friend Zola. On the contrary, in there he cultivated his hatred for the cassock and observed the hypocrisy and the

---

[1061] Halina Suwala: **Autour de Zola et du Naturalisme**, chapter: *Maupassant et le naturalisme*, op.cit, p. 290.
[1062] **Ibidem**, p. 292.
[1063] **Ibidem**, p. 291.
[1064] For David Baguley, Maupassant was effectively much closer to Flaubert than to Zola, in **Naturalist Fiction. The Entropic Vision**, op. cit. p. 49.

intolerance of priests. Very quickly, he was dismissed from the seminary for disciplinary reasons and, by the age of sixteen, he was deeply debauched. He contracted syphilis at the age of twenty-six and ended up becoming a madman.

It is vital to also recognise that Maupassant was not only a realistic author, because he wrote fantastic works, like **Une Main Écorchée** in 1875, and **Le Horla** in 1887. He was also and above all an emeritus storyteller and a novelist. His first short story, ***Boule de Suif***, was published in **Les Soirées de Médan** in 1880, followed in 1881 by his first collection of short stories, **La Maison Tellier**, which achieved great success. Another collection of short stories followed in 1886, **Toine**. In terms of tales, **Les Contes de la Bécasse** were a masterpiece in 1884, followed by thirty additional tales published in 1885. Maupassant died as a madman at the clinic of Dr. Blanche on July 6th, 1893, after spending many months in delirium and in complete isolation. Despite the indisputable success of his novels, **Une Vie** (1883), **Bel Ami** (1885), **Mont-Oriol** (1887) and **Notre Cœur** (1890), he will always be remembered more as a storyteller and short stories writer than a novelist. There is no doubt in any case that none of his works enter into the canonical mould of the experimental novel as drawn up by Zola, even though he observed the three rules: look, observe and dissect before writing.

Was this not the general characteristic of the realistic authors that were the likes of Balzac, Flaubert, Goncourt, Zola[1065] and Daudet?

3.4. Zola, the atheist and lonely writer

It has already been shown that Zola was a natalist, a believer in fertility. However, the principles advocated by natalism oppose the cult of Virgin Mary – and even the virginity of the secular individual. They also oppose the celibacy of priests, which is advocated by the Catholic Church. While the church vehemently opposes abortion and contraception today, the observation of these two dogmas - virginity and celibacy -, on a large scale, would consecrate the death and disappearance of the human species in Zola's eyes. So, for him, Catholicism is a << *religion de mort* >>[1066], to borrow the word of F. Hemmings: << *or le chaste, n'est-il pas celui qui se refuse à engendrer la vie? La vierge, celle qui se dérobe aux devoirs de la maternité ? Religion de mort aussi parce que, pour un Zola qui ne croyait pas à la résurrection, c'est un dieu mort que semble glorifier le catholicisme en la personne du crucifié* >>[1067].

[1065] In **Naturalist Fiction. The Entropic Vision**, David Baguley established that the balzacian description, which is characterised by the extreme sordid, is opposed to the description in Zola's works, which is marked by its strangeness and its excentricity. Huysmans description, however, is supposed to be marked by etiolation and liquefaction, whereas the Goncourt brothers' is marked by the grey colour and by dissolution, op. cit. pp. 198-200.

[1066] F.W.J. Hemmings: *Zola et la religion. À Propos de* **La Faute de l'Abbé Mouret**, article published in **Europe : Zola**, op. cit. p. 132.

[1067] **Ibidem**, p. 132.

When analysing **La Faute de l'Abbé Mouret**, Hemmings finally found paganism as Zola's only religion: << *Oui, Zola, [...] a été un grand païen [...] culte secret, enfoui dans son inconscient, et dont il avait un peu honte* >>[1068]. For Hemmings, therefore, it is inaccurate to consider that novel as an anti-religious book: << *Mais, pour en finir avec La Faute de l'Abbé Mouret, cet ouvrage prétendu antireligieux, ne faudrait-il pas conclure, au contraire, que c'est de tous ses livres, celui qui témoigne le plus clairement du sentiment religieux de l'auteur ?* >>[1069]. Note also that this idea of Zola's paganism appears in David Baguley's writings about **La Terre** : << *le culte païen de la fécondité domine ce roman* >>[1070]. Such paganism implies the renunciation to the old **Bible** since Baguley sees in the tender romance between Clotilde and Pascal, a << *nouvelle Bible de l'Humanité* >>[1071].

I have already noted, in my opening remarks, Bertrand-Jennings' point of view with regards to the rejection of the Church in Zola's novels, as well as that of Jean Borie, which goes in the same direction. That idea of the negative Church, which is the symbol of death, is also present in Philippe Hamon's works[1072] and in Jean-François Tonard's[1073]. Let us therefore agree, from all this and from the study of the characters of the priests and other assimilated religious figures, as I did in this study as well as that of the episode of the destruction of the church of the Father Mouret, that Zola was not a Christian. In fact, he was a fierce opponent to the Catholic Church in particular. In his biography, no religious practice[1074] is attributed to him to the point where one must admit to his atheism[1075]. For Zola, faith in man and in science was the guarantor of human happiness.

[1068] F.W.J. Hemmings: *Zola et la religion. À Propos de La Faute de l'Abbé Mouret*, article published in **Europe : Zola**, op. cit. p. 135.

[1069] **Ibidem,** p. 135.

[1070] David Baguley: **Zola et les Genres**, chapter IX : *Le réalisme grotesque et mythique de La Terre*, op. cit. p. 95.

[1071] **Ibidem**, chapter XI: *Du naturalisme au mythe : l'alchimie du Docteur Pascal*, op. cit. p. 133.

[1072] Philippe Hamon: **Le Personnel du Roman. Le Système des Personnages dans les Rougon-Macquart d'Émile Zola**, op. cit. p. 228.

[1073] J.-F. Tonard: **Thématique et Symbolique de l'Espace Clos dans le Cycle des Rougon-Macquart d'Émile Zola**, op. cit. p. 299.

[1074] Roger Ripoll recalled that Zola was influenced by the Catholic teachings – that he received during his younger years – and the menace of eternal damnation in **Réalité et Mythe chez Zola**, op. cit. p. 98. However, the critic claims that the adult Zola was not a practising Catholic.

[1075] Émile Zola wrote: << *De nos jours, le protestantisme est donc devenu, en morale et en littérature, un épouvantail bien autrement gênant que le catholicisme ; nous nous entendrons encore avec un catholique, tandis que je défie un artiste de jamais faire bon ménage avec un protestant. Il y a là une antipathie de cerveaux. Nous autres romanciers naturalistes, observateurs et expérimentateurs, analystes et anatomistes, nous sommes surtout en guerre ouverte avec le protestantisme, par notre enquête continuelle qui dérange les dogmes et les principes, qui passe outre aux axiomes de morale. Notre ennemi est là. Je le sens depuis longtemps* >>, in **Documents Littéraires** : *De la moralité en littérature*, article published for the first time in **Le Messager de l'Europe** in October 1880, and reproduced in **Le Roman Naturaliste**, Henri Mitterand (éd.), op. cit. p. 110. This apparent ceremonious treatment of Catholicism must not mislead anyone, for

Finally, in view of all the above, it is fair to argue that Zola was a lonely writer[1076] whose itinerary as a man and as a literary figure was sanctioned by many meetings. His hundreds of correspondents certainly testify to that. But also, and above all, he built some sincere friendships such as with Paul Alexis'. Unfortunately, though, he experienced some disappointments in his friendships just like he abruptly fell out with Cézanne the day after the publication of **L'Œuvre**[1077]. Some of his friendships were short-lived just like his relationship with Huysmans, whereas some were hypocritical like his accointance with the Goncourt[1078] brothers. He was betrayed by some so-called friends that betrayed him outright like the authors of the **Manifesto of Five**. It seems indisputable that Zola fulfilled his statement of loneliness made on August 19th, 1897, when he wrote to Henry Bauer, since his retirement home in Médan: << *J'ai toujours été affamé de solitude et d'impopularité, à peine ai-je quelques amis, et je tiens à eux* >>[1079].

Basically, one can summarise Zola's situation by saying that he was accompanied, at some point in his naturalistic journey, and then he got abandoned on the way by Huysmans. At some point in time, Maupassant took a path next to his, often going in the same direction, but refusing to walk on the same path as him[1080]. As for Edmond de Goncourt, he preferred to walk parallel to Zola, in slow motion, refusing to follow him on the overtaking lane that he liked. As for the five, according to Zola himself, he barely knew them: << *Heureusement, aucun des cinq signataires n'est de mon intimité, pas un n'est venu chez moi, je ne les ai jamais rencontrés que chez Goncourt et Daudet. Cela m'a rendu leur manifeste moins dur* >>[1081]. Abandoned or marginalised by those he believed to be his literary friends, Zola was similar to Labdacus, who was publicly immolated by those who claimed to be his heirs, the new Oedipuses.

Did that not make Zola equally a tragic and a mythical hero in his own right?

Zola was simply not a believer in the Christian dogmas generally speaking, no matter which Christian denomination was promoting them.

[1076] Colette Becker : *Introduction biographique* in Émile Zola: **Correspondance, volume VII, juin 1890- septembre 1893,** Montréal/Paris, les Presses de l'université de Montréal/Éditions du CNRS, 1989, pp. 19-22.

[1077] Henri Mitterand: *Préface* in Émile Zola: **Correspondance, volume VI, 1887-1890**, Montréal/Paris, Les Presses de l'université de Montréal, Éditions du CNRS, 1987, p.12.

[1078] **Ibidem**, p. 12.

[1079] **Ibidem**, p. 168.

[1080] Henri Mitterand writes in this aspect: << *Il a été déçu par l'incapacité de ses premiers disciples les plus proches (Alexis, Céard, Hennique) à produire des œuvres nombreuses et fortes, et par l'éloignement de ses amis les plus talentueux (Huysmans, Maupassant)* >>,in **Le Roman Naturaliste** by Émile Zola, Henri Mitterand (éd.), op. cit. p. 133.

[1081] Émile Zola: **Correspondance, Tome VI, 1887-1890**, *Lettre du 19 août 1887 adressée à Henry Bauër,* op. cit. p. 168.

CONCLUSION

CONCLUSION

This study tried to look at the current state of the literary criticism on Zola's fiction works in the context of sexuality and fate in order to evaluate the limits of those previous studies and to see what is at stakes in this current approach.

The first part of the work, by superimposing the author's texts, showed that the choice of sexuality as the unifying theme of the **Rougon-Macquart** was not the result of a fantasy on the artist's part. On the contrary, Zola had some religious, sociological, ideological, and epistemological reasons that justified the preponderant place awarded to sexuality in the naturalistic novel. Subsequently, it has been established that in Zola's novels, sexuality is shown in a generally bad or even a morbid light for Zola did have an animalistic, a perverse, a mythical and an apocalyptic approach[1082] to sexuality, which consolidated the idea of a social catastrophe that was both imminent and inevitable [1083]. Such was the sentence of the god Zola levied on the Second Empire through his romantic cycle subtitled << *l'histoire naturelle et sociale d'une famille* >>.

The second part was devoted to the study of the characters facing sexuality and fatality. The characters are indeed the first elements of legibility of the literary text and they were apprehended in their intrinsic being and their different deeds in the strict framework of the sexuality. In fact, the being of the characters constituted a narrative programme by itself. That is why the onomastic transparency was sometimes so manifest[1084] in the corpus. Once the actantial diagram was laid bare, the plot of the narrative did emerge by itself, at least as far as the being, the deeds and the becoming of the characters is concerned. It was then that I took interest in their sanctions in terms of crack, hereditary diseases, follies, early and/or atrocious deaths. Basically, the fatum that strikes the Zolan characters has nothing to do with that which hit the Ovidian or the Racinian heroes for example. Here, the inevitability of the fatality hanging over the heads of the characters is no longer of divine order, but rather of scientific, literary and artistic nature[1085]. In this, one can appreciate the originality of the fatality of Zola's conscious naturalism, which is no longer the fault of the ancient Greek gods.

The discovery of Zola's personal myth was based on the study of the metalinguistic and the poetic functions, notably by questioning the haunting

---

[1082] Jacques Noiray: **Le Romancier et la Machine, I : L'Univers de Zola**, op. cit. p. 508 and Roger Ripoll: **Réalité et Mythe chez Zola**, op. cit. p. 101.
[1083] Maarten Van Buuren: **Les Rougon-Macquart d'Émile Zola. De la Métaphore au Mythe**, op. cit. p. 187.
[1084] Philippe Hamon: **Le Personnel du Roman. Le Système des Personnages dans Les Rougon-Macquart d'Émile Zola**, op. cit. p. 108 et p. 116, and Claude Seassau : **Émile Zola, Le Réalisme Symbolique**, op. cit. pp. 37-61
[1085] **Réalité et Mythe chez Zola** by Roger Ripoll, op. cit. p. 78.

mythical, metaphorical and synecdochic figures. I was able to admit, on the basis of that analysis, that Zola was obsessed with sex, obsessed with the reproductive process, obsessed with the haunting of nothingness and death. I was strengthened in this position by the recurrence and the convergence of the same figures of rhetoric towards those same fatal goals, both within a given novel and at the level of the entire series.

The third part dealt exclusively with the problem of the relevance of the immanent spatio-temporal component in the fatality linked to sexuality. The relationship between this component and the anthropomorphic agents convinced me that the literalness of any text, notably a novelistic one, depended to a great extent on the treatment of temporality on the one hand, and on that of the spatial component on the other hand. Indeed, the character and their spatio-temporal environment are indissociable as they influence one another, and they reflect and incarnate each other. In **Les Rougon-Macquart**, the study of the external times and the internal ones - the verbal tenses of enunciation and the temporal symbolism - shows that various sexual situations ranging from convergence to divergence, and passing through ambivalence are brought about by the temporal component. Then, at the same time, time is the sexual agent's accomplice and it also denounces the debauchery that characterises the protagonists. Time also works hand in hand with the space that is sometimes protective, or persecuting the sexual subjects. The latter is sometimes attacked and defeated by their space. In that case, they end up taking revenge on their space by turning into pyromaniac nihilists, thus confirming Zola's obsession with nothingness and atrocious death. That is why I found it regrettable to notice so little interest on the critics' part for they have vastly ignored the temporal component in naturalistic fiction in general, and in Zola's works in particular.

Nevertheless, I could not stop there because in the fourth part, I showed that the theme of sexuality was very fruitful. That is why I found it quite natural to invest myself in putting that fertility under the spotlight, in order to enlighten it as best as I could, humbly and concisely. That way, I discovered that sexuality allowed a renewal of novel writing. Also, the allusion and the half-words, the mises en abyme or the repetition, the opulence of the discursive anachronisms and "*l'hypertrophie du détail vrai*" and significative, all constituted the categorical fundamentals of that new writing technique, at least in the understanding of the master of naturalism.

Beyond that purely aesthetic aspect, I discussed at the same time Zola's autobiography, the criticism of the author. This, it must be clearly stated, led me to highlight the strengths and the weaknesses of a man, an author with prodigious talent, but a very controversial one. Ideologically, Zola was a natalist and a republican[1086] who loved justice. All his journalistic and literary production

---

[1086] Émile Zola insiste: << *Je suis un républicain de la veille. Je veux dire que j'ai défendu les idées républicaines dans mes livres et dans la presse, lorsque le Second Empire était encore*

can be summed up in a single word: struggle. He was a fierce wrestler obsessed with the denunciation of the privileges of the elite of imperial society and the various injustices of which the little people were the resigned victims[1087]. His tireless struggle against those two scourges that were unbearable in his eyes, had the sole purpose of putting an end to them so that progress and social welfare would benefit all his fellow citizens, his contemporaries, without exception.

Zola was indeed a passionate and an indefatigable worker. He was above all a theoretician of heredity, of which he made his creed, replacing, so to speak, the biologist and the geneticist. That disciplinary transgression - from literature to science - has not gone unhindered, however, because of the different nature of the two domains[1088] of knowledge. As a consequence, the scientism of Zola's naturalism was approximate, especially in view of the new developments that genetic science has recorded since the late nineteenth Century. At the time of Zola already, so many voices were raised to attack the author on this sensitive issue and the controversy quickly arose between the detractors and the defenders of naturalism. Zola found himself at the forefront of the apologists of his literary movement to defend himself and his ideas against attacks targeted him and his novels. The defenders categorically condemned the extremism of a literary movement entirely focused on sex, filth and immorality, while his defenders praised the powerful genius and the insightful analysis of the author of the **Rougon-Macquart**. This part also brought to light the paganism and the loneliness of Zola, that scholar who did not believe in Catholic dogmas and whose literary friendships were crumbling along the way. At that stage, I praised the author's courageous attempt at combining the two domains of knowledge - literature and science[1089] - to analyse and to explain the world.

---

debout. J'aurais pu être de la curée, si j'avais eu la moindre ambition politique. Il me suffisait de me baisser pour ramasser les épis, après les avoir fauchés.

Ainsi donc, ma situation est nette. Je suis un républicain qui ne vit pas de la République. Eh bien ! l'idée m'est venue que cette situation est excellente pour dire tout haut ce que je pense >>, dans La République et la littérature, article published in August 1879, in **Le Messager de l'Europe**, and later on reproduced in **Le Roman Expérimental**, and lastly in the **Œuvres Complètes, volume 9: Nana 1880**, op. cit, p. 488.

[1087] Colette Becker wrote the following about Zola: << *Très tôt deux images apparaissent sous sa plume: celle d'une meute lancée à la curée, et celle, consécutive, de la pourriture, de la gangrène, qui gagne le corps social promis à la débâcle* >>, in Zola, article published in the **Dictionnaire des Littératures de Langue Française, tome 4**, op. cit. p. 2693.

[1088] Refer to Roger Ripoll, in **Réalité et Mythe chez Zola**, volume II, op. cit. p. 922.

[1089] In **Naturalist Fiction. The Entropic Vision**, David Baguley affirms that naturalism could well be defined as the sum of a rigorous scientism and of the individual genius of an author, op. cit. p. 57.

In the same sens, by opposing the romantic poets - considered as deistics and idealists – to the naturalist novelists, Émile Zola claimed: << *Les naturalistes, au contraire, vont jusqu'à la science ; ils nient tout absolu, et l'idéal n'est pour eux que l'inconnu qu'ils ont le devoir d'étudier et de connaître ; en un mot, loin de refuser Dieu, loin de l'amoindrir, ils le réservent comme la dernière solution qui soit au fond des problèmes humains. La bataille est là* >>, in Le Naturalisme,

Anyway, Zola was and still remains an outstanding author that is important to know for those interested in the modern novel in general, and the French novel in particular. Zola was, in fact, a great author, even an inescapable novelist that deserves respect. It would not be honest, from the sexual characteristics found in this study, to peremptorily assert that he merely produced putrid literature, because this man did indeed have an ideal of beauty, an ideal of justice and humanism; ideals that he tried to defend until his accidental or criminal death on September 28th, 1902. In his epic battles, he spared no weapon: romantic cycles with **Les Rougon-Macquart, Les Quatre Évangiles, Les Trois Villes;** and journalistic biases with the numerous press articles against the imperial society and especially his famous *J'accuse!* in the Dreyfus Affair.

Evidently, those controversial columns testify to his total commitment to taking part in all the major struggles of his time. That alone can justify his celebrity among the people and his reputation as an irreducible polemicist. Today, Zola is probably one of the most read French novelists and he still is amongst the bestsellers. Certainly, each of his novels has their own destiny. For example, **Germinal** is the second most read French novel of all times after Stendhal's **Le Rouge et le Noir**, while some other titles have sold more than one million copies in France according to Professor Colette Becker, in her *Audience d'Émile Zola*[1090]. Such a performance is only justice rendered to a great servant of humanity; a man who basically, << *était bon* >>, according to Anatole France[1091]. That statement is of such importance in the mouth of someone who was, in 1887, one of the most ardent critics of Zola.

It should also be recognised in Zola, one of the authors who have particularly contributed to the rehabilitation of the novel as a literary genre and its emancipation[1092].

However, one could question the particular interest that led me to undertake this study on sexuality in the works of Zola, i.e. the originality of this work in the concert of the countless Zolian studies. For me, instead of tackling the roots of naturalism, the works on Zola often approach it from a fragmentary angle - and it is probably not a bad thing, though. Indeed, while specialists such as Lethbridge, Hamon, Serres and Todorov - to name but a few - are tackling, who,

---

article published for the first time in **Le Voltaire** on 17th January 1881, and then in **Une Campagne** (1882), and lastly, in **Le Roman Naturaliste**, Henri Mitterand (éd.), op. cit. p. 128.
[1090] Colette Becker : Zola in **Dictionnaire des Littératures de Langue Française**, volume 4, op. cit. p. 2714.
[1091] Anatole France: "*Discours d'oraison funèbre*" pronounced at the funeral of Zola in 1902, partially reproduced by Marcel Girard in his *Archives de l'œuvre* in **La Terre** de Zola, op. cit. p. 502.
[1092] Émile Zola: *Le Naturalisme au théâtre*, article published in **Le Messager de l'Europe** in June 1879, and then in **Le Roman Expérimental** and in **Le Roman Naturaliste**, Henri Mitterand (éd.), op. cit. p. 76.

to the composition of some novels of the author, who, to the system of characters, who, to the myths in his novels, practically none of them has studied the literary movement that is naturalism in what is at its core: Nature and sexuality.

The specialists who, like Bertrand-Jennings, were interested in the thorny issue of sexuality, did so from a partisan perspective, starting from the segregationist principle that sexuality is first and foremost a womens' affair. That assertion can lead to an insufficient study that would marginalise all male characters[1093] and the non-anthropomorphic[1094] ones. However, they too have a sexuality that is proven and varied in the works of Zola. Studying the sexuality of those non-anthropomorphic characters is an unavoidable necessity in my eyes. So, I think it is appropriate to restore **Les Rougon-Macquart** in their initial context, that of fundamental naturalism. In Zola's works, naturalism results from the concomitance of two fundamental aspects: firstly, sexuality - which allows the reproduction of human beings with its corollary of hereditary genetic transmissions – and, secondly, the natural environment – the spatio-temporal and social components. Man is fatally and doubly the victim of his hereditary inheritance - which he has no capacity to choose, or to cherry pick - and of the omnipotence of the natural time and space - which he can scarcely tame. In addition to all these burdens, he finds it difficult to get rid of the social body to which he originally belongs.

My aim was therefore to study the masterpiece of naturalism, **Les Rougon-Macquart**, not from the basis of any particular novel anymore - such a choice would necessarily be arbitrary - even less by attacking a particular theme that the author would have addressed in it, but to study its cornerstone that is sexuality, the source of all fatalities. Once sexuality is removed from this romantic cycle, the **Rougon-Macquart** family immediately ceases to exist. Such a demolition would make me lose Ariadne's thread and without doubt, Zola would no longer succeed in writing one of the twenty novels that the theme of sexuality has generated.

Unlike previous studies that touched the themes of fatality and of sexuality in Zola's works, I took up the challenge, not only to unify them, but also to apprehend them from a broader angle. Indeed, I took interest as much in the sexual agents as a whole as in the myths and the metaphors that are attached to them. Then I took a special interest in the times and spaces of sexuality, which are sometimes extremely significant. Unfortunately, so far, critics have neglected these last two components in explaining the theme of sexuality in Zola's naturalism. This contribution repairs that injustice while federating previous studies, which are sometimes brilliant, but often sectarian too. That is

---

[1093] This is exactly the main reproach one can direct at Chantal Bertrand-Jennings.
[1094] Let us remember that Philippe Hamon had made that very same mistake, by claiming that the non-anthropomorphic entities were asexual.

why this study is timely as it comes to show that the theme of sexuality is unifying and that it should be considered from a unifying point of view.

Nonetheless, the fact that, overall, critics have almost ignored sexuality that is so bright and so blatant in Zola's novels, is undoubtedly surprising, given the iterative nature and the special importance that it has in his works. But it must probably be due to the fact that sexuality still remains taboo today. The preconceptions attached to it may have scared researchers off, consciously or unconsciously. I refuse, for my part, to participate in this *"conspiration du silence*[1095]*"* and I am committed to shedding a bright light on naturalism. And all the better if sexuality, which is its fundamental element, is finally illuminated in a new light and that it can be appreciated in all its nakedness.

[1095] This expression is borrowed from Robert Lethbridge: *Une "conspiration du silence"? Autour de la publication de **La Curée***, article published in the **Lettres Romanes, XXXI, no. 3**, August 1977 issue.

BIBLIOGRAPHY

SELECTIVE BIBLIOGRAPHY[1096]

I. CORPUS OF THIS THESIS

ZOLA, ÉMILE : **Les Rougon-Macquart, Tome I**, édition dirigée par Armand Lanoux et Henri Mitterand, Paris, Éditions Fasquelle et Gallimard, 1961, comprenant :
La Fortune des Rougon, pp. 1-315.
La Curée, pp. 317-600.
La Faute de l'Abbé Mouret, pp. 1213-1527.

ZOLA, ÉMILE : **Les Rougon-Macquart, Tome II**, édition dirigée par Armand Lanoux et Henri Mitterand, Paris, Éditions Fasquelle et Gallimard, 1961, comprenant :
Nana, pp. 1092-1485.

ZOLA, ÉMILE : **Les Rougon-Macquart, Tome III**, édition dirigée par Armand Lanoux et Henri Mitterand, Paris, Éditions Fasquelle et Gallimard, 1964.

ZOLA, ÉMILE : **Les Rougon-Macquart, Tome IV**, édition dirigée par Armand Lanoux et Henri Mitterand, Paris, Éditions Fasquelle et Gallimard, 1966, comprenant :
L'Œuvre, pp. 9-363.
La Terre, pp. 365-811.
La Bête Humaine, pp. 995-1331.

ZOLA, ÉMILE : **Les Rougon-Macquart, Tome V**, édition dirigée par Armand Lanoux et Henri Mitterand, Paris, Éditions Fasquelle et Gallimard, 1967.

II. OTHER WORKS BY ZOLA

2.1. NOVELS :

ZOLA, ÉMILE : **La Confession de Claude**, Paris, Lacroix, 1865.
ZOLA, ÉMILE : **Le Vœu d'une Morte**, Paris, 1866.
ZOLA, ÉMILE : **Thérèse Raquin**, Paris, Fasquelle, 1867.
ZOLA, ÉMILE : **Madeleine Férat**, Paris, Librairie Internationale, 1868.

2.2. TALES :

ZOLA, ÉMILE : **Contes à Ninon**, Paris, Hetzel et Lacroix, 1864.
ZOLA, ÉMILE : **Les Mystères de Marseille**, Paris, Arnaud, 1867

2.3. PLAYS

ZOLA, ÉMILE : **Thérèse Raquin**, Paris, Charpentier, 1873.
ZOLA, ÉMILE : **Les Héritiers Rabourdin**, Paris, Charpentier, 1874.
ZOLA, ÉMILE : **Le Bouton de Rose**, Paris, Charpentier, 1878.
ZOLA, ÉMILE : **L'Assommoir**, Paris, Charpentier, 1879.

[1096] For the complete bibliography of the studies on Zola's works, please refer to the excellent research and publication by Baguley, David: **Bibliographie de la Critique sur Émile Zola: 1864-1970**, Toronto, University of Toronto Press, 1976 and **Bibliographie de la Critique sur Émile Zola: 1971-1980**, Toronto, Buffalo, London, University of Toronto Press, 1982. For the period going from 1981 to 2000 and beyond, visit the following Website:
http://www.dur.ac.uk/SMEL/depts/french/Baguley/Bibliog/index.htm

ZOLA, ÉMILE :   **Lazare**, Paris, Charpentier, 1893.

2.4. ESSAYS :

ZOLA, ÉMILE :   **Mes Haines**, Paris, Lacroix, 1865.
ZOLA, ÉMILE :   **Mon Salon**, Paris, Librairie Internationale, 1866.
ZOLA, ÉMILE :   **Édouard Manet**, Paris, Dentu, 1867.
ZOLA, ÉMILE :   **Le Roman Expérimental**, Paris, Charpentier, 1880.
ZOLA, ÉMILE :   **Les Romanciers Naturalistes**, Paris, Lacroix, 1881.
ZOLA, ÉMILE :   **Les Auteurs Dramatiques**, Paris, Charpentier, 1881.
ZOLA, ÉMILE :   **Le Naturalisme au Théâtre**, Paris, Charpentier, 1881.
ZOLA, ÉMILE :   **Le Roman Naturaliste**, édité par Henri Mitterand, Paris, Librairie Générale Française, collection classiques de poche, 1999.

2.5. FICTIONAL SERIES:

2.5.1. THE THREE CITIES:

ZOLA, ÉMILE :   **Lourdes**, Paris, Charpentier, 1894.
ZOLA, ÉMILE :   **Rome**, Paris, Charpentier, 1896.
ZOLA, ÉMILE :   **Paris**, Paris, Charpentier, 1898.

2.5.2. THE FOUR GOSPELS :

ZOLA, ÉMILE :   **Fécondité**, Paris, Charpentier, 1899.
ZOLA, ÉMILE :   **Travail**, Paris, Charpentier, 1901.
ZOLA, ÉMILE :   **Vérité**, Paris, Charpentier, 1902.
ZOLA, ÉMILE :   **Justice**, inachevé et non édité.

2.5.3. CORRESPONDANCE :

ZOLA, ÉMILE :   **Correspondance, Tome 1 : 1858-1867**, Édition Bakker, Becker, Mitterand, Presses de l'université de Montréal, Éditions du CNRS, 1978.

ZOLA, ÉMILE :   **Correspondance, Tome II : 1868-mai 1877**, Édition Bakker, Becker, H. Mitterand, Presses de l'université de Montréal, Éditions du CNRS, 1980.

ZOLA, ÉMILE :   **Correspondance, Tome III : juin 1877-mai 1880**, Édition Bakker, Becker, H. Mitterand, A. Pagès, Albert Salvan, Presses de l'université de Montréal, Éditions du CNRS, 1982.

ZOLA, ÉMILE :   **Correspondance, Tome IV : juin 1880-1888**, Édition Bakker, Becker, H. Mitterand, D. Speirs, J. Walker, Presses de l'université de Montréal, Éditions du CNRS, 1983.

ZOLA, ÉMILE :   **Correspondance, Tome V : 1884-1886**, Édition Bakker, Becker, H. Mitterand, O. Morgan, A. Pagès, Presses de l'université de Montréal, éditions du CNRS, 1985.

ZOLA, ÉMILE :   **Correspondance, Tome VI : 1887-mai 1890**, Édition B.H. Bakker, O. Morgan, B. Sanders, Dorothy Speirs, H. Mitterand, Presses de l'université de Montréal, Éditions du CNRS, 1987.

ZOLA, ÉMILE :   **Correspondance, Tome VII : juin 1890- septembre 1893**, Édition B.H. Bakker, Owen Morgan, H. Mitterand, Presses de l'université de Montréal, Éditions du CNRS, 1989.

ZOLA, ÉMILE :   **Correspondance, Tome VIII : octobre 1893-septembre 1897**, Édition B.H. Bakker, O. Morgan, D. Speirs J. Walker, H.

	Mitterand, Presses de l'université de Montréal, Éditions du CNRS, 1991.
ZOLA, ÉMILE :	**Correspondance, Tome IX : octobre 1897-1899**, Édition B.H. Bakker, O. Morgan, A. Pagès, H. Mitterand, Presses de l'université de Montréal, Éditions du CNRS, 1993.
ZOLA, ÉMILE :	**Correspondance, Tome X : octobre 1899-septembre 1902**, Presses de l'université de Montréal, Éditions du CNRS, Édition B.H. Bakker, O. Morgan, J. Walker, D. Speirs, H. Mitterand, 1995.

2.5.4. COMPLETE WORKS

ZOLA, ÉMILE :	**Œuvres Complètes**, Paris, Tchou, Cercle du Livre Précieux, édition Henri Mitterand, 15 volumes, 1966-1970.
ZOLA, ÉMILE :	**Œuvres Complètes,** sous la direction de Henri Mitterand, **Tome 1 : Les Débuts**, Henri Mitterand (éd.), Paris, Nouveau Monde Éditions, 2002.
ZOLA, ÉMILE :	**Œuvres Complètes,** sous la direction de Henri Mitterand, **Tome 2 : Le Feuilletoniste (1866-1867)**, Colette Becher (éd.), Paris, Nouveau Monde Éditions, 2002.
ZOLA, ÉMILE :	**Œuvres Complètes,** sous la direction de Henri Mitterand, **Tome 3 : La Naissance du Naturalisme (1868-1869)**, Jean-Louis Cabanès, Colette Becher (éds.), Paris, Nouveau Monde Éditions, 2003.
ZOLA, ÉMILE :	**Œuvres Complètes,** sous la direction de Henri Mitterand, **Tome 4 : La Guerre et La Commune (1870-1871)**, Patricia Carles, Béatrice Desgranges (éds.), Paris, Nouveau Monde Éditions, 2003.
ZOLA, ÉMILE :	**Œuvres Complètes,** sous la direction de Henri Mitterand, **Tome 5 : Thiers au Pouvoir 1871-1873**, Patricia Carles, Béatrice Desgranges (éds.), Paris, Nouveau Monde Éditions, 2003.
ZOLA, ÉMILE :	**Œuvres Complètes,** sous la direction de Henri Mitterand, **Tome 6 : L'Ordre Moral 1873-1874**, Daniel Compère, Jean-Pierre Leduc-Adine (éds.), Paris, Nouveau Monde Éditions, 2003.
ZOLA, ÉMILE :	**Œuvres Complètes,** sous la direction de Henri Mitterand, **Tome 7 : La République en Marche (1875-1876)**, Jean-Pierre Leduc-Adine, Marie Scarpa (éds.), Paris, Nouveau Monde Éditions, 2004.
ZOLA, ÉMILE :	**Œuvres Complètes,** sous la direction de Henri Mitterand, **Tome 8 : Le Scandale de l'Assommoir (1877-1879)**, Marie-Ange Voisin-Fougère, Paris, Nouveau Monde Éditions, 2004.
ZOLA, ÉMILE :	**Œuvres Complètes,** sous la direction de Henri Mitterand, **Tome 9 : Nana - 1880**, Chantal Pierre-Gnassounou (éd.), Paris, Nouveau Monde Éditions, 2004.
ZOLA, ÉMILE :	**Œuvres Complètes,** sous la direction de Henri Mitterand, **Tome 10 : La Critique Naturaliste - 1881**, François Marie Mourad, Paris, Nouveau Monde Éditions, 2007.
ZOLA, ÉMILE :	**Œuvres Complètes,** sous la direction de Henri Mitterand, **Tome 11 : La Fortune d'Octave Mouret (1882-1883)**, David Baguley, François Marie-Mourad, Paris, Nouveau Monde Éditions, 2005.
ZOLA, ÉMILE :	**Œuvres Complètes,** sous la direction de Henri Mitterand, **Tome 12 : Souffrance et Révolte - 1884-1885**, Olivier Lumbroso, Paris, Nouveau Monde Éditions, 2005.
ZOLA, ÉMILE :	**Œuvres Complètes,** sous la direction de Henri Mitterand, **Tome 13 : <<Naturalisme poas mort !>> - 1886-1888**, Olivier Got, Paris, Nouveau Monde Éditions, 2006.

ZOLA, ÉMILE :	Œuvres Complètes, sous la direction de Henri Mitterand, **Tome 14 : Le Sang et l'Argent - 1889-1891**, Guy Larroux, Paris, Nouveau Monde Éditions, 2006.
ZOLA, ÉMILE :	Œuvres Complètes, sous la direction de Henri Mitterand, **Tome 15 : La Clôture 1892-1893**, Jean-Sébastien Macke, Jean-Louis Cabanès, Paris, Nouveau Monde Éditions, 2007.
ZOLA, ÉMILE :	Œuvres Complètes, sous la direction de Henri Mitterand, **Tome 16: De Lourdes à Rome : Les Trois Villes [1] - (1894-1896)**, Jean-Louis Cabanès et Jacques Noiray, Paris, Nouveau Monde Éditions, 2007.
ZOLA, ÉMILE :	Œuvres Complètes, sous la direction de Henri Mitterand, **Tome 17 : Paris fin de siècle : Les Trois Ville [2] - 1897**, Jacques Noiray, Jean-Louis Cabanès, Paris, Nouveau Monde Éditions, 2008.
ZOLA, ÉMILE :	Œuvres Complètes, sous la direction de Henri Mitterand, **Tome 18 : De l'Affaire aux Quatre Évangiles - 1897-1901**, Alain pagès, Paris, Nouveau Monde Éditions, 2008.
ZOLA, ÉMILE :	Œuvres Complètes, sous la direction de Henri Mitterand, **Tome 19 : La Critique Naturaliste - 1881**, François Marie Mourad, Paris, Nouveau Monde Éditions, 2007.
ZOLA, ÉMILE :	Œuvres Complètes, sous la direction de Henri Mitterand, **Tome 20 : Vérité et Justice : Les Quatre Évangiles [3] - 1902-1903**, Be2atrice Laville, Paris, Nouveau Monde Éditions, 2009.
ZOLA, ÉMILE :	Œuvres Complètes, sous la direction de Henri Mitterand, **Tome 21 : La Critique Naturaliste - 1881**, François Marie Mourad, Paris, Nouveau Monde Éditions, 2007.

III. CRITICAL BOOKS ON ÉMILE ZOLA AND THE ROUGON-MACQUART IN GENERAL

ALEXIS, PAUL :	Émile Zola, Notes d'un Ami, Paris, Charpentier, 1882.
BAGULEY, DAVID:	**Naturalist Fiction. The Entropic Vision**, Cambridge, Cambridge University Press, 1990.
BECKER, COLETTE :	**Les Critiques de Notre Temps et Zola**, Paris, Garnier, 1972.
BECKER, COLETTE :	*Zola* dans **Dictionnaire des Littératures de Langue Française**, Paris, Bordas, pp. 2685-2715, 1987.
BECKER, COLETTE :	*Introduction Biographique* dans la **Correspondance** de Zola, Tome VII, Montréal/Paris, Les Presses de l'Université de Montréal/Éditions du CNRS, 1989.
BECKER, COLETTE :	**Les Apprentissages de Zola**, Paris, PUF, 1993.
BERNARD, MARC	**Zola par Lui-même**, Paris, Seuil, 1952.
BERTRAND-JENNINGS, CHANTAL :	**L'Éros et la Femme chez Zola**, Paris, Klincksieck, 1977.
BONNEFIS, PHILIPPE :	**L'Innommable, Essai sur l'Œuvre de Zola**, Paris, SEDES, 1984.
BORIE, JEAN :	**Zola et les Mythes**, Paris, Seuil, 1971.
BRUNET, ÉTIENNE :	**Le Vocabulaire de Zola**, Genève-Paris, Slatkine-Champion, 3 Volumes, 1985.
CARLES, PATRICIA et DESGRANGES, BEATRICE :	**Zola**, Paris, Nathan, 1991.
COGNY, PIERRE :	**Zola et son Temps**, Paris, Larousse, 1976.
COLIN, R.P. :	**Zola et le Coup de Force Naturaliste**, Tusson, Charente, Édition du Lérot, 1991.
COLLECTIF :	**Cahiers de l'U.E.R. Froissart, no 5 : Zola**, Paris, 1980.
COLLECTIF :	**Europe : Zola**, 46ème Année, **no. 468-469**, Europe et les Éditeurs Français Réunis, Avril-Mai, 1968.

COLLOT, SYLVIE :	**Les Lieux du Désir. Topologie Amoureuse de Zola**, Paris, Hachette, collection Université, recherches littéraires, 1992.
DECAUDIN, MICHEL et LEUWERS, DANIEL :	**Littérature Française, T 8 : De Zola à Apollinaire**, Paris, Arthaud, 1968.
DELEUZE, GILLES :	**La Logique du Sens**, Paris, Édition de Minuit, 1969.
DEZALAY, AUGUSTE :	**Lectures de Zola**, Paris, Armand Colin, 1973.
DEZALAY, AUGUSTE :	**L'Opéra des Rougon-Macquart**, Paris, Klincksieck, 1983.
DEZALAY, AUGUSTE (Éd.) :	**Zola sans Frontières. Actes du Colloque International de Strasbourg (mai 1994)**, Strasbourg, Presses Universitaires de Strasbourg, 1994.
EVRARD, MICHEL :	**Émile Zola**, Paris, Éditions Universitaires, 1967.
DE FARIA, NEIDE :	**Structure et Unité dans Les Rougon-Macquart, (La poétique du cycle)**, Paris, Nizet, 1977.
GUILLEMIN, HENRI :	**Présentation des Rougon-Macquart**, Paris, Gallimard, 1964.
HAMON, PHILIPPE :	**Le Personnel du Roman. Le Système des Personnages dans Les Rougon-Macquart de Zola**, (seconde édition) Genève, Droz, 1998.
HEMMINGS, F.W.J.:	**Émile Zola**, London-Oxford, Blackwell, 1966.
HEMMINGS, F.W.J. :	**Zola**, Paris, Hachette, 1969.
HUYSMANS, JORIS-KARL :	**Émile Zola et L'Assommoir**, Bruxelles, L'Artiste du 18 et du 27 mars, 1877.
KAEMPEER, JEAN :	**Émile Zola. D'un Naturalisme Pervers**, Paris, Corti, 1989.
LANOUX, ARMAND :	**Bonjour Monsieur Zola**, Paris, Amiot-Dumont, 1931.
LEBLOND-ZOLA, DENISE :	**Zola Raconté par sa Fille**, Paris, Fasquelle, 1931.
LEPELLETIER, EDMOND :	**Émile Zola, sa Vie, son Œuvre**, Paris, Mercure de France, 1908.
MITTERAND, HENRI :	**Zola Journaliste**, Paris, Armand Colin, 1973.
MITTERAND, HENRI :	**Zola et le Naturalisme**, Paris, PUF, 1986.
MITTERAND, HENRI :	**Zola : l'Histoire et la Fiction**, Paris, PUF, 1990.
MITTERAND, HENRI :	**Zola. Tome 1. Sous le Regard d'Olympia (1840-1871)**, Paris, Fayard, 1999.
MITTERAND, HENRI :	*Préface* de la **Correspondance** de Zola, tome VI, Montréal/Paris, Les Presses de l'Université de Montréal/Éditions du CNRS, 1987.
MORGAN, OWEN et SANDERS, JAMES :	*Introduction Biographique* dans la **Correspondance** de Zola, tome VI, Montréal/Paris, Les Presses de l'Université de Montréal/Éditions du CNRS, 1987.
NELSON, BRIAN:	**Zola and the Bourgeoisie**, London, MacMillan, 1983.
NOIRAY, JACQUES :	**Le Romancier et la Machine : L'Image de la Machine dans le Roman Français (1850-1900), T. 1 : L'Univers de Zola**, Paris, José Corti, 1981.
PAGÈS, ALAIN :	**Émile Zola, Bilan Critique**, Paris, Nathan, collection université, 1993.
PIERRE-GNASSOUNOU, C. :	**Zola. Les Fortunes de la Fiction**, Paris, Nathan, collection Le Texte à l'Œuvre, 1999.
POLLARD, PATRICK (Éd.):	**Émile Zola Centenary Colloquium 1893-1993**, London, The Émile Zola Society, 1995.
PROULX, A. :	**Aspects Épiques des Rougon-Macquart**, Paris, Mouton, 1966.
RIPOLL, ROGER :	**Réalité et Mythe chez Zola**, Paris, Champion, 1981.
ROBERT, GUY :	**Émile Zola, Principes et Caractères Généraux de son Œuvre**, Paris, Belles Lettres, 1952.
SAMAKÉ, FAMAHAN :	**Fondements, Caractéristiques et Fatalité de la Sexualité dans Les Rougon-Macquart d'Émile Zola**, Abidjan, Université de Cocody, D.E.A., 1996.

SCHOR, NAOMI:	Zola's Crowds, Baltimore and London, The Johns Hopkins University Press, 1978.
SEASSAU, CLAUDE :	Émile Zola, Le Réalisme Symbolique, Paris, José Corti, 1989.
SERRES, MICHEL :	Feux et Signaux de Brume : Zola, Paris, Grasset, 1975.
SIGNORI, D.A. et SPEIRS, D.E. :	Émile Zola dans la Presse Parisienne (1882-1902), Toronto, University of Toronto Press, 1985.
TERNOIS, RENÉ :	Zola et son Temps, Paris, Belles Lettres, 1961.
TONARD, JEAN-FRANÇOIS :	Thématique et Symbolique de l'Espace Clos dans le Cycle des Rougon-Macquart d'Émile Zola, Frankfurt, Berlin, Bern, New York, Paris, Wien, Peter Lang, collection Publications Universitaires Européennes, 1994.
VAN BUUREN, MAARTEN :	Les Rougon-Macquart d'Émile Zola : De la Métaphore au Mythe, Paris, José Corti, 1986.
VAN DER BEKEN, M. :	Zola, le dessous de la femme. Essai, Bruxelles, Le Cri, 2000.
WARREN, PAUL (Éd.) :	Zola et le Cinéma, Laval/Paris, Presses de l'université de Laval/Presses de la Sorbonne Nouvelle, 1995.

IV. BOOKS AND CRITICAL ARTICLES ON NATURALISM

BAGULEY, DAVID:	Zola et les Genres, Glasgow, University of Glasgow French and German Publications, 1993.
BAGULEY, DAVID :	Le Naturalisme et ses Genres, Paris, Nathan, 1995. (version française de Naturalist Fiction : The Entropic Vision, Cambridge, Cambridge University Press, 1990).
CHEVREL, YVES :	Le Naturalisme, Paris, PUF, 1982.
COLLECTIF :	La Revue des Sciences Humaines no. 4, Le Naturalisme, Paris, 1976.
COUTY, P. :	Naturalisme dans Dictionnaire des Littératures de Langue Française, Paris, Bordas, 1987.
DE LATTRE, ALAIN :	Le Réalisme selon Zola, Paris, PUF, 1975.
HUYSMANS, JORIS-KARL :	Préface d'À Rebours, pp. 55-77, Paris, Gallimard, 1977.
MARTINO, PIERRE :	Le Naturalisme Français, Paris, Armand Colin, 1973.
MITTERAND, HENRI :	Zola et le Naturalisme, Paris, PUF, collection Que-Sais-Je ? (Seconde édition) 1999.
PAGÈS, ALAIN :	Le Naturalisme, Paris, PUF, 1989.
SUWALA, HALINA :	Naissance d'une Doctrine. Formation des Idées Esthétiques de Zola (1859-1865), Varsovie, Thèse de l'université de Varsovie, no. 109, 1976.
SUWALA, HALINA :	Autour de Zola et du Naturalisme, Paris, Honoré Champion Éditeur, 1993.

V. BOOKS AND CRITICAL ARTICLES CRITIQUES ON VARIOUS NOVELS FROM THE ROUGON-MACQUART SERIES

1. On La Fortune des Rougon

ARMSTRONG, MARIE-SOPHIE :	Une Lecture << Hugo-centrique >> de La Fortune des Rougon dans The Romanic Review, LXXXVII, no. 2, mars 1996, pp. 271-283.
CHAITIN, GILBERT:	The Voices of the Dead: Love, Death and Politics in Zola's La Fortune des Rougon dans Literature and Psychology, XXVI, no. 3 et 4, Fairleigh Dickinson University, 1976, pp. 131-144; et pp.148-158.

DEZALAY, AUGUSTE :	*Ordre et Désordre dans* Les Rougon-Macquart ; *l'exemple de* La Fortune des Rougon dans Travaux de Linguistique et de Littérature XI, no. 2, 1973, pp.71-81.
DEZALAY, AUGUSTE :	*Commentaires* dans La Fortune des Rougon de Zola, Paris, Fasquelle, 1985.
GERHARDI, G. C. :	*Zola's Biological Vision of Politics : Revolutionary Figures in* La Fortune des Rougon *and* Le Ventre de Paris dans Nineteenth Century French Studies II, no. 3 et 4, printemps-été 1974, pp. 164-180.
GOT, OLIVIER :	*L'Idylle de Miette et de Silvère dans* La Fortune des Rougon, *Structure d'un mythe* dans Les Cahiers Naturalistes, XIX, no. 46, 1973, pp.146-164.
MITTERAND, HENRI :	Le Discours du Roman, Paris, PUF, 1980.
PETREY, SANDY :	*From Cyclical to Historical Discourse : The* Contes à Ninon *and* La Fortune des Rougon dans Revue de l'Université d'Ottawa XLVIII, no. 4, octobre-décembre, 1978, pp. 371-381.
SCHOR, NAOMI :	*Mythes des Origines, Origine des Mythes :* La Fortune des Rougon dans Les Cahiers Naturalistes XXIV, no 52, 1976, pp. 124-134.

2. On La Curée :

ALLAN, J. A. :	*Narcissism and the Double in* La Curée dans Stanford French Review, V, no. 3, Winter 1981, pp. 295-312.
ALCORN, CLAYTON :	La Curée *: Les deux Renée Saccard* dans Les Cahiers Naturalistes, XXIII, no 51, 1977, pp. 49-55.
BERTA, MICHEL :	*Une pièce dans un roman de Zola. << Les Amours du Beau Narcisse et de la Nymphe Écho >>* dans Excavatio, VIII, 1996, pp. 8-16.
BORIE, JEAN :	*Préface* de La Curée de Zola, Paris, Gallimard, 1981.
COLLECTIF :	La Curée de Zola ou la Vie à Outrance, Colloque du 10 janvier 1987, Paris, Sedes, 1987.
DEZALAY, AUGUSTE :	*La << Nouvelle Phèdre >> de Zola ou les Mésaventures d'un Personnage Tragique* dans Travaux de Linguistique et de Littérature IX, no. 2, 1971, pp.121-164.
DUCHET, CLAUDE :	*Préface* de La Curée de Zola, Paris, Garnier-Flammarion, 1970.
LAVIELLE, VERONIQUE and BECKER, COLETTE:	Émile Zola. La Curée, Rosny-sous-Bois, Bréal, collection : Connaissance de l'œuvre, 1999.
LETHBRIDGE, ROBERT :	*Du Nouveau sur la Genèse de* La Curée dans Les Cahiers Naturalistes XIX, no. 45, 1973, pp. 23-30.
LETHBRIDGE, ROBERT :	*La Préparation de* La Curée *: Mise au Point d'une Chronologie* dans Les Cahiers Naturalistes XXXIII, no 51, 1977, pp. 37-48.
LETHBRIDGE, ROBERT :	*Autour de la Publication de* La Curée *: Une conspiration du Silence ?* dans Les Lettres Romanes, XXXI, no. 3, août 1977, pp. 203-219.
LUTAUD, CHRISTIAN :	Sur Émile Zola, La Curée, Paris, Ellipses, collection : Résonances, 1999.
MITTERAND, HENRI :	*Notes* et *Notice* dans La Curée de Zola, Paris, Gallimard, 1981.
NELSON, BRIAN:	*Speculation and Dissipation: A Reading of Zola's* La Curée dans Essays in French Literature, no. 14, (University of Western Australia) novembre 1977, pp.1-33.
NELSON, BRIAN:	*Zola's Metaphoric Language: A Paragraph round* La Curée dans Modern Languages, LIX, no. 2, juin 1978, pp. 61-64.

PETREY, SANDY:	*Sociocriticism and Les Rougon-Macquart* dans **L'Esprit Créateur, XIV, no. 3**, automne 1974, pp. 219-235,
PETREY, SANDY:	*Stylistics and Society in La Curée* dans **Modern Language Notes, LXXXIX, no. 4**, mai 1974, pp. 626-640.
RIPOLL, ROGER :	*L'Histoire du Second Empire dans La Curée* dans **Revue d'Histoire Moderne et Contemporaine, XXI**, janvier-mars 1974, pp. 46-57.
SCARPA, MARIE :	*Le Carnaval des Halles. Une Ethnocritique du Ventre de Paris de Zola*, Paris, CNRS Éditions, collections CNRS littérature, 2000.
VIA, SARA :	*Une Phèdre Décadente chez les Naturalistes* dans **Revue des Sciences Humaines, XXXIX, NO. 153**, 1974, pp. 29-38.

3. On Le Ventre de Paris

BESSE, LAURENCE :	*<< Le feu aux graisses >> : la chair sarcastique dans Le Ventre de Paris* dans **Romantisme, no. 91**, 1er trimestre 1996, pp. 35-42.
DEZALAY, AUGUSTE :	*Les Mystères de Zola* dans la **Revue des Sciences Humaines, no. 160**, octobre-décembre 1975, pp. 475-487.
GAILLARD, JEANNE :	*Zola et l'ordre moral*, dans **Les Cahiers Naturalistes, XXVI, no. 54**, 1980, pp. 25-32.
GURAL-MIGDAL, ANNA :	*Représentation utopique et ironie dans Le Ventre de Paris* dans **Les Cahiers Naturalistes, XLVI, no. 74**, 2000, pp. 145-161.
NIESS, ROBERT :	*Émile Zola : la femme au travail* dans **Les Cahiers Naturalistes, XXII, no. 50**, 1976, pp.40-58.
PETREY, SANDY:	*Historical reference and Stylistic Opacity in Le Ventre de Paris* dans **Kentucky Romance Quarterly XXIV, no 3**, 1977, pp. 325-340.

4. On La Conquête de Plassans

BAGULEY, DAVID :	*Les Paradis Perdus : Espace et regard dans La Conquête de Plassans* dans **Nineteenth Century French Studies, VII, no 1-2**, Autumn- Winter 1980, pp. 80-92.
DEZALAY, AUGUSTE :	*Gobineau et Zola au rendez-vous de Stendhal* dans **Études Gobiniennes, VIII**, Paris, Klincksieck, 1975, pp. 165-176.
FERNANDEZ-ZOÏLA, ADOLFO :	*Effets de Pouvoir et Espace de deux Folies à Plassans* dans **Les Cahiers Naturalistes, XXX, no 58**, 1984, pp. 43-62.
RIPOLL, ROGER :	*La Vie Aixoise dans Les Rougon-Macquart* dans **Les Cahiers Naturalistes, XVIII, no. 43**, 1972, pp. 39-54.
SCHOR, NAOMI :	*Le Délire d'Interprétation : Naturalisme et Paranoïa* dans **Le Naturalisme**, Colloque de Cerisy, Paris, U.G.E., 1978, pp. 237-255.
SLATER, J. A. :	*Echoes of Balzac's Provincial scenes in La Conquête de Plassans* dans **Modern Language, IX, no. 3**, septembre 1979, pp. 156-161.

5. On La Faute de l'Abbé Mouret

BERTRAND-JENNINGS, CHANTAL :	*Zola ou l'Envers de la Scène : De La Faute de l'Abbé Mouret au Docteur Pascal* dans **Nineteenth Century French Studies, IX, no. 1-2**, Automne-Hiver 1980, pp. 93-107.

BONNEFIS, PHILIPPE :	*Le Descripteur Mélancolique* dans La Description. Nodier, Sue, Flaubert, Hugo, Verne, Zola, Alexis, Fénélon. Université de Lille III, Paris, Éditions Universitaires, 1974, pp. 103-151.
BONNEFIS, PHILIPPE :	*Intérieurs Naturalistes* dans Intime, Intimité, Intimisme, Université de Lille III, Paris, Éditions universitaires, 1976, pp. 163-198.
GENGEMBRE, GÉRARD :	*Préface* et *Au Fil du Texte* dans La Faute de l'Abbé Mouret de Zola, Paris, Éditions Pocket Classiques, 1993.
GREAVES, A.A. :	*Zola féministe : de la femme fatale à la femme libérée* dans Les Cahiers de l'U.E.R. Froissart (Valenciennes), no. 5, automne 1980, pp. 47-52.
HARDER, H. MARKLAND:	*The Woman Beneath: The femme de marbre in Zola's La Faute de l'Abbé Mouret* dans Nineteenth-Century French Studies, XXIV, no. 3-4, printemps-été, 1996, pp. 426-439.
LEMARIÉ, YANNICK :	*Jules Derville et Ovide Faujas : deux curés en enfer* dans Cahiers Mirbeau, VI, 1999, pp. 100-121.
LOVERSO, ROSABIANCA :	*Le Péché et la Divinité dans La Faute de l'Abbé Mouret* dans Studies in Language and Literature, Eastern Kentucky Universty, 1976, pp. 347-351.
MINOGUE, VALÉRIE:	*Zola's Mythology: That Forbidden Tree* dans Forum for Modern Languages Studies, XIV, no. 3, juillet 1978, pp. 217-230.
ORMEROD, BEVERLEY:	*Zola's enclosed Gardens* dans Essays in French Literature no. 11, University of Western Australia, novembre 1974, pp. 35-46.

6. On Son Excellence Eugène Rougon

BAFARO, GEORGES :	*Quelques aspects du pouvoir dans Son Excellence Eugène Rougon* dans Les Cahiers Naturalistes, XLIV, no. 72, 1998, pp. 305-316.
BAGULEY, DAVID :	*Histoire et Mythe dans Son Excellence Eugène Rougon* dans Les Cahiers Naturalistes, XXVIII, no. 56, 1982, pp. 46-60.
CLAVERIE, MICHEL :	*La Fête Impériale* dans Les Cahiers Naturalistes, XIX, no 45, 1973, pp. 31-49.
LETHBRIDGE, ROBERT :	*Zola et la fiction du pouvoir, Son Excellence Eugène Rougon* dans Les Cahiers Naturalistes, XLIV, no. 72, 1998, pp. 291-304.

7. On L'Assommoir

ALLARD, JACQUES :	*Zola, le Chiffre du Texte. Lecture de L'Assommoir*, Montréal, Presses Universitaires de Grenoble, 1978.
BAGULEY, DAVID:	*Event and Structure: The Plot of Zola's L'Assommoir* dans Publication of the Modern Languages Association of America, XC, no. 5, octobre 1975, pp. 823-833,
BECKER, COLETTE :	L'Assommoir, Paris, Hatier, 1972.
BONNAFOUS, S. :	*Recherche sur le Lexique de L'Assommoir* dans Les Cahiers Naturalistes, XXVII, no 55, 1981, pp. 52-62.
CASSARD MARIE-JOSÉE et JOINVILLE, PASCALE :	*Le Thème de l'Eau dans L'Assommoir* dans Les Cahiers Naturalistes, XXVII, no 55, 1981, pp. 63-73.
DUBOIS, JACQUES :	L'Assommoir de Zola, Société, Discours, Idéologie, Paris, Larousse, 1973.
GUILLAUME, ISABELLE :	Étude sur Zola. L'Assommoir, Paris, Ellipses, collection : Résonances, 1999.

GROBE, EDWIN. P. :	*Narrative Technique in L'Assommoir* dans L'Esprit Créateur, XI, no. 4, hiver 1971, pp. 56-66.
LEDUC-ADINE, JEAN-PIERRE :	*L'Assommoir d'Émile Zola*, Paris, Gallimard, 1997.
MITTERAND, HENRI :	*Programme et Préconstruit Génétiques : Le Dossier de L'Assommoir* dans Essais de Critique Génétique, Paris, Flammarion, 1979, pp. 193-226.
NEWTON, JOY et SCHUMACHER, CLAUDE :	*Le Rouge et le Noir dans L'Assommoir* dans Cahiers U.E.R. Froissart no. 5, Valenciennes, automne 1980, pp. 59-64.
PLACE, DAVID:	*Zola and the Working Class: The Meaning of L'Assommoir* dans French Studies XXVIII, no. 1, 1974, pp. 39-49.

8. On Une Page d'Amour

KIMBALL, M. DOUGLAS :	*Zola's Une Page d'Amour. Pictures and Exhibitions* dans Proceedings: Pacific, Northwest Conference on Foreign Languages 33 rd Annual Meeting, (Oregon State University), April 28-29, 1972, pp. 123-126,
KRAKOWSKI, ANNA :	Paris dans les Romans d'Émile Zola, Paris, PUF, 1968.
MAX, S. :	Les Métaphores de la Grande Ville dans Les Rougon-Macquart, Paris, Nizet, 1966.
NELSON, BRIAN:	*Zola and the Ambiguities of Passion. Une Page d'Amour* dans Essays in French Literature, no 10, University of Western Australia Press, novembre 1973, pp. 1-22.
SCHOR, NAOMI :	*Le Sourire du Sphinx. Zola et l'Énigme de la Féminité* dans Romantisme, no. 13-14, 1976, pp. 183-195.

9. On Nana

BAFARO, GEORGES :	Nana, Zola, Paris, Ellipses, 2000.
BARTHES, ROLAND :	*La Mangeuse d'Hommes* dans Guide du Livre, XX, Paris, Seuil, 1955.
BERTRAND-JENNINGS, CHANTAL :	*La Symbolique de l'Espace dans Nana* dans Modern Language Notes, LXXXVIII, no. 4, mai 1973, pp. 764-774.
BESNIER, PATRICK :	*Lulu et Nana, Visage de la Femme Fatale* dans Interférences, Rennes, janvier-juin 1978, pp. 19-37.
CHEVREL, YVES :	*La Leçon d'Histoire de Nana : Structure Romanesque et Instruction du Lecteur* dans Cahiers UER Froissart, no. 5, Valenciennes, automne 1980, pp. 73-80.
CONROY, JUNIOR V.P.:	*The Metaphorical Web in Zola's Nana* dans University of Toronto Quarterly, XLVII, no 3, printemps 1978, pp. 239-258.
DANOW, DAVID:	*The Spirit of Carnival. Opening Remarks. Nana's World* dans Excavatio, VIII, 1996, pp. 194-204.
HOFMANN, WERNER:	Nana: Mythos und Wirklichkeit, Cologne, Schauberg, 1973.
LAPP, JOHN C.:	*The Jealous Window-Watcher in Zola and Proust* dans French Studies, XXIX, no. 2, avril 1975, pp. 166-176.
RIPOLL, ROGER :	*Introduction* dans Nana de Zola, Paris, Garnier-Flammarion, 1968.
ROBERTS, J. L.:	Nana, Lincoln, Nebraska, Cliffs, 1967.

10. On Pot-Bouille

ARMSTRONG, JUDITH:	The Novel of Adultery, London, Macmillian, 1976.

BACCARD, ALIA :	*Le Thème de l'Éducation de la Jeune Fille d'après les Romanciers du 19ème siècle et d'après Émile Zola en particulier* dans **Les Cahiers de Tunisie, XXII, no. 87-88**, 3ème et 4ème trimestre 1974, pp. 155-165.,
HAMON, PHILIPPE :	*Le Personnage de l'Abbé Mauduit dans* Pot-Bouille *: Sources et thèmes* dans **Les Cahiers Naturalistes, XVIII, no. 44**, 1972, pp. 201-211.
LAVIELLE, VERONIQUE and BECKER, COLETTE:	*Émile Zola.* **Pot-Bouille**, Rosny-sous-Bois, Bréal, collection : Connaissance de l'œuvre, 1999.
NELSON, BRIAN:	*Black Comedy: Notes on Zola's* Pot-Bouille dans **Romance Notes, XVII, no. 2**, hiver 1976, pp. 156-161.
NELSON, BRIAN:	*Zola and the Bourgeoisie: A Reading of Pot-Bouille* dans **Nottingham French Studies, XVII, no. 1**, mai 1978, pp. 58-70.
NELSON, BRIAN :	*Pot-Bouille, Étude Sociale et Roman Comique* dans **Les Cahiers Naturalistes, XXVII, no. 55**, 1981, pp. 74-92.
MAROTTE, PIERRE :	*Commentaires* dans **Pot-Bouille** de Zola,
SPENSLEY, R.M.:	*Zola and Conrad: The influence of Pot-Bouille on The Secret Agent* dans **Conradiana**, Texas Technical University, XI, no. 2, 1979, pp. 185-189.
VOISIN-FOUGÈRE, M-A. :	*Ironie et intertextualité dans Pot-Bouille. Désirs, tendresses et haines zoliennes* dans **Les Cahiers Naturalistes, XLII, no. 70**, 1996, pp. 35-44.

11. On Au Bonheur Des Dames

BECKER, COLETTE et GAILLARD, J. :	Au Bonheur des Dames, Profil d'une Œuvre, Paris, Hatier, 1982.
BELGRAND, ANNE :	Étude sur Zola. Au Bonheur des dames, Paris, Ellipses, collection : Résonances, 2000.
CNOCKAERT, VÉRONIQUE :	*Denise, ou la vertu attentatoire dans Au Bonheur des Dames* dans **Excavatio, X**, 1997, pp. 40-47.
COUDERT, PIERRE-EMMANUEL :	*Le mythe dans Au Bonheur des Dames*, dans **Excavatio, X**, 1997, pp. 189-195.
LE BAIL, STÉPHANE :	*Au Bonheur des Dames*, dans **Les Cahiers Naturalistes, XLV, no. 73**, 1999, pp. 195-197.
KAMM, LEWIS:	*People and Things in Zola's Rougon-Macquart: Reification Re-humanized* dans **Philological Quarterly, LIII, no. 1**, janvier 1974, pp. 100-109.
NEWTON, JOY:	*Zola* dans **The Year's Work in Modern Language Studies, volume XXXIX**, année 1977, The Modern Humanities Research Association, pp. 208-211.
NIESS, ROBERT:	*Zola's Au Bonheur des Dames: The Making of a Symbol* dans **Symbolism and Modern Literature: Studies in Honor of Wallace Fowlie**, Edition M. Tétel, Durham, D.C. Duke University Press, 1978, pp. 130-150.
PIHAN, YVES :	*Étude de Texte. Émile Zola : l'Emprise d'un Grand Magasin*, dans **L'École des Lettres, LXIX, no. 7**, 1er janvier 1978, pp. 11-16.
SIMOUNET, A. :	**Au Bonheur des Dames**, Paris, Édition Pédagogique Moderne, 1977.

THOMPSON, HANNAH :	*Une perversion du désir, une névrose nouvelle : Female sexuality in Zola's Au Bonheur des Dames*, dans **Romance Studies**, no. 32, automne 1998, pp.81-92.
ZEISLER, MARIE-CLAUDE :	**Lecture Suivie et Dirigée. Zola : Au Bonheur des Dames** dans **L'École des Lettres, LXVII, no. 4**, 1er novembre 1975, pp. 19-27.

12. On La Joie de Vivre

BAGULEY, DAVID :	*De la Mer Ténébreuse à l'Eau Maternelle : Le Décor Symbolique de La Joie de Vivre* dans **Travaux de Littérature et de Linguistique, XII, no. 2**, 1974, pp. 79-91.
BORIE, JEAN :	**Le Tyran Timide**, Paris, Klincksieck, 1973.
COLIN, R. P. :	**Schopenhauer en France : Un Mythe Naturaliste**, Presses Universitaires de Lyon, 1979.
FRANZEN, N-O. :	**Zola et La Joie de Vivre. La Genèse du Roman, les Personnages, les Idées**, Stockholm, Almquist et Wicksell, 1958.
PREISS, AXEL :	*Aux Sources de La Joie de Vivre : une lettre inédite d'Émile Zola à Edmond Perrier* dans **Les Cahiers Naturalistes, XXV, no. 53**, 1979, pp. 132-137.

13. On Germinal

ABASTADO, CLAUDE :	**Germinal : Analyse Critique**, Paris, Hatier, 1970.
BECKER, COLETTE :	**Germinal**, Paris, PUF, Études Littéraires, 1984.
BECKER, COLETTE :	De nombreux articles sur **Germinal** dans **La Revue d'Histoire de la France** (mai-juin 1985, numéro spécial sur le Centenaire de l'œuvre) et dans **Les Valenciennes no. 10**, puis dans **Les Cahiers Naturalistes, no. 59**.
BERTRAND, DENIS :	**Germinal. Émile Zola**, Paris, Bertrand-Lacoste, 2000.
BONDARENCO, ANNA :	*Le Stéréotypé et l'Événementiel dans Germinal d'Émile Zola*, texte inédit, **New Approaches to Zola**, colloque international de l'Université de Cambridge, 17 avril 2002.
DUCHET, CLAUDE :	*Le Trou des Bouches Noires. Parole, société, révolution dans Germinal* dans **Littérature, no. 24**, décembre 1976, pp. 11-39.
FRANDON, I.-M. :	**Autour de Germinal. La Mine et les Mineurs**, Genève, Droz, 1955.
GIRARD, MARCEL:	**Germinal de Zola**, Paris, Hachette, 1973.
GRANET, E.M.:	**Zola's Germinal. A Critical and Historical Study**, Leicester, Leicester University Press, 1962.
MITTERAND, HENRI :	*Germinal et les Idéologies* dans **Les Cahiers Naturalistes, XVII, no. 42**, 1971, pp. 141-152.
MITTERAND, HENRI :	*Fonction Narrative et Fonction Mimétique. Les Personnages de Germinal* dans **Poétique, IV, no. 16**, Paris, Seuil, 1973, pp. 477-490.
MITTERAND, HENRI :	Deux Études sur **Germinal** dans **Le Discours du Roman**, Paris, PUF, Écriture, 1980.
MOREAU, P. :	**Germinal d'Émile Zola**, Paris, CDU, 1954.
PETREY, SANDY :	*Discours Social et Littérature dans Germinal* dans **Littérature, no. 22**, mai 1976, pp. 59-74.
SMETHURST, COLIN:	**Émile Zola: Germinal**, London, Arnold, 1974.
VAN TIEGHEM, P.:	**Introduction à l'Étude d'Émile Zola : Germinal**, Paris, CDU, 1954.
VIAL, MARC-ANDRÉ :	**Germinal et le << Socialisme >> de Zola**, Paris, Éditions Sociales, 1975.

14. On L'Œuvre

BALIGAND, RENÉE : *Lettres Inédites d'Antoine Guillemet à Émile Zola (1866-1870)* dans **Les Cahiers Naturalistes**, XXIV, no. 52, 1978, pp. 173-205.

BARDET, GUILLAUME
Et CARON, DOMINIQUE : *Étude sur Émile Zola. L'Œuvre*, Paris, Ellipses, collection : Résonances, 1999.

BECKER, COLETTE : *Un Ami de Jeunesse d'Émile Zola : Georges Pajot. Lettres Inédites* dans **Les Cahiers Naturalistes**, XXV, no. 53, 1979, pp. 95-123.

BRADY, PATRICK : *L'Œuvre d'Émile Zola*, Genève, Droz, 1967.

BRADY, PATRICK : *Pour une Nouvelle Orientation en Sémiotique. À Propos de L'Œuvre d'Émile Zola* dans Rice University Studies, LXIII, no. 1, hiver 1977, pp. 43-84.

GENDRAT, AURÉLIE : Zola. *L'Œuvre*, Rosny-sous-Bois, Bréal, collection : Connaissance de l'œuvre, 1999.

NEWTON, JOY et
FOL MONIQUE : *L'Esthétique de Zola et de Rodin, Zola et la Sculpture* dans **Les Cahiers Naturalistes** XXV, no. 53, 1979, pp. 75-80.

NIESS, ROBERT.J. : Zola, Cézanne and Manet. A Study of L'Œuvre, University of Michigan Press, 1968.

OLRIK, HILDE : *Œil Lésé, Corps Morcelé. Réflexions à Propos de L'Œuvre d'Émile Zola* dans Revue Romane, XI, (Copenhague) no. 2, 1976, pp. 334-357.

PASCO, ALLAN : *The Failure of L'Œuvre* dans L'Esprit Créateur, XI, no. 4, hiver 1971, pp. 45-55.

SOLARI, JEAN : *Philippe Solari* dans **Les Cahiers Naturalistes**, XXV, no. 53, 1979, pp. 214-218.

STEINMETZ, JEAN- LUC : L'Œuvre dans Le Naturalisme, Colloque de Cerisy : Paris, UGE, série 10/18, 1978, pp. 415-431.

15. On La Terre

BRACHET, PIERRE : *Zola et Hauptmann : Rose Bernd et La Terre*, dans Les Cahiers Naturalistes, XXI, no. 43, 1975, pp.149-167.

CESBRON, GEORGES : *La Terre de Zola : Capitalisme ou Socialisme ?* dans **Les Humanités**, XIV, no. 10, juin 1971, pp. 18-23.

DONNARD, JEAN-HERVÉ : *Les Paysans et La Terre* dans L'Année Balzacienne 1975, Paris, Garnier, 1975, pp. 137-148.

GIRARD, MARCEL : *Chronologie* dans **La Terre** de Zola, Paris, Garnier-Flammarion, 1973.

GIRARD, MARCEL : *Préface* et *Archives de l'œuvre* dans **La Terre** de Zola, Paris, Garnier-Flammarion, 1973.

MITTERAND, HENRI : *Étude* dans Les Rougon-Macquart de Zola, tome IV, édition Armand Lanoux/Henri Mitterand, Bibliothèque de la Pléiade, Paris, Gallimard, 1966.

OLORENSHAW, R. : *Lisibilité, Structures Globales et Méta-discours Critique dans La Terre* dans **Les Cahiers Naturalistes**, XXV, no. 53, 1979, pp. 46-52.

ROBERT, GUY : La Terre d'Émile Zola, Étude Historique et Critique, Paris, Les Belles-Lettres, 1952.

ZAKARIAN, RICHARD : *Zola's La Terre* dans The Explicator, XXXVI, no. 2, hiver 1978, pp. 11-13.

16. On Le Rêve

BILODEAU, LOUIS : *Le Rêve. Des Rougon-Macquart à la scène lyrique* dans **Les Cahiers Naturalistes, XLIII, no. 71,** pp. 239-250.

DALLENBACH, LUCIEN : Le Récit Spéculaire. Essai sur la Mise en Abyme, Paris, Seuil, 1977.

DALLENBACH, LUCIEN : *Le Rêve dans l'œuvre chez Zola* dans **Le Naturalisme,** colloque de Cerisy, édité par Pierre Cogny, Paris, Union Générale d'Éditions, 1978, pp. 125-139.

COUILLARD, MARIE : *La ''Fille-Fleur'' dans Les Contes à Ninon et dans Les Rougon-Macquart,* Revue de l'Université d'Ottawa/University of Ottawa Quarterly, XLVIII, no. 4, 1978, pp. 398-406.

FERRAND, NATHALIE : *Le Rêve de Zola à Weimar : des épreuves inédites* dans **Genesis, no. 11,** 1997, pp. 143-148.

GREAVES, A.A. : *A Question of Life and Death: A Comparison of Le Rêve and La Faute de l'Abbé Mouret* dans **Nottingham French Studies, XIX, no. 2,** automne 1980, pp. 47-52.

17. On La Bête Humaine

BAROLI, MARC : Le Train dans la Littérature Française, Paris, Éditions N. M., 1963.

BONNEFIS, PHILIPPE : *L'Inénarrable même* dans **Les Cahiers Naturalistes, XX, no. 48,** 1974, pp. 125-140.

DELEUZE, GILLES : *Zola et la Fêlure* dans La Logique du Sens, Paris, Éditions de Minuit, 1969.

DUCHET, CLAUDE : *La Fille Abandonnée et La Bête Humaine : Éléments de Titrologie Romanesque* dans **Littérature, no. 12,** décembre 1973, pp. 49-73.

DUGAN, RAYMOND : *La Psychologie Criminelle dans Thérèse Raquin et La Bête Humaine d'Émile Zola* dans **Travaux de Linguistique et de Littérature, XVII, no. 2,** 1979, pp. 131-137.

FRANCHI, DANIÈLE et
RIPOLL, ROGER : *Douceur et Intimité dans La Bête Humaine* dans **Les Cahiers Naturalistes, XXIII, no. 51,** 1977, pp. 80-90.

RIPOLL, ROGER : *Originalité de l'œuvre* dans La Bête Humaine de Zola, Paris, Librairie Générale de France, 1984.

HAMON, PHILIPPE : **Philippe Hamon Présente La Bête Humaine d'Émile Zola,** Paris, Gallimard, 1994.

JAGMETTI, A. : **La Bête Humaine d'Émile Zola. Étude de Stylistique Critique,** Genève, Droz, 1955.

KANES, MARTIN : **La Bête Humaine. A Study in Literary Creation,** University of California Press, Berkeley and Los Angeles, 1962.

LABESSE, JEAN : **Étude sur Émile Zola. La Bête Humaine,** Paris, Ellipses, collection : Résonances, 1999.

NOIRAY, JACQUES : *L'angoisse de la chair dans La Bête Humaine,* dans **Voix de l'Écrivain. Mélanges Offerts à Guy Sagnes,** Toulouse, Presses Universitaires du Mirail, 1996, pp. 163-177.

WOOLLEN, GEOFF (Éd.) : **Zola, La Bête Humaine : Texte et Explication,** colloque du centenaire à Glasgow, University of Glasgow French and German Publications, 1990.

WOOLLEN, GEOFF : *What's (in) a Bête humaine?* dans **Bulletin of the Émile Zola Society, no. 13,** mars 1996, pp. 20-22.

18. On L'Argent

AHEARN, EDWARD J.:	*Monceau, Camondo, La Curée, L'Argent: History, Art, Evil* dans **The French Review**, LXXIV, no. 6, 2000, pp. 1100-1115.
DUBOIS, JACQUES :	*Oxymores et Incestes : la Folie et les Crises dans Les Rougon-Macquart* dans **Marche Romane**, LXVII, no. 1-2, 1977, pp. 67-73.
HENNESSEY, SUSAN :	*La maternité stérile : une analyse des mères spirituelles dans Au Bonheur des Dames, La Joie de Vivre, Le Rêve et L'Argent* dans **Excavatio**, II, automne 1993, pp. 103-109.
JOHN, ELERIUS:	*L'Argent d'Émile Zola* dans **Calabar Studies in Modern Languages**, I, no. 1, 1977, pp.1-10.
LEBRON, MONICA :	*Madame Caroline. Expéditions discursives dans L'Argent* dans **Les Cahiers Naturalistes**, XLV, no. 72, 1999, pp.217-225.
McQUEEN, ANDREW:	*The Wild Child in Zola's L'Argent*, dans **Excavatio**, XII, 1999, pp.53-59.
MITTERAND, HENRI :	*Notes* dans L'Argent d'Émile Zola, Paris, Gallimard, 1980.

19. On La Débâcle :

BAGULEY, DAVID :	*Le Récit de Guerre : Narration et Focalisation dans La Débâcle* dans **Littérature**, no. 50, mai 1983, pp. 77-90.
BAGULEY, DAVID :	*Formes et Significations : sur le Dénouement de La Débâcle* dans **Cahiers de l'U.E.R. Froissart**, no. 5, Valenciennes, automne 1980, pp. 65-72.
LUMBROSO, OLIVIER :	*Topologie d'un champ de bataille. L'exemple de La Débâcle* dans **Poétique**, no. 12, novembre 1998, pp. 447-460.
McLYNN, PAULINE:	*The Franco-Prussian war in La Débâcle. An Examination of Zola's Method* dans **Nottingham French Studies**, XX, no. 2, 1981, pp. 25-36.
PETREY, SANDY :	*La République de La Débâcle* dans **Les Cahiers Naturalistes**, XXVI, no. 54, 1980, pp. 87-95.
SACKVILLE, WEST E.:	**Zola's La Débâcle, Inclinations,** London, Secker and Wartburg, 1949.
SAMINADAYAR, CARINNE :	*La Débâcle, roman épique* dans **Les Cahiers Naturalistes**, XLIII, no. 71, 1997, pp. 203-219.

20. On Le Docteur Pascal :

BACHELARD, GASTON :	**La Psychanalyse du Feu**, Paris, Gallimard, 1938.
BUTOR, MICHEL :	*Émile Zola, romancier Expérimental et la Flamme Bleue* dans **Répertoire IV**, Paris, Éditions de Minuit, 1974, pp. 259-291.
FERNANDEZ-ZOÏLA, A. :	*Le Docteur Pascal et Lourdes : une transvaluation des imaginaires* dans **Les Cahiers Naturalistes**, XLII, no. 2, 1996, pp. 45-66.
GAILLARD, FRANÇOISE :	*Genèse et Généalogie ; le cas du Docteur Pascal* dans **Romantisme**, no. 31, 1981, pp. 181-196.
GENGEMBRE, GÉRARD :	*Préface* et *Dossier* dans **Le Docteur Pascal** de Zola, Paris, Éditions Pocket Classiques, 1995.
GRANET, MICHEL :	**Le Temps Trouvé par Zola dans son Roman Le Docteur Pascal. Nouvelle Lecture de l'Œuvre Zolienne**, Paris, Les Publications Universitaires, 1980.
KRUMM, PASCALE :	*Le Docteur Pascal : un (dangereux) supplément ? La problématique féminine dans le cycle zolien* dans **Les cahiers Naturalistes**, XLV, no. 72, 1999, pp. 227-240.

MITTERAND, HENRI :	*Préface* du **Docteur Pascal** de Zola, Paris, Édition Folio Classiques, 1991.
MOUCHARD, CLAUDE :	*Naturalisme et Anthropologie* dans **Le Naturalisme**, Colloque de Cerisy, Paris, UGE, série 10/18, 1978.
PETRONE, MARIO :	*Inceste et pureté dans* **Le Docteur Pascal**. *Remarques sur le personnage de Clotilde* dans **Les Cahiers Naturalistes**, XLV, no. 72, 1999, pp. 241-245.
PREISS, AXEL :	*Pascal ou la Biodicée Médicale* dans **Les Cahiers Naturalistes**, XXIX, no. 57, 1983, pp. 116-131.
SERRES, MICHEL :	**Feux et Signaux de Brume**, Paris, Grasset, 1975.
TOUBIN, CATHERINE. et MALINAS, YVES :	*Les Clés et les Portes : Essai sur la Symbolique du* <u>Docteur Pascal</u> dans **Les Cahiers Naturalistes**, XVII, no. 41, 1971, pp. 15-21.

VI. THESES ET DISSERTATIONS ON THE ROUGON MACQUART

1. Theses:

BAILES, J.M.:	The Naturalist Novel: Realism, Irony or Myth? An Archetypal Study of Zola's *La Curée*, Rice University, 1980.
BECKER, COLETTE :	*Pot-Bouille* d'Émile Zola. Genèse du Roman, Édition et Commentaire du Dossier Préparatoire, Paris, 1970.
BUVIK, PER : Mythe et Mythologie. Essai d'Analyse de *Nana* d'Émile Zola, Université de Bergen, 1972.
CHAROZ, JEAN-CLAUDE :	*Les Rougon-Macquart et les Visages du Temps : Étude de l'Imaginaire Zolien*, Université de Grenoble III, 1977.
CHEHAYED, JAMAL :	La Conscience Historique dans *Les Rougon-Macquart* d'Émile Zola et dans les romans de Nagib Mafuz, Université de Paris III, 1974.
CHEVREL, YVES :	Le Roman et la Nouvelle Naturalistes Français en Allemagne : **1870-1893**, Université de Paris, 1980.
COUSINS, F. RUSSELL:	The Genesis of Zola's *L'Argent*, Birmingham University, 1972-1973.
FINCH R, CLARENCE:	The Genesis of Émile Zola's *Nana*, Pennsylvania State University, 1974.
KELLNER, S. :	*Le Docteur Pascal*. Rétrospective des *Rougon-Macquart*, Livre de documents, Roman à Thèse, Lund, 1980.
LETHBRIDGE, ROBERT:	The Genesis of Émile Zola's *La Curée*, University of Cambridge, 1974.
NAGDI, D. EL :	Étude sur le Vocabulaire des Sensations dans *Le Ventre de Paris*, Université de Paris IV, 1974.
NGUYEN, Q. :	Étude Historique et Critique d'*Une Page d'Amour*, Paris, Sorbonne, 1965.
OUVRARD, PIERRE :	Le Personnage du Prêtre dans l'Œuvre Romanesque d'Émile Zola, Université de Paris XII, Val- de- Marne, 1983
WALKER, P.D.:	A Structural Study of Zola's *Germinal*, Yale University, 1956.
ZAKARIAN, R.H.:	Zola's *Germinal*. A Critical Study of its Primary Sources, Genève, Droz, 1972.

2. Master Degree Dissertations

RONDEAU, D. :	*Au Bonheur Des Dames*, Paris, 1958
SAMAKE, FAMAHAN :	Procès du Second Empire dans *La Curée* d'Émile Zola, Université d'Abidjan Cocody, 1995.

VII. BOOKS AND CRITICAL ARTICLES ON LES TROIS VILLES (LOURDES, PARIS, ROME)

BANCQUART, M.-C. :	*Un Adieu à Paris, Paris de Zola : un présent figé, un dynamisme tellurique, deux gravures décalées,* dans **Les Cahiers du XX ème Siècle, no 2, 1974, pp. 69-83.**
NIESS, ROBERT:	*Zola's Paris and the Novels of the Rougon-Macquart series* dans **Nineteenth Century French Studies IV, no. 1-2,** automne-hiver 1975-1976, pp. 89-104.
TORNOIS, RENÉ :	Zola et son Temps : Lourdes, Rome, Paris, Paris, Les Belles-Lettres, 1961.
TISON-BRAUN, M. :	La Crise de l'Humanisme [...] T 1, Paris, Nizet, 1958.
THEIS, RAIMUND :	*Paris, Rome bei Zola* dans **Zur Sprache der Cité in der Dichtung Unterstudien zum Roman und zum Prosagedicht,** Frankfurt, Klostermann, 1972, pp. 74-93.
THOMSON, CLIVE :	*Discours Littéraire et Discours Idéologique* dans **Les Cahiers Naturalistes, XXII, no. 50, 1976, pp.202-212.**
THOMSON, CLIVE :	*Une Typologie du Discours Idéologique dans Les Trois Villes* dans **Cahiers Naturalistes, XXVI no. 54, 1980, pp. 96-105.**
THOMSON, CLIVE :	*Zola et la IIIème République, Étude Idéologique de Paris* dans **Cahiers de l'U.E.R. Froissart, no. 5,** Valenciennes, automne 1980, pp. 19-26.

VIII. BOOKS AND CRITICAL ARTICLES ON THE QUATRE ÉVANGILES (FÉCONDITÉ, VÉRITÉ, TRAVAIL)

BAGULEY, DAVID :	*Fécondité d'Émile Zola. Roman à Thèse, Évangile, Mythe,* University of Toronto Press, 1973.
BAGULEY, DAVID :	*Du Discours Polémique au Discours Utopique. L'Évangile Républicain de Zola* dans **Les Cahiers Naturalistes, XXVI, no. 54, 1980, pp. 106-121.**
CASE, FREDERICK. I. :	La Cité Idéale dans *Travail* de Zola, University of Toronto Press, 1974.
GOT, OLIVIER :	Le Paria et le Prophète ou l'Université selon Zola dans **Les Cahiers Naturalistes, XXVI, no. 54, 1980, pp, 127-137.**
KACZYNSKI, M. :	Les Quatre Évangiles de Zola : Entre la Vision Catastrophique et la Vision Utopique, Paris, Lublin, 1979.
MITTERAND, HENRI :	*L'Évangile Social de Travail : un anti-Germinal* dans **Roman et Société,** Paris, Armand Colin, 1973.
PELLETIER, JACQUES :	*Zola Évangéliste* dans **Les Cahiers Naturalistes, XX, no. 48,** 1974, pp. 205-214.
ROSS, PETER:	*Émile Zola, the Teachers and the Dreyfus Affair* dans **Nottingham French Studies, XIV, no. 2,** octobre 1975, pp. 77-85.
SPEIRS, DOROTHY :	*État Présent des Études sur Les Quatre Évangiles* dans **Les Cahiers Naturalistes, XX, no. 48, 1974, pp. 215-235.**
STEINS, MARTIN :	*L'Épisode Africain dans Fécondité de Zola* dans **Les Cahiers Naturalistes, XX, no. 48, 1974, pp. 164-181.**

IX. THESES ON LES TROIS VILLES AND LES QUATRE ÉVANGILES

THOMPSON, CLIVE :	Étude Critique de *Paris* d'Émile Zola, Toronto, University of Toronto, 1970.
PELLETIER, JACQUES :	Zola Évangéliste, Aix-Marseille, 1972.

SPEIRS, DOROTHY:	Étude Critique de *Travail*, Toronto, University of Toronto, 1977.

X. BOOKS AND CRITICAL ARTICLES ON TALES OF ZOLA

COUILLARD, MARIE :	*La Fille-Fleur dans les Contes à Ninon et Les Rougon-Macquart* dans **Revue de l'Université d'Ottawa**, Vol. 48, no. 4, octobre-décembre 1980, pp. 398-406.
LAPP, JOHN :	**Les Racines du Naturalisme. Zola avant Les Rougon-Macquart**, Paris, Bordas, 1972.

XI. BOOKS AND CRITICAL ARTICLES ON ZOLA'S PHOTOGRAPHY

ÉMILE-ZOLA, FRANÇOIS et MASSIN :	**Zola Photographe**, Paris, Denoël, 1979.
MITTERAND, HENRI et VIDAL, JEAN :	**Album Zola**, Paris, Gallimard, 1963.
MITTERAND, HENRI :	**Images d'Enquête d'Émile Zola. De la Goutte-d'Or à l'Affaire Dreyfus**, Paris, Presses Pocket, Album Terre Humaine, 1987.

XII. BOOKS AND ARTICLES ON THE AUDIENCE OF ZOLA

ALLARD, JACQUES :	**Zola, le Chiffre du Texte**, Presses Universitaires de Grenoble, 1978.
BAGULEY, DAVID :	**La Bibliographie de la Critique sur Émile Zola : 1864-1970**, Toronto, University of Toronto Press, 1976.
BAGULEY, DAVID :	**La Bibliographie de la Critique sur Émile Zola : 1971-1980**, Toronto, Buffalo, London ; University of Toronto Press, 1982.
BECKER, COLETTE :	**Émile Zola et les Critiques de Notre Temps**, Paris, Garnier, 1972.
BECKER, COLETTE :	*L'Audience d'Émile Zola* dans **Les Cahiers Naturalistes**, XX, no. 47, 1974, pp. 40-69.
BECKER, COLETTE :	**Trente ans d'Amitié. Lettres de l'Éditeur Charpentier à Émile Zola**, Paris, PUF, 1981.
DEZALAY, AUGUSTE :	**Lectures de Zola**, Paris, Armand Colin, 1973.

XIII. BOOKS ON ZOLA'S PLAYS

GUIEU, JEAN-MAX :	**Le Théâtre Lyrique d'Émile Zola**, Paris, Librairie Fischbacher, 1983.

XIV. BOOKS ON ZOLA'S JOURNALISM

MITTERAND, HENRI:	**Zola Journaliste**, Paris, Colin, 1963.

XV. BOOKS ON THE LITERARY THEORIES AND METHODOLOGY

ARAGON, LOUIS :	**Je n'ai jamais appris à écrire, ou les incipits**, Genève, Skira, 1969.
AUEURBACH, FRANK :	**Mimésis : la Représentation de la Réalité dans la Littérature Occidentale**, Paris, Gallimard, 1946.
BACHELARD, GASTON :	**Psychanalyse du Texte Réaliste**, Paris, Vrin, 1947.
BAKTINE, MIKHAIL :	**Esthétique et Théorie du Roman**, Paris, Gallimard, 1978.
BARTHES, ROLAND :	**Le Degré Zéro de l'Écriture**, Paris, Gonthier, 1966.
BARTHES, ROLAND :	**S/Z**, Paris, Seuil, 1970.

BARTHES, ROLAND (Éd) :	**Essais Critiques**, Paris, Seuil, 1964.
BOURNEUF, ROLAND :	**L'Univers du Roman**, Paris, PUF, 1985.
BRECHT, B. :	**Sur le Réalisme**, Paris, L'Arche, 1970.
COLLECTIF :	**Communications, 4**, Paris, Seuil, 1964.
COLLECTIF :	**Théorie de la Littérature**, Paris, Seuil, 1966.
COLLECTIF :	**Littérature 1**, février 1970.
COLLECTIF :	**Communications 8**, Paris, Com, 1966, (seconde édition : Paris, Seuil, 1982).
COLLECTIF :	**Communications 19**, Paris, Seuil, 1972.
COLLECTIF :	**Poétique 12**, Paris, Seuil, 1972.
COLLECTIF :	**Sémiotique Narrative et Textuelle**, Paris, Larousse, 1974.
COLLECTIF :	**Poétique du Récit**, Paris, Seuil, 1977.
COLLECTIF :	**Littérature et Réalité**, Paris, seuil, 1972.
COLLECTIF :	**Poétique 49**, Paris, Seuil, 1982.
COLLECTIF :	**Esthétique et Poétique**, Paris, Seuil, 1992 (Textes réunis et présentés par Gérard Genette).
COLLECTIF :	**Pratiques no. 10**, Paris, Seuil, 1976.
FAYE, JEAN-PIERRE :	**Théorie du Récit**, Paris, UGE 10/18, 1978.
FLAUBERT, GUSTAVE :	**Correspondance**, Paris, Édition du Centenaire, Librairie de France, 1993.
GENETTE, GÉRARD :	**Figures 1**, Paris, Seuil, 1966.
GENETTE, GÉRARD :	**Figures 2**, Paris, Seuil, 1969.
GENETTE, GÉRARD :	**Figures 3**, Paris, Seuil, 1972.
GOLDENSTEIN, LUCIEN :	**Pour Lire le Roman**, Bruxelles, De Boeck-Duculot, 1989.
GREIMAS, ALGIRDAS JULIEN :	**Sémantique Structurale**, Paris, Larousse, 1966.
GREIMAS, A. J. :	**Maupassant : La Sémiotique du Texte**, Paris, Larousse, 1976.
GREIMAS, A. J. et COURTÈS, J. :	**Sémiotique. Dictionnaire Raisonné de la Théorie du Langage**, Paris, Hachette, 1979.
GREIMAS, A. J. :	**Du Sens II : Essais Sémiotiques**, Paris, Seuil, 1983.
GONCOURT, EDMOND et JULES HUOT DE :	**Journal. Mémoires de la Vie Littéraire**, édition Robert Ricatte, Paris, Fasquelle-Flammarion, 4 volumes, 1956.
GROUPE D'ENTREVERNES :	**Analyse Sémiotique des Textes**, Presses Universitaires de Lyon, 1984.
HAMON, PHILIPPE :	**Introduction à l'Analyse du Descriptif**, Paris, Hachette, 1981.
HENAULT, ANNE :	**Narratologie, Sémiotique Générale 2**, Paris, PUF, 1983.
JENNY, L. :	*La Stratégie de la Forme* dans **Poétique no. 27**, Paris, Seuil, 1976.
KRISTEVA, JULIA :	**Séméiotikè : Recherches pour une Sémanalyse**, Paris, Seuil, 1989.
LASOWSKI, PATRICK WALD :	**Syphilis. Essais sur la Littérature Française du XIXème Siècle**, Paris, Gallimard, 1980.
LUKACS, GEORGE :	**Balzac et le Réalisme Français**, Paris, Maspéro, 1967.
LUKACS, GEORGE :	**Problèmes du Réalisme**, Paris, L'Arche, 1975.
MARTINO, PIERRE :	**Le Naturalisme Français**, Collection U2, Paris, Armand Colin, 1969.
MITTERAND, HENRI :	**Le Discours du Roman**, Paris, PUF, Écriture, 1980.
POUILLON, JEAN :	**Temps et Roman**, Paris, Gallimard, 1946.
PROPP, VLADIMIR :	**Morphologie du Conte**, Paris, Seuil, 1970.
RAIMOND, MICHEL :	**Le Roman**, Paris, Armand Colin, 1989.

THIBAUDET, ALBERT : Réflexions sur le Roman, Paris, Gallimard, 1968.
TODOROV, TZVETAN : Introduction à la Littérature Française, Paris, Seuil, 1970.
VALÉRY, PAUL : Tel Quel T 2, Paris, Gallimard, 1960.
WEINRICH, HARALD : Le Temps du Récit, Paris, Seuil, 1979.

XVI. GENERAL BOOKS

BENVENISTE, ÉMILE : Problème de Linguistique Générale, Paris, Gallimard, 1966.
COLLECTIF : Pratiques, no 1, Paris, 1976.
FREUD, SIGMUND : Trois Essais sur la Théorie de la Sexualité, Paris, Gallimard, 1981, (I ère édition : Vienne, 1905).
FREUD, SIGMUND : Cinq Leçons de Psychanalyse, Paris, Payot, 1966, 1 ère Édition : Vienne, 1909.
FOUCAULT, MICHEL : Histoire de la Sexualité : 1, La Volonté de Savoir, Paris, Gallimard, 1976
JAKOBSON, ROMAN Essais de Linguistique Générale, Paris, Minuit, 1968.
LALAIRE, LOUIS : Le Verbe et le Classement Syntaxique du Verbe, collection Les Cahiers de Grammaire, Abidjan, ENS, 1990.
LIDSKY, PAUL : Les Écrivains contre La Commune, Paris, François Maspero, 1982.
MAURON, CHARLES : Des Métaphores Obsédantes au Mythe Personnel, Paris, José Corti, 1952.
METZ, CHRISTIAN : Essais sur la Signification au Cinéma, Paris, Klincksieck, 1968.
SAUSSURE, FERDINAND DE : Cours de Linguistique Générale, Paris, Payot, 1972.

XVII. HISTORY AND MYTHOLOGY

BONIN-KERDON, BURLOT, NONJON, NOUSCHI et SUSSEL : Héritages Européens, Paris, Hachette, 1981.
BOUILLON, SOHN et BRUNEL : 1848-1914 : Histoire, Paris, Bordas, 1978.
CARATINI, ROGER : Histoire de la France Urbaine, T4, Paris, Seuil, 1983.
COLLECTIF : Histoire, Collection GREHG / Seconde, Paris, Hachette, 1987.
COMMELION, P. : Mythologie Grecque et Romaine, Paris, Garnier, 1960.
DUBY, GEORGES et MANDROU, ROBERT : Histoire de la Civilisation Française, T 2, Paris, Armand Colin, 1968.
GRIGORIEFF, VLADIMIR : Mythologie du Monde Entier, Belgique, Alleur, 1987.

XVIII. DICTIONARIES

CHEVALIER, JEAN et GHEERBRANDT, ALAIN : Dictionnaire des Symboles, Paris, Laffont, 1982.
COLLECTIF : Dictionnaire des Littératures de Langue Française, Paris, Bordas, 1987.
LITTRÉ, M. P. ÉMILE : Dictionnaire de la Langue Française, A-C, Paris, Librairie Hachette et Cie, 1883.
LITTRÉ, M. P. ÉMILE : Dictionnaire de la Langue Française, D-H, Paris, Librairie Hachette et Cie, 1883.
LITTRÉ, M. P. ÉMILE : Dictionnaire de la Langue Française, I-P, Paris, Librairie Hachette et Cie, 1883.
LITTRÉ, M. P. ÉMILE : Dictionnaire de la Langue Française, Q-Z, Paris, Librairie Hachette et Cie, 1883.

LAROUSSE, PIERRE :	**Grand Larousse de la Langue Française VI**, Paris, Librairie Larousse, 1977.
LAROUSSE, PIERRE :	**Grand Larousse de la Langue Française VII**, Paris, Librairie Larousse, 1978.
ROBERT, PAUL :	**Le Petit Robert 1**, Paris, Robert, 1979.
ROBERT, PAUL :	**Le Nouveau Petit Robert 1**, Paris, Robert, 1994.
ROBERT, PAUL :	**Dictionnaire Universel des Noms Propres**, Paris, Robert, 1989.
ROBERT, PAUL :	**Le Grand Robert de la Langue Française, Tome I**, Paris, Dictionnaires Robert, 1992.
ROBERT, PAUL :	**Le Grand Robert de la Langue Française, Tome II**, Paris, Dictionnaires Robert, 1992.
ROBERT, PAUL :	**Le Grand Robert de la Langue Française, Tome III**, Paris, Dictionnaires Robert, 1992.
ROBERT, PAUL :	**Le Grand Robert de la Langue Française, Tome IV**, Paris, Dictionnaires Robert, 1992.
ROBERT, PAUL :	**Le Grand Robert de la Langue Française, Tome V**, Paris, Dictionnaires Robert, 1992.
ROBERT, PAUL :	**Le Grand Robert de la Langue Française, Tome VI**, Paris, Dictionnaires Robert, 1992.
ROBERT, PAUL :	**Le Grand Robert de la Langue Française, Tome VII**, Paris, Dictionnaires Robert, 1992.
ROBERT, PAUL :	**Le Grand Robert de la Langue Française, Tome VIII**, Paris, Dictionnaires Robert, 1992.

XIX. SACRED BOOKS

Les Saintes Écritures :	Traduction du Monde Nouveau, Watch Tower Bible and Tract Society of Pennsylvania, 1974, Association des Témoins de Jéhovah, Boulogne-Billancourt, France, 1995.
La Sainte Bible :	Traduction de Louis Segond, Genève-Paris, Société Biblique de Genève, seconde édition, 1979.

TABLE OF CONTENTS

	Pages
ABSTRACT	3
STATEMENT OF THE CANDIDATE	4
DEDICATION	5
ACKNOWLEDGEMENTS	6
PREAMBLE	8
SUMMARY	9
INTRODUCTION	11
INTRODUCTORY CHAPTER: STATUS OF ZOLA'S CRITICISM IN RELATION TO SEXUALITY AND FATALITY	18
PART ONE: THE FOUNDATIONS AND THE CHARACTERISTICS OF SEXUALITY IN THE ROUGON-MACQUART	28
CHAPTER 1: THE FOUNDATIONS OF SEXUALITY IN THE ROUGON-MACQUART	29
1. THE RELIGIOUS FOUNDATIONS	29
2. BIOLOGICAL AND SOCIOLOGICAL FOUNDATIONS	30
3. LITERARY AND IDEOLOGICAL FOUNDATIONS	32
4. THE EPISTEMOLOGICAL FOUNDATIONS	34
CHAPTER 2: CHARACTERISTICS OF SEXUALITY IN THE CORPUS	40
1. THE HEREDITARY DISEASES AND THE NARRATIVE GRAMMAR	40
2. THE SEXUAL ABERRATIONS	43
2.1. The deviations from the sexual object	43
2.1.1. The absolute inversions	43
2.1.2. The amphigenic inversions	45
2.1.3. The occasional inversions	49
2.2. The deviations from the sexual purpose	49
2.2.1. The anatomic transgressions	49

2.2.2. The stops at intermediate relations	51
3. THE ANIMALISTIC APPROACH TO SEXUALITY	52
3.1. The female characters and animalisation	54
3.2. Male characters and animalisation	57
4. THE SATANIC AND THE DIABOLICAL APPROACH TO SEXUALITY	60
5. THE MYTHICAL APPROACH TO SEXUALITY	64
6. THE APOCALYPTIC APPROACH TO SEXUALITY	67
PART TWO: SEXUAL AGENTS AND THE QUESTION OF SEXUALITY	71
THE GENEALOGICAL TREE OF THE ROUGON-MACQUART	72
CHAPTER 1: THE BEING OF THE CHARACTERS OR THE EXPANSION OF PUPPETS	73
1. THE MANIPULATION OR THE *ÊTRE DU FAIRE*	74
1.1. The author and his characters	74
1.2. The identification and the classification of the sexual agents	75
1.2.1. The Anthropomorphic characters	75
1.2.1.1. The Anaphoric characters	75
1.2.1.2. The clutch characters or the ''personnages embrayeurs''	79
1.2.1.2.1. The animalisation of the clutch characters	80
1.2.1.2.2. The Reification of the Clutch and the Anaphoric Characters	82
1.2.1.3. The referential characters	83
1.2.2. The Non-anthropomorphic characters	85
1.2.2.1. Natural non-anthropomorphic characters	85
1.2.2.1.1. The Earth	85
1.2.2.1.2. The woods	86
1.2.2.1.3. Paris	87
1.2.2.2. The Non-Anthropomorphic Non-Natural Characters	88
2. THE COMPETENCE OF THE SEXUAL AGENT	89
2.1. The decomposition of nominal lexemes	89
2.1.1. The Absolute absolute names	90
2.1.2. Names accompanied by an article or an adjective	94
2.2. The Being versus the appearance of the characters or the category of truthfulness	96
3. THE ACTANTIAL DIAGRAM ON THE AXIS OF SEXUALITY	98
CHAPTER 2: THE DOING AND THE BECOMING OF THE CHARACTER OR THEIR PERFORMANCE AND THEIR SANCTIONS	105

1. THE FAIRE-ÊTRE OF THE CHARACTER OR THEIR PERFORMANCE	105
1.1. The system of operations related to sexuality	105
1.1.1. Conjunction and disjunction	105
1.1.2. The gift	106
1.1.3. The exchange or the contract	107
1.1.4. The virtuality	108
1.1.5. The actuality	108
1.1.6. The reality	109
1.2. The system of modalities	110
1.2.1. The passive obedience	110
1.2.2. The active obedience	111
1.2.3. The passive resistance	112
1.2.4. The active resistance	112
1.3. Studying some specific performances	114
1.3.1. The "virtuous and chaste" characters	114
1.3.2. The evil characters	118
1.3.3. The vicious characters	121
1.3.4. The incestuous characters	122
1.3.4.1. The pseudo incest or incest by allegory	123
1.3.4.2. The true Incest	124
2. THE RECOGNITION AND THE SANCTION OF THE CHARACTER	126
2.1. The miscarriages	126
2.2. The hereditary diseases	128
2.3. The amorphous children	129
2.4. The mad and/or crazy characters	131
2.5. The characters lacking intelligence	135
2.6. Early and untimely death	137

CHAPTER 3: THE METALINGUISTIC AND THE POETIC FUNCTIONS IN THE ROUGON-MACQUART OR THE PREVISIBILITY OF THE FATALITY OF SEXUALITY   141

1. THE METALINGUISTIC FUNCTION OR THE MYTHS AND THEIR ''SIGNIFIÉ''	141
IN THE LOGIC OF SEXUALITY	141
1.1. The identification and the classification of the myths	142
1.1.1. The Christian myths	142
1.1.1.1. The Garden of Eden and the Original Sin	142
1.1.1.2. The punishment or the penalty for disobedience to God	146
1.1.1.3. The damnation of the sexual subject	147
1.1.1.4. The devil, death and hell	149
1.1.1.5. The opposition Christian myths and nature	150
1.1.2. The pagan myths	154
1.1.2.1. The Roman myths	154
1.1.2. 2. The Greek myths	156

1.1.2.2.1. The myths of unfulfilled sexuality	159
1.1.2.2.2. The myths of the flourished and the triumphant sexuality	160
1.1.2.2.3. The myths of vicious sexuality	160
1.1.2.2.4. The myths of the perverted sexuality	161
1.2. The relevance of those myths	161
1.2.1. The sacralisation of the chimeric	161
1.2.2. The process of discursive and narrative intensification	162
2. THE POETIC FUNCTION OR THE FIGURES OF RHETORIC SERVING THE THEME OF SEXUALITY	165
2.1. The functions	166
2.1.1. The metonymy	166
2.1.2. The synecdoche	169
2.2. The Indices	170
2.2.1. The Metaphors	170
2.2.2. The comparisons	171
2.2.3. The periphrases	172
3. DISCOVERING THE PERSONAL MYTH OF THE AUTHOR	173
PART THREE: THE RELEVANCE OF THE SPATIO-TEMPORAL COMBINATORICS IN RELATION TO THE FATALITY OF SEXUALITY	**177**
CHAPTER 1: TIME IN THE ROUGON-MACQUART: THE PROGRAMMED AND TIMED-OUT SEXUALITY	**178**
1. THE EXTERNAL TIME	179
1.1. The author's time	179
1.1.1. The time he lived: 1840-1902	179
1.1.2. The time of the production of the ROUGON-MACQUART: 1870-1893	179
1.2. The historical time or the time of the fiction: 1852 -1870	180
1.3. The reader's time	181
2. THE INTERNAL TIME	181
2.1. The time of the narrative enunciation	181
2.1.1. Order in Zola's LES ROUGON-MACQUART	182
2.1.2. The duration	183
2.1.3. The frequency	186
2.1.4. The mode	187
2.1.4.1. The distance	187
2.1.4.2. The perspective or the point of view	188
2.1.4.3. The voice	189
2.2. The verb tenses of the enunciation in Zola's fiction works	193
2.2.1. The present of the indicative	193
2.2.2. The simple past	195
2.2.3. The imperfect and the pluperfect	196

2.2.4. The conditional mode	199
2.2.5. The simple future of the indicative	200
3. The temporal symbolism in LES ROUGON-MACQUART	201
3.1. The night or the time of the convergent sexuality	201
3.2. The day or the time of the divergent sexuality	203
3.3. The symbolism of colours (vivid versus dark)	204
3.4. The opposition continuous times versus discontinuous times	205
3.5. Seasons and sexual ambivalence	207

CHAPTER 2: THE SPACE IN THE ROUGON-MACQUART: THE FRAGMENTED BUT THE DELIMITED SEXUALITY — 209

1. THE SPATIAL CONFIGURATION AND THE MUTATION OF THE SEXUAL AGENT	209
1.1. The open spaces or the unprotected sexuality	210
1.2. The confined spaces or the intense and protected sexuality	214
1.3. The closed-open spaces or the morbid sexuality	218
1.4. The couple surface spaces/deep spaces: the descent into hell?	219
2. THE SITUATION OF THE CONFLICT SPACE/CHARACTER	221
2.1. The Space and the aggression of the sexual agent	221
2.2. The defeat of the sexual agent	226
2.3. The revenge of the sexual agent on their space or the emergence of pyromaniacs	228
2.4. Highlighting another personal myth of the author and its psychoanalytic interpretation	228

PART FOUR: FERTILITY OF THE THEMATICS OF SEXUALITY IN THE ROUGON-MACQUART — 233

CHAPTER 1: SEXUALITY AND THE RENEWAL OF THE FICTION WRITING TECHNIQUES — 234

1. THE ALLUSIONS AND THE SAYINGS WITHOUT HAVING TO SPELL THINGS OUT	235
2. THE MISE EN ABYME OR THE REPETITION	237
3. THE OPULENCE OF THE DISCURSIVE ANACHRONISMS	237
4. THE HYPERTROPHY OF TRUE DETAIL	240

CHAPTER II: ZOLA AND NATURALISM — 244

I. THE AUTOBIOGRAPHY OF ZOLA: AN AUTHOR CONCERNED BY SEXUALITY	244
1.1. The natalist? Certainly, but a socialist?	244
1.2. Zola: The anti-communard	250
1.3. The workaholic or work seen like a libido	252

1.4. The theorist of heredity	256
II. THE CRITICISM OF ZOLA	259
2.1. The rough scientism of Zola's naturalism	259
2.1.1. Critics of naturalism	260
2.1. 2. The extremist naturalism or the curiosity of a voyeur	262
2.1.3. Zola, the talentless novelist ?	265
2.1. Tributes pouring in	266
III. ZOLA, THE LONE WRITER OR THE LITERARY SCHOOL CHIEF?	271
3.1. Huysmans and naturalism	272
3.2. The Goncourt brothers and naturalism	275
3.2.1. The Goncourts' relationship with Zola at the human level	276
3.2.2. The literary conceptions or the similarity source of conflict	276
3.3. Guy de Maupassant	278
3.4. Zola, the atheist and lonely writer	280
CONCLUSION	283
BIBLIOGRAPHY	290
TABLE OF CONTENTS	312

www.ingramcontent.com/pod-product-compliance
Lightning Source LLC
Chambersburg PA
CBHW051751100526
44591CB00017B/2658